INVASION
1940

INVASION 1940

The Nazi Invasion Plan
for Britain

SS-General Walter Schellenberg

Introduction by
Professor John Erickson

ST ERMIN'S
PRESS

A *St Ermin's Press* Book

First published in this form in Great Britain in 2000
by St Ermin's Press
in association with Little, Brown & Company
and the Imperial War Museum

Introduction and footnotes copyright © 2000 by St Ermin's Press and John
Erickson
Preface copyright © 2000 by Westintel Research Ltd
English language translation copyright © 2000 by St Ermin's Press
Introduction by Terry Charman © Imperial War Museum 1989

Moral right has been asserted.

A CIP catalogue record for this book
is available from the British Library.

ISBN: 0 9536151 2 X

Typeset in Imprint by M Rules
Printed and bound in Great Britain
by Clays Ltd, St Ives plc

St Ermin's Press
in association with
Little, Brown and Company (UK)
Brettenham House
Lancaster Place
London WC2E 7EN

Contents

Introduction

By all accounts, his own included, Walter Schellenberg cut quite a dash in the world of Nazi Germany's secret service. Trained as a lawyer, recruited to the SS out of blatant careerism and avoidance of the SA riffraff, Schellenberg quickly attracted the attention of faceless but influential men in the Nazi Party's new-found security and intelligence service, the SD (*Sicherheitsdienst*). Schellenberg moved on and up, melodramatically impressed that his movements were seemingly 'being plotted as though by an unseen hand'. One of those 'unseen hands' quickly showed itself: Reinhardt Heydrich, founder and head of the SD. He drew Schellenberg closer to, and finally headlong into, the piranha-pool which was Nazi Party politics and intelligence intrigues.

Heydrich's patronage, if it can be called that, carried with it great dangers of which Schellenberg quickly became aware. Added to these were other enmities, such as that of Gestapo chief Heinrich Müller to be considered. Surrounded by 'nonentities and bandits', a cause of his frequent complaints, Schellenberg nevertheless made rapid progress in his career. By his own account he was involved in several intelligence coups: the planting of false evidence against the Soviet high command in 1937, 'active espionage' at Dakar, breaking a Polish spy ring, travels with Himmler.[1]

On 27 September 1939 Heinrich Himmler set up the Main

1 Walter Schellenberg, *The Schellenberg Memoirs*, Intro. Alan Bullock (trans. Louis Hagen, London 1956), Chs I–II The Makings of a Nazi and Under Heydrich's Order. Further on Schellenberg and Nazi intelligence, Reinhard Spitzy, *How We Squandered The Reich* (trans. G.T. Waddington, Norwich 1999).

Office for Reich Security (*Reichssicherheitshauptamt*), a security and intelligence monopoly which combined within itself the Gestapo, the Criminal Police (*Kripo*) and the Nazi Party's security organisation, the SD. Heydrich, the brain behind this centralising machine and its overlord, took the title of Chief of the Security Police and the Security Service (*Chef der Sicherheitspolizei und des SD*) for himself. Under the new organisation Schellenberg was appointed to *AMT IVE* (part of Müller's *AMT IV* bailiwick 'combating opposition to the state'), responsible specifically for counter-espionage in Germany and subsequently in occupied countries. In this position Schellenberg was a member of a tight if fractious Nazi 'inner circle' with power of life and death, predominantly the latter, over millions.

Such association brought Schellenberg into contact with Himmler and Hitler himself, with most of the grandees of the Nazi political and military machine, but what evidently captivated him was the 'derring-do' aspect of his work, the excitement of the counter-espionage chase and being in at the kill. A dramatic illustration of this is in the 'Venlo incident': the kidnapping and extraction from neutral Holland to Germany of two British secret agents in October 1939, the implications and consequences explored in the Introduction. At the beginning of 1940 Schellenberg set about reorganising the counter-espionage department, finding time though 'overburdened with work' to cosy up to Admiral Canaris, head of the *Abwehr,* rival intelligence agency to the SD.

Overburdened but far from overwhelmed, Schellenberg plunged into the work of activating German intelligence and security resources for the invasion of Denmark and Norway, dredging the 'Venlo incident' prior to the German attack to prove Dutch violation of neutrality to favour Britain. He drew on the prophecies of Nostradamus among much else to demoralise French civilians in a series of propaganda and 'disinformation' broadcasts during the German advance. The nature of other 'special assignments' he does not disclose.

Like so many others, Schellenberg was stunned by the fail-ure to attack 'Anglo-French forces at Dunkirk from the west', in obedience to Hitler's 29 May 1940 order to hold off the attack for two days. By way of explanation he recounted what Hitler told him 'personally' in 1939, that he, the *Führer,* had no wish to destroy the British, rather that the British must be humbled, taught to 'see things from a Continental-European point of view', just as the Germans see them. In unity Germany and Britain could rule Europe together, at which time 'the East will no longer be a danger'.[2]

Schellenberg relies on this explanation to clarify the con-trast between the 'typical Prussian thoroughness' of preparations for an invasion of Britain, Operation Sea Lion *(Seelöwe),* and Hitler moving only 'very hesitantly', finally bringing the whole thing to naught. This bland over-simplifi-cation fell far short of explaining the complicated evolution of an invasion plan first bruited as early as November 1939 by Admiral Raeder. The naval staff submitted that a major seaborne assault across the North Sea could well be a 'possible expedient' to force Britain to come to terms. The German army and the *Luftwaffe* evidently reacted with varying degrees of hostility and scepticism.[3]

The possibility or contingency of a German seaborne inva-sion had not escaped the notice of the British War Cabinet. Preceding Raeder's preliminary order by a month, on 30 October the prospect of a German invasion was examined after 'a spate of diplomatic and SIS reports' on German inten-tions.[4] In November the Chiefs of Staff evaluated the likelihood of invasion, discounting it as long as British naval and air forces remained largely intact. In May 1940 the posi-tion changed dramatically. The Chiefs of Staff, prompted by

2 *The Schellenberg Memoirs*, p. 123.

3 Peter Fleming, *Invasion 1940* (London 1958), pp. 34–5.

4 F.H. Hinsley *et al., British Intelligence in the Second World War* (London HMSO 1979), Vol. 1, p. 165.

SIS reports, set up the Home Defence Executive to co-ordi-nate anti-invasion measures among both military and civilian organisations. British intelligence calculated that Germany would have no difficulty in assembling the necessary troops and shipping for an invasion. It was assumed late in May that with fully developed plans Germany could invade at any time, given suitable conditions.[5]

Those 'fully developed plans' nevertheless seemed at this point to be wanting. Hitler learned only on 21 May from Admiral Raeder that preliminary plans for an invasion did exist. What they had disclosed even at the very earliest stage was that invasion would be a formidably difficult undertaking and that no meeting of minds over such a project existed within the German armed forces. At this moment, with the battle of France as yet undecided, Hitler evidently showed little interest in and no enthusiasm for 'details concerning the invasion of England' presented by Raeder. At Raeder's next meeting with Hitler on 4 June the subject of invasion simply did not come up, nor on 20 June did Raeder make any further progress with a non-committal Hitler. General Warlimont, deputy to General Alfred Jodl at Operations, learned on 17 June that with regard to any landing in Britain 'the *Führer* has so far *not* uttered any such intention', conscious as he was of the 'extreme difficulties' involved in an invasion. *No* studies had been set in train or preparations authorised by the high command.

Jodl, Chief of the Operations Staff *(Wehrmachtführungsstab)*, was obviously anxious to have the situation clarified. In pre-senting his proposals for future action to Hitler on 30 June he trod warily, aware of what lukewarm reception Raeder's pro-posals had received and in what direction 'diplomatic soundings' were moving. Jodl therefore presented the invasion of Britain as 'the last resort'. German victory was now inevitable, but there was need to minimise risk and economise with the armed forces.

---

5 *British Intelligence in the Second World War*, Vol. 1, p. 167.

The *Luftwaffe* would eliminate the Royal Air Force, co-ordinated air and sea attacks would seriously damage British supplies and supply routes, terror attacks would be aimed at centres of population. Invasion would be the *coup de grâce*, mounted only when the Government was on the verge of capitulation, the people demoralised. Set immediately in train, this course of action should yield results by the end of August or early September. The essence of Jodl's plan was that the actual landing should be merely 'the last and the least important' aspect of other measures, responsibility for which devolved primarily on the *Luftwaffe*. This order of priorities and proposed sequence of events was evidently better suited to Hitler's appetite, ambitions and aspirations.[6]

Hitler lingered long over his desire for an 'understanding' with the British, averse at this stage to authorise more extreme methods of warfare such as poisoning the food supply or bacteriological war. Only towards the end of June did Hitler come to a reluctant conclusion that the British were not at all inclined to make peace or accept the compromise he was suggesting. A situation could well develop requiring a 'show of force'. To meet this contingency Hitler now ordered a start upon preparations for an invasion. It was at this juncture that Schellenberg received orders to prepare 'a small handbook for the invading troops and the political and administrative units accompanying them'. The purpose was to provide the invasion force with information on the most important British political administrative and economic institutions. It would also be furnished with information on 'leading public figures' and the procedures to be adopted in taking over the Foreign Office, the War Office, the Home Office and the 'various departments' of the Secret Service and Special Branch.

Added to Hitler's ambivalence was the ambiguity which lay

6 Walter Warlimont, *Inside Hitler's Headquarters 1939–1945* (trans. R.H. Barry, London 1964), p. 107.

behind the perception of the method, the timing and the
objectives of the actual landing. It was assumed on the one
hand that winning air superiority over Britain was simply the
essential precondition for a successful landing, the landing
itself being the decisive element in the whole operation. Jodl
and Raeder on the other hand, with Hitler a sympathetic listener, argued for a landing as a 'last resort', the air offensive
occupying pride of place in reducing British resistance. The
German navy and the *Luftwaffe* reposed little faith in the
notion of a landing, either in the prospect of it materialising or
in its success should it do so. At the end of June General
Jeschonnek, *Luftwaffe* Chief of Staff, reportedly refused to
lend his aid in the army's invasion planning, dismissing the
whole idea that the *Führer* had any intention of mounting an
invasion. So why waste time in planning one![7]

In Ronald Lewin's phrase, it was 'with mincing steps' that
Hitler advanced towards the idea of a landing.[8] On 2 July he
made the first of a series of tentative decisions, admitting the
possibility of a landing in England but hedging this about
with the caveat that air superiority must first be attained and
'certain other necessary conditions' met. The three Services
were to report to him, but whatever preparations they had in
mind or had committed to paper were to be understood
against the background of 'a possible operation' only. Two
weeks later, after yet another mental wresting-match of trying
to solve the riddle of British unwillingness to make peace, he
issued Directive No. 16, *On preparations for a landing against
England*. Its substance was the result of the Berghof conference held with the army C-in-C Walther von Brauchitsch and
Franz Halder, Chief of the General Staff. It also signalled the
German army rather than the navy taking poll position in the
planning and preparation of this 'possible operation'.

Directive No. 16 can hardly be described as a ringing

---

7 Quoted in David Irving, *Hitler's War* (London 1977), p. 135.
8 Ronald Lewin, *Hitler's Mistakes* (London 1984), p. 112.

clarion-call to action. Hitler declared himself ready to prepare a landing against England and, '*if necessary*', carry it out, an operation designed to eliminate 'the English homeland' as a base which, '*if necessary*', may have to be occupied in its entirety. The landing itself would be a surprise crossing on a broad front from 'about Ramsgate to the area west of the Isle of Wight'. Conceivably a *limited operation*, possibly the seizure of the Isle of Wight or Cornwall, mounted before the general crossing could be useful, depending on what the three Services thought, but Hitler himself would decide. All preparations for what was now code-named Operation Sea Lion were to be completed by the middle of August.

The German army's task was to draft the operational and crossing plans for all formations of the first wave of the invasion, the navy's to 'procure the means for invasion', taking them to points allocated by the army. The air force's role was designed to 'prevent interference by the enemy Air Force', attack infrastructure and reserves, and explore the possible use of parachute troops. Preliminary planning envisaged an invasion force of some 25–40 divisions, mechanised and enjoying numerical superiority, requiring for its movement about 4,000 naval units, landing craft, barges and tugboats. Admiral Raeder had from the outset expressed grave doubts about the feasibility of invasion. He emphasised the importance of air supremacy, vital not only for the Channel crossing itself but also to ensure the deployment of the transport fleet and the minesweeping operations. For him, the landing had to be 'a last resort'. Additionally there was the risk to German industry involved in withdrawing a thousand heavy barges for the invasion, but more important, sheer logistics would make it impossible to commit the second and third waves of the invasion force for more than a week after the first wave. Though Hitler had specified 15 August by which time preparations must be complete, what he subsequently learned from Raeder made this patently impossible.

On 19 July Hitler delivered his long-awaited, long-delayed

speech to the *Reichstag*, the 'more in sorrow than anger' passages directed to the British. However, he knew full well that this was pointless and his appeal fruitless. He seized the occasion to announce twelve promotions to field marshal and Goering to *Reichsmarshall*. He also used the occasion to give private assurance to Field Marshal von Rundstedt that he had no real intention of embarking on a wholly superfluous operation, namely, the invasion of England.[9]

Two days later Hitler assembled a command conference with the C-in-Cs of the *Wehrmacht* services, Raeder, Brauchitsch and Jeschonnek. In an ideal world the war could and should be ended with the invasion of Britain, but this was not an ideal world and a cross-Channel attack was daunting in the extreme. Hitler wanted a report within a week from Raeder about the feasibility of a cross-Channel attack completed by 15 September. Not surprisingly Raeder scarcely exuded optimism, at which Hitler observed that if preparations were not complete by the beginning of September, then 'other plans' would have to be considered. 'Other plans' referred to postponing a decision about Britain until 1941, but attacking Russia this coming autumn.

What 'other plans' really signified was disclosed to senior planning officers on 29 July by the newly promoted full General Jodl: nothing less than Hitler's decision to rid the world 'once and for all' of the menace of Bolshevism. This was to be accomplished by a surprise attack on Russia to be launched at the earliest possible moment, namely, May 1941.[10] The clash with Bolshevism was inevitable. By the autumn of 1941 the *Luftwaffe*, strengthened by its victories in the east, would be an even more formidable instrument for use against England. Instructions went out to draft orders to implement *Aufbau Ost*, the transfer of substantial army and air-force units to western Poland. It was little consolation that Hitler, made

9 Quoted in *Hitler's War*, p. 147.
10 *Inside Hitler's Headquarters 1939–1945*, p. 111.

aware of the time factor, the climate and transportation problems, had at least been dissuaded from hurling himself
precipitately on Russia. What now impressed itself upon some
German planners was the urgent necessity to 'keep the way
open for Operation Sea Lion' as the only possible way of out-
flanking the Russian 'adventure' and its potential for disaster.[11]

The command conference on 31 July was a further demon-
stration of Hitler's wavering over a decision on a
cross-Channel attack, contrasting sharply with the energy he
devoted to justifying an attack on Russia. Raeder duly reported
on Sea Lion as ordered, conveying an impression of the navy's
readiness to meet the mid-September deadline but advancing
arguments which favoured a postponement of the cross-
Channel attack to May 1941 and the onset of fair weather.
Presently only two favourable tidal periods in late August and
the third week in September could be reckoned on. Even then,
the navy could not meet the first date, while the second usually
brought heavy weather. Raeder also questioned the tactical
soundness of proposing an assault across a broad front.[12]

Technical difficulties, not insurmountable but plausible
enough, thus provided Hitler with another refuge from actually taking a decision, deferred this time in the guise of
establishing 'the necessary conditions for the final conquest of
England', embodied in the 1 August Directive No. 17, *For the
conduct of air and sea warfare against England*. One of those
'necessary conditions' was the defeat of the British air force, a
task assigned to Goering and the *Luftwaffe*. The German air
offensive, already delayed, finally opened on 15 August,
though the previous day, 14 August, Hitler had expressed his
doubts about the success of the air offensive: in the event of
failure, a decision about invasion would be put off to May
1941. 'We must see what the *Luftwaffe* can do. . . .'[13]

11 *Ibid.*, p. 115.
12 *Hitler's War*, p. 150.
13 *Ibid.*, p. 157.

At the beginning of September Hitler had still not reached a decision, increasingly persuaded that Britain could be brought to heel without an invasion. Although Raeder informed him on 10 September that the navy would be ready with the transports on the date stipulated, 15 September, he procrastinated for a further three days before informing his commanders that while the *Luftwaffe* had scored 'enormous successes' as yet one of the 'necessary conditions', indeed the primary condition, defeat of the British air force, had not been established. The moment had not yet come to issue the ten-day warning order for the invasion. This crucial moment was postponed for a further three days on 14 September, precluding any invasion attempt before 27 September. Raeder now suggested the next favourable date, 8 October, but like Goering he was fully conscious that there was little likelihood of an actual landing taking place. Hitler had already ordered a partial dispersal of the *Transportflotte* and a halt to further shipping movements on 19 September, designed to reduce losses inflicted by British air attacks. Nevertheless re-assembly within the given warning period (S-10) could be facilitated by favourable weather.[14] Bomber attacks and the threat of invasion were to be the main instruments to weaken British resistance. Directive No. 18 dated 12 November referred only obliquely to Sea Lion: changes in the situation 'may make it possible, or necessary to revert to Operation Sea Lion in the spring of 1941'. The three Services would meanwhile continue to improve 'the conditions for such an operation'.

The German army, upon whom much of the planning and preparation for Sea Lion devolved, took the whole enterprise very seriously, unlike the scepticism which pervaded the navy

14 *Kriegstagebuch des Oberkommandos der Wehrmacht (Wehrmachtfuhrungsstab) 1940–1945*. Vol. 1 August 1940–31 December 1941. Ed. H-A. Jacobsen (Frankfurt am Main 1965), entry 19 September 1940, p. 82.

and the air force. The divisions of Army Group A's Ninth and Sixteenth Armies would constitute the actual invasion force. Army Group A undertook the identification of the available sea and river craft in Germany and in the occupied countries, and organised the requisite exercises to familiarise troops with embarkation and disembarkation procedures from these craft. The Germany army, among several other agencies, had also to attend to the framing of occupation policy, though the immediate requirements of the invading force were met with handbooks, geographical guides and phrase books, their strengths, weaknesses and idiosyncrasies wittily and shrewdly analysed by Peter Fleming in *Invasion 1940*.

The *Informationsheft GB*, a classified compilation for which Schellenberg claims a large share of the credit, was a different matter, proof that whatever delays, imprecisions and vagaries Hitler imposed on Sea Lion, there were influential circles which took it seriously and laboured as best they might to ensure its success, or at least their part in it. What Schellenberg called 'a small handbook' is belied by the facts. *Informationsheft GB* is actually a substantial compendium covering virtually every aspect of British life, of little use to the front-line soldier fighting his way in but indispensable to those setting up a German-dominated administration and an occupation regime. What will they find, assuming much remained essentially intact, and how is it organised? At the outset any user of the handbook would be supplied with the 'basic statistics' of the country, its size, topography and climate, the economy, transportation, population and language affiliation. Presumably this data was compiled with recourse to standard reference works, though its compactness would make it a handy tool for a quick check of items such as: population figures, principal cities. I see that my birthplace is mentioned, its population of the time accurately recorded.

The section on 'Constitutional Structure' provides a brief history lecture on the monarchy and what appears to be a 'parliamentary monarchy' but where in fact 'parliamentary and governmental absolutism prevail'. In terms of 'the pursuit of national interests Royalty is obsolete'. There is an interesting speculative twist to explaining the abdication of Edward VIII. Parliament and the Cabinet are 'vigilant in protecting their rights'. Should the King attempt to break out of his role of 'mere representation', he will be forced back into it or made to abdicate. 'This may well have been the real cause' of Edward's abdication 'in favour of his more passive brother George VI'. Precisely what a German Gauleiter or *SS* officer would make of this is open to question. He could scan a list of members of the British Government, several of whose names would be familiar to him from headlines, and he would learn that 'democratic freedom in Britain' is a sham. Military law (*sic*) has been imposed on the entire country, which, 'in its dictatorial application, defies all acknowledged democratic principles'. This lesson in civics may well have startled some German readers.

Britain, unlike Germany, lacks codified law, a criminal and a civil code. Nor does Britain enjoy a 'tradition bound civil service' such as exists in Prussia. Thus, the lower ranks of the Civil Service are pronouncedly 'trade unionist in character', the strongest 'anti-Conservative force' apart from Labour. When is a town not a town but a borough, how is the term 'city' used? Very possibly this convoluted section would simply cause a German official's eyes to glaze over, though he might pay livelier attention to 'ceaseless' criticism of the British legal system and the high costs of court proceedings, costs which 'make it impossible for the less affluent classes to gain their rights in court'.

The section on the organisation of central and local government is straight 'handbook' material, listing ministries and illustrating local administration with a flowchart. Much the same applies to the listing under 'Armed Forces', manpower strengths and basic organisation of the army, navy and air force, all 'linked through the King', the Imperial General Staff and the Imperial Defence College in London the providers of uniforms, weapons and training. Perhaps the compiler here found brevity preferable to exactitude. Those who needed specific information and had appropriate access could consult the various classified General Staff/*Fremde Heere West* files, such as *Grosses Orientierungsheft des englischen Heeres* or their naval and air-force equivalents.

Next came the serious business of seeking out Germany's foes, firstly those entrenched in 'universities and enemy cultural institutes'. Of twenty-five British universities, Oxford, London and Bristol were those 'active in political propaganda'. Oxford was singled out as being the home of the new series of 'Oxford Pamphlets' directed against Germany. Among particular authors were: R.C.K. Ensor, J.W. Brierly, A.E. Zimmer, G.F. Hudson and R.R. Kuczynski. The Cobden Club in London must be identified as a famous institution treating Germany as an adversary; its publications designed to prove the superiority of British culture over that of Germany, the eradication of science from the *Reich* one of its international slogans. The Royal Institute of International Affairs is an excellent source of information on international politics, 'shaping' opinion against Germany 'in terms of colonial policy'. The Central Committee for National Patriotic Associations based in London had widespread contacts with neutral countries, providing material and speakers. The Institut Français in London 'requires special attention'. The Academic Assistance Council in London (an association of German scientists abroad) finances research and 'propaganda assignments' for émigré scientists. 'A very valuable institute' but one little known is located within the Information Bureau of the City of Birmingham, producing 'vast amounts of statistical material' on the city and also 'German propaganda material'.

At this point the German official or officer would be introduced to the mystique of the public schools system, repositories of 'important anti-German material which is politically and historically significant'. One half of a percent of children attend public schools, yet these same children will eventually occupy 'about 80%' of all important social and political posts. To have attended one of these schools is the pride of any upper-class Englishman. Children are registered at birth with the father's old school. If the German invader had conceivably any pretensions in that direction, he was speedily disabused of them, advised that Eton College was 'sold out until 1949'. The judgement on the system is quite severe. Here the future English gentleman is educated, 'the gentleman who has never thought about philosophical issues, who has hardly any knowledge of foreign culture, who thinks of Germany as the embodiment of evil but accepts British power as inviolable'.

Whoever compiled the section on the International Boy Scout Movement clearly let his imagination run a little wild, branding the movement as 'a disguised instrument of power for British cultural propaganda', additionally an excellent information source for the British Intelligence Service. Central headquarters of the movement, the 'so-called International Bureau', managed until recently by 'a half-Jew, Mr Martin', head of the Passport Office, is now in the hands of John Wilson also of the Passport Office. The reports compiled by individual International Commissioners, data on economic and political conditions, are passed to the International Bureau. Perfect for intelligence gathering! Given the Nazi predilection for raiding the national treasures of occupied countries, 'Important Museums in England' (to which a somewhat confused entry on Scotland was tacked on) provides a quick but well-informed 'check-list' of major national holdings, what cultural artefacts and works of art to look out for, not least those prime candidates for repatriation, German documents and art 'of special interest' to the *Reich*.

It is obvious from the style and the contexts that many hands had been at work on the *Informationsheft*. For example, the section on the press provides some general background followed by straight listings of titles and ownership which distinguishes those newspapers run by the 'seven big groups or trusts' dominating the English press. Then come the 'independents', *Observer, Manchester Guardian, The Times,* Sir Oswald Mosley's *The Blackshirt, The East London Pioneer, Action* and *The British Union Quarterly,* plus *The Fascist* (Leese).

Apart from an opening jab about English radio broadcasting's well-known penchant for 'anti-German agitation and propaganda', this compilation follows the pattern set by the analysis of the press: structure of the BBC, leading personalities, organisation of regional broadcasting. Much of this, as with the press, simply meant reaching for the reference books, though this does not seem to have been the case with a somewhat bizarre item on 'Ethnographic Research', probably compiled by an academic or political analyst with a special interest in this field. Pride of place goes to Chatham House with its intensive work on *Mitteleuropa* or *Osteuropa,* problems of the 'Polish Corridor', Sudetenland and Germans in the east. Important figures in this work, men who possibly 'have important material in their private homes', are listed as Dr A. Toynbee, 'personally obliging, skilful man', Sir Albert Zimmerman at Oxford, Dr Allan Fisher, Sir John Hope Simpson and Lionel Curtis. Margaret Cleeve is singled out as the 'indispensable manager for special events'. Other 'important institutes for political work' include the School of Slavonic and East European Studies (the original has the title in the wrong order) housing 'very important material'. Professor R. Seton-Watson is significant in his own right. Other named centres include: Newbattle Abbey College in Dalkeith financed by Lord Lothian, Selly Oak College in Birmingham established by the Quakers and the Cambridge Slavonic Society associated with Professor W.J. Reddaway. Among prominent individual scholars identified under the curious rubric of 'English work' on east central Europe are C.A. Macartney on Hungary, and R.C.K. Ensor, 'one of the toughest opponents of National Socialism', yet undertaking in-depth studies of the '*Führer*'s European politics'. Even more bizarre in this somewhat eclectic assemblage, as if the author was seeking some pattern or arrangement of the agencies and persons connected with east central Europe, is the item on 'Ukrainians in England'. What purpose this might have served is obscure.

Josef Lisnowskyj 'should not be anti-German'. Stefan Dawidowytsch is 'doubtlessly pro-German', a member of the Ukrainian nationalist organisation, the OUN. Both held out the promise of co-operation. That may have been one motivation for including the Ukrainians in England, co-operation, or following up intelligence leads, counter-espionage business involving one Makohin, owner of the Ukrainian Bureau in London, connected with 'American espionage'. He could have acquired through the magazine *Investigator* material proving the 'disloyalty' of Hetman Paul Skoropadskij presently in Berlin.[15] It is possible that German counter-intelligence wanted this material included, since these were cases 'on file', identified from the huge card-index system in which Schellenberg took such pride. So this was partly unfinished business, partly a fishing expedition.

Nor surprisingly religion gets short shrift, drafted by an unsympathetic, hostile Party ideologue. First, however, an academic was obviously assigned to provide historical profiles of the Anglican Church, English Catholicism and the Methodist Church. The stolid factual material is precisely that, but the political interpretation put upon it is another matter, warped, derisive and malignant. The 'Religious division' of the Ministry of Information labours to 'ignite anti-German sentiment'. Given this remit, the German security authorities deemed it mandatory to 'take possession of this department's material'. The Archbishop's Commission on Relations of Church and State, enjoining 'leading British politicians and

15 On Hetman Skoropads'kyi, links with the senior German leaders, also the differences between the 'Hetmanites' and the Nationalists of the OUN, see John A. Armstrong, *Ukrainian Nationalism* (Columbia University Press, 2nd edn, 1963), pp. 26–33.

economists', is identified as a very efficient propaganda machine, portraying Germany as the enemy of all Christian states, and arguing that the totalitarian state and Christianity are incompatible. But 'the worst anti-German agitators within the Anglican clergy' are to be found in the Church of England Council on Foreign Relations, another organisation whose 'materials' must be seized. The Student Christian Movement of Great Britain and Ireland, leading member of the Christian World Union of Students, 'pretends to work for the spread of Christianity among students' but in reality has 'strong political tendencies' and is often critical of Germany. The Oxford Group is the third association to be marked down for mandatory seizure of its materials, indeed physical occupation of its 'main bureau', precisely because here may well be yet another outpost or offshoot of British Intelligence.

The analysis of the Communist Party of Great Britain is extremely thorough and remarkably free of extraneous or irrelevant comment. Obviously a special effort has been made to identify the role and importance of German émigré organisations, such as the German Freedom Party, a mass movement created solely for the 'elimination of National Socialism', welcomed by the Marxist camp as a participant in the struggle against the Third *Reich* but 'not given great prominence since these circles [the Marxists] believe the bourgeoisie to be too cowardly to support actively a struggle against the Third *Reich*'.

The treatment of the Trade Union movement is not dissimilar, though perhaps a little too sanguine in stating that 'English trade unions are not concerned with politics. . . .' Reference and address books were obviously extensively quarried, down to the National Society of Packing Case Makers (Wood and Tin), Box Makers, Sawyers and Mill Workers and the National Society of Brushmakers.

Not unexpectedly émigré organisations come in for close scrutiny. The number of German émigrés settled in Great Britain 'is relatively small', the permanent settlement of

émigrés 'unwanted'. The anti-German emigration in England
is divided into three groups: first the Jewish organisations,
second 'pacifist, liberal, religious' and other organisations
fighting Germany 'under the cover of ideology', and third the
Labour Party and unions. The World Jewish Organisations in
England are identified in the 'Special Wanted List'. The compiler then returns to the reference books, listing refugee
organisations. The Czech Émigré Organisation is singled out
for special attention, listing the membership of the Czech
government in exile. Masaryk is identified as the individual
responsible for intelligence, involving support for 'the highly
treacherous organisations and operations in the Protectorate',
plus arranging 'unscrupulous agitation and horror propaganda'. Elements of the former Czech Legion in France are
present in England though they are small in numbers: 'A
return of these legionnaires is not sought.'

'England is the country of Freemasonry.' It is, furthermore,
'a dangerous weapon in the hands of Britain's plutocrats
against National Socialist Germany'. What follows is a historical account of Freemasonry, its organisation and structure,
the Lodge in all its varieties and the inclusion of all known
British Lodges in the Special Wanted List. The section on
'The Jews in Britain' follows, designed to confirm a conspira-
torial combination, Freemasons and Jews lurking in unison.
The foundation of the 'Anglo-Jewish alliance' is attributed to
Cromwell, who recognised the affinity of the English scheme
for world domination and 'the Jewish version'. The compilers
adhere to the usual pattern of presentation, first a historical
introduction describing the place of the Jewish community
in Britain, followed by a review of the Jewish presence in politics, business, press and films, rounded off with a list of
Jewish organisations – not included in the 'Special Wanted
List'. Presumably the list of organisations and agencies in the
body of the text *was* the 'special wanted list'.

The organisation and structure of the British Police is yet
another 'reference book' compilation: facts, figures, the

Railway Police, Ports Police, location and classification of the fingerprint collection, the Special Branch ('political police'), many of whose officers have evidently shown a particular interest in studying German. The would-be German occupying authority was especially anxious to lay its hands on the ten-digit fingerprint collection (New Scotland Yard), the 'nominal' and 'wanted' indexes from the Criminal Record Office, the Forensic Science Institute, records of the Special Branch, the Information Room (supervising radio patrols), the register of aliens, the latter especially of consuming interest if only out of German awareness of what damage émigrés and exiles had inflicted.

The text of the *Informationsheft GB* ends on a dramatic note, possibly just what the compiler intended, nothing less than an account of the British secret service. Peter Fleming found the section 'marred by inaccuracy and pedantry', the approach 'novelettish', in contrast to the author of the Introduction here who is confident not only of the accuracy of the analysis of the structure of the SIS but also of the sensitivity of the information. What was known to German intelligence in 1940, the name of an SIS chief, was not vouchsafed to the British public until 1966 and then only through inadvertence. One intriguing aspect of the discussion of British secret intelligence is the complication which wells up over terminology or designation. Clearly the amorphous English phrases, deliberately enigmatic, presented something of a problem when rendered into German, and the author or authors of this section took great and necessary care to emphasise that the British service was not like the German. In order to understand the structural essence of British Intelligence, 'right at the beginning we have to free ourselves of conventional ideas of strict organisation, from the particularly German need for precise detail, separation and definition'. What seems to have impressed German Intelligence, or counter-intelligence, is the contribution of 'voluntary effort', the involvement of 'civilians' of independent means, even heads of state, an enviable attribute or facility largely denied the Germans. Though written fifty-nine years ago, whatever its occasional 'novelettish' imaginings (by no means confined then and even now to German Intelligence) or the misspellings, this is an account which has a quite a contemporary ring to it.

What, therefore, does this handbook amount to? Though sometimes compared to a 'snapshot' of Britain in 1940, it is more like a slowly unwinding video with 'educational' sub-titles, historical background, statistics, passages resembling garish film cartoons, social portraits, institutional description, geographical information, demographic profiles and economic analysis. Inevitably the Nazi ideological bias intrudes, the 'Jewish conspiracy' and the incubus of Freemasonry. Add to this a peculiarly envenomed view of the British plutocratic 'ruling class' and a distorted, frequently inaccurate view of the endemic 'Marxism' of the trade unions.

The 'Special Wanted List' (*Die Sonderfahndungsliste GB*) is literally the 'sharp end' of the handbook, a list of 2,820 British subjects and European aliens or exiles plus institutions and establishments of special interest to the Nazi occupation forces. At the front of the 'Special List' a note draws attention to a 'special, "special list"', identifying thirty individuals, with accompanying photographs, to be seized on sight, *'Lichtbilder festzunehmender Personen'*. The list had obviously been compiled for quick reference, since each name bears its corresponding Gestapo file reference, no doubt a product of that 'huge circular table . . . on which the files were placed'. An electrically powered system, Schellenberg took obvious pride in it, particularly since at the press of a button one man could access any one of 500,000 cards. The system must obviously have worked overtime to compile the list with its appropriate references. The 'usual suspects' are well represented within the names: Prime Minister Winston Churchill, British government ministers, politicians, journalists, financiers. Noël Coward, it seems, was marked down for possible dusty death. What the 'Special Wanted List' did disclose, as the Introduction amply demonstrates, is the degree to which the Germans had managed to penetrate SIS and individual spy-rings (*Täterkreise*) identified, for example, 'd'Alton, Leiter d. Intellig. Serv. I. Rotterdam (Taterkreis: Egon Rohr) RSHA IV E4'. The reference RSHA IV E4 indicated an intelligence connection or association on the part of the individual named, generating a strong interest from German counter-intelligence. On the other hand, the fabulous card index could not spell the first name of the 'Führer d. Labour Party', one Clemens Attlee, yet managed it successfully with 'Attlee, Clement Richard, 3.1.83, Major Wohng.: Heywood, Stanmore (Middlesex). . .'.

The 'Special Wanted List' was evidently compiled with an eye to the zealous, possibly overworked member of the *Einsatzgruppe*. The second part identifies those agencies and institutions which were of special significance, embassies and legations, firms, trade unions, the press, Grand and provincial Masonic Lodges.* In an impressive piece of cross-referencing the *SS Standartenführer* can assign his subordinates to localities spread from Aberdeen to Alloa, Ashbourne-Derbyshire, Llanelly, London (with its giant cross-reference system), Wimslow/Prov. Cheshire, closing alphabetically with York, all with assigned targets referenced to the main personnel list plus the appropriate Gestapo mark. Planning envisaged basing 'search and destroy' *Einsatzgruppen* in London, Bristol, Birmingham, Liverpool, Manchester and Edinburgh. In brief, search missions had no need of the elaboration and quasi-academic meandering which fill the formal text. In any event what did *SS* officers care for Cromwell's perception of the shared affinity between the English view of world domination and that of the Jews? This was a manual for total occupation, for the ruthless elimination of any who stood in its way or who had shown any hint of a propensity to opposition, resistance to

---

* This edition reproduces only the first part of the List, identifying personalities to be arrested.

or revulsion at the sights and sounds of National Socialism, with a candidate list for the *Knickschuss*.

It would be easy enough to mock the *Informationsheft GB* as Teutonic thoroughness taken to extremes, presenting a warped picture of Britain further distorted by misinformation and mis-understanding, cluttered with a near-obsessional urge to peer into every local nook and cranny. The British Union of Fascists does not merit a mention, not even *honoris causa*. As for some of the more recondite listings, maybe the RSHA ran a competition to discover who could furnish the longest, fattest dossier, for much of the material resembles nothing so much as a straight 'print-out' from a ready-made card index or a gazetteer. What cannot be denied is that while Hitler dithered and procrasti-nated over issuing the S-10 warning order for the invasion, the Gestapo and its associates worked furiously and assiduously on preparing a document *to be used* in the field, their view of Sea Lion being one of near imminent realisation and subse-quent total occupation of the length and breadth of Britain.

Even at this distance in time *Informationsheft GB* remains a somewhat eerie and slightly unnerving document, not so much because of what our would-be German masters did not know but rather for reasons of how much and exactly what they did know.

JOHN ERICKSON
University of Edinburgh

Preface

Among the most extraordinary documents to be recovered by the Allies at the end of the Second World War was the Gestapo's contribution to the planned invasion of England's south coast, a handbook classified 'secret' bearing the title *Informationsheft GrossBritannien*.

Precisely who wrote the whole of this report remains unclear to this day. In his post-war *Memoirs, SS Brigadeführer* Walter Schellenberg of the *Sicherheitsdienst* asserted that

> At the end of June 1940, I was ordered to prepare a small handbook for the invading troops and the political and administrative units that would accompany them, describing briefly the most important political, administrative and economic institutions of Great Britain and the leading public figures. It was also to contain instructions on the necessary measures to be taken in occupying the premises of the Foreign Office, the War Office, the Home Office and the various departments of the Secret Service, and Special Branch. This task occupied a great deal of my time, involving the collection and assembly of material from various sources by a selected staff of my own people.

Thus Schellenberg claimed he had supervised much of the work, although he was based in Lisbon for some of the relevant period, arriving in Madrid on 26 July and returning to Berlin on 6 August, apparently hatching an abortive plot to abduct the Duke of Windsor and bring him to Berlin. Another candidate as co-collaborator is Schellenberg's subordinate in *AMT VI*, Major Walter zu Christian, who had been

transferred to the SD's foreign intelligence branch after
having collected intelligence about Gibraltar and Britain
before the war. Claiming to have been educated at Seaford,
near Brighton, zu Christian has been credited with collating
the handbook's contents, although little can be verified
because, according to Schellenberg, almost all of the 20,000
copies printed were destroyed in an air-raid on his Berlin
office in 1943.

Whatever the truth, only the names of Schellenberg and
zu Christian have ever been publicly linked to the handbook.
Certainly Schellenberg was well-informed about the British
Secret Intelligence Service, to which the handbook devotes a
full, largely accurate, chapter. Although the spelling of some
surnames is unreliable, the rest of the data is authentic, which
raises the issue of the sources used in its compilation. The
internal evidence points to several references to Captain
Sigismund Payne Best and Major Richard Stevens, both SIS
officers who were seized while on an ill-advised visit to the
Dutch frontier in November 1939. While Stevens was relatively inexperienced, serving in The Hague under the
semi-transparent cover of the British Passport Control
Officer, Best had spent much of his career in SIS, having
joined the organisation during the First World War. Since
1936 he had operated for SIS as part of the 'Z' network which
had been intended, by its architect Colonel (Sir) Claude
Dansey, to act in parallel with, but in isolation from, the local
PCO. However, upon the outbreak of war the fateful decision
was taken to combine both organisations, and this led to Best
approaching Stevens and mounting a joint operation to recruit
a purportedly senior anti-Nazi dissident within the *Luftwaffe*.
Unfortunately this project was doomed from the outset
because it was nothing more than an elaborate scheme devised
by Schellenberg to tempt SIS into the open and thereby to
penetrate and disrupt its activities in the Netherlands. This
objective changed when an attempt was made on Hitler's life
in a Munich beer cellar, and Schellenberg arranged for the

two hapless SIS men to be dragged across the border into Germany as a reprisal for what was claimed to have been a British assassination plot. In reality the entire episode had been stage-managed to enhance the *Führer*'s status, but nevertheless Best and Stevens had been drawn into a complex deception scheme which left them in the SD's custody, where they were to remain until the very last days of the war.

Remarks attributed to both in the text imply that under interrogation they had supplied accurate answers to some apposite questions. As a consequence they faced a hostile reception upon their release from German captivity in 1945, and were regarded with considerable suspicion and contempt in London. Best, who wrote about his experiences in *The Venlo Incident* in 1950, subsequently was declared bankrupt, and Stevens scraped a living as an interpreter at NATO headquarters before his premature death in Brighton in 1965. Best lived until 1978, always embittered by the treatment he had received from SIS, and particularly resentful that he had been obliged to fight to be included in the list of those compensated for their imprisonment by the Nazis.

However, some years after both men had died new evidence emerged which suggested that the *Abwehr* had acquired much of its comprehensive knowledge of SIS's structure and operations from Colonel C.H. ('Dick') Ellis, an experienced intelligence officer who admitted after his official retirement that he had sold vast quantities of information about his employers, for whom he had worked since 1923, to the Germans. Ellis's confession to a large part explained the depth of the enemy's understanding about what was supposed to be a very secret service. Not only does the handbook demonstrate an impressive insight into SIS's pre-war operations, but careful analysis of the Special Wanted List shows that the Germans had accumulated a remarkable quantity of authentic material relating to SIS personnel and the addresses at which they lived and worked. All those listed were to be arrested. Accompanied by photos and even card registration numbers, the list bears eloquent testimony to the extent to which SIS had been penetrated and shows that several networks run from Passport Control Offices on the Continent were thoroughly compromised.

Typically an entry gave the full name of an arrestee, his date of birth, his cover-name, a last known current address and his car's index number, followed by the name of the espionage organisation with which he was associated. This impressive documentation was far more extensive than anything the British had learned about the *Abwehr*, so the question arises as to how the leak occurred.

Undoubtedly Best disclosed much of what he knew about the parallel 'Z' organisation, which had been intended to work independently, in isolation of the more overt SIS structure based on the vulnerable and conspicuous Passport Control Offices, which had to close down as the enemy swept through France, Belgium and Holland. It is also clear that Stevens did little to mislead his inquisitors, and after the war he blamed Best for his loquacity in the belief that his fellow prisoner's talkativeness had severely compromised his room to manoeuvre. Of course, neither realised that their much more senior colleague, Dick Ellis, had haemorrhaged more than enough to enable the SD to put the most pertinent questions to its two wretched prisoners. Much of the enemy's data can be traced to these three men but, intriguingly, some documents recovered after the war suggest that there might have been another source.

Before the outbreak of war German espionage in Britain, as indicated by the prosecution of Hermann Goetz in 1936, seems to have been conducted at a low level, principally by amateurs, and it is now an established fact that MI5 quickly gained control of the *Abwehr*'s entire network so that by January 1941 it was running a stable of double agents based on recently arrived parachutists and other longer-term spies. Messages transmitted by these men and women were carefully supervised by specially appointed Security Service case officers, as documented by Sir John Masterman in *The Double Cross System of the War of 1939–45*, leaving MI5 confident that every enemy agent had operated under its direct control. This, however, fails to explain the origin of some of the *Abwehr*'s information dating from September 1940, and in particular a report of the defences at Beachy Head and Rye dated 2 September 1940, and captured in Germany at the end of the war. Allegedly 'the agent was not able to give a clearer account of the number of armoured cars in the different localities, or of the regiments he saw there', but the very fact that a spy was at large in the area is highly significant. The context of the agent's report, which inexplicably places Tunbridge 'on the railway line from Hastings to London', suggests strongly that it was not an item manufactured by MI5's deception experts to mislead the *Abwehr*, and was most likely an authentic if mistaken signal from a genuine, if not very well-informed, agent. No message transmitted by an MI5 double agent would have been allowed to contain an error that could be verified so easily, by reference to an ordinary road map. While the Security Service was anxious to deceive the enemy about troop strengths and other military matters, it did not seek to undermine the credibility of its deception campaign by inserting patently bogus information.

The proposition that in early September 1940 there was an independent spy at liberty in southern England is quite novel, and on the evidence that the Soviet military intelligence service, the GRU, is known to have well-established networks functioning at that time, may be interpreted as evidence that some intelligence collected for Moscow was actually reaching Berlin. Such a development would demand a complete reassessment of how Britain in 1940 was viewed by Stalin, but the recently decrypted VENONA intercepts prove conclusively that the GRU was extremely active in managing several networks that were reporting on military deployments in England.

Whether or not this is the explanation for the mysterious

spy who reported from Rye in September 1940, there can be
no doubt about the quality of information contained in the
Gestapo handbook. There are, of course, quite a few factual
errors, such as the inexplicable assertion that the diplomat Sir
Robert Vansittart had acted as a front bench spokesman for
the Foreign Office in the House of Commons, when he was
never elected to Parliament, and the somewhat fanciful view of
the English character as inherently perfidious and untrust-
worthy, but the mistakes and the denigrating perspective shed
fascinating light on the then current German opinion about
the British and their Empire. The compilers rightly concluded
that most British expatriates and travellers were likely to be
well-disposed towards their country's ubiquitous intelligence
agencies, whereas by contrast German refugees could only be
relied upon to be critics of the Nazi regime. While it might
now seem somewhat paranoid to have suspected the international Boy Scout movement as an SIS appendage, it is a fact
that the organisation's founder, Robert Baden-Powell, took
espionage very seriously and wrote several books on the topic.
Indeed, as the handbook points out, its leader in the immediate pre-war era, Colonel John Wilson, was not unconnected
with intelligence, and was to be appointed head of the
Scandinavian Section of Special Operations Executive.

The handbook's analysis of the structure of SIS was
not just accurate, despite some eccentric spelling, such as
'Winter-Bottom' for Wing Commander Fred Winterbotham,
then head of SIS's Air Section, but was considered sufficiently sensitive post-war to ensure that the document was
kept under wraps for years after it had fallen into Allied hands.
Indeed, SIS's Chief was correctly identified as Stewart
Menzies (his Christian name being miss-spelt 'Stuart'), a fact
that was to remain concealed from the British public until
1966. SIS was presented as a ubiquitous, amorphous organisation with a reach that extended into the War Office, Shell
Oil and the Metropolitan Police, and to a large extent the picture presented was true. City institutions and British

businesses abroad were generally willing to share information
with SIS, and many SIS retirees had acquired new careers in
which they were occasionally asked to give help and advice to
the modern service. A certain class and generation, regardless
of occupation, saw a call from Broadway Buildings as an
opportunity to serve their country, whereas elsewhere on the
Continent, as the handbook's author commented ruefully,
such conduct was considered highly disagreeable, almost as
the equivalent of consorting with rogues and cut-throats.

The handbook remains an unique snapshot of how the
Nazis perceived Britain, certainly by today's standards a
myopic misconception of the influence of the Jews and
Freemasonry over local government, Parliament and the
Empire. However, for all its misconceptions, it provides an
intriguing insight into how Hitler's regime saw its perfidious
opponents from across the English Channel.

NIGEL WEST

PART 1

The Gestapo Handbook
for the Invasion of Britain

General Survey of Great Britain
(England, Scotland and Northern Ireland)

a) Size

		km2
1.	England	131,761
	Wales	19,343
	Scotland	71,171
2.	Northern Ireland	13,564
3.	Isle of Man	572
4.	Channel Islands	195
		242,606 [*sic*]

b) Topography

South-east: lowlands
North, West and South-west: hilly country
North and Scotland: mountainous and moors.

c) Climate

In general, a sea climate prevails in Britain. The west is mild
and humid in winter, cool and a little dryer in summer. The
east is cool and dry in winter and spring, hot and a little less
dry in summer and autumn. The most humid region is the
seaside district of Cumberland, the most arid the mouth of
the Thames, and Lincolnshire.

d) Economy

Economic districts:
In north-western Cumberland, ore mining.
In north-eastern Durham, coal-mining (the area around

Middlesborough being Britain's most modern iron and
steelworks).

In South Wales, coal depots (mainly bunker coal which is
shipped from Newport and Cardiff).

In the Midlands (from Bristol to Hull), different small industries, namely knitwear factories, iron and steel products
(Leicester, Nottingham, Derby, Burton, Sheffield).

In the area of Manchester and Lancashire, major cotton industry with Liverpool as collecting point of raw material.

At the mouth of the Clyde-Firth (Scotland), the most important district of coal and heavy industries of Lanarkshire;
the site of the world's biggest shipyards.

London, as enormous warehouse.

The south-eastern lowlands is the only larger agricultural area.

Employment in Great Britain (1931)

England, Wales and Scotland show the lowest number of agricultural and forestry workers in Europe, and the highest
number of employees in industry and mining, trade and
transport, civil service and the self-employed.

Percentage of employees in:

	England and Wales	Scotland	Northern Ireland
Agriculture, forestry and fishing industry	6.2	9.5	26.3
Industry and mining	48.2	47.5	43.7
Trade and transport	27.1	26.8	18.2
Armed forces	1.0	0.3	0.8
Civil service and self-employment	10.2	10.0	5.3
Domestic service	7.3	5.9	5.5

e) Industry and Mining

Highly industrialised Great Britain does not possess any

significant amount of minerals or industrial raw materials in the British Isles, except for hard coal and iron ore. On the other hand, the British Empire can supply British industry with all raw materials it requires. The main industries of Britain are coal, iron, cotton and textiles.

f) Trade

Great Britain still holds the leading position in world trade, even though its share has been falling over past decades. Its share in the world trade fleet has declined mainly due to the growth of the American fleet. However, Britain is still pre-eminent in shipbuilding.

Britain shows a substantial balance-of-trade deficit, i.e. imports are considerably higher than exports. This imbalance is corrected mainly through sea freight, interest and dividends paid by those companies active abroad, insurance and cable companies and the London market as an auction centre for raw materials. London is the centre of international financial transactions.

Important Imports:	Important Exports:
Wheat and flour	Cotton products
Fat and meat	Iron products
Fruit	Coal
Tea	Woollen products
Sugar	Yarn
Tobacco	Machines
for industrial purposes:	Leather
Cotton	Glass
Wool	Stoneware
Jute and flax	Ships
Ore	
Wood	
Rubber	
Mineral oil	

g) Agriculture and Forestry

Agriculture and forestry are severely neglected in Great Britain, only 5.4% (in the German Reich 27.5%) of its overall surface is woodland. Although 80.6% of its surface is agriculturally exploited, a mere 21.5% (in the German Reich 38.6%) of the total is arable. The remainder consists of meadows and pastures. Wheat, rye, barley, oats, potatoes and sugarbeet are cultivated. Britain's livestock, including horses, cattle, pigs and goats, is extremely low. Only the stock of sheep is very high, with over 20 million.

h) Fisheries

Great Britain has Europe's biggest fishing industry. Its fishing fleet has caught 920,900 tonnes of fish in 1937 worth 318,000,000 Reichsmarks. It is outdone only by Japan and the USA. (Germany, 1937: 627,400 tonnes.)

i) Transport

Mail, telegraphy and telephone are nationalised. On the other hand railways (London Midland and Scottish, LMS; London and North Eastern, LNER; Great Western, GWR; Southern, SR) are fully licensed private enterprises.

The once excellent waterway network has been neglected in coastal areas, and because of the growth of the railway network, is no longer sufficient to meet modern requirements. Submarine cables are mostly privately owned. Since all British trunk lines, as well as many foreign lines, cross British territory, Britain dominates international communications, with the exception of wireless transmission.

Road networks and air routes are well developed.

Population

1.	England	37,789,700
	Wales	2,158,200
	Scotland	4,812,600
2.	Northern Ireland	1,293,000
3.	Isle of Man	49,300
	Channel Islands	93,100
		46,225,900 [*sic*]

Language Affiliation

Exclusively Welsh languages (in Wales and Monmouthshire) are spoken by	78,000
English and Welsh are spoken by	811,000
Gaelic is spoken exclusively (in Scotland, Ross and Cromarty, Inverness and Argyll) by	7,000
English and Gaelic are spoken by	137,000

Three languages are spoken in Great Britain apart from English. They represent different groups of the Celtic proto-language:

1. Scottish Gaelic
2. Welsh Gaelic
3. Irish Gaelic

In the Free State of Ireland, Gaelic is used now with remarkable devotion. The constitution for 'The Republic of the Whole of Ireland' (in force since the end of December 1937) proclaims that 'Gaelic is, as the national language, its first official language, in addition English is recognised as its second.'

List of Principal Cities

England and Wales (residents in thousands)

London (with suburbs)	8,204	Birkenhead	148
(without suburbs)	4,397	Brighton	147
Birmingham	1,003	Derby	142
Liverpool	856	East Ham	142
Manchester	766	Rondda	141
Sheffield	521	Oldham	140
Leeds	482	Middlesborough	138
Bristol	397	Wolverhampton	133
Kingston-upon-Hull	314	Walthamstow	131
Bradford	298	Ilford	131
West Ham	294	Leyton	128
Newcastle-upon-Tyne	283	Norwich	126
Stoke-on-Trent	277	Stockport	125
Nottingham	269	Blackburn	123
Portsmouth	252	Gateshead	122
Leicester	239	Southend-on-Sea	120
Croydon	233	Preston	119
Cardiff	224	Ealing	118
Plymouth	208	Bournemouth	117
Willesden	184	Hendon	116
Bolton	177	Huddersfield	113
Southampton	176	South Shields	113
Coventry	167	Saint Helens	107
Swansea	165	Walsall	103
Tottenham	158	Blackpool	102

Scotland

Glasgow	1,088	Dundee	176
Edinburgh	439	Aberdeen	167

Northern Ireland

Belfast	438

Constitutional Structure

The claim that Britain had the earliest and most liberal constitution has always played an important role in British
constitutional politics. However, up to now Britain has not pos-
sessed a written body of laws in a constitutional sense; the legal
basis of its governmental system consists of conventions and
historical customary rights, which are difficult to categorise.

Great Britain (England, Wales and Scotland) and Northern
Ireland is a hereditary constitutional monarchy, headed by the
House of Windsor (until 17 July 1917 the House of Saxe-
Coburg-Gotha). George VI, formerly the Duke of Windsor,
has been King since the abdication of his brother Edward
VIII (on 10 December 1936).

Nowadays Britain appears as a parliamentary monarchy,
but in spite of the democratisation of its constitution, parliamentary and governmental absolutism prevail. Today's state
organisation is maintained by the monarchist and bureau-
cratic elements. The King (known respectfully as the Crown)
heads constitutional life but nowadays, in terms of the pursuit
of national interests, royalty is really obsolete. But within the
British Empire the King is the only link between the mother
country and its dependent dominions and colonies. According
to constitutional law, the King represents the executive and
the Parliament the legislative in political life. In reality, however, the King's executive powers are very limited and have
long been passed to the Cabinet and to Parliament. It is possible that a stronger King could secure more influence for
himself in the affairs of the state and the government, but
Parliament and the Cabinet are vigilant in protecting their
rights and would force the King back into his role of mere
representation, or even bring about his abdication. This
might have been the real cause of Edward VIII's abdication
in favour of his more passive brother George VI in the
autumn of 1936.

In theory, based on the royal prerogative, the Crown even now has the right to convene and dissolve Parliament, to determine Britain's foreign policy, to nominate the Prime Minister and fill the most important government posts. Assisting the King is the secret crown council, the Privy Council, where all laws passed by the Parliament are enacted. The Privy Council is composed of some 300 members. Apart from archbishops, the senior judges and some aristocracy, out-standing personalities from the worlds of politics and culture belong, as do all past and current members of the Cabinet. At the moment the former Prime Minister Chamberlain is its president bearing the title 'Lord President of the Council'. All members of the Privy Council have the honorary title 'Right Honourable' in front of their names. Apart from fulfilling some important judicial functions, the Privy Council is now only a figurehead: all its important tasks have been transferred to the Cabinet, which in historical terms emerged from the Privy Council.

The Prime Minister is nominated by the King, who cannot exercise free choice. The Prime Minister emerges from the strongest Party in Parliament and chooses his fellow Ministers from among the members of this Party. About 15–20 Ministers are part of the Cabinet. Under-Secretaries of State as well as some senior public servants also have the title minister, but without having a seat in the Cabinet. As happened during the last war at the Opposition's demand, the principle of one party govern-ment has given way to a Coalition Cabinet. In his Cabinet reshuffle of May 1940 Churchill included the Labour leader Attlee and others from the Labour and Liberal Parties, and even put them in his War Cabinet, which is composed of just six members.

Composition of British Government (as of 13 May 1940):

1. Prime Minister and First Lord of the Treasury: Winston Churchill – 1911–15 First Lord of Admiralty, 1918–21 Minister of War and Aviation, 1924–9 Chancellor of the Exchequer, currently 65 years of age. 10 Downing Street, Whitehall, SW1.

2. Chancellor of the Exchequer: Sir Kingsley Wood – 1931–5 Postmaster General, 1939–40 Lord Privy Seal, 59 years of age. 11 Downing Street, Whitehall SW1.

3. Lord President of the Council: Neville Chamberlain – during the war Mayor of Birmingham, 1923, 1924 and 1931–7 Chancellor of the Exchequer, 1924–9 Minister of Health, 1938–40 Prime Minister, 71 years old. Downing Street, Whitehall SW1.

4. Lord Chancellor (similar to a Minister of Justice): Sir John Simon – 1913–16 Minister of Justice and later Home Secretary, 1931–5 Foreign Secretary, until 1940 Chancellor of the Exchequer, 66 years of age. House of Lords, London SW1.

5. Secretary of State for Home Affairs: Sir John Anderson – since 1905 officer of the British Colonial Service, 1922 Under-Secretary of State in the Home Office, 1932–7 Governor of Bengal, 58 years of age. London SW1.

6. Secretary of State for Foreign Affairs: Viscount Halifax (Edward Frederick Lindley Wood) – 1922–4 Minister of Education, 1924–5 Minister of Agriculture, 1926–31 Viceroy of India, 59 years of age. 10 Downing Street, London SW1.

7. Lord Privy Seal (an insignificant court appointment and honorary office): Major C.R. Attlee (Leader of the Labour Party) – 1931 Deputy Leader of the Labour Party, 57 years of age. Treasury Chambers, London SW1.

8. Secretary of State for the Dominions: Viscount Caldecote – 1935 Governor of Hong Kong, 56 years of age. Dominions Office, Downing Street, London SW1.

9. Secretary of State for the Colonies: Lord Lloyd – 1929 High Commissioner of Egypt, 61 years of age. Colonial Office, Downing Street, London SW1.

10. Secretary of State for India and Burma: L.S. Amery – 1929 Secretary of State for the Dominions, 67 years of age. King Charles Street, Whitehall, London SW1.

11. Minister for the Co-ordination of Defence: Winston Churchill (see above). 2 Whitehall Gardens, London SW1.

12. First Lord of the Admiralty: A.V. Alexander – 1928–31 First Lord of the Admiralty. The Board of Admiralty, Whitehall SW1.

13. Secretary of State for War: Anthony Eden – 1926–9 Foreign Office Under-Secretary of State, 1931–3 Lord Privy Seal, 1934–5 Minister for Affairs of the League of Nations, 1935–8 Foreign Secretary, 1940 Secretary of State for the Dominions, 43 years of age. The War Office, Whitehall SW1.

14. Secretary of State for Air: Sir Archibald Sinclair (Representative Peer for Scotland). Adastral House, Kingsway WC2.

15. Secretary of State for Scotland: Rt Hon. Ernst Brown (1935 Minister of Labour). Office of the Secretary of State for Scotland. Dover House, Whitehall SW1; Scottish Office, 28 Drumshengh Gardens, Edinburgh.

16. President of the Board of Trade: Sir Andrew Duncan – 1920–7 Deputy Chairman of the Employers' Federation of Shipwrights, President of the Executive Committee of the British Iron and Metal Union, Member of the Bank of England's Board of Directors, 36 years of age. Great George Street, SW1.

17. Minister of Agriculture and Fisheries: Robert Hudson – Parliamentary Secretary and Minister of Health (1936).

18. President of the Board of Education: Herwald Ramsbotham – since 1911 lawyer, ex-serviceman, since 1936 Pension Minister, later Minister of Education. Whitehall, London SW1.

19. Minister of Health: Rt Hon. Malcolm MacDonald (Secretary of State for Dominion Affairs 1935), 39 years of age. Whitehall, London SW1.

20. Minister of Labour: Ernest Bevin. Montagu House, London SW1.

21. Minister of Transport: Sir John Reith (Senior Director of the British Broadcasting Corporation).

22. Chancellor of the Duchy of Lancaster: Lord Hankey (London Naval Conference).

23. Ministry of Information: Duff Cooper (Secretary of State of War 1935).

24. Minister for Economic Warfare: Hugh Dalton – 1929–31 Member of the Board of Trade, 53 years of age.

25. Minister for Aircraft Production: Lord Beaverbrook – 1918 Minister of Information, 61 years of age.

26. Minister for Food and Nutrition: Lord Woolton – businessman from Liverpool, General Director of the Lewis's Stores, during the war Government Adviser for questions on raw materials, included into the Cabinet in April 1940, 57 years of age.

27. Minister of Supplies: H. Morrison – 1931 Minister of Transport.

28. Minister for Overseas Trade: J.H. Shakespeare (joint Department under the Foreign Office and the Board of Trade) – ex-serviceman, 1921–3 Private Secretary to Lloyd George, later Chief Whip of the National Liberal Party, 1931–5, later Parliamentary Secretary of the Ministry of Health and Education, since 1936 Parliamentary and Finance Secretary of the Navy, 47 years of age. Old Queen Street, London SW1.

29. Minister without Portfolio: Anthony Greenwood – 1931 Minister of Health, 52 years of age.

30. Postmaster General: Sir William Morrison – 1923 lawyer, Private Secretary, later Parliamentary Private Secretary to the Crown Advocate, Attorney-General, Conservative MP since 1927, ex-serviceman, 1936–40 Minister of Agriculture, later Postmaster-General. St Martin-le-Grand, London WC1.

31. Minister for Shipping: Ronald Cross – banker, 44 years of age.

32. Minister of Public Works: Lord Tryon – 1935 Minister for the Dominions.

33. Minister of Pensions: Sir Walter Womersley – (first factory worker, then shop assistant, later retail store manager, self-employed at 21) Mayor of Grimsby, Deputy Chairman of the British Chamber of Commerce, Unionist representative since 1924, 1931 Sir Kingsley Wood's Parliamentary Private Secretary, 1931–5 Second Lord of the Exchequer.

34. Attorney-General: Sir Donald Somervel.

35. Solicitor-General: Sir William Jovitt.

36. Paymaster-General: Lord Cranborne.

(The above are at the same time members of the War Cabinet.)

All ministers are Members of one of the two Houses of Parliament. In spite of the general right to the vote, which has existed since 1918, Parliament is still linked to the class system. It is composed of the 'Upper House', the House of Lords, and the 'Lower House', the House of Commons. The Upper House holds the Royal Princes, the hereditary Peers, the Peers of Scotland and Ireland, the highest Church dignitaries and the senior judges. The total number of Upper House members is around 750. Due to heredity of the majority of Upper House seats and the one-sided representation of high finance and the major industries, the character of the House of Lords is fundamentally Conservative. Since the introduction of the 1911 Parliament Act, it has lost most of its political power, since the Lower House can, under certain circumstances, pass laws without seeking its approval. Nevertheless the significance of the House of Lords as representative of the British aristocracy, with its vast political connections and capitalist networks, should not be underestimated.

The House of Commons has a constant number of 615 members, and its appearance is determined by its party structure. The seating order of rows in the chamber makes a major fragmentation into different parties impossible. The two main adversaries, originally the Whigs and the Tories, later Liberals and Conservatives (Unionists), are now the strongest party, the Conservatives, and its Opposition, Labour. The Conservative Party has divided into groups of partly moderate and partly ultra-conservative and chauvinist orientation. Since Munich, one of these groups of the extreme right diehards concentrated around Churchill has become prominent because of its warmongering. More centrist, but still part of the government party, are the National Liberal groups around Sir John Simon and the National Labour MPs. By joining the coalition government the Opposition has abandoned its main duty: criticism of the party in power. Even in normal times the British Opposition, which calls itself 'His Majesty's Most Loyal Opposition', and whose leader is paid by the government, holds a peculiar position. The British parties are not ideological or programme-based parties in our sense of the terms. None of today's parties has a written, rigid manifesto. While they undoubtedly represent certain interests, the party structure is just a vessel into which new content flows every five years with the parliamentary elections. The last parliamentary election took place in the autumn of 1935, so at the very latest there should be a new election by the autumn of 1940. However, to avoid disturbing the domestic political equilibrium during the war, the parliamentary term has been extended indefinitely, as happened during the First World War. In spite of the elimination of the Opposition, the left-wing parties will try to replace the government at the first opportunity. Accordingly the Labour Party, which has formed the government only twice, in 1924 and 1929–31, has already drawn up a manifesto to address peacetime social injustice. However, the Labour Party will never achieve a revolutionary change because its leaders have, like their Conservative opponents, mainly attended feudal public schools, and so are too rooted within this system. When leading Labour Party personalities really have worked their way up from the lower social ranks, as in the case of Ramsay MacDonald, the system of British society usually absorbs them socially as well as ideologically. The Labour Party's membership is smaller than is generally assumed. Trade union members and members of co-operative societies are numerically the strongest components within the Party. When it became the official Opposition after the First World War, the Liberals lost their significance as the biggest opposition party and have now lost much of their importance. The far left wing of the Opposition consists only of the Independent Labour Party MPs and the single Communist, whose insignificance follows their paucity of number. The major universities send their own representatives to the House of Commons, who join the respective parties according to their views.

The current state of war clearly illustrates how much democratic freedom in Britain there really is. An Enabling Act at the beginning of the war has allowed the government to impose military law on the entire country, which, in its dictatorial application, defies all acknowledged democratic principles.

Law and Administration

The British system of justice and local government are, even for the English, very complex matters and differ greatly from the system in Germany and other European countries. These systems have developed historically, one law following another, without completely doing away with previous regulations and institutions. The administration has never been organised to establish a uniform system, or to delineate individual authority. In Britain, in spite of all efforts, there is no codified law and no criminal or civil code as there is in Germany.

The British Civil Service is the apolitical, expert and permanent element in the state, in contrast to the ministers who come and go with each electoral shift. A tradition-bound civil service, like the Prussian one, does not exist in England; in its lower ranks the civil service has a pronounced trade unionist character which makes it the strongest anti-Conservative force, apart from Labour.

Administratively England (actually England and Wales without Scotland and Northern Ireland) is subdivided into 83 county boroughs and 61 administrative counties. London, which is further subdivided into the City of London and 28 metropolitan boroughs, is a county borough as are England's major 83 cities. The official administrative term for the cities is therefore not 'town' but 'borough'. The term 'city' is only applied to those which are the seat of a Bishop or have a Royal Charter. In the County boroughs administration lies in the hands of County Councils (in London: London County Council).

Administrative counties are bigger units of administration. They again subdivide into urban and rural districts with corresponding authorities, and vary greatly in size. So, generally named by its historical appellation of county, Oxfordshire forms an 'administrative county' (the City of Oxford is a 'county borough' and therefore independent), while the county borough of Yorkshire is split into three 'administrative counties': North, West, and East Riding. The administrative counties, like the cities, have their county councils, headed by an elected chairman, who, in the case of bigger cities, holds the title of Mayor or Lord Mayor.

In each county the King, respectfully known as the Crown, is represented by a Lord Lieutenant and a Sheriff, whose functions are insignificant compared with their former glory, when they surrounded themselves with great pomp. The entire local administration with its different, overlapping authorities does not, as one would expect, come under the jurisdiction of the Home Office, but first of all of the Ministry of Health, while the Home Office, the Ministries of Education and Agriculture etc. also intervene. Regulations for Scotland and Northern Ireland are generally similar to those in England and Wales, but again we have different terms for the divisions into districts and administrative authorities.

For a foreigner (a non-British subject) the system of the English administration of justice is as difficult to understand as that of local administration. The training of English jurists is not provided by universities (where they follow general philosophical courses), but at the Inns of Court, after graduation from university. The latter have mainly social functions and serve to build a social network of relationships enabling the young jurists to develop a practice. In England there is no distinction between lawyer or solicitor or barrister, judge, and public prosecutor as there is in Germany. After completing his education, the young jurist is called to the bar and then carries the title of barrister. The highest stage of a legal career is the 'King's Counsel'.

The High Court in London is the highest court for most of the civil and criminal cases. The lower court system is subdivided into two different stages of appeal for civil and criminal jurisdiction. The highest court for criminal appeals is the High Court of Justice, but for civil law appeals the House of Lords is the highest court. There are also county courts and Justices of the Peace for the regulation of petty offences. Their competence is limited. Scotland and Northern Ireland have a special jurisdiction.

Criticism of the English legal system is ceaseless, and usually begins with the high cost of court proceedings. In spite of the attested rights which should guarantee each citizen a fair trial by his equals, i.e. a jury, the high costs make it almost impossible for the less affluent classes to gain their rights in court.

Central and Local Government

a) Central Administration

Great Britain lacks parallelism of governmental and local administration down to the lowest offices. There is no decentralised lower level of the state, and all local authorities administer themselves. Apart from the ministries there is no central state apparatus. Among others, e.g. the ministries for transport, trade, agriculture, labour and education as well as the Treasury, two ministries perform the main central administrative tasks in matters concerning local government.

The Home Office (Ministry of the Interior)
Apart from being responsible for internal security (known as the King's Peace), the Secretary of State for Home Affairs controls the organisation of parliamentary and local elections, the entire police force, the prisons, psychiatric asylums, naturalisation and immigration, the licensing of restaurants and public houses, theatres, the vice squads, trade schools and trading inspections. Recently the Home Office acquired a whole new range of responsibilities, and today it supervises civil defence and air-raid precautions, which the local authorities are required to organise so that they may receive government grants. The Home Office provides gas-masks for the population and equips the local civil defence organisations.

The Ministry of Health
Its area of responsibility includes:

1. the health service,
2. the general insurance business,
3. public welfare,
4. general supervision and audit of the local financial administration.

Legally the central authority has no official power over local government and its civil servants. In legal terms there is only local supervision. State inspection, meaning the supervision by travelling departmental officials, is the only link between the instruments of governmental supervision, the ministries and the community. This system allows only supervision; ministerial direction of local authorities is illegal.

b) Local Administration

England and Wales with exception of London
  Structure by areas of the English local authorities:

	County	
Rural District	Urban District	Non-County Borough
Rural Parishes	Urban Parishes	Urban Parishes
	County Borough	
	Urban Parishes	

Except for the County Borough and the County, all area local administrative units form parts of the related bigger unit.

The biggest unit of administration is the County, of which England and Wales currently have 62. Within these are included most of the smaller cities (306 Non-County Boroughs) and the urban and rural districts. Furthermore the Counties contain 575 urban districts and 475 rural districts.

The three communities – the cities, rural and urban districts – are answerable to the County. They are themselves again subdivided into parishes. The number of parishes fluctuates with the frequent changes in local areas. Nowadays there are almost 11,000 of them, and they are the smallest local administrative units. Apart from the Counties, there are 83 County Boroughs. These are cities equal to a County, over which the County has no authority.

All of these local administrative units have elected bodies, the Councils (consisting of Aldermen and Councillors). These county, city, district and parish officials are citizens of the communities and form the local administration in an honorary capacity. Their honorary leaders are selected from among them: the Mayor in towns, or Lord Mayor for bigger cities, and the Chairman of the Council in the counties and rural districts. The Councils act as local parliaments and create standing committees which are responsible for the execution of specific tasks. The local administration's civil servants and local officials, appointed by these elected bodies, are under their control. The most important of these local officials are the County Clerk and the Town Clerk, who are employed as administrators, but as their influence grows they act increasingly as the political authority's expert advisers.

London
The structure of London's administration is different:

1. The County of London subdivides into 27 Metropolitan Boroughs, which work in the same way as the rest of the local administration, the individual Metropolitan Borough Councils and the London County Council (LCC) being the highest administrative authorities.
2. The City, the old part of London, relies on old privileges which allow administration through the authority of the Lord Mayor, the Common Council, the Court of Aldermen and the Court of Common Hall.

Special authorities responsible for the entire area of London
are: the Metropolitan Water Board, the Gas, Light and Coke
Company, the London and Home Counties Joint Electricity
Authority, the London Passenger Transport Board, and the
Port of London Authority.

Armed Forces

The armed forces are composed of

1. the national forces,
2. the British fleet,
3. the British Air Force,
4. the national forces of the Colonies, Protectorates and
    Mandates,
5. the armed forces of Ireland and the Dominions.

These are not directly subordinate to the War Office, but first
to their respective government department, so are linked
through the King. The Imperial General Staff and the
Imperial Defence College in London provide uniforms,
weapons and training.

Recently Great Britain introduced universal conscription
and compulsory military service, but have applied it only to
some of the younger age groups. The regular Army, which is
voluntary and professional, with a period of service of twelve
years, operates in parallel with the Territorial Army, a voluntary militia. The former has about half of its forces in Britain
and the other half in the colonies, protectorates and mandates
on a system of rotation. In addition, a voluntary supplemen-
tary reserve consisting of engineers, technicians and railway
staff fills shortages in the technical units. Military youth training is not a legal obligation, but is widely practised by about
two million members.

The country is subdivided into six military districts: Aldershot, North, South, East, West and Scotland.

The Dominions are not automatically required to participate in war. If they agree, about 1 million white and 3 million coloured able-bodied men are at the UK's disposal.

a) Army

The regular Army's power of command and administration is executed by the Army Council, under the leadership of the Minister for War. The regular army (with a peacetime strength of 133,000 men and an additional reserve of 149,000) is structured into 5 infantry divisions and 1 armoured division. The Territorial Army (with a peacetime strength of 187,000) consists of 12 infantry sections and 5 anti-aircraft units.

b) Royal Navy

The Admiralty commands and administrates. The First Lord of Admiralty is accountable to Parliament as Minister for the Navy (he is usually not a naval officer but a parliamentarian). Subordinate, but independent, are the six Lords Commissioners (two Civil and four Navy Lords). The Admiralty handles mobilisation and war plans.

Main war ports are: Chatham, Sheerness, Dover, Portsmouth, Rosyth in Scotland, and Scapa Flow in the Orkney Islands.

Personnel (about 125,000 men) are volunteers, mostly from the seafaring population; the new generation of non-commissioned officers consists partly of ship's boys from the Merchant Navy.

c) Royal Air Force

Britain aspires to have an Air Force equal to the strongest, and the authority is the Air Ministry. The Royal Representative

(Air Force Commander) is the head of staff in the Ministry. As recently as the spring of 1939, there were 123 squadrons, 1,750 front line aircraft ready at home, and at least as many in reserve. Total strength is 125,000 officers and men. About 80 airbases are planned in Britain and most are already completed. An Air Force Voluntary Reserve (RAFVR) is being trained at schools: Air Academy in Andover, Royal Defence Academy (together with the Army and the Royal Navy) in London, Central Flying School in Upavon, 11 military and 13 civil flying schools etc. In addition, torpedo squadrons operate under Coastal Command. Nationality marking: a blue, white and red roundel on wings and fuselage.

Air defence: England is structured into three areas – London, Portsmouth and the North. Two air defence sections have been newly established (4 groups, anti-aircraft units and engineer battalions). Coastal Command is subordinate to the Admiralty.

Universities and Enemy Cultural Institutes

Among a total of about 25 universities, Oxford, Bristol and London have been specifically active in political propaganda.

Oxford University helped British propaganda during the First World War, when it published a series of 87 so-called Oxford Pamphlets. Since the spring of 1939, before the start of the current war, a new series of these Oxford Pamphlets have been issued, directed against Germany. The following publications appeared: R.C.K. Ensor, *Mein Kampf*; A.G.B. Fisher: *Economic Self-Efficiency*; J.W. Brierly: *The Revision of Versailles*; A.E. Zimmer: *Law of Force in International Relations*; H.V. Hodson: *Imperial Relations*; H.D. Henderson: *Colonies and Raw Material*; G.F. Hudson: *Turkey and the Balkans*; R.R. Kuczynski: *Population Problems* [Lebensraum].

The Universities of Oxford and London are co-operating closely with the Ministry for Information, created from the private Wellington House.

Under Churchill's protection, Bristol University has also been taken into confidence for political reasons and used to co-operate in propaganda.

Of the scientific, political and cultural institutions which deal with Germany as an adversary, the Cobden Club in London is most famous. Its publications attempt to prove the superiority of English culture over German culture. (The assertion that after 1933 science was eradicated from the Reich is one of its international slogans.)

The Royal Institute of International Affairs is subordinate to the British Council which in turn depends directly on the Foreign Office and co-operates closely with the latter as well as with the Ministry for Information. Its principal task is research in all questions concerning foreign countries and, from an English standpoint, it has achieved excellence, being a major source of information on international and political questions and territorial conflict. In terms of colonial policy, it has shaped opinion against Germany. The institute holds a lot of extremely important political material.

The Central Committee for National Patriotic Associations in London has special political significance. It is linked to many cultural societies and associations in neutral countries and from time to time provides them with material and speakers. Some old data and figures may give an indication of its activities: during the First World War the Committee had at its disposal 250 speakers who spoke at 1,500 meetings. It distributed 850,000 leaflets to school children and 900,000 to workers at important industrial centres. A total of 250,000 pamphlets, tracts and books were sent to neutral countries.

The Institut Français in Kensington requires special attention. It is the centre of French cultural propaganda in Great Britain and works with the British universities.

The Public Record Office in Chancery Lane, London

WC2, was founded in 1838 and is of great interest. It has had its own museum since 1902.

The Academic Assistance Council (an association of German scientists abroad) at 12 Clement's Inn Passage, Clare Market, London WC2, is a focus of German émigrés who contributed to the 1937 émigrés' register. It corresponds to the local German research council and finances research and propaganda assignments for emigrant scientists.

The Information Bureau of the City of Birmingham in the Council House is a very valuable institute which gets little public attention. The Bureau corresponds more or less to our statistical offices and is a public body which distributes vast amounts of statistical material about Birmingham. It also produces German-language propaganda material.

Educational System

1. Public Schools

These are the best-known English schools. They merit special attention in so far as they have for centuries educated and politically orientated the country's political leadership. Important anti-German material, which is politically and historically significant, can be found in their documents and collections.

There are about 150 Public Schools. In social standing the most distinguished are Eton, Harrow and Winchester, then Westminster, Rugby, Charterhouse, Marlborough, Clifton, etc. Hardly one per cent of all children currently go to a Public School, but they will eventually occupy about 80% of all politically and socially important posts. They are the schools of the English upper class, and to have attended one of these schools is still the pride of any Englishman who is a member of that class. Fathers often register their children at birth with the Public School they had previously attended (Eton College is sold out until 1949). However, wealth alone is not sufficient grounds for admission; the father must be politically or socially important.

The first generation of English Labour leaders all came from ordinary backgrounds and for the most part acquired political status as political secretaries. Prominent among today's Labour Party leaders are public schoolboys Major Attlee, Arthur Greenwood, Dr Dalton and Sir Stafford Cripps.

Chamberlain was a pupil at Rugby, while Ministers John Hankey, Halifax, Eden, Oliver Stanley and Duff Cooper all went to Eton. The current Viceroy of India, Lord Linlithgow, and Sir Robert Vansittart, the government's foreign policy adviser, were also educated at Eton. Sir Samuel Hoare attended Harrow, as did Winston Churchill. Hore Belisha went to Clifton College, Bristol, and Sir John Simon attended Fettes College in Edinburgh. All of these are boarding schools, and some were founded as long ago as the 14th Century. They are almost completely independent of the state, are based on old financial foundations, and have served to perpetuate the traditions of the ruling class. It is here that the future English gentleman is educated, the gentleman who has never thought about philosophical issues, who has hardly any knowledge of foreign culture and who thinks of Germany as the embodiment of evil, but accepts British power as inviolable. The entire system's purpose is to train those of strong willpower and boundless energy, who consider spiritual issues a waste of time, but know man's nature and understand how to rule. These are educated people who in conscienceless manner represent English ideals and see the meaning of their lives in the promotion of the interests of the English ruling class.

2. The International Boy Scout Movement

This was created in 1907 by the English military officer Lord Baden-Powell, who defended Mafeking in the Boer War. His organisation first limited its activities to England, later expanded over Europe (1911) thanks to propaganda from the British government and finally extended to the whole world. The Boy Scout Movement was established in the Dominions only after pressure from the English authorities.

Lord Baden-Powell is, as World Chief Scout, the leader of the International Boy Scout Movement. Its central headquarters is in London, in the so-called International Bureau which until recently has been managed by a half-Jew, Mr Martin, who was simultaneously the head of the Passport Office. The current manager of the International Bureau, John Wilson, also works at the Passport Office; for the previous eight years he was Chief of Police in Calcutta. It is possible that his successor there is a certain Mr Lunt. The International Bureau builds links between the individual national scout associations. An International Commissioner heads each national association and is responsible for maintaining the link with the International Bureau in London. The International Commissioner is required to draft monthly and quarterly reports on the economic, cultural and political situation of the relevant country and pass them to the International Bureau. In addition, any personal or written contact between groups have to go through him. The individual national Boy Scout sections are structured similarly to the International Bureau.

Although the individual Boy Scout organisations are ostensibly almost entirely devoted to pre-military youth education, the Boy Scout Movement is a disguised instrument of power for British cultural propaganda, and an excellent source of information for the British Intelligence Service. Lord Baden-Powell was run as an agent against Germany during the last war. The dissolution of the Austrian boy scout association has, among other things, provided proof of the link between the Boy Scout Movement and the Secret Service.

The English Boy Scout Movement follows a similar model, altered to fit English circumstances, to the German Free Youth Movement. Accordingly, there has been close personal contact between members of the German Free Youth Movement and the English Boy Scout Movement.

The 1926 Kandersteg Agreement on Minorities has special significance for international relations since it guarantees the constitution of minority scout groups in every country with a national scout association. The German Youth Front, a gathering of émigré youth leaders, also enjoys close ties with the International Bureau. Furthermore, it is suspected, due to its numerous connections abroad, that the International Bureau works for British Intelligence.

Important Museums in England

England has some of the largest museums in the world. Art treasures and cultural valuables have been collected or stolen for decades. They also contain documents and works of art from German history, in which the German Reich must have a special interest. The biggest collections are to be found in the British Museum in London, which is organised with an international perspective and exhibits collections and treasures from all over the world, generally the very best that could have been obtained or stolen. Its valuable manuscript collection, with some very important historical documents, has to be particularly emphasised. The building's central block contains a giant library for all sections and collections.

Apart from the British Museum, the South Kensington Museum has to be mentioned since it houses valuable art objects and items from Europe, including wood-carvings, woven articles and embroideries, the world's most beautiful and precious pieces of ivory, iron and most of all gold and silver. The London Museum illustrates the City's history and presumably there are also objects of general interest to be found. The Guildhall Museum houses medieval finds and treasures from England and Scandinavia. London's New Burlington Gallery held the

anti-German exhibition of 'degenerate art'. The National
Gallery has among 4,000 paintings many portraits of English
personalities, as well as a series of Jews. Apart from these
museums some churches possess considerable treasure vaults.

Almost every English county has similar smaller collections
and among them the Yorkshire Museum must be stressed.
Further museums are located in Cambridge and Oxford (e.g.
the Ashmolean Museum with Director Leeds). Collections of
objets d'art and ancient manuscripts are to be found in the different colleges of Oxford and Cambridge.

In Scotland the National Museum of Scotland and
Edinburgh in Queen Street must be pointed out. The current
Director Edwards is said to have been sympathetic to
Germany. The museum contains, among other things, a col-
lection of ancient Celtic artefacts.

Among the libraries and societies in London, the most
important are: the Royal Society of Arts, The International
Society for Contemporary Music, The British Music Society,
The Museums Association, University College Arts Libraries,
Royal Academy of Music Library, Library of the Royal
Academy of Arts.

Using international funds, the Societies have supported the
fight against Germany. The libraries contain the most important documents of European, and especially German
historical and cultural development.

The Press

The English press consists mainly of popular newspapers and
is the result of decades of liberal press management in pursuit
of vast sales to make large profits from advertising. The advertising business is dependent upon commercial clients with
offers of insurance, crossword puzzles and competitions etc.
The editorial content is secondary.

There are several noticeable trends among the many titles. The *Daily Herald* hardly resembles the British party press; it existed in Germany before 1933. The editor was changed in the spring of 1937: Percy Cudlipp, who hitherto had been editor of a Conservative paper, the *Evening Standard*, replaced Francis Williams at the top of this socialist organ. The publisher simply explained that business considerations accounted for the appointment of a Conservative editor.

The historical origins of the current English press date back to the second half of the last century. After the businessmen had succeeded in making newspapers tax efficient and politically more independent, the way was paved for an injection of purely private capital. Of the three men who decisively dominated this development, the most significant is Alfred Harmsworth, later Lord Northcliffe. With the acquisition of the *Evening News* (1896) and the founding of the *Daily Mail* England acquired its first modern daily press. Northcliffe also created the English illustrated daily with the establishment of the *Daily Mirror*. At the peak of his power he succeeded in bringing the English quality newspaper *The Times* under his influence. The tough competition in the English newspaper market has two distinctive phenomena as consequence:

1. In England there are few extremely high circulation papers. With 47m inhabitants in England and Northern Ireland, there are only 150 dailies among the 1,877 newspapers published; eleven of which are entirely sport-oriented, and four devoted to finance and trade. There is only one daily newspaper for every 150,000 people, therefore circulations are correspondingly high. The *People* has the highest circulation, not only in Britain but in the entire world, with 3,250,000 copies.
2. The other distinctive phenomenon is the concentration of ownership of English newspapers in a few big groups or trusts.

Only a few newspapers, principally *The Times*, avoid developing into the popular press, which is aimed at a mass readership, and succeeded in maintaining a separate identity. In spite of its low circulation, it is the most important vehicle for influencing political opinion.

The Sunday papers are a special feature of the English press. There are seven, with a total circulation of around 16,500,000. This high circulation is explained by the fact that the usual dailies are not printed on Sundays. The English, and especially those who live in the cities, read papers only in the morning, and there are only a limited number of evening newspapers, especially in London. A greater number of these appear only in the rural areas.

Seven big groups or trusts dominate the English press. Their dependence on financial considerations has meant that, especially in times of economic fragility, their property and financial holdings often vary, but without changing the basic structure. The major conglomerates are:

1.   Rothermere conglomerate (Harmsworth family) under the management of Lord Rothermere, Lord Northcliffe's brother; with his friendly attitude towards Germany, he is an exception among the press tycoons. It controls the *Daily Mail, Daily Mirror, Evening News* and *Sunday Dispatch*.

2.   The Berry conglomerate is split into 3 groups:
   a)   Lord Camrose (William Ewart Berry), controls *Daily Telegraph* and *Financial Times*.
   b)   Lord Kemsley (James Gomer Berry), controls *Daily Sketch, Sunday Times, Sunday Graphic*.
   c)   Lord Iliffe.

3.   The Westminster Group, owned by the Morrel and Rowntree families, controls about fifty newspapers in the North of England, among them the *Birmingham Gazette*.

4.   The Beaverbrook conglomerate, managed by Lord Beaverbrook, controls the *Daily Express, Evening*

Standard, *Sunday Express* and, together with the Rothermere Group, various agricultural publications.

5. The Inveresk Paper Company (William Harrison, family name Grotrian) is managed by William Harrison, controls over ten newspapers and magazines, e.g. the *Yorkshire Evening News*.
6. Since November 1936, the Cadbury Family has owned the *News Chronicle* and the evening paper the *Star*.
7. Elias conglomerate (manager Julius Salter Elias). Its most important subsidiary company is Odhams Press Ltd which holds 51% of the capital of the socialist *Daily Herald* (circulation 2 million), the balance is owned by the English Trades Union Congress.

Among the newspapers which have kept their independence are:

1. The *Observer* (Lord Waldorf Astor)
2. The *Manchester Guardian* (Scott Family)
3. *The Times*, which was bought back after Lord Northcliffe's death by the founding family Walter and the Astor family. In 1922, they set up a control committee whose task was to see that *The Times* remained an 'institution of public interest'. Among the committee members are the Bank of England's governor, a senior judge and the director of the All Souls College in Oxford.
4. The papers under Sir Oswald Mosley's authority, *The Blackshirt*, *The East London Pioneer*, *Action* and *The British Union Quarterly*.
5. *The Fascist* (Leese).

The main press agencies working with the English press are:

1. Reuters Ltd (owned by Press Association and Sir Roderick Jones, General Manager for Europe, and W.L. Murray, who is a Knight of the French Legion of

Honour). Specialises in foreign news and news related to the Empire.

2. Press Association (controls Reuter's). Specialises in news of the United Kingdom and Northern Ireland.
3. Exchange Telegraph Company Ltd.
4. Central News Ltd.

There is no press law in England, and there are no constitutional or other rules governing the relationship between the press and the state. The interests of journalists are looked after by:

1. The National Union of Journalists, founded in 1907, is concerned with legal and economic issues.
2. The Institute of Journalists deals mainly with the new generation of journalists and with general questions of news media and therefore admits non-writers into its ranks.
3. The National Guild of Catholic Journalists, founded in 1935.

On the other side of the profession there are organisations for the editors and associations for the newspaper entrepreneurs for London: The Newspaper Proprietors' Association, the provinces: The Newspaper Society, and Scotland: The Scottish Daily Newspaper Society.

The English provincial press takes London's press as its model, but without the same circulation or significance. Of importance is, among others, the *Manchester Guardian*. Each English paper has on its own, or, in association with other provincial papers, a correspondent in London. Advertising is, in most cases, assigned to an agency.

London is also the centre of economic and political life for dominion and colonial papers, who also have permanent representatives in the capital. In order to look after their economic interests they have, in many cases, set up communities of interests and societies, for example:

1. The Argus South African Newspaper Ltd (community of interest for South African dailies)
2. The South African Morning Newspaper Ltd.

A visible link of the Empire's English-language press is the Empire Press Union, founded in 1909 and located in London. It handles all legal issues concerning problems related to press, news, cable and radio media, and is responsible for fostering imperialism. There are also regional associations for the individual dominions.

Radio

The extent to which English radio broadcasting has supported anti-German agitation and propaganda is well known, and accordingly this is only a brief overview of the organisation and structure of English broadcasting.

English radio is similar in organisation to its counterpart in Germany. Based on the 1904 Wireless Telegraphy Act, the state exercises total control over radio broadcasting, which is assigned to the Postmaster-General. The current organisation and its legal basis are determined by the Royal Charter of 20 December 1926. At the same time a contract between the Postmaster-General and the new corporation was established in conformity with English constitutional custom. The corporation is named the British Broadcasting Corporation (BBC), a company governed under public law which is supposed to act as a 'trustee of the national interest'. It has a concession for ten years, which was renewed for the same amount of time in 1936.

The corporation does not have any capital, but it has the right to edit magazines and hold copyrights and patents. Its task is to establish radio stations and to run them, renting the necessary connecting cables from the Post Office. Its income comes from radio licence fees, of which it receives 75%.

The BBC has a chairman and a vice-chairman, but the 'highest executive official of the corporation', the General-Director, has decisive influence, since the BBC, founded by the Crown, is fundamentally independent, not subordinate to a change of government, and subject to minimal parliamentary control. Radio broadcasting is available to the Government as well as to the Opposition. This, however, presupposes goodwill. The Postmaster-General has the power to decide the BBC's life or death, since he can withdraw the concession at any time.

Since its creation in 1927 until recently, Sir John Charles Walsham Reith was General-Director. It is now F.W. Ogilvie, Ll.D.; his deputy is Sir Cecil Graves. The BBC's headquarters are in Broadcasting House, London W1.

The Board of Governors, consisting of seven members in peacetime and of two during the war, controls the BBC. The General-Director is accountable to the Board of Governors.

In each of its seven population centres (London, Midland, Northern, West, Wales, Scotland and Ireland) the BBC has two radio channels, one broadcasting the national programme from London, the other transmitting a regional programme. Thus the listener can switch from one medium wave channel to the other which is transmitted from: Midland Regional, London National, London Regional, North National (Huddersfield), North Regional (Huddersfield), Scottish National (Falkirk), Scottish Regional (Falkirk), Northern Ireland Regional (Lisburn), West National (Watchett), West Regional (Watchett), Aberdeen, Bournemouth, Newcastle, Plymouth.

In the national programme the musical content is about 60% of the broadcast, and news about 22%. The regional programmes are dominated by music with 75% of the content. Radio plays and cabaret are frequent, and political and sports reports are, of course, priorities. Religious programmes still occupy about 4.16% (according to the *Handbook of Worldwide Broadcasting*, 1937–8).

Apart from the medium-wave channels the BBC also runs a long-wave station in Droitwich and a short-wave channel in Daventry, maintaining links between the UK and the British Empire.

The production of BBC programmes is supervised by special advisory committees, headed by the General Advisory Council, which is composed of several Members of Parliament, some members of the aristocracy and the Bishop of Winchester. There are also advisory committees for each of the regional channels and for individual types of programmes, especially music, educational programmes and religious transmissions.

Ethnographic Research

Chatham House:

On ethnographic issues, Chatham House is of the utmost importance. Its full name is The Royal Institute of International Affairs, 10 St James's Square, London SW1. It has in the past few years been engaged intensively with questions of eastern middle Europe, especially with the problems of the corridor, Bohemia, and Germans in the East. Chatham House has not only undertaken studies but has often held debates. The following men have played significant roles, and presumably also have important material in their private homes:

a)   Dr A.J. Toynbee, Professor at University of London. Personally an obliging and skilful man.
b)   Sir Albert Zimmern, Professor, holding the Montague Burton Chair for International Relations at Oxford.
c)   Dr. Allan G.B. Fisher, Professor of World Economics. In the past Fisher was in Australia and New Zealand, but in the last few years he has studied intensively economic issues of South-Eastern Europe.

d) Sir John Hope Simpson. Mainly looked into the 'persecution of Jews' and the problem of refugees, used to work in Palestine, China and Newfoundland.

e) Lionel Curtis, one of the founders of Chatham House. Specialist on South Africa. A believer that the British Empire corresponds particularly well to God's will. Has travelled the entire globe and lectured about the topic of his treatise in three volumes: *The Commonwealth of God*.

f) Margaret E. Cleeve. In charge of all the Institute's publications and indispensable for managing special events.

The Institute has a series of international links, particularly with similar institutes in Canada, South Africa, New Zealand, India, the USA and France. In the past few years connections have also been made with the Polish Baltic Institute in Godingen. The Institute's publications are mostly issued through Oxford University Press, Amen House, London EC4.

Further Important Institutes for Political Work, especially concerning Eastern Europe:

1. The School of Eastern European and Slavonic Studies at London University is the political and scientific centre for British research on Poland and Czechoslovakia, not only linguistic and Slav, but historical and political and with reference to cultural geography. Very important material. A significant name is Professor R. Seton-Watson.

2. Newbattle Abbey College, Dalkeith (Scotland). School of Politics with very big influence, deeply Christian orientation. Lord Lothian is its financier. Studies on France and Germany.

3. Selly Oak College, Woodbroke (near Birmingham). School of Politics set up by the Quakers, with important material on their international lateral connections.

Perhaps this material is located at friends' Service Council in London.

4. Cambridge Slavonic Society, Cambridge. Close co-operation with Poland, led by Professor W.J. Reddaway.

English Work on Eastern Middle Europe

Important individuals in politics concerning eastern middle Europe are:

1. C.A. Macartney, All Souls College, Oxford, who is a specialist on Hungary with important connections to Madjar circles.
2. Dr B. Manilowski, Professor of Anthropology at London University. One of the Polish contacts.
3. R.C.K. Ensor, Vice-President of Corpus Christi College, Oxford. One of the toughest opponents of national socialism in England, but who has dealt in depth with the Führer's European politics.
4. Dr Williams F. Reddaway, Professor at King's College, Cambridge, specialising in Polish and Baltic questions. Honorary Doctor of Dorpat; co-operating member of the Baltic Institute in Godingen.
5. Dr Alexander Bruce Boswell, Liverpool University, Professor for Russian and Polish. Connections to the Baltic Institute in Godingen.
6. Dr Kenneth C. Edwards, Professor of Geography, University College Nottingham. Plays an important role at Le Play Society. Strong connections with Poland.
7. Baron Marcellus von Redlich, address unknown. Foreign Service College; important contact of the Foreign Office. Co-operation with anti-German Polish Combat Institutes.
8. Dr Eric J. Patterson, University College of the South West of England, Exeter. Connections to Polish Combat Institutes.

Ukrainians in England

The Ukrainian group in England does not have the political significance enjoyed by Ukrainian émigrés in Paris. It has mainly to do with establishments created by western Ukrainians to acquaint the Anglo-American world with Ukrainian issues.

The following interrelations are of importance:

1. Ukrainian Bureau, London. The owner is the American citizen Makohin, a very dark personage who apparently serves American espionage. There are documents about the Bureau and Makohin at III B 15.
2. The magazine *Investigator*. Published in the past to inform the English about the Ukrainian Hetman Group. Korostowec was crucial. It can be assumed that some most important material is accessible through him, which proves the disloyalty of Hetman Paul Skoropadskij, living in Berlin.
3. The magazine *Contemporary Russi*. Editor: Professor Lancelot Lowton. The magazine propagated the break-up of Russia and had very good connections to numerous anti-Bolshevik circles. Documents of the magazine are of great interest for further Eastern European work. In Germany a certain Mr Kaskel once appeared on behalf of Professor Lowton.
4. Josef Lisnowskyj, Manchester. Plays a certain role in Manchester's Ukrainian community and was in contact with the magazine *Meta*, of Lemberg. Should not be anti-German. Possible co-operation. Presumably with strong religious (Greek-Uniate) interests.
5. Stefan Dawidowytsch, London. Member of OUN, doubtlessly pro-German. Came to London from Canada some years ago and directs an Information Bureau of the Ukrainians in Canada. Co-operation.

The Anglican Church (Church of England)

Historical Development

Reformation of the English Church has developed independently and has played a role in the general spiritual movement and opposition to the Pope. The external cause for the introduction of reformation was the behaviour of Henry VIII.

English reformation involved four main stages:

1. Split from Rome under Henry VIII, 1529–47.
2. The Reforms of Edward VI.
3. Reaction under Queen Mary.
4. Reinforcement and reconstruction under Queen Elizabeth.

1. Under Henry VIII, the Reformation, in its most intense initial stage, was a national operation executed by the King and Parliament. The first step was the abolition of papal supremacy and the institution of royal supremacy over the Church of England. The Catholic clergy were accused by the King of Treachery to the Court. They were forced to endorse the King's supremacy with the following words: 'We recognise His Majesty as the sole protector, only and highest ruler and, as far as the law of Jesus Christ permits, as the supreme head of the Church of England and its clergy.'

   Henry VIII's conservative attitude became imposing for a characteristic side of the Church of England. All earlier forms for the election, confirmation and consecration/ordination of bishops, for the offer of sacraments and for the Church service were kept. The most significant act of reformation was the wide spread of the 'holy scripture'. Cranmer, Archbishop of Canterbury, also revised the Common Prayer Book.

2.   Under Edward VI's government, the Protestant party dominated. The remission of royal injunctions in 1547, followed by a royal and episcopal visitation of the different dioceses led to iconoclasm which changed the external appearance of the places of worship as well, with the destruction of icons, windows, garments and other adornments.

   In the meantime Cranmer developed and widened his contacts with Protestant circles on the Continent, and the Common Prayer Book, which had appeared as early as 1549, was revised again in 1552 in the Protestant tradition.

3.   Queen Mary (1553–8), a convinced Roman Catholic, reinstated Rome's full authority and the anti-Roman laws were revoked. This was the government of the burning and the martyrs.

4.   With Elizabeth's coming to power in 1558 two decided factions, the followers of Rome and the Puritans, were at odds. By revoking Mary's pro-Roman legislation, she opposed the intentions of the reformers who had fled the country under Mary's rule and had now returned to build the Reformed Church of England following Zwingli's and Calvin's patterns. Her goal was 'the appropriation of the achievements of the new teachings and the conservation of what had been since primeval times'.

   The conflict with the followers of Rome reached its height with the bull by Pope Pius V, *Regnans in Excelsis* (1570), which excommunicated Queen Elizabeth. The Puritans, who first remained with the Church, worked towards the elimination of the episcopate and the introduction of the new Church order and a new instruction for the Church service, which would be binding on everyone. After disagreeing with this demand, they separated from the Church of England. The Anglican Church developed into the main ecclesiastic system: The Kingdom by Divine creation, population and Parliament obliged to God's obedience; the Church as second heavenly institution, with its hierarchy instilled in the population and governed by the King. With this the Church of England became the national Church.

In the eighteenth century, a reaction against the influence of Enlightenment philosophy, which became apparent in the form of the so-called Latitudinarianism, developed. Methodism, introduced by the brothers John and Charles Wesley and Whitefield, stimulated a deep renewal of religious and moral life in England, strongly influenced by German Pietism.

Royal belief led the teachings closer to the Protestant profession of the Continent, partly Lutheran, partly Protestant. This gives the Anglican Church its unique position between Catholicism and Protestantism. In its constitution and cult it reminds one of Catholicism while continued emphasis is put on its independence from the Pope, and its connection with the medieval Church of England is stressed. Close to Protestantism is the view that its profession, apart from constitution and cult which fundamentally inform the essence of the Anglican Church, has never played the role it held in the German Church. In its attitude to life, Calvinism has had its effects within the Anglican Church.

The specificity of the Anglican Church gives it a world-wide span leaving room for different kinds of conviction, as long as the four cornerstones of Anglican religious community persist. These are:

a) The Episcopal constitution with special emphasis on deriving the consecration from the time of the apostles (apostolic succession);

b) The use of the Bible in a reformed interpretation with specific worth attached to the Old Testament;

c) The Common Prayer Book, the prayer book of the Church of England which outlines the formal structure of services and contains the creed in 39 articles;

d) The recognition of royal supremacy.

There are three orientations within the Anglican Church:

1. The 'High Church' which feels related to Roman Catholicism though not subordinated to the Pope. It stresses the independence and significance of the Church in its entire hierarchical structure to the state as well as the Free Churches. Special emphasis is put on the arrangement of the religious order following the old customs of Catholicism (frankincense, coloured attire, veneration of the Virgin Mary and Saints, auricular confession, monasteries and convents, spiritual exercises).

    Apart from the more elevated classes, who are members of it, the High Church has got through to the broader layers of the population with its rituals and its Anglo-Catholic tendencies.

    Outside its religious order, the High Church has constructed new churches and is a hive of social activities. It often intervenes in social disputes (strikes, etc.). The High Church's alignment is organised within the 'English Church Union'.

2. The 'Low Church' includes the Evangelicals within the Anglican Church, who also originate from the middle classes. Supporters of this orientation, which developed from Puritanism, feel close to the Free Churches with whom they have many things in common. Their devoutness is related to Pietism and they strongly rely on the Bible. From these circles, the 'British and Foreign Bible Society' was founded in 1804. They take part in missionary projects, and their organisations are the Church Association and the National Church League.

3. The 'Broad Church', called into life by S.T. Coleridge (the 'English Lessing'), represented the scientific tendency within the Anglican Church. It assembled those who sought to combine a philosophically and scientifically liberal attitude with a conscious Christian religiousness.

Here also a progressive outlook and outright conservatism hold the balance.

The Broad Church has captured the lower bourgeoisie, the distinguished upper class, the lowest social stratum and intellectual circles. Thereby the Anglican Church acquired elements of English Catholicism and spiritual atomism.

Organisation

The Church of England put special emphasis on the Episcopal constitution and consecration, which gave full powers to perform ecclesiastical duties only to the ordained.

The Church of England is the national Church. The King is its 'highest leader', but is not allowed to interfere in issues relating to the Church service. As 'Visitator' he can merely make inquiries and demand an account of conducting of services. In part the powers have been transferred to Parliament.

As the legally recognised Church, the King has to be in touch with the Church of England. At his coronation, he promises to support the teachings, discipline and direction of the Church. He is crowned by the Archbishop of Canterbury.

The Crown nominates Bishops and other high pontiffs; among these 2 Archbishops and 24 diocesan Bishops represent the clerical Lords in the Upper House. At the top, the Church of England is divided into two provinces, a southern under the Archbishop of Canterbury, and a northern under the Archbishop of York; the first takes precedence. He is the Empire's peer and has the right to crown the King and to issue dispensations.

In total the Anglican Church embodies 38 Episcopal dioceses: Canterbury, York, London, Durham, Winchester, Bath and Wells, Bristol, Carlisle, Chester, Chichester, Ely, Exeter, Gloucester, Hereford, Lichfield, Lincoln, Liverpool, Manchester, Newcastle, Norwich, Oxford, Peterborough,

Ripon, Rochester, St. Albans, Salisbury, Sodor and Man, Southwell, Truro, Wakefield, Worcester, Birmingham, Bradford, Chelmsford, Coventry, St Edmundsbury and Ipswich, Sheffield, Southwark. The last seven are newly founded or rather re-establishments since 1900. At the top of each diocese there is a Bishop consecrated according to apostolic succession, and his Dean, who takes care of the cathedral service. Their tasks are the direction and visitation of dioceses, undertaking confirmation ceremonies and ordination, spiritual jurisdiction and general administrative duties.

The selection of the Bishops is made on advice of the Crown whose First Minister initially gets in touch with the clerical authorities via a type of cathedral chapter. Bishops, priests and deacons form three layers of the churchly classes. Those holding parishes are called rector, vicar, incumbent, and are assisted by curates. For the most part the parishes are under the patronage of the monarch, private persons or institutions and public corporations. Apart from the parish clergy, there are chaplains of different sorts, in the army, within institutions and prisons, etc. A specific novelty in the Church's Constitution is the 'National Assembly of the Church of England', which emerged in 1921 as the first parliamentary representation of the national Church. The 'Assembly' combines the Church into a parliamentary body, structured into the three Houses of Bishops, lower clergy and laity. The 'Assembly' merely has discussion and proposal rights for the laws of the Church remaining to be put into force by Parliament.

A priest's educational background can be diverse; there is no regular required theological study course. There are two kinds of candidates for ordination: graduate candidates (those who have attended a three to four years' study course at university and have obtained an academic degree), and non-graduate candidates, who are those that have not obtained any academic degree.

The guiding principles are that graduate candidates have to

undertake at least 18 months' theological, practical and Church service instruction at a theological college or other authorised guidance, whereas non-graduate candidates have to attend three years of education at a theological college, and have to possess the Higher School Certificate.

There are about 23 theological colleges reflecting different schools of thought. They attach great importance to inner strengthening of character, devotion and seriousness about the profession. Regular dutiful church service in the college chapel, classes in meditation and leisure and pastoral advice support this. Examinations are not held uniformly; chaplains test the candidates on behalf of the Bishops. Before the ordination of a priest (laying on of hands by the Bishop), he is ordained as a deacon, whose duties are limited to the holding of the sacraments. The deaconate usually lasts for a year.

Funding

In a sense, the Church of England does not possess any assets. The term 'Church property' designates merely the belongings of different ecclesiastical and other corporations such as bishops, chapter, priests, etc.

In contrast to earlier years, the fundamental arrangement (funding of the Church through Queen Anne's Bounty) has been changed by the creation of an ecclesiastic commission, in part due to measures of the Church assembly pointing towards a stronger centralisation, in part due to the creation of a central financial committee and diocese committees.

Church possessions can be structured into the following main groups:

1. vicarages and land,
2. possessions belonging to the bishops or deans and chapters,
3. tithes or equivalents of these,

4. funds which are administered by the Church
    Commissioners or Queen Anne's Bounty on behalf of
    priests, etc.
5. possessions and funds from the Queen Anne's Bounty and
    the Church Commissioners.

Anglican Communion

Having acquired worldwide significance through its long
standing expansion in the British colonies and dominions, the
Church of England is in close contact with all Anglican
Churches throughout the world. Although the Church has its
own constitution and that the Common Prayer Book has been
revised differently in, for example, Scotland, Canada, Ireland,
South Africa and North America, there is spiritual affinity
due to the use of the Common Prayer Book and another cult,
which we may call 'Anglican Communion'. The representatives of the Anglican Communion meet every ten years at the
Lambeth Conference, where they are invited by the
Archbishop of Canterbury. Since 1867 there has been such a
conference every ten years, which takes its name from the
London palace of the primate of the Anglican Church, the
Archbishop of Canterbury. The Lambeth Conference is only
of a representative and advisory character and deals mainly
with issues of unity (pan-Anglicanism), and its unification
efforts play a leading role.

At its seventh conference in 1930 the following issues were
on the agenda:

I. Christian religion:
    a) with regard to modern ways of thinking;
    b) with regard to non-Christian perspectives;
    c) as determining for the character of the Christian
        cult;
    d) the evaluation of this discipline by the Church in edu-
        cation and science.

II. Influence of the Christian community on sexual issues, the problem of racism and questions of peace and war.

III. Unity of the Church:
- a) Reports on the successes of the Lambeth Appeal and the world conference for creed and Church constitution;
- b) plans and proposals for unification;
- c) Relations of the Anglican Church to the separate/special churches and their relationships with the Anglican Church.

IV. The Anglican communion:
- a) its ideals and future;
- b) its organisation: central; national or provincial; in missionary or extra-provincial dioceses.

V. The office:
- a) the new generation of ecclesiastical office and education before and after ordination,
- b) substitute and assistance office in the Church.

VI. Youth and vocation.

Additionally, a permanent committee (Consultative Body) is composed of representatives from different provinces and churches; it does not have or demand executive or administrative powers. It meets at irregular intervals between Lambeth Conferences. The following churches or provinces compose the Anglican Communion and as such are represented in the council: The provinces of Canterbury, York, Wales; The Church of Ireland; The Episcopal Church in Scotland; The Protestant Episcopal Church in the United States of America; The Church of England in Canada and in Australia; The Church of the Provinces of New Zealand, the West Indies, South Africa and India; The Church in China and Japan. (The last two were recognised as constituent churches by the 1930 Lambeth Conference.)

The Oxford Group

The current Oxford Group is not to be mistaken for the 'Oxford Movement' founded a hundred years ago by the subsequently Roman Catholic Bishop I.H. Newman, with the objective of creating Anglo-Catholicism. The new Oxford Group made its first public appearance in 1928 in the English university town of Oxford, and is led by the American Lutheran priest Frank Buchman. The starting-point of the Oxford Group is England, which at the present time is also the centre of its worldwide activities.

The movement does not support any single teaching, but superficially calls for a general Christendom with an early Christian character. It wants to 'work in Churches of all creeds, lead the outsiders back into the church again and recall the ecclesiastic Christians to their duty'. The movement spread among intellectuals. It has known rapid and wide expansion due to its apparently suggestive method of work, the zealotry of each member, who is bound to further try to get support, and modern ways of defining religious principles.

In England the movement has found its support mainly from influential personalities of public and political life, high finance and aristocracy. For example, Lord Salisbury declared during a Group social event at the beginning of 1939: 'We are quite strongly represented in British diplomacy, we can therefore build important and valuable connections there.' Lord Addington and former Foreign Secretary Lord Halifax are among the closest advisers to Buchman. At a convention in 1938 Lord Addington explained: 'The Oxford Group is the spiritual Geneva. It's not the history of a group, but history in general.'

Leading English Group Members:

1. Lord Halifax – (former) Minister of Foreign Affairs
2. Lord Addington – member of the House of Lords

3. Bernhard Bourdillon – participant in the British delegation at Versailles
4. Earl of Athlone – personal ADC to the King since 1936
5. Lord Bicester – Lord-Lieutenant of Oxfordshire
6. Earl of Clarendon – Lord Chamberlain to the King
7. Earl of Cork and Orrery – Admiral of the Fleet, Commander in Chief, Portsmouth
8. Viscount Fitzalan of Derwent – Viceroy of Ireland 1921–2
9. Lord Kennet – Minister of Health 1931–5
10. Earl of Midleton – Secretary of State for War 1903–5
11. Earl of Munster – Under-Secretary of State for War
12. Marquess of Salisbury – Leader of the House of Lords, 1929–31
13. Viscount Trenchard – Marshal of the Royal Air Force, Commander of the Air Staff 1918–29.

The Anglican Church is positive about the Oxford Movement, and a considerable number of the clergy is active within it.

The world conference at Interlaken was held under Frank Buchman's motto of 'moral rearmament'. This slogan has been over-used for the purposes of English politics, and found easy acceptance in the Western democracies for anti-German propaganda. The Oxford Group has proved itself a tool of British diplomacy.

Summary

It could be said that the Anglican Church is an instrument of British imperial political power. National Church and state become one, which means that the world's Protestantism is influenced significantly by England. This is helped by the fact that the Swedish orientation of world Protestantism, after Bishop Söderblom's death, has faded into the background.

The different orientations within the Church, such as Puritans, Presbyterians, etc., are rudely pushed to the rear when confronting the foreign political power of world Protestantism.

Catholicism

After much turbulence, the liberalism of the nineteenth century brought good prospects for the Roman Church in England: 1829 saw the abolition of the anti-Catholic laws and in 1850 the Pope re-established his hierarchy. The number of faithful grew from 60,000 in 1850 to about three million now. Hierarchical structuring in Britain divides into the Roman Church in England and Wales and the Roman Church in Scotland. In 1937 there were 5,500 Roman clergy in England and Wales, of whom about 2,000 were from a religious order. The number of monasteries was about 1,000 in 1935.

English Catholicism is clearly missionary Catholicism, i.e. it strives to convert the English to the Roman Church. The number of conversions fluctuates around 10,000–12,000 each year. The Roman Church in England is unified and assertive, not least with its special influence on public life. Similarly, English Catholics are very willing to make sacrifices.

The centre of Catholic life in England is the school system. Some few years ago there were 14,300 Catholic primary schools and 537 Catholic secondary schools with a total of about 450,000 pupils. In spite of this expansion the Catholic private school system is the biggest worry of English Catholicism, since the grants of support from the state are. often disputed, which leads to powerful confrontations, mainly in the North of England. Normal secondary schools supported by the municipalities do not enjoy a high reputation with English Catholics because there is too much time for recreational activities. In contrast, there are the educational institutions led by religious orders (Jesuits, Benedictines, etc.) of which non-Catholic pupils make up for 80%. The Catholic representative on the national schools inspectorate of the British Board of Education is suffragan Bishop Myers of Westminster, whose activity has influenced favourably the development of the Catholic school system in the British Empire.

Since 1937, the Catholic Action [CA] in England, based on Vatican principles, has opened the School of the CA in Liverpool for education and further training of future Catholic leaders.

Different organisations deal with the spread of Catholic teachings. Among them the Catholic Evidence Guild, a lay organisation which preaches to the community in public squares; the Catholic Missionary Society, an organisation of priests which handles issues of Catholic world-view in churches or other assembly rooms, especially within the diaspora. The Apostolic League, a lay organisation, performs in the same way. The following organisations are specifically concerned with the question of conversion: Guild of Our Lady of Ransom and the Messengers of the Face, as well as the Converts Aid Society. Apart from these organisations there are, as in all other countries, a great number of Catholic professional and functional associations, youth organisations, etc.

In England, the Catholic press is also very evident. In 1936 alone, 320 Catholic press titles in English were published. The most significant are the weeklies: *The Universe* (117,000 copies), *The Catholic Times* (43,000), *The Catholic Herald* (20,000), *Dublin Review*, *The Tablet* and *The Month*. The latter two are published by the Jesuits.

The development of Roman Catholicism in England has been enhanced by Catholics occupying senior state and private office. The high percentage of Catholics in the Foreign Office is striking. The Privy Council had fifteen Catholic members in

1935, among them the Earl Marshal, the Duke of Norfolk; the former Viceroy of Ireland, Lord FitzAllan; the former Ambassador in Washington, Lord Howard of Genrith; the former Ambassador in Paris, Lord Tyrell; the former Prime Minister of Australia, Lyons; and the King's former senior equerry, the Earl of Granard. At the 1935 general election, 38 Catholics were nominated out of a total of 1,346 parliamentary candidates, and only 18 were elected. Concerning the question of abolishing the anti-papal formula in the Oaths of Coronation, there is a disagreement between the Catholic Church and Anglicanism. At the coronations of George V and VI this oath was considerably shortened.

The Vatican established a papal legation in London in 1938. Catholicism in England is to a large extent practised by people of Irish descent, and therefore there are only limited opportunities to use Catholicism as a weapon against Anglicanism.

Apart from the Vatican's delegate, the representative of the Catholic Church in England is the Cardinal Archbishop of Westminster, Hinsley. In the current conflict with Germany, Hinsley is one of the most notorious anti-German agitators in the Catholic Church. It is he who has called for an anti-parachute defence organisation under the name of 'sword of the spirit'.

Religious orders and associations are widespread in England and this is especially true of the Jesuits. In the appendix there is a list of their establishments. Some of these establishments of religious orders are branches of German organisations. For example the two houses of the Association of the Word of God have their mother houses in Steyl, in Hadzor and Donamon Castle. The number of convents in England is remarkable. Female education in elementary schools and nursing are nearly exclusively in the hands of nuns. Also orphanages, asylums and poorhouses are almost all run by Catholic orders.

The Methodist Church

The Methodists are a religious community which split from the Anglican Church after 1738. Its religious teachings resemble those of the Reformed Church and the church was founded by John Wesley. It accounts for about six per cent of the population. It is primarily directed through the 'Conference' and further through synods held in May and September. Both synods are subordinate to the Conference which has the legislative and judicial powers. The Reverend W.L. Wardle, who has his seat in Manchester, is president of the Conference. The church is closely linked to ecumenical movements and supports the Freemasons' idea of a World Council of Christian Churches; it took an active part in the conferences of Oxford and Edinburgh.

Apart from these groups which are the strongest in number, there are the following sects and groups in England: Congregationalists, Baptists, Presbyterians, Church of Christ, Moravians, Brethren, Catholic Apostolic Church, Swedenborgians, Society of Friends (called Quakers), Unitarians, Christian Scientists, etc.

Young Men's Christian Association and Salvation Army

Among the many secular organisations with religious connections, the YMCA and the Salvation Army have to be mentioned.
The YMCA, Young Men's Christian Association, Great Russell Street, London WC1. President: Sir Henry McMahon. Treasurer: R. Austin Pilkington. Secretary-General: F.J. Chamberlain. The YMCA is entirely in the hands of the Freemasons.

The Salvation Army. The Salvation Army was founded in the East End of London in July 1867 by General William Booth and is currently led by General Evangeline Cory Booth. A 1931 parliamentary regulation decreed that in future the general has to be elected by the High Council of the Salvation Army. The Salvation Army's headquarters are at 101 Queen Victoria Street, London EC4. It covers the whole globe, and its objective is to alleviate the suffering of the poor.

Division according to Church membership (1930)

England, Wales and Channel Islands:

Anglicans	2,300,000
Catholics	2,200,000
Methodists	1,150,000
Congregationalists	500,000
Baptists	400,000
Jews	300,000
Salvation Army	260,000
Presbyterians	85,000

Scotland

United Free Churches	1,300,000
Catholics	600,000
Episcopal Church	60,000

Northern Ireland

Catholics	420,400
Protestant Episcopal Church	340,000
Methodists	50,000
Other	55,000

The following will be due for consideration shortly:

1. Secretariat of the Archbishop of Canterbury, Lambeth Palace, London SW1.

2. Secretariat of the Archbishop of York, Bishopthorpe, York.

3. Secretariat of the Bishop of Chichester, The Palace, Chichester.

4. Secretariat of the Bishop of Gloucester, The Palace, Gloucester.

5. Bishop Harold Jocelyn Buxton, diocese of Gibraltar, 35 Wood Street, London SW1. Buxton is the contact to the Orthodox Churches of the Balkans and was a leading member in the visit to the Balkans of the Anglican Church in April. Spain, Portugal, Greece, Romania, Bulgaria, Yugoslavia and Asia are part of his diocese.

6. The British Ministry of Information, at the outbreak of war, established a special department, the Religious Division. This department attempts, with the support of an information service in many neutral countries, to ignite anti-German sentiment. Announcements from leading personalities as well as extracts from ecclesiastical literature are broadcast by this department – proof that the Christian Churches of England recognise the British government's efforts and objectives as political war theses and Christian matters, and as tasks for Churches to commit themselves to carrying out. Taking possession of this department's material would be absolutely necessary.

7. Anglican and Eastern Churches Association. Pursues and encourages the connection between the English and the Orthodox Church. Presidents are the Bishop of London, Winnington-Ingram, and the Metropolit of Thyatira, Germanos. Secretary-General: Rev. R.M. French. General Secretariat: St James Vicarage, West Hampstead, London NW6.

8. Church Esperantists League. Secretary-General: Rev. A.J. Ashley, St John's Vicarage, Rastrick, Brighouse, Yorkshire. The League strives to introduce Esperanto as a world language. It has connections to pacifist associations all over the world.

9. Archbishop's Commission on Relations of Church and State. Presidents: Viscount Cecil of Chelwood, Sir Philip Baker-Wilbraham, Professor E.F. Jacob, Marquess of Hastington. General Secretariat: 2 Little Smith Street, London SW1. Leading British politicians and economists work for it. The World Conference of Churches in Oxford made it clear that the Commission has strongly criticised national socialism and indicated that the totalitarian state and Christianity are incompatible. Germany should therefore be seen as enemy of all Christian states. In this way the commission has made propaganda very efficiently against Germany.

10. Church of England Council of Empire Settlement. President: Archbishop of Canterbury. Chairman: Brig. Gen. Sir George MacMunn. Secretariat: 39 Victoria Street, London SW1. This council's task is to maintain links between the English government and the Dominions and Churches overseas. It is characteristic that the Archbishop of Canterbury is president, and he tries to reinforce the political influence of Britain through connections with the Dominions and overseas.

11. Church of England Council on Foreign Relations. Presidents: Archbishop of Canterbury, Bishop of Gloucester. Chairman: Lord Charnwood. Secretary-General: J.A. Douglas. General Secretariat: 535 Grand Buildings, Trafalgar Square, London WC2. It is the Council's task to maintain the relations with the Orthodox Churches; the Assyrian Church; the Coptic Church; the Syrian-Orthodox Church; the Armenian Church; and the Protestant Churches of the Continent. Within this Council are the worst anti-German agitators within the Anglican clergy. Taking possession of the Secretariat's material is vital.

12. Church Socialist League. Secretary: Rev. Paul Stacy. Secretariat: St Peter's Vicarage, Coventry.

13. Macedonian Guild. Secretary-General: The Rev. Rosslyne Bruce. General Secretariat: Herstmonceux Rectory, Sussex. This association has defined its task as to orientate the attention of British churchgoers to the Churches of Eastern and South-Eastern Europe. It holds lectures about the ecclesiastical situation in the Balkans.

14. Modern Churchmen's Union for the Advancement of Liberal Religious Thought. Chairman: The Rev. E. St G. Schomberg. Secretariat: 520 Grand Buildings, Trafalgar Square, London WC2.

15. South African Church Institute. Director: Rev. L.E. Parsons, 40 Wood Street, London SW1. Maintains connections between the churches of South Africa and the Anglican Church. There are annual conferences to which priests and laymen from South Africa are invited to England. With this institute the English Church tries to reinforce Britain's influence in South Africa.

16. Spanish and Portuguese Church Aid. Secretary-General: The Rev. F. Bate. General Secretariat: 13 Sergeants Inn, Fleet Street, London EC4.

17. Church Army. Secretary-General: Wilson Carlisle. General Secretariat: Bryanston Street, Marble Arch, London W1.

18. Church Self-Government League. President: Viscount Wolmer. Secretary: Arthur B. Thornhill. Secretariat: Room 507, Grand Buildings, Trafalgar Square, London WC2.

19. Church Lads' Brigade. Secretary: H.F. Peerless, General Secretariat: St Margaret's Rectory, Ironmonger Lane, London EC2. The Church Lads' Brigade is concerned with religious youth work. It has good connections abroad, especially with South Africa and India.

20. British Christian Council for International Friendship, Life and Work. The head office of the World Alliance for churches' international friendship work is located in

Geneva. In the World Alliance's council, English clergymen hold leading positions and try to gain influence over other states through the centre in Geneva.

Members of the English council are the Bishops of Chichester and Fulham; Bishop Dickensen; and the Rev. Burlingham and Rev. H.W. Fox. Secretariat: 1 Arundel Street, London WC2.

21. Friends of Reunion. Chairman: Bishop of Southampton. Secretary-General: Rev. Eric Hamilton. Secretary: Rev. Trevor Kilborn. Secretariat: Annandale, North End Road, London NW11. It works for the amalgamation of all Church associations in England.

22. League of Nations Union. Head office: Geneva. It contributes primarily to keeping the League of Nations alive in the individual countries. There are annual conferences in Geneva, and a committee of the League of Nations Union and the Anglican Church has been established; the chairman is the Bishop of Chichester, Arthur Steward Duncan-Jones. In the committee's office there is valuable material for the political assignment of the Anglican Church. The office is at 15 Grosvenor Crescent, London SW1.

23. Missionary Film Committee. President: Rev. Dr Scott Lidgett. Secretary: T.H. Baxter. Secretariat: 104 High Holborn, London WC1. The Film Committee produces missionary films. It would be valuable to take possession of this film material.

24. Socialist Christian League. Secretariat: Huddersfield, 318 Almondbury, Bank.

25. Student Christian Movement of Great Britain and Ireland. Secretary-General: Canon Tissington Tatlow. Secretary: Rev. R.D. Mackie. Secretariat: Annandale, North End Road, London NW11. In the Christian World Union of Students the British association holds a leading position. The World Union is an international association of democratic pacifist character, and it pretends to work

for the spread of Christianity among students. But from the past few world conferences it has become clear that the World Union under English leadership has strong political tendencies and at different times members have sharply criticised Germany.

26. Young Men's Christian Association. Secretary: F.J. Chamberlain. Secretariat: Great Russell Street, London WC1.

27. Young Women's Christian Association. Secretary-General: Miss May Curwen. Secretariat: 4th Floor, Central Buildings, Great Russell Street, London WC1.

28. The Oxford Group Movement. Leading politicians and economists in England were included in the Oxford Group and committed themselves to it with zeal. Since it is suspected that the Oxford Group has been exploited by the Intelligence Service, immediate possession of the main bureau is to be accomplished. The office is in Brown's Hotel, Dover Street, London W1.

The Communist Party of Great Britain (CPGB)

Historical Development

The CPGB was established at a meeting of revolutionary groups in London in 1920. Based on a resolution of the Comintern, it was called the British Section of the Third International. The CPGB's core came from the British Socialist Party and left-wing extremists. The Socialist Party was called upon to amalgamate with the CPGB, but refused. The founders were: Gallacher; J.T. Murphy; Harry Pollitt of the Shop Steward Movement; MacManus; Tom and Harry Quelch; Tom Mann of the Socialist Labour Party; Albert Inkpen; and W. Paul of the British Socialist Party.

Apart from the CPGB there was a second Communist Party

at that time, which was under the control of Sylvia Pankhurst, former leader of the suffragette movement. This group was of no importance. In spite of the incredible sums of money the CPGB received from Moscow and which increased annually (in 1936 alone it received £100,000 in subsidies), it has not achieved any major successes in its organisational work. In the first few years after its creation its membership never exceeded 5,000. Only in 1926, the year of the coal miners' strike, did it suddenly jump to over 10,000 members. Subsequently this number dropped dramatically; in 1931 the CPGB had 2,756 registered members. From then on a steady upward trend set in. From the time of the Seventh World Congress, the membership rose from 7,700 to nearly 18,000 in 1939.

Organisation

Its organisational structure resembles other divisions of the Comintern. The Central Committee (CC) is elected at the National Congress and is the leading executive organ. Known members of the Central Committee are Harry Pollitt, William Gallacher, R. Palme-Dutt and Tom Mann.

Great Britain's Communist Youth Association (GBCYA)

The GBCYA does not publicly identify itself as the Youth Organisation of the Communist Party and has few members, although it has increased in size in the past few years. It strives in all sorts of ways to approach non-Communist youth organisations in order to exploit them: its call to English Catholic youth to join the peace movement is typical. The district divisions arrange musical and theatre events to facilitate access.

At the last Youth Conference in 1939, attended by about 200 delegates, the Secretary of the GBCYA, John Gollan, demanded the resignation of Chamberlain's government and its replacement with an administration which would call for peace. Another leading personality in the Communist youth movement is Alex Massi.

A large number of the English Sports Associations are under direct influence of conservatives or reactionaries, but most of the workforce take the view that sports have to be independent from politics. The same conviction is shared by the top of the Labour Party and the trade unions. Accordingly, they are not vulnerable to the GBCYA's influence.

Press and Theatre

The central organ of the GBCYA is the *Daily Worker*, with a circulation of 150,000 copies. There are also other newspapers, such as *Russia Today*, *The Communist International* (weekly paper dedicated to international politics), *The Communist Review* (a monthly magazine), and innumerable leaflets and pamphlets deal with daily problems.

Apart from the press, the theatre and the films also feature Communist propaganda. For example, biased sketches are acted out in the streets, which have a revolutionary content and are very popular, especially in working-class areas. Individual towns are toured with trucks purpose-built to be transformed into stages.

Films are also used for propaganda. In spite of severe film censorship, 'private film societies' can show movies of any inclination within closed groups. This opportunity is exploited to show the most notorious Soviet movies. Tickets are sold at counters neutrally disguised, where, of course, Communist propaganda is displayed. This form of agitation has achieved a certain success.

Cover Organisations

Due to the special situation which is in part due to the conservatism of the English and partly caused by the enormously

strong position of the English trade unions, the Communist
Party has adopted a methodology which distinguishes it from
other divisions of the Comintern. The development of the
Party's organisation has shown that the main strata of the
English working class have not yet been entrapped by the
Communist Party because the English worker is not amenable
to loud and bloodthirsty propaganda and has dissociated himself from the Communist Party. The latter has thus changed
its tactics fundamentally by establishing a series of social, cultural, economic and political organisations which appear to
be independent, but are really controlled by the GBCYA.

It was the goal of these organisations to include all strata of
the English population, to undermine their confidence in the
institutions of public life and in the government, to systemat-
ically influence their political views, and thereby subvert the
population from within. At the same time they hoped to tie
them to the Comintern through discreet Communist influence.

Several organisations of this kind are, including the Rank
and File Movements, a successor to the National Minorities
Movements. The leadership of this organisation is composed
exclusively of Communists who minutely follow the Party's
principles. The movement's publications are the *Rail Figiland*
(circulation of 12,000), *The Busmen's Punch* (about 5,000),
and *The Seafarer*, which is distributed in ports. Membership
of the Rank and File Movement is 250,000.

The National Unemployed Workers' Movement (NUWM)
was founded in 1921 and is an important support organisation
of the CPGB. It organised hunger marches, which often
clashed with the police. The movement's mouthpiece is *The
Unemployed Worker*.

The Hands Off Russia Committee was created by the
CPGB and discourages action against the Soviet Union.

The Society for Cultural Relations with Russia is the reception organisation for revolutionaries who do not want to be
identified, externally, with the Communist Party. Many well-
known personalities in public life are members.

The Friends of Soviet Russia works on the same principles but with a different membership, namely the working class. Its most influential representative is Norman Angell of London.

The Workers' International Relief originally collected money for the hungry in Russia and later for the 'victims of capitalist oppression'. It has merged into the International Labour Defence, which now also takes care of the 'victims of capitalist oppression'.

The Educational Workers' League members are supposed to influence their students with Communist ideas, while The League against Imperialism stirs up populations in the Colonies and Dominions to break with English domination.

The Anti-Fascist League is supported specifically by Jews and is supposed to be the defence organisation against the British Fascist Union. Many of its members are well-known personalities, mostly Jews. The best known anti-Fascists are Harald Barry, Sir Bernhard Baron, Lord Marley, Professor Harold Laski, etc.

The League of Socialist Freethinkers has made great progress in the recent past. Its main goal is the conversion of youth to its organisation. It is not part of the Communist Party, but is of Communist orientation.

The Fight for Peace was established at the CPGB's last Party Congress and is the CPGB's vanguard.

German Emigration

The foreign management of the KPD (German Communist Party) in London has been directly subordinate to the Central Committee in Paris, where it received its orders until the fall of France. The Central Committee sent instructors to London for training purposes from time to time. The training included political, economic and cultural daily issues. There is no official association with the CPGB so as to avoid contact with the British police.

All Jewish émigrés, regardless of political orientation, are taken care of by Woburn House, 1 Woburn Place, London. All Aryan émigrés, Communists, Marxists and others are taken care of by the Quakers' Association, Peace House, Euston Road, London.

Tactics

For a long time the CPGB has attempted to build a popular front with the most diverse reasons and slogans in order to encourage the masses to come under its leadership. For this reason a league named the Peace Bloc was created. Its goal was to subvert the workers' parties and overthrow their leadership to realise a merger of the Labour Party with the Communists. This has not led to any co-operation because the leaders of the Labour Party, the trade unions and the Co-operative societies fundamentally oppose the CPGB.

At one of the most recent Party conferences, Sir Stafford Cripps, leader of the Social Democratic Workers' Party, made an application for the creation of a Unitary Front with the CPGB. This was refused by a big majority. The trade union leader Clynes and representative Morrison voted against the application.

The swing in Soviet politics has also caused differences within the English Communist Party during which Pollitt was relieved of his post as the CPGB Secretary-General. Nevertheless he remained an executive member and was given other functions within the Party.

After the surrender of France, the CPGB's politburo issued a manifesto which said, among other things: 'Politics of the leading classes in Great Britain lead from one defeat to another. Today the English population can expect either a catastrophe or the prospect of endless war. The interests of the population require the fastest possible ending of the war, but not through capitulation in front of fascism, but by organising the defence of the free people and the creation of movements for a peace agreement as well as with the establishment of unity with the workers of all countries.'

In detail the manifesto asked for (1) elimination of all supporters of Fascism and the Munich policies; (2) mobilisation of the capital, nationalisation of industry, creation of workers' control committees and guarantee of an even distribution of food; (3) increase of individual earnings and sufficient support for their families; (4) arming of industrial workers; (5) elimination of the class principle for promotion in the army and the navy; (6) fraternal relations with the Soviet Union. To support these demands large rallies were organised by the Communist Party with support from over 7,000 participants. In Glasgow 2,500 people gave a standing ovation to the Communist representative Gallacher when he said: 'Our primary task consists in the elimination of the current government from its office and its replacement though a people's government.'

The Communist Party of Ireland (CPI)

The CPI was founded in the period after the Sixth World Congress of the Comintern. At its first Party Congress in 1932 it proclaimed the necessity to fight against English imperialism and Irish capitalism with its national-reformist parties. Only through this fight could it reach its goal of national liberation and the creation of a workers' and peasants' republic.

The CPI organised mass strikes of railway workers, the agricultural industry and of the emergency workers in 1932, and in 1935 the printers went on strike for two months in Dublin, when no newspapers were published. The same year saw the strike of the tram and bus workers which paralysed traffic in Dublin for eleven weeks. Even if these strikes had not been inspired by the Communist Party, they always supported them in time to use them for propaganda. There are no accurate statistics about the exact strength of the organisation but there is no detectable increase in the membership. Murray plays a leading role.

Marxist Parties and Trade Unions

I. Marxist Parties (legal)

1. Labour Party

The Labour Party was started in February 1920 at the Trades Union Congress in Plymouth following a successful motion to create a parliamentary workers' movement. It is thus a creation of the trade unions. Also present at its founding conference were delegates from several socialist organisations, namely the Social Democratic Federation (SDF, established in 1882), the Fabian Society (established in 1884) and the Independent Labour Party (ILP, established in 1893), and these three organisations were included as components of the Labour Party.

Initially, in contrast to all other political parties, the Labour Party consisted exclusively of trade unions and socialist organisations and not of individual members. A worker or socialist was part of the Labour Party only if he was already a member of a trade union or of one of the three socialist organisations. The trade unions as a whole and the socialist organisations as a whole paid annual contributions to the Labour Party based on the size of their membership. The trade unions joined Labour by a majority decision, leaving in almost every union a minority who disagreed with the association but was obliged to accept the majority's decision to be counted as part of the Labour Party's membership.

The Labour Party takes two forms: a) the association of entire unions and socialist organisations; b) local organisations made up of individual members. The latter is important because of the resolution which excludes Communists from the Labour Party. The Labour Party therefore is a trade union party led by social democrats and differs from the continental European social democratic parties in that it does not strictly tend to class-struggle perspectives.

Trade union members are the political reservoir of the Labour Party, and its growth therefore corresponds largely to the growth of the trade union movement. Within Labour there are two main currents:

1. The democratic current which has opposed any dictatorship from the right or the left for years, and has made democracy its political standard. This counts among its representatives, Major Attlee, Party leader in the Commons, Middleton, an ardent defender of the democratic principles, and Herbert Morrison, President of the City of London.
2. The left wing, which aspires to co-operation with the Communists and strives for the construction of a popular front. Among its members are intellectuals who attack the Party leadership and demand effective agitation and propaganda.

There is nothing positive to say about the current strength of the democratic and left wings, since the different votes of delegates at Party Conferences or Trade Union Congresses do not give complete numbers of the diverse streams. The Party Chairman is Major Attlee, his deputy Greenwood.

2. The Independent Labour Party (ILP)

The Independent Labour Party, i.e. of England, is not to be confused with the independent socialist of the Continent where 'independent' generally stands for an inclination more revolutionary and Marxist than the socialists. In Great Britain the Independent Labour Party meant no more than 'independent from the liberals'. The ILP did not want to know about class-struggle theories but in practice was a class-struggle party. It sought close contact with organised workers, especially young trade union leaders.

In 1933 the ILP departed from the Second International

and sought admission to the Third International. Vivid correspondence with Moscow ended with the Comintern's request for the resignation of Maxton and Fenner Brockway. At the ILP's Congress in York in March 1934, a policy of cooperation was adopted to prepare the membership for closer ties with Moscow, but the leadership distanced itself from any formal association with the Comintern.

The Party has been in a state of constant crisis with many changes in the leadership. At the May 1939 Conference MacGovern, Campel, Stephan, Aplen failed to be re-elected. Maxton resigned as leader and was replaced by a university teacher, A. Smith. Brockway remained editor of the *New Leader* and became the Party's Political Secretary. John MacNair replaced him as Secretary-General. Elected into the leadership were Ballantyne, executive member of the Railway Workers Union, and Gibson, a city councillor in Glasgow.

This Conference put an end to any claim to lead the working masses in England. Consequentially, the ILP's Country Council decided in August 1939, with a big majority, to rejoin the British Labour Party, from which it had split in 1932.

3. International Bureau for Revolutionary Unity, called the 'London Bureau'

Little is known about the London Bureau, and the date of its establishment is unclear. Nor can it be determined what arguments led to its creation, nor which parties participated. Nevertheless it is assumed that the Bureau was built upon Marxism although Communists seem to have joined only in 1933. The Bureau's leadership was ILP, but since 1938 there has been an effort to link the Bureau to communism.

After 1939, the following parties were part of the London Bureau: the ILP, the Swedish Party, the Dutch RSAP, POUM (Spanish Party), the Italian Socialist Party (Maximalists), the Archeo-Marxist Party and the International Youth Office.

Until the autumn of 1938 the German SAP had also been part of the Bureau.

II. Marxist Organisations of (illegal) German Émigrés

1. German Freedom Party

The German Freedom Party is understood among the émigrés as the most politically influential. In contrast to all existing émigré groups it does not define itself as a party, but as a mass movement which was created solely for the elimination of national socialism. It is welcomed by the Marxist camp as a comrade-in-arms against the Third Reich, but is not given great prominence, since these circles believe the bourgeoisie to be too cowardly to support actively a struggle against the Third Reich.

Democrats would have a great interest in any possible subversion of the German bourgeoisie, and the Party's financial support is said to come partly from government sources in London and Paris. The so-called Baldwin Fund, which was intended to aid émigrés and fund their accommodation in Europe, is seen as a further source of money. Hitherto it has been based in Paris, with London as a strong centre of support.

Management: Dr August Weber, born in Oldenburg 4 February 1871, retired Bank director, auditor and provincial tenant said to be in England since 31 May 1939.

Ministerial Director (retired): Karl Spiecker, born in München-Gladbach 7 January 1888, formerly living in Paris, current whereabouts unknown.

Dr Hermann Rauschning, former President of the Senate in Danzig, born in Thorn 7 August 1888, living in Paris up to now, current whereabouts unknown.

Gottfried Treviranus, born 20 March 1891 in Schieder/Lippe, retired Minister of the Reich, based in London.

Otto Klepper, born in Brotterode 17 August 1888, former Prussian Finance Minister, lawyer, apparently living in Basle.

Hugo Simon, born in Usch 1 September 1880, former Finance Minister, banker, last known living in Paris, current whereabouts unknown, probably London.

2. Revolutionary Socialist Party of Austria (RSÖ)

The RSÖ emerged from the left wing of the Social Democratic Party of Austria after the 1934 February uprising. Soon after the rebellion the social democrats who had emigrated to the Czech Republic under the leadership of Dr Otto Bauer and Dr Julius Deutsch gathered members and supporters of the SPÖ's left wing and in Brünn founded the so-called Foreign Bureau of Austrian Socialists (Alös) and established so-called border stage sites. Later a group of former social democratic editors and lower officeholders became allied to Alös, and it was from these groups that the Central Committee of Austrian Social Democracy was constituted. At the September 1934 Conference in Vienna all revolutionary oriented groups finally joined together to form the United Socialist Party of Austria. Its supporters called themselves socialist revolutionaries. Later on the name was changed into Revolutionary Socialist Party of Austria. On 1 January 1938 the Party officially entered the Second International.

Goal: Violent overturn, establishment of the 'proletarian dictatorship' in a common action with the Communists. The planned united front, however, has not been accomplished in practice. Josef Buttinger, born in Reichenbrunn 30 April 1906, was its leader.

In February 1938 an RSÖ émigré living in England established a foreign branch in London, led by Rudolf Geissner, Toynbee Hall, 28 Commercial Street, London. Later the Jewess Dr Marie Lazarsfeld-Jahoda, born in Vienna 26 January 1907, was made manager of the foreign post, which in

1939 included the collaborators Dr Th. Zerner, Karl Zernitz and Dr Hans Hirsch.

With special instructions for the RSÖ, Manfred Mann, born in Nikolburg 1 November 1889, and Emil Sladky, born in Vienna 11 January 1905, were temporarily living in London.

II. Trade Unions

English Trade Unions

English trade unions go back as far as to the middle of the last century and are the oldest organisations of their kind. At the beginning only highly qualified workers were members, but unqualified workers were included later. This also led to the problem of which group individual workers should join. Up to now this problem has not been completely solved. In general, three orientations are distinguished:

a) The Craft Union Association which receives craftsmen and qualified workers from different trades (professional associations).

b) The 'Union-by-Industry' tries to embody all workers who are employed in companies such as the railways, urban businesses, etc.

c) The General Workers' Unions which are rounded up in the 'National Federation of General Workers' which the unskilled labourers have mainly joined.

The proportion of women in trade unions is not insignificant. Most of them are affiliated to either the textile trade unions or to the National Union of General Workers.

English trade unions are not concerned with politics and refuse to deal with them. The political strength of the workers in the Labour Party is therefore concentrated away from the trade unions, which are at the same time members of the

International Trade Union Alliance.

English Trade Unions of Marxist Foundation:

National Centre: The Trade Unions Congress, Transport House (South Block), Smith Square, London.

Associations:

1. Food Industry:
   Amalgamated Union of Operative Bakers, Confectioners and Allied Workers, Union House, 8 Guildford Street, London WC1.
   National Union of Distributive and Allied Workers, Oakley, 122 Wilmslow Road, Fallowfield, Manchester.
2. Building Workers:
   National Federation of Building Trades Operatives, 20a Ceders Road, Clapham, London SW4.
3. Woodworkers:
   Amalgamated Society of Woodworkers of Great Britain and Ireland, 131 Wilmslow Road, Withington, Manchester.
   National Society of Brushmakers, 15 Hackney Road, London E2.
   National Society of Packing Case Makers (Wood and Tin), Box Makers, Sawyers and Mill Workers, 95 Farringdon Road, London EC1.
4. Pottery Workers:
   National Society of Pottery Workers, 5a Hill Street, Hanley, Stoke-on-Trent.
5. Goods Workers:
   Amalgamated Society of Journeymen Felt Hatters, 113 Manchester Road, Denton near Manchester.
6. Leather Workers:
   Amalgamated Society of Leather Workers, Hepworth Chambers, Briggate, Leeds.

National Union of Boot and Shoe Operatives, 28 Bedford Square, London WC1. (Also office of the International Professional Secretariat.)
The Rossendale Union of Boot, Shoe and Slipper Operatives, 7 Tenterfield Street, Waterfood, Rossendale, Lancashire.
Amalgamated Society of Boot and Shoe Makers and Repairers, 7 Cartwright Gardens, London WC1.

7. Diamond Trade Workers:
   The Society of Goldsmiths, Jewellers and Kindred Trades, 9 Belgrave Street, Euston Road, London WC.

8. Privately Employed Workers:
   National Union of Distributive and Allied Workers, Oakley, 122 Wilmslow Road, Fallowfield, Manchester.
   Association of Engineering and Shipbuilding Draughtsmen, 96 St George's Square, London SW1.
   National Amalgamated Union of Shop Assistants, Warehousemen and Clerks, Dilke House, Malet Street, London WC1.
   The Mental Hospital and Institutional Workers Union, 1 Rushford Avenue, Levenshulme, Manchester.

9. Civil Servants:
   Civil Service National Whitley Council, Victoria Street, Parliament Mansions, London SW1.

10. Garment Workers:
    National Union of Tailors and Garment Workers Chambers, 20 Park Place, Leeds.
    National Union of Distributive and Allied Workers, Oakley, 122 Wilmslow Road, Fallowfield, Manchester.

11. Lithographic Printers:
    Amalgamated Society of Lithographic Printers of Great Britain and Ireland, Whitworth Park, 70 Cecil Street, Manchester.
    Amalgamated Society of Lithographic Artists, Designers, Engravers and Process Workers, 54 Doughty Street, London.

12. Engineers and Stokers:
    The National Union of Enginemen, Firemen, Mechanics
    and Electrical Workers, 228 Wellgate, Rotherham.
13. Metal Workers:
    British Section of the IMF, 93 Borough Road, West
    Middlesbrough.
14. Miners:
    Miners' Federation of Great Britain, 55 Russell Square,
    London.
15. Painters:
    National Amalgamated Society of Operation House and
    Ship Painters and Decorators, 4 Camp Street, Lower
    Broughton, Manchester.
16. Stone Workers:
    Amalgamated National Union of Quarryworkers and
    Settmakers, 167 Hinckley Road, Leicester.
17. Bookbinders:
    National Union of Printing, Bookbinding and
    Paperworks, 88 Nightingale Lane, London SW12.
18. Public Service:
    National Union of General and Municipal Workers, 28
    Tavistock Square, London WC1.
19. Tobacco Workers:
    National Cigar Makers and Tobacco Workers Union, 19
    Great Prescott Street, London E.
20. Agricultural Workers:
    Scottish Farm Servants Union, Dalmacoulter, Airdrie,
    Lanarkshire.
21. Textile Workers:
    United Textile Factory Association, 77 St George's
    Road, Bolton.
    National Association of Unions in the Textile Trade,
    Central Chambers, 84 Godwin Street, Bradford.
    Bureau of the International Secretariat of Textile
    Workers, Transport House, 2 Smith Square, London
    SW1.

22. Transport Workers:
    National Union of Railwaymen, Unity House, Euston Road, London NW1.
    The Railway Clerks Association of Great Britain and Ireland, 25 Euston Road, London NW1.
    Transport and General Workers' Union, Transport House, Smith Square, Westminster, London SW1.
    National Union of Distributive and Allied Workers, Oakley, Wilmslow Road, Fallowfield, Manchester.
    Cardiff, Renarth and Barry Coal Frimmers Union, 13 Bute Crescent, Cardiff.
23. Factory Workers:
    National Union of Distributive and Allied Workers, 122 Wilmslow Road, Fallowfield, Manchester.
    National Union of General and Municipal Workers, 28 Tavistock Square, London SW1.
24. Glass Workers:
    The National Federation of Glass and Allied Trade Unions, 2 Wesley Street, Castlefort.

Transport and General Workers' Union

The most significant trade union of Marxist orientation is the Transport and General Workers' Union. Its main office is located in London, in Smith Square, Westminster, where the organisation owns so-called Transport House. The leading officials are: Secretary-General: Ernest Bevin; Deputy Secretary-General: Arthur Deakin; and Finance Secretary: Stanley Hirst. There are also three authorised representatives: F.F. Beechey, W.H. Green and W. John.

The Union splits up into twelve so-called National Secretariats. These are a subdivision according to professional categories. The names of the individual groups and their representatives are as follows:

1. Docks Group, Head: D.W. Milford, London.

2. Waterways Group, Head: D.W. Milford, London.
3. Passenger Services Group, Head: H.E. Clay, London.
4. Commercial Service Group, Head: J.E. Corrin, London.
5. General Workers Group, Head: L.H. Pearmaine, London.
6. Flour Milling and Allied Group, Head: T.H. Hodgson, London.
7. Building Trades Group, Head: T. Pugh, London.
8. Administrative, Clerical and Supervisory Group, Head: C.E. Akroyd, London.
9. Metal, Chemical and Engineering Group, Head: A. Dalgleish, London.
10. Power Workers Group, Head: I.J. Hayward, Rotherham.
11. Quarryman's Group, Head: R.W. Williams, Carnarvon.

Additionally there are five so-called Departmental Secretariats. These are the Legal Department, Head: Frank Tillwell; National Health Insurance Department, Head: W. Page; Convalescent Home Department, Head: S. Hirst; Record Dept, Head: J. Gill; Political and Research Department, Head: John Price.

All officials have their facilities at Transport House in London. The Union runs twelve District Secretariats in various parts of the United Kingdom:

1. London, Woodberry, 218 Green Lane, Head: J.T. Scoulding
2. Southampton, 80a High Street, Head: A. Waygood
3. Bristol, Broad Street, Head: J. Donovan
4. (South Wales), Cardiff, 42 Charles Street, Head: H. Batey
5. Birmingham, 211 Broad Street, Head: J. Blewitt
6. Salford, The Crescent Transport House, Head: J.A. Webb
7. Glasgow, 24 Circus Park, Head: J. Veitch
8. Newcastle, 72 Jesmond Road, Head: J. White

9. (Yorkshire), Leeds, 22 Blenheim Terrace, Head: A.J. Heal
10. Hull, 152 George Street, Head: G.E. Farmery
11. Dublin, Marlborough Street 112, Head S. Kyle
12. Liverpool, 35/37 Islington, Head: H.O. Pugh.

Émigré Organisations

In contrast to France which accepted émigrés not only for political reasons but because of population policies, in England political reasons were all-important in the admission of emigrants. Accordingly, the number of German émigrés settled in Britain is relatively small. At the beginning of February 1940 the Home Secretary, Sir John Anderson, estimated the number of emigrants from the old Reich living in England at 62,244, with 11,989 Austrians. A deduction concerning the low number of foreigners in England in general can be made according to the same minister's statement that most of the foreigners living in England were German émigrés. In contrast to this, the number of foreigners, about 3.5m to 4m people, does not appear too high. Certainly a feature of British politics is the need to try to get a grip on all strands of immigration, and this objective was pursued, too, by the League of Nations' Commissioner for German Emigration, Sir Macdonald. Another means was the financial support which flowed from England to émigré organisations under the cover of 'Christian compassion'.

The permanent settlement of émigrés, however, was unwanted. As early as on 30 July 1934 the current Lord Privy Seal, Mr Eden, replied to a Commons petition on the same subject and disclosed that the High Commissioner for Refugees had been told the British government was prepared to be as generous about permanent resettlement of individual refugees as was economically possible, but that the government had to retain the right to refuse individual refugees because, due to severe unemployment, the work available to foreigners was restricted.

The anti-German emigration in England divides up into three main groups:

1. The Jewish organisations, who are mainly accountable for the boycott movement and agitation in the press against Germany,
2. The pacifist, liberal, religious and other organisations which fight Germany under the cover of ideology,
3. The Labour Party and trade unions.

The Jewish organisations have their headquarters in the so-called Jewish Board of Deputies, Woburn House, Upper Woburn Place, WC1. Here, a number of German Jews work as secretaries or other contributors. Among them Dr Gustav Warburg, the former editor of SPD's *Hamburger Echo*, must be noted. He used to live at 1 Woodside, Ersken Hill, London NW11. The Jewish émigré David Yaskiel has also to be named, living in London at 25 Southampton Street, Fitzroy Square, telephone: Museum 0446. He trades under the name of the British International Jewish Agency and has connections with Münzenberg. Also, Dr Hans Preiss living in London at 41a Museum Street should be mentioned. A list of the Jewish World Organisations in England is comprised in the Special Wanted List.

The pacifist, liberal, religious and other organisations are, compared to the total number of émigrés settled in England, relatively numerous, but have not achieved the same political influence as émigré organisations in France. Among the members of these organisations Dr Rudolf Olden, formerly an editor at the *Berliner Tagblatt*, is especially notable. Also Prince Löwenstein and Otto Lehmann-Russbueldt were active as officers. One of the centres of work of these organisations was the salon of a Hungarian-born Countess, wife of Labour

Lord, the Earl of Listowel, 36 Onslow Gardens, Kensington SW7. The Earl of Listowel has repeatedly led protest delegations to the German Embassy.

Special support for emigration is given by the Quakers through the English High Church. For this purpose it used International Friendship through the Churches, 1 Arundel Street; The organisation Friends of New Europe, 97 St Stevens House, Westminster SW1, also supported the emigrants' anti-German activities. In this, the Secretary Rennie Smith is said to have distinguished himself. This organisation is also said to have maintained connections with Germany, but no evidence has been found for this claim up to now. The journalist Wickham Steed, Lansdown House, Holland Park, London W11 also moves in these circles. The pacifist organisations, especially Friends of New Europe, are said to have had close ties with Military Intelligence.

The Labour Party and trade unions employed the former leader of the Reichbanner, Höltermann, and the former legal adviser of the SPD, Dr jur. Franz Neumann. Höltermann is said to be accessible via the Foreign Political Secretary of the Labour Party, Mr Gillies, Transport House, London. The address of Dr Franz Neumann, who is a reader at the School of Economics, is 52 Doughy Street, London WC1, telephone: Holborn 0747.

The Labour Party is also said to have maintained links with the other émigré groups abroad. One of the most active of agitators against Germany in the Labour Party is Victor Schiff, Paris correspondent of the *Daily Herald*, 12 Wilson Street, London EC2. The Aid Committee for the Relief of the Victims of German Fascism, Anglo House, Litchfield Street, Charing Cross Road, London WC1, was also a centre for anti-German activities, which produced the petitions in favour of Thälmann and show trials, as well as the horror stories about German concentration (KZ) camps (Mrs Seeger, Mrs Seifert).

About the Labour leader Major Attlee, the connections lead to the delegate of the Saar's miners, Kurt Thomas, who was also received by the former Minister Sir John Simon.

Through Höltermann the ties went to Matz Braun, who received financial support, and Wickham Steed also maintained relations with Thomas. He is also said to have given Steed a memorandum about the burning of the Reichstag.

The Earl of Listowel maintained connections with the Austrian journalist Baron von Kühnelt-Lehdin, who at that time claimed to have close ties to the Vatican.

One of the main financial sources of the émigré organisations was the Rockefeller Foundation which has granted organisations and individuals financial aid to allow them to pursue their studies. Its address is University College, Gower Street, London WC1; its Secretary was the Labour Party MP, Mrs Ellen Wilkinson.

Another organisation which has put aside large sums of money for German émigrés is the Society of Friends (Quakers). G.P. Gooch is its Secretary. Leading elements are members of the families Cadbury, Rowntree and Fry, who are very rich. The organisation's address is: Friends House, Euston Road, London N1.

Support is also given by the World Non-Sectarian Anti-Nazi Organisation to Secure Human Rights. This organisation's Secretary is at the same time Secretary-General of the British Trades Union Congress, Sir Walter Citrine. The address is Transport House, Smith Square, London SW1. Another of the organisation's directors is Lord Marley, so it can be safely assumed that the organisation receives Communist support. Sir Walter Citrine is connected to the International Federation of Trade Unions whose international Secretary is Edo Fimmen. The British section of this organisation is the Trades Union Congress where Sir Walter Citrine is Secretary-General.

The amicable attitude of English trade unions towards the émigrés lasted until recently. So in August 1938, on the eve of the English Trade Unions Congress, the Labour MP Morgan Jones accurately explained in a leading article published in the magazine *Labour* that the trade unions want to exert their political influence in favour of a generous attitude to German émigrés. It was the task of the democracies, and particularly English democracy, not to let the victims of fascism suffer.

Officially, England's attitude was generally opposed to this view. For example, when the Labour MP Colonel Wedgwood lobbied to speed up the naturalisation process for the émigrés, Sir Samuel Hoare, on behalf of the Home Office, refused to do so. One of the Home Office officials consulted by a member of the German Embassy described the Labour Party's action as being intended solely to create occasions for political speeches. At the same time the impression has been created that official circles, especially those around Sir Robert Vansittart and the Secret Service, and with the Labour Party's assistance, are seeking to use émigré organisations as instruments of English politics and strategic defence planning.

At the beginning of the war, England set up special law courts to investigate refugees and decide to to which of three categories they belonged. Category A refugees were detained immediately. Category B were not imprisoned but were still classified as 'Enemy Alien' and were submitted to limitations on enemy foreigners. Category C émigrés lost the individual rights to which a neutral foreigner in Britain is usually entitled, a stamp in their passports confirms their status as political exiles and refugees from Nazi oppression. Most of the German émigrés were classified under Category C. The principal aim was to try to integrate this group into the national defence system and, if desired, into the armed forces.

Émigré Organisations

a) For émigrés in general:
Committee for Mass Colonisation, Anthony de Rothschild, New Court, London EC4.

Co-ordinating Committee for Refugees, Domestic Department, Mecklenburgh Square off Guildford Street, London WC1.

Federation of Polish Jews in Great Britain, 24 Oldgate, London EC3.

Intergovernmental Committee, Central Building, Westminster, SW1. Director: George Rublee.

International Committee for Employment of Refugees (Professional Workers), 38 Primrose Hill Road, London. President: Mr Edgar Dugdale. Honorary Secretary: Miss Mary Omerod.

International Student Service (ISSO), Co-operating Committee for England and Wales, 49 Gordon Square, London WC1. Chairman: Dr Tissington Tatlow. Chairman for England: Sir Walter Moberly. Treasurer: Professor Ernest Barker. Treasurer for Support Organisation: Mr Gareth Maufe. Secretary for Support Organisation: Miss Christina Ogilvy.

Jewish Professional Committee, Woburn House, London. Chairman: A.J. Makower. Vice-Chairman: Sir Philip Hartog.

Jewish Refugees Committee, Woburn House, London. Chairmen: Otto M. Schiff and Leonard M. Montefiore.

Jewish Resettlement, Woburn House, London. Chairman: Sir Robert Waley Cohen. Director: Mayer Stephany.

Refugees Co-operative Housing Scheme, 124 Westbourne Terrace, London W2.

The Jewish Association for the International Protection of Jewish Girls, Women and Children, 45 Great Prescott Street, Aldgate, London E1. President: Mrs N. Charles Rothschild. Vice-Presidents: Dr Claude Montefiore, Artur R. Moro. Secretaries: Mrs L. Pyke, S. Cohen.

The Society for the Protection of Science and Learning (formerly: Academic Assistance Council), 12 Clement's Inn Passage, Clare Market, London. Chairman: Lord Rutherford of Nelson.

International Student Service, 3 West Castle Road, Edinburgh. Contact: J. de Gaudin.

Glasgow Jewish Council for German Refugees, Queens Square, Glasgow S1.

b) For German émigrés:

The High Commission of the League of Nations for Refugees from Germany, 16 Northumberland Avenue, London WC2. President: Major-General Sir Neill Malcolm. Representative: Lord Duncannon.

British Movement for the Care of Children from Germany, 69 Great Russell Street, London WC1.

Central British Fund for German Jewry, Woburn House, Upper Woburn Place, London WC1. Chairman: Sir Osmond E. d'Avigdor Goldsmid.

Council for German Jewry, Woburn House, London. Chairman: Viscount Samuel of Mount Carmel.

Central Bureau for the Settlement of German Jews in Palestine, 77 Great Russell Street, London. Division of the Jewish Agency. President: Dr Chaim Weizmann. Director of the London office: Dr Martin Rosenblüt.

Council for German Jewry (Agricultural Committee), Bentinal House, 46 Southampton Row, London WC1. President: Dr Karl Kapralik, 49 Eton Place, London. Secretary: Stephany.

German Jewish Aid Committee, Bloomsbury House, London.

Inter-Aid Committee for Children from Germany, 21 Bedford Row, London, WC1. Chairman: Sir Wyndham Deedes. Secretaries: Gladys Stelton, Francis Bendet.

Notgemeinschaft Deutscher Wissenschaftler im Ausland (Emergency Community of German Scientists Abroad), 12 Clement's Inn Passage, Clare Market, London. Chairman: Privy Councillor Dr Demuth.

Union for Displaced German Scholars, 12 Clement's Inn Passage, Clare Market, London.

Czech Émigré Organisation

After the fall of France the majority of the Czech émigrés in France moved to England. Previously, Czech activity in Britain had been restricted to the cultural influence of the Czech Foreign Institute, whose English offices had branches at 26 Gloucester Road, London NW1, and 26 Ann Street, Jersey. The Foreign Institute started political work only after the CSR's collapse. Thereafter, the intelligence activity of these clubs has had to be taken into account.

At the end of July of that year the circles around Benesch-Masaryk succeeded in obtaining official British recognition of a Czech government and from that moment Benesch was considered to be the legal President of the CSR and Sramek became Prime Minister, the Foreign Minister being Jan Masaryk. The other members of the Czech government in exile were: Jan Becko, Feierabend, Necas, Osusky, Outrata, Ripka, Slavik, Viest as well as the former chief commander of the Czech Legion in France, General Ingr. Intelligence work was left in the hands of Masaryk, and its main activity was to support the highly treacherous organisations and operations in the Protectorate, as well as arranging unscrupulous agitation and horror propaganda.

According to English radio, part of the former Czech Legion in France continues to exist in Britain, but it is relatively certain that it is only a small percentage of the original Czech Army. A return of these legionnaires is not sought.

Apart from these legionnaires, about 1,000 Czechs have been living in England for many years and can be defined as politically indifferent. It is probable that only the small circle of the Czech government and an insignificant group of journalists and former Czech diplomats now live in England, presumably in London or its immediate surroundings.

Freemasonry

England is the country of Freemasonry; English clerics of the Enlightenment era were the foundation upon which the Freemasons' ideology was built. However, it was not only organisation which enabled Freemasonry to spread overseas so extensively; it was Britain's overseas trade and political power, and cultural influence, which enabled Freemasonry to follow Britain's success. Today English Freemasonry is far greater in number and in reputation than its Latin branch. Highlighting the grand lodges, its membership is found in Germanic and Anglo-Saxon countries as well as in the Empire and South America. Single lodges are found all over the world, especially in areas under the influence of the UK.

The historical significance of Freemasonry, which spread from England to the Continent, is the advancement of Jewish emancipation in Europe, born from the intellectual and political heritage of the Freemasons. They include a large number of the social-political leaders and are the carriers of British imperialism. The Field, Colonial and Military lodges play an especially important part as gateways for colonial and political enterprises, and as bases of English lifestyle across the Empire. The Freemasons' lifestyle in the colonial lodges attracts the natives in an imperceptible way to a close 'apolitical' link with the rulers of their country and puts them under the spell of England's political grandeur and its noble traditions. With their adaptation to the English style of life, they become denationalised and fall more and more into political sterility. But the lodge is not only a connection between the natives and the English, servants and masters, but represents a binding link between Britain and her Dominions. The King and his family are the strongest connection between Britain and the member states of the Empire by being simultaneously the Empire's political and masonic leadership. Freemasons drawn from the political classes provide the link between

politics and the royal family. The deep roots of this ruling
class in the English population, and their complete acceptance, is due to a large extent to tradition and to masonic
solidarity. The numerous and politically significant middle
classes provide the main constituency of Freemasons in
England, and are bound by their masonic leadership. Apart
from the Society and its following, masonry links Scotland
and Ireland (whose Grand Lodge, in contrast to its national
divide into Irish Free State and Ulster, unites the whole of
Ireland) with England.

Unique to English Freemasonry are the lodges whose members are composed of people from the same professions or the
same areas. They build these masonic bases in individual
areas, and through them the possibility of influencing that
area – or even the entire life of the British Empire – is made
relatively easy. There are lodges which are composed mainly of
members of the royal family and members of Society. The
university lodges in Oxford and Cambridge and the public
school lodges (especially those of Eton and Harrow) form
masonic centres for the socio-political ruling classes. Apart
from these, there are lodges of purely political significance:
the New Welcome lodge unites the parliamentary members of
the Labour Party. In the military lodges and masonic temples,
where only members of specific professions or professional
groups can work, there are fraternal committees which influence political life on behalf of Freemasonry.

Freemasonry is thus an invisibly effective, important political instrument for the internal structure of Great Britain and
its Empire, and for British imperialism. What concerns us is
that in its ideological orientation and its political effective-
ness – as long as it lasts – it is a dangerous weapon in the
hands of Britain's plutocrats against national socialist
Germany.

To what degree English attitude and masonic spirit have
coalesced became clear with the establishment of lodges in
England. Then English Freemasonry sought to hold all the

most important political posts in State and Church as well as in economy and culture. Freemasonry stood for the liberal and democratic tendencies which spread from England over France and finally over the whole of Europe in the eighteenth century. The connection between masonic ideas and English Liberalism became closer in the nineteenth and twentieth centuries. The belief in a world religion purely based on reason, in which all people were equal, irrespective of racial and national differences, had particular influence on Jewish emancipation. The lodges defended the equality of the Jews, and their unconditional acceptance into the lodges helped their social and civic emancipation in England, because in the Freemasons' organisations the Jews were able to get in touch with the leading classes of English society.

Freemasonry maintained not only close contact with the Jews but with the English churches and sects. This is linked to the essence of Puritanism which is close to ideas from Judaism and the Old Testament. The Jews saw themselves as the chosen people on earth and in consequence of this Puritan tradition the English regarded themselves as the chosen people of the world. This belief in being chosen is the basis of England's world rule and therefore of a world empire. English Freemasonry regards itself as the organisation for the realisation of this idea. From this stems a particular spiritual Christianity of the English, which has also left its mark on Freemasonry. In the lodges the open Bible lies as a symbol on the altar, and all lodge members have to obey the omnipotent builder of all worlds through the moral laws set out in the Bible. Indicative of the close connection between Freemasonry and the English Church is the fact that a great number of bishops, many clerics and the laity are Freemasons.

Even at the beginning of its development English Freemasonry was extraordinarily adroit politically. Like the Jesuits, the Freemasons sought to penetrate the higher political classes. Slowly, it won over nobility, leading statesmen, politicians and diplomats, the senior officers of the armies and the navy, leaders of trade and the economy, captains of industry and principal businessmen, parliamentarians and journalists, and finally advocates and the clergy. It paid special attention to getting as many members as possible of the royal family, and to understand the position of English royalty towards Freemasonry the close synthesis of masonic politics with politics of English imperialism must be considered. In theory, there should have been opposition between purely humanitarian politics and power politics, but in practice these contrasts were eliminated through Freemasonry. Humanity became a power-political slogan against states which opposed England's claim to world domination, or stood in the way of English politics in general. This became obvious in the English press's propaganda against Germany during the First World War. Over and over again, the old (but for ever new) slogan of Freemasons about the struggle of 'democracies' against 'autocracies' was used. There were endless calls for the 'liberation' of the 'suffering peoples', and so often the 'freedom of the world' threatened by autocratic states was defended. This struggle of English Freemasonry is unchanged; autocracies have been replaced by 'authoritarian states'.

The close connection between English Freemasonry and imperialism is especially clear in the development of the English military and colonial lodges. A short time after the establishment of Freemasonry in England in 1717 – similar lodges also developed in Ireland and Scotland – the lodges tried to acquire connections to senior military personnel, and these attempts were well received not only in England, Ireland and Scotland, but in Canada and the former English colonies in North America through regiments of the British army. Special military and field Lodges were founded within individual garrisons and at more senior levels in headquarters.

These lodges often recruited almost the entire officer corps of the regiments or military headquarters where they were

established. The lodges accompanied the units in their different military operations and thus played a significant role in the
growth of English Freemasonry in countries outside of
England, Ireland and Scotland. English field lodges also
accepted civilians as members; when the regiments departed,
those left behind created civil lodges. Relations between the
army and Freemasonry in Britain became ever tighter during
the eighteenth and nineteenth centuries, with many high-
ranking officers playing a leading role in Freemasonry, as
Great Master or Grand Lodge Officer.

Lodges developed not just for the land forces, but in the
navy. At an early stage there were special ones for naval officers in Bristol and Liverpool.

The list of military, field and navy lodges increased year by
year and through these lodges Freemasonry established itself
not only on the American continent, but in the British possessions in Asia, and especially in India. The establishment of
Freemasonry was also promoted by the regiment lodges of
the British units deployed there. In English colonial politics
these military lodges were the ideological and political centres
for the expansion of British interests. Wherever English businessmen, soldiers or colonists settled, the founding of lodges
followed. They offered a social and cultural centre for colonial
pioneers in foreign countries, and association and uniform
spiritual convictions within British Freemasonry gave this
work extraordinary impetus. Above all, it enabled English
colonists to confront the native population with a united front.
Simultaneously, it also maintained contact with the motherland.

At the beginning, only whites were admitted as members of
the colonial lodges, natives being excluded, but this arrangement was in direct contradiction to the most basic masonic
principles. Thus, during the course of the nineteenth century
the Grand Lodge of England decided to allow full access to
Indians. This acceptance of natives conferred on British colonial politics an advantage not to be underestimated. Not only

were leading Indians admitted, but the blacks in the African possessions who had attended English schools and universities. They too became part of the society of English Freemasons, some in lodges purely for the coloured, and some in mixed race lodges. The Indians, who had been brought up in the English tradition, through their attendance at English schools, were excluded from Indian nationalism and were alienated from their own Indian traditions.

Here English Freemasonry can be seen to have used the same political tactics as practised by the English government, and to have attempted to win over to their organisation India's most important princes and other leading figures.

British lodges in the overseas possessions obey the principles of the English mother lodges in their activities. Considering English domination of vast areas of the world, it is not surprising that world Freemasonry is also under English control. This is mainly due to the fact that England is the motherland of modern Freemasonry. Not only in Europe but in Africa, Asia, America and Australia there are Grand Lodges, which are now independent, but owe their original establishment to the activities of British Freemasons. In the United Grand Lodge of England they still worship the 'Mother Grand Lodge' of world Freemasonry. Even if there have been tensions between the English and the Scottish and Irish Grand Lodges, they form a complete unity in a spiritual sense. Characteristic of the dominant position that English Freemasonry holds within worldwide Freemasonry is the fact that the Highest Council for Britain and its overseas possessions is a member of the international organisation, the Confederation of Lausanne, but up to now it has never participated in the congresses held by the Confederation. Here the English group does not have as dominating an influence as the Johannis Freemasonry.

With its multiple connections and relations, British Freemasonry can afford to portray itself as apolitical. It does not require specific political goals, since it significantly controls the domain of English politics. Under the guise of a humanitarian welfare organisation, English Freemasonry is a pivotal element of English Imperialism and therefore of the British World Empire.

A list of the known British lodges is contained in the subject index of the Special Search List.

The Jews in Britain

I. Jews in British History

Exactly when the Jews first appeared in England cannot be positively determined. They were mentioned for the first time in a Christian ordinance in which the Church opposed the mixing of Christian and Jewish holidays. In the Middle Ages the Jews were granted the King's direct protection but had to succumb to high taxation. Nevertheless they acquired great wealth, to the extent that a Jew could finance the construction of ten monasteries. The levies that the Jews had to pay the King were recovered through extortion and other financial business from the broad mass of the population.

Under Richard the Lionheart, Judaism was awarded a significant broadening of its rights and Jews were granted a special court to settle their business disputes. This preferential treatment engendered opposition within the general population and developed into public protests against Judaism. The Church intervened to oblige the Jews to wear badges, and at the same time banned Christians from any contact with them. In the wars of the barons against the King the junior aristocracy takes up an extremely anti-Jewish position and in 1250 its leader, Simon de Montfort, secured a significant reduction in the rights of Jews in the Magna Carta. After the Jewish question had been so addressed, the Kingdom could not ignore the Jewish movement any longer and in 1290 all the Jews were expelled from England.

The few who remained after converting to Christianity soon regained their power, the most famous among them being Perkin Warbeck, who became pretender to the Crown against Henry VII and was executed when his plan failed.

The rise of Puritanism brought about a revival of Jewish influence in England, and Cromwell recognised the similarity of the English scheme for world domination and the Jewish version. Cromwell was convinced his people were the chosen ones, just as the Jews were. This set the foundations for an Anglo-Jewish alliance. The relationship between the Jews and the English was reinforced by an old tale that the English people were one of the lost tribes of Israel, a myth which still has supporters in England and is deliberately propagated by the Jews.

Negotiations for a return of the Jews to England were led by the Dutch Rabbi Manasseh Ben Israel, and were successful within a few years. The advantage of the Anglo-Jewish connection became clear to Cromwell in his wars against Spain and Holland, and it was then that the ideological basis for the English attitude to Zionism was formed. Disraeli later pushed through the legal standing of Jews and also established Judaism's position of power in England. The overlap of English and Jewish interests becomes evident with the English approach to the problem of Palestine.

Under considerable pressure in 1915, England promised the Arabs Palestine in return for help in the war against Turkey. Two years later, when England was in need of the support of world Judaism, the then Colonial Secretary Balfour promised in a solemn declaration to create a 'national homeland' for the Jews in Palestine at the end of the First World War. In the aftermath of the Balfour Declaration the Jewish Agency was formed to represent Judaism and Jewish interests in Palestine, and was recognised by the League of Nations. It is also the working committee of the Zionists, led by Chaim Weizmann, and is a combination of a series of larger Jewish organisations.

II. *Judaism's Current Situation*

There is no exact estimate of the number of Jews now living in England. Officially there are said to be 300,000, but in reality the number is significantly higher.

Politics

Since Disraeli (Lord Beaconsfield), the Jews have held a powerful position in politics. As Prime Minister, he accomplished the takeover of the Suez Canal shares for Britain and thus secured the most important waterway to India. At the Berlin Conference in 1878, he pushed through the incorporation of Cyprus into the British Empire and laid the foundation for English domination of the Near East.

Disraeli was always conscious of his Jewish descent. This is most evident in his novels where he defines racial issues as the key to understanding world history. After Disraeli, Isaac Rufus (later Lord Reading) was the most conspicuous representative of Judaism in England. In 1921 he was made Viceroy and Governor-General of India, and held this post until 1926. He was also an outstanding representative of the Jews and until 1921 was Vice-President of the Anglo-Jewish Association and supported, as the British government's representative, the Jewish Agency's work in Palestine.

Thereafter no new Cabinets were formed without including Jews. Baldwin's last Cabinet contained two Jews from the financial world who also held managing positions at Baldwins Ltd. When Neville Chamberlain announced his Cabinet before the outbreak of this war he took two Jews into the government: Sir Philip Sassoon as Minister of Works, and Hore-Belisha as War Minister. Additionally several Jews held influential positions: the President of the Post Office Savings Bank was, for example, the well-known Zionist Leon Simon, and one of the most senior officials in the Home Office was the Jew Sir Cecil Kisch, whose counsel in turn were the Jews Sir Henry Strakosch and T.E. Gregory-Gugenheim. The current Churchill Cabinet does not include Jews at ministerial level, but Eden, Cooper and Churchill himself have to be seen as representatives of Jewish interests. At the beginning of the war, when Eden was in Opposition, he was supported by the so-called Fabian wing of the Socialists under the leadership of the Jew Israel Sieff. At the same time Duff Cooper undertook a lecture trip through North America where he expressed his support for the Judaism at every opportunity.

Today the number of Jews in Parliament is 19 or 20. The best-known among them are Thomas Levy (Conservative), leader of the Textile Committee in the Commons; L. Silkin is the leader of an important committee of London's local government; the Jew Isadore Salomon is chairman of the very important Select Committee on Estimates, which deals with the most secret concerns of the state in the distribution of the two budgets. The power of the Jews within the Cabinet depends on the representation of several economic organisations which gain considerable advantage from the fact that their respective director or chairman is a Member of Parliament. For example in 1934, 581 MPs held 646 management posts or were members of a board of directors.

Judaism is very influential in local government and Jews are most evident in Greater London. Sir Percy Simmons has been a councillor for a long time, and has been Chairman of the London County Council, the Fire Brigade, the Committee for Theatre and Music Halls, of the Improvement Committee, etc. Sir Samuel Joseph was also a councillor and a Sheriff of London for a considerable time.

Finance

Jewish status in politics corresponds to their standing in the financial world. The influential Jews C. J. Hambro and Goschen are directors of the Bank of England, and Jews also hold leading positions in the so-called 'big five' banks. Sir Victor Schuster is a director of the National Provincial Bank Ltd (Capital: £60,000,000); Lord Bearstead in Lloyds Bank Ltd (Capital: £74,000,000); Lord Goschen in the Midland Bank Ltd (Capital: £45,200,000); and Lord Goschen, Sir George Schuster and Lord Melchett in Barclays Bank (Capital: £20,000,000). Sir Leonard Cohen is seen as a powerful financier in India, where he is the director of the Bengal and North-Western Railway Company (£4,800,000 capital), and Lord Bearstead, together with two other Jews, F.D. and Peter Montefiore-Samuel, is a director of the most significant bank, Samuel & Co. Its capital of £2,000,000 does not begin to reflect the huge influence this company exercises on international finance.

The same is true for the companies Samuel Montagu & Co., with Jewish directors E.L. Franklin, L.S. Montague, S.E. Franklin, Lord Swaythling and C.M. Franklin. Japhet & Co. has the Jew Sammy Japhet as chairman and the Jews Paul Lindenberg, Max Frontheim and Gottfried Loewenstein as directors. The Jewish company Erlangers Ltd has Emile d'Erlanger as chairman, with Baron Frederic d'Erlanger and Leo F.A. d'Erlanger as his representatives. The individual families have further directorships in sixteen different transport companies. Another well-known banking family is that of Sir Albert Stern whose company headquarters is Stern Brothers. Sir Albert is a director of seven other financial companies. Sir Osmond Elim d'Avigdor-Goldsmid, as head of the family, is active in seven different trading companies.

Economy

Jews also hold significant positions in the economy of the British Empire directly corresponding to their economic influence. The two directors of the biggest oil company, Shell Transport and Trading Co. Ltd, which is seen as a world power and has a capital of £43,000,000, are the Jews Peter

Montefiore-Samuel and Sir Robert Waley. The latter is chairman and director of 26 different oil companies. Other significant Jews in the oil industry are B. Maisel and Johanna Maisel, the directors of Petroleum Trust and Orient Oil and Finance Co. Ltd.

To a large extent the British food industry is supposed to be in Jewish hands. Sir George Schuster is chairman of big conglomerates: Home and Colonial Stores Ltd, Lipton Ltd, Maypole Dairy Co. Ltd and Allied Suppliers. These companies have branches all over England and more or less hold a monopoly position. The same is also true for Lyons & Co. Ltd, which apart from food distribution owns a big number of restaurants and hotels and whose share capital amounts to £10,000,000. Sir Isidore Salomon is chairman of this company, has direct control over other financial institutes, and owns two of the largest and most modern London hotels, the Strand Palace and the Cumberland.

In the insurance business, Alliance Assurance Co. has a near monopoly and is an amalgamation of nine large insurance companies. Its chairman is Lionel de Rothschild, with Lord Bearstead and Lord Roseberry as directors. The Jews Sir George Schuster and Sir Charles Seligman are directors of the Commercial Union Assurance Co. Ltd, which runs twelve other companies.

The gold and diamond industries are almost entirely Jewish – Sir George W. Albo is chairman and manager of General Mining and Finance Corporation Ltd and is also a director of six other gold and diamond companies. Geoffrey Joel is director of De Beers Consolidated Mines who have taken over thirteen diamond mines and have leased a great number. Joel is also director of numerous other South African diamond companies. Sir Ernest Oppenheimer is director and respectively chairman of 24 South African gold and diamond companies.

Press, Radio and Film

The anti-German attitude of these instruments of propaganda is mainly due to the large number of Jews working for them. The English press, apart from a few important exceptions, is dominated by six large groups: Odhams, Beaverbrook, the Berry Group, News Chronicle, Daily Mail and Westminster Press.

In all of these corporations Jews either hold leading posts or finance the enterprises. Baron Southwood of Fernhurst, formerly Julius Salter Elias, exerts a dominant influence over the Odhams Group, which publishes the *Daily Herald*, with a circulation of over two million, and is the official mouthpiece of the Marxist Labour Party. The *Daily Express*, *Sunday Express* and *Evening Standard* are part of Beaverbrook Press. Lord Beaverbrook, who owns this group, is a close friend of the Jew Melchett and is completely pro-Jewish. In 1930 he wrote: 'The commercial and intellectual capabilities of the Jews are so abundant in Britain because they are held back by neither ban nor barrier. Here the Jewish question is solved by their complete integration in our varied activities, and the nation is therefore richer and happier. The Continent will eventually discover that there is no other solution.' Lord Roseberry, a half-Jew, has a large interest in the Westminster Press and acts as one of its directors.

One of the first directors of the radio company, the British Broadcasting Corporation, was Godfrey Isaacs. Since then Jewish influence on British broadcasting has changed very little.

Two Jews Ivor Montagu and S. Bernstein are mainly responsible for the many anti-German films produced in England in the past few years. In England they hold positions akin to film censors.

There are also numerous Jewish-owned film companies. The largest and most important is owned by the brothers Ostrer, who also own several hundred cinemas and music-halls.

Isidore Ostrer is president of six movie corporations, Mark
Ostrer is director and respectively chairman of 26 film businesses, and the third brother, Maurice Ostrer, as well as being
involved in his brothers' enterprises, has a share in twelve other
film companies. Since British Gaumont merged with Odeon
Theatres under the presidency of Oscar Deutsch, this Jew controls 500 cinemas and a big share of the British cinema
industry.

The Jews have formed a series of organisations in England,
the most important of which is the Board of Deputies. The
Zionists also have their headquarters in England, as do other
Jewish international press offices and anti-German propaganda institutes.

Jewish Organisations

The Jewish Defence Committee, Woburn House, Upper
    Woburn Place, London WC1. First Secretary: Sidney
    Salomon.

Bnei Brith, Woburn House, Upper Woburn Place, London
    WC1.

District Grand Lodge of Great Britain and Ireland, address as
    above. Grand-President: Julius Schwab; Grand Vice-
    President: Mrs V. Hassan and Professor S. Brodetzky;
    Grand Treasurer: Harry Samuels.

European Committee, address as above. President: Julius
    Schwab, 180 Goldhurst Terrace, London NW6.

Agudas Israel, 53 Queens Drive, London N16. President:
    Jacob Rosenheim; Treasurer: Ludwig Strauss; Political
    Secretary: H. Goodman; Organisation Secretary: Henry
    Pels.

Keren Hayishuv Co. Ltd, 19 London Wall, London EC2.
    Chairman: J. Rosenheim; Secretary: M.L. Halpern.

Freeland League for Jewish Territorial Colonisation, 69
    Aberdare Gardens, London NW6. Treasurer: Dr Myer S.
    Nathan; Secretary: Dr I.N. Steinberg.

Jewish Colonisation Association, 16 Old Broad Street, London EC2. President: Sir Osmond D'Avigdor Goldsmid; Vice-President: Jules Philippson; Main management: Dr Louis Oungre.

Maccabi World Union, 37 Museum Street, London WC1. Presidents: Rt Hon. Lord Melchett, Professor. S. Brodetzky; Chairman: Dr H. Lelewer; Treasurer: Dr K.F. Jacobowitz; Organisation manager: Dr W.W. Meisl.

World Jewish Congress, 150 Dudden Hill Lane, London NW10. President: Marchioness of Reading; Chairman: Rev. M.L. Perlzweig; Treasurer: L. Gildesgame; Secretaries-General: N. Barou, Prof. E. Cohn.

Anglo-Jewish Association, Woburn House, Upper Woburn Place, London WC1. President: Leonard J. Stein; Vice-Presidents: Sir Osmond E. D'Avigdor Goldsmid, Rev. Dr H.I. Hertz, Lionel de Rothschild; Treasurer: Leonard G. Montefiore.

Joint British Committee for the Reconstruction of East European Jewry (Ort-Ose), Central Office: Premier House, 150 Southampton Row, London WC1. President: Lord Rothschild; Chairman and Treasurer: I.H. Levey.

ORT, address see above. Chairman: A.I. Halpern; Treasurer: S. Beloff; Secretary: P.I. Rogers.

Jewish Agency for Palestine (Zionist), 77 Great Russell St, London WC1. President: Dr Chaim Weizmann; Executive Member: Prof. S. Brodetzky; Director of Information: Rev. M.L. Perlzweig; Secretary: A. Lourie (political department), Israel Cohen (information department), J. Hodess (editor of the *New Judea*), I. Linton (finance and administration).

British Section, address see above. Chairman: Lord Melchett; Secretaries-General: L. Bakstansky, A.G. Brotman.

Keren Hayesod Committee, address see above. President Gen.: Sir Osmond d'Avigdor-Goldsmid; President: Simon Marks; Chairman: The Marchioness of Reading; Secretaries-General: Rev. M.L. Perlzweig, L. Bakstansky;

Treasurers: Dennis M. Cohn, A. Le Vay Lawrence.

The World Zionist Organisation, 77 Great Russell St, London WC1. President: Dr Chaim Weizmann; Chairman of the Executive: D. Ben Gurion.

Keren Kayemet Leisrael Ltd (Jewish National Fund), 65 Southampton Row, London WC1. President: Prof. Samson Wright; Treasurer: Albert van den Bergh; Secretary: Maurice Posette.

The Jewish State Party, 6 Queensdown Road, Clapton, London E5. Chairman: Dr I.M. Machover; Secretary-General: E. Livny.

World Mizrachi Organisation, 78 New Oxford St, London WC1. President: Dr I.H. Hertz; Vice-President: Salomon Wolfson; Chairman: S.E. Sklan; Representative Chairman: Dayn M. Gollop; Treasurer: W.N. Williams; Secretaries-General: F.N. Landau, W. Frankel.

Poale Zion, 134 Goldhurst Terrace, London NW6. Secretary General: Dr S. Levenberg.

Habonim (Zionist Youth Organisation), 65 Southampton Row, London WC1. President: Dr Nathan Morris; Vice-Presidents: J.C. Gilbert, Rev. B. Cherrick.

Women's International Zionist Organisation (WIZO), 75 Great Russell St, London WC1. President General: The Viscountess Samuel; Vice-President: Mrs H. Irwell; Chairs: I.M. Sieff, Mrs Weizmann; Organisation and Propaganda Department: P. Goodman; Treasurers: H. Irwell, Olga Alman.

New Zionist Organisation, 47 Finchley Road, London NW8. President: Vladimir Jabotinsky; Presidential Members: A. Abrahams, E. Ben-Horin, Dr I. Damm, Dr S. Klinger, A. Kopelowicz; Secretary-General: I. Benari.

Independent Order of Bnei Brith, 118 Great Ducie Street, Strangeways, Manchester. President General: M. Redstone; Secretary-General: D. Dolovitz.

The Board of Deputies, Woburn House, Upper Woburn Place, London WC1. President: Prof. S. Brodetzky;

Vice-Presidents: Sir Robert Waley Cohen, Dr Israel
Feldmann; Treasurer: Gordon Livermann; Secretary:
A.C. Brotman; Syndic: Charles H.L. Emanuel.
London Area Council, 43 Prescot Street, London E1.
Chairman: Cyril M. Picciotto; Secretary: Councillor
Henry Solomons.
Sephardi World Union, Heneage Lane, Bevis Marks, London
EC3. President General: Charles E. Sebag-Montefiore;
President: David Vaz Nunes da Costa; Financial
Secretary: David Berio.
The Zionist Federation of Great Britain and Ireland,
Woodside, Hinksey Hill, Oxford. President: Dr Chaim
Weizmann; Vice-President: Lord Melchett; Executive:
I.K. Goldbloom; Treasurer: Paul Goodman; Secretaries-
General: M.L. Perlzweig, L. Bakstansky. Mrs A. Harris,
94 Clive Road, London NW2. Miss Nathan, c/o 29 Palace
Road, London SW2. J. Samuel, 32 North Villas, Camden
Square, London NW1. J. White, 5 King Edward's
Gardens, London W13. Mrs S.W. Magnus, 55 Wolmer
Gdns. J. Rosen, 24 Vaughan Ave, London NW4. A.
Sheinwold, 108 Clarence Road, London E5. D. Benjamin,
367 Queen's Road, London E13. Mrs G. Karsberg, 134
Broomwood Road, London NW11. R. Gale, 220
Stamford Hill, London N16. Dr H. Capell, 121 Parkside
Way, London N. Harrow. Miss J. Goldberg, 33 Wickford
St, London E1. Miss S. Klein, 79 Chalkhill Rd, Wembley
Park. I.J. Miller, 1 Green's Court, London W1. O. Rose,
19 Colville Road, London W11. A. Sheinwold, 108
Clarence Road, London E5.
Federation of Women Zionists of Great Britain and Ireland,
75 Great Russell St, London WC1. President: Mrs I.M.
Sieff; Chair: R.B. Solomon; Vice-Chair: Mrs M.D. Eder;
Secretaries-General: Mrs J. Hodess, M. Liebster.
New Zionist Organisation in Great Britain, 47 Finchley Road,
London NW8.
Brit Trumpeldor, address see above. President: Vladimir

Jabotinsky; Secretary-General: M. Katz; Navy Dept: I.
Helpern; Cultural Dept: I. Remba.
Student Corporations, address see above.
British Maccabi Association, 34 Clarendon Road, London
W11. President: Lord Melchett; Chairman: I.H. Levey;
Treasurer: R.R. Curtis; Secretaries: Rev. E. Levine, G.H.
Gee, Hyman Cen, M. Lam, Maccabi House, 73 Compayne
Gdns, London NW6. Alfred Cohen, 154 George Lane,
London SE13. A. King, 83 Baston Road, London N16.
M. Swerdlin, 91 Clarence Road, London E5.
The Joint Foreign Committee, Woburn House, Upper
Woburn Place, London WC1. Secretary: A.G. Brotman;
Members of the Board of Deputies: Neville J. Laski, Sir
Osmond E. d'Avigdor-Goldsmid, Israel Cohen, Lionel
L. Colmen, S. Robert Waley Cohen, Barnett Janner, H.L.
Nathan. Members of the Anglo-Jewish Association:
Leonard Stein, Sir Philip Hartog, Leonard G.
Montefiore, Sir P. Magnus.

The British Economic Structure

England is extraordinarily industrialised. In spite of its size it
is, together with Germany and the USA, at the top of the
league of industrialised countries, though no longer in the
lead. Until the start of the war England dominated the world
market in textiles.

Almost all raw materials have to be imported; only coal is
available domestically in abundance. Food and wood are particularly short and there is no source of oil. Quite apart from
investment in its Dominions, England has large financial holdings in South America and in all the oil-producing countries.
English banks are responsible for reinforcing the country's
economic influence.

The English economy is dominated less by Trusts which

control only a limited number of economic branches – for example, Imperial Chemical Industries – than by individuals. This is because there are men in England who are on the boards of more than a hundred of the larger companies. The lack of a national economic organisation, influenced by the state, has led to the absence of a supply economy which, together with the lack of domestic raw material, has caused serious disruption in production. The Federation of British Industries is the only organisation which encompasses all branches of the economy, which externally seems similar to the German organisation of commercial economy, but which goes beyond our understanding of the term 'industry'. It also includes, for example, the fishing and printing industries and is subdivided into 24 main groups and regionally into 22 district groups. The significance of this federation should not be overestimated, however, because it cannot impose binding regulations, and membership is not compulsory. Similarly, the Chambers of Commerce in England do not have the same significance as their German counterparts.

The Trusts have a greater impact. Imperial Chemical Industries, in the chemical field, or the Imperial Smelting Corporation in the non-ferrous metal industry, are dominant. Most of the Trusts are formed by investment organisations, most of which are called Investment Trusts. There is no limit to their activities and the individual investment organisations or Trusts participate in almost all areas of the economy; in general, however, they prefer railway companies, mostly in South America, banks and oil corporations. More than 50% of their investment is abroad. Even if the amount of disposable capital varies, its distribution according to discipline and country is invariably similar to that of the Industrial & General Trust, which we offer as a model:

Distribution by Discipline: **per cent**

Industry   63

Banks and insurance   12.7

American and foreign railways   11

National securities   6.6

English Dominions and Colonial Railways   3

Land and other ownership   2

Shipping   1

Urban transport   0.7

                                                  ─────

                                                  100

Distribution by Country: **per cent**

Great Britain   45.2

Dominions   21

South America (without Argentina)   10

USA   7.6

Argentina   6.6

Asia and Africa, excluding Dominions   4.6

Europe excluding Great Britain   4.5

Mexico and Central America   0.5

                                                  ─────

                                                  100

Even including the Dominions, one third of capital remains outside the British Commonwealth. This share is disproportionately high and is only achieved by perhaps the USA, but not by all Trusts there. The so-called Fixed Trusts are pure investment companies and cannot be compared in any way with those above. The Fixed Trusts have much tighter bonds: the bonds of Investment Trusts and investment companies exist only on a personal level when a member of the board of directors simultaneously has a place on the board of directors of another, comparable enterprise; in the Fixed Trusts there is a genuine organisation. Characteristic for the Fixed Trust is the extremely low capital and the small individual investments, which are never more than the £500 limit. The share of a single Fixed Trust can therefore be seen as irrelevant. They gain significance only through the already mentioned organisation. Individual Fixed Trusts are combined into groups:

1. Municipal & General Securities Group
2. National Group
3. Dawney Day Group
4. Keystone Group
5. British Industries
6. British Empire Group
7. First Provincial Group
8. British General Group
9. Insurance Group
10. Selective Group
11. Protected Group.

The Municipal & General Securities Group is also at the top of the individual groups. The disposable capital of the individual groups amount to between £20,000 and £95,000. The only exception is the National Group which has a disposable capital of over £250,000. The organisation gains importance because in the individual trusts, almost without exception, the same companies appear all the time. An influence on the economy as a whole or just on individual companies happens only through the Fixed Trusts.

The food industry has a special significance in the English economy thanks to Lever Bros and Unilever Ltd as well as Van den Bergh & Jurgens, both chemical enterprises devoted primarily to the production of margarine. They control not only Dutch and French margarine production, but own an important portion of shares issued by the two German companies: Margarine Union and the soap factory, Sunlicht AG.

The chemical industry is dominated by Imperial Chemical Industries Ltd, which has succeeded in acquiring more and more chemical businesses, and perpetually increases its prominence and influence. Imperial Chemical Industries was founded in 1926 by the Jew Sir Alfred Mond, initially as a conglomerate of the large groups: Brunner Mond & Co., Nobel & Explosives Co., United Alkali Co. and the British Dyestuffs Corporation. By 1927 it had acquired forty companies, and had capital of £58 million; by 1939 its capital had increased to £95 million. ICI employs in total about 65,000 workers. Alfred Mond's son sits on the board of ICI under the name of Lord Melchett. The new coal liquefaction processing machines are of special significance.

The Association of British Chemical Manufacturers, which has special authority from the English Board of Trade, is also of particular importance in the industry and includes 132 firms.

The English public utilities of gas, water and electricity show strong personal connections between the members of the boards of the gas works and other public utilities. The electricity industry has a stronger participation on the enterprise level. Whereas many individual gas works can be seen as completely independent, most electricity works have lost their autonomy.

England does not have a single transport company which covers the whole of the country, such as the German Reichsbahn. Here only four companies are of greater importance: The Great Western Railway Company, the London & North Eastern Railway Company, the London, Midland and Scottish Railway Company, and the Southern Railway Company. Again, a remarkable characteristic of the railway companies, and to an even larger extent in shipping, is the strong personal connections between members of the boards, in their association with the oil companies and the banks. At the outbreak of the war England's shipping companies totalled 18 million tonnes. Because a large part of the merchant fleet is devoted to passenger transport, at the outbreak of war it could not cope with the increased quantity of freight under war conditions, which involve longer shipping routes and loss of time through participation in convoys. Importance is given to the passenger sector, notably the White Star Line, Cunard Steam Ship Company and the Peninsular & Oriental Steam Navigation Co.

London's transport is dominated by the London Passenger Transport Board, which supervises trams, buses and the underground train system.

Domestic air traffic is run or controlled by British companies, as in Ecuador, Egypt, Iran, Burma, Venezuela, Peru, Romania, Russia (Shell Transport & Trading Co.), North and South Sumatra, Borneo, Java, Ceram, Mandoel, Trinidad and North America. The larger British oil corporations exert great influence on the English transport system.

British shipyards have large capacities but are unable to begin to meet wartime loss of shipping. The large weapons manufacturer Vickers-Armstrong also has a strong interest in shipyards.

The British motor industry, especially in car and aircraft production, was regarded as a world leader until 1934–5, when it was overtaken by Germany and Italy, not only in performance but in capacity. Most significant are the Armstrong Siddeley Development Co., Austin Motor Co., Birmingham Small Arms Co., Bristol Airplane Co. (Bristol-Blenheim), Ford Motor Co., Hawker Siddeley Aircraft Co. (Hawker-Hurricane), Morris Motors, de Havilland Aircraft and Rolls Royce (luxury cars). British engineering also had to give up its leading position in the world to the United States and Germany. Nevertheless firms such as Vickers, Baldwins, Babcock & Wilkinson, and the General Electric Co. are still prominent.

The textile industry has special importance, both in spinning mills and textile processing. The largest English firm is Courtaulds Ltd (textiles and yarns) which has spinning mills in seven locations. The company is controlled by the Courtauld family, who is represented by three members on the board of directors. In the current war the textile industry has had to lower its capacity (leading in the world!) since the supply of raw material has been greatly reduced in favour of more important goods, and insufficient stocks had been held in reserve.

England held the world's leading position in coal mining for a long time, but had to surrender that position to Germany. Nevertheless coal remains England's only locally produced abundant raw material. Pure coal mining companies are rare; they are usually combined with iron ore. Coal for shipping is mainly provided by the Powell Duffryn Steam Coal Co., which also supplies heating installations and electricity works.

A number of companies mine iron ore and are (in contrast to the coal mining companies) exclusively concerned with the extraction of iron ore. The most important are: the Consett Iron Co. (whose board of directors includes men from all branches of the economy), and Pease & Partners, as well as Stanton Ironworks Co. In contrast to coal mining, iron ore extraction in England is not self-sufficient, and in wartime about one third of the volume consumed will have to be imported.

Britain also held the top place in world steel production, but was pushed aside by Germany and the USA. United Steel are the absolute leaders in England, and Baldwins Ltd are also concerned with the production of steel.

As chairman of the two largest cement companies, Sir Malcolm Stewart dominates almost the entire production of cement in England, which is substantial (Associated Portland Cement Manufacturers and British Portland Cement Manufacturers).

English insurance companies have always been of considerable international significance, especially in shipping and most special fields. The men on the individual insurance companies' boards of directors are to be found in all sections of the economy (Sir E. Horne, Lord Balfour of Burleigh, Sir Goschen, Sir Royden, J.J. Astor [The Times], F. D'Arcy Cooper, Earl of Dudley, R.O. Hambro, L. Rothschild).

The largest and most influential of Britain's banks, the 'Big

Five', are Barclays Bank, Lloyds Bank, Midland Bank, National Provincial Bank and the Westminster Bank. English banks are particularly important because of their vast holdings in the most diverse areas of English economy, and they or their directors dominate the banking system in the Dominions and in other countries. Among them are the Bank of Romania, the Ottoman Bank, the Hong Kong and Shanghai Banking Corporation, etc.

A special appendix notes the particular connections between the following establishments: Petschek-Concern, Steel and Industrial Works, Unilever, Lloyds, Merton, Royal Dutch Shell, Imperial Chemical Industries and Coates. Also mentioned is the Department of Overseas Trade, and a list of German firms whose shares are either completely or partly in British ownership.

Structure and Organisation of the British Police

The following is only a very brief outline from the mass of material at the disposal of Amt V. Comparisons with the German Criminal Police cannot be made because of the entirely different – and for us inexplicable – organisation and activities of the British police.

A. General Structure:

In England and Wales the police are subordinate to the Home Office, and in Scotland to the Scottish Office, but police command lies with the local authorities, with the exception of the Greater London Police District. The local police system follows the country's national characteristics, and is retained with conservative tenacity.

I. Metropolitan Police (Greater London)

This is the only police force directly subordinate to the Home Office, and its jurisdiction includes the counties of London and Middlesex as well as parts of Kent, Surrey, Essex and Hertford, an area of around 1,700 square kilometres and a population of about 8.25 million.

The City of London (centre and business district, roughly 3 square kilometres) has its own local police, the City of London Police, headed by a Commissioner and consisting of approximately 1,100 men.

The Metropolitan Police has more than 20,000 police officers and is headed by a Commissioner. Its central authority, the police headquarters, is located at New Scotland Yard on the Victoria Embankment. Headquarters are subdivided into four major departments: A Department: Administration Section; B Department: Traffic Section; C Department: Criminal Investigation Department (abbreviated to CID); D Department: Organisation Section. There is also L Department, the Legal Section, and S Department, the Secretariat (headquarters office).

The Receiver's Office holds a particular responsibility as the financial and economic department. Other branches affiliated to the headquarters are a medical department, the Police College in Hendon (for higher ranks), the Police Training School (for lower ranks) and the Special Constabulary (the auxiliary police).

The Greater London Police District is subdivided into four districts, each headed by a Deputy Assistant Commissioner. Every district is further divided into divisions (identified by letters), which in turn are each headed by a superintendent. All divisions include sub-divisions and police stations. In total there are twenty-two divisions, plus the TA Division, which covers the Thames river police, as well as 183 sub-divisions and police stations.

The organisation of the Metropolitan Police is shown in

detail in the appendix (as of the summer 1937). This outline also contains the names of all police officers in charge of London's police force, the location of the police stations and telephone boxes. (The single letters behind the names of the officers indicate their decorations.)

The classification by rank of the uniformed police is: Commissioner (1), Deputy Commissioner (1), Assistant Commissioners (3), Deputy Assistant Commissioners (4), Chief Constables (8), Superintendents (28), Chief Inspectors (60), Sub-Divisional Inspectors (115), Station Inspectors (95), Junior Station Inspectors (95), Inspectors (459), Station Sergeants (460), Sergeants (1,900), Constables (16,000).

For the Criminal Police: Assistant Commissioner (1), Chief Constables (4), Superintendents (8), Chief Inspectors (15), 1st Class Inspectors or Divisional Detective Inspectors (170), Detective Inspectors (170), Detective Sergeants (470), Detectives (500). The numbers in brackets indicate the approximate strength at the beginning of 1939.

II. The Police Forces in England and Wales

Local police forces divide into:

1. County Police Forces, whose area of jurisdiction comprises the area of a county with the exception of those cities and communes which operate their own forces. In England and Wales there are sixty county forces, the strongest being Lancashire, Yorkshire West Riding, Durham and Staffordshire. The central main office (the police headquarters) is normally located in the county's principal town.

2. City Police Forces or Borough Police Forces in larger and middle-sized cities run their own force, independent of the County Police. In England and Wales there are 121 such forces, the strongest being in Liverpool, Birmingham and Manchester.

Classifications by rank of the local police are (by agreement with the Home Office Minister): Chief Constable, Assistant Chief Constable, Chief Superintendent, Superintendent, Chief Inspector, Sub-divisional Inspector, Inspector, Sub-Inspector, Sergeant, Station Sergeant, Acting Sergeant, Constable.

The strength of each County Police Force lies between 20 and 2,100 men; in total there are around 19,000 men. The number of each City Police Force is between 15 and 1,800 men. In total the City and Borough Police Forces have more than 21,000 men at their disposal. Cities with a population below 20,000 cannot have their own police force. The larger police forces are again divided up into divisions and police stations.

Local police forces are independent of one another but there are universal regulations covering management, co-operation of the individual forces, training, pay, care, uniform, employment conditions, etc. In addition, local police forces are constantly supervised by state inspectors (Inspectors of Constabulary) who have to produce a report to Parliament via the Home Office about their status and fitness for duty. Should any mismanagement be exposed, the relevant local authority can lose the state subsidy, which is half the cost of the police. The requirement for police authorities to fulfil their legal obligations has led to uniformity within the police system. The Inspectors are responsible for all branches of police duty, including the criminal police.

III. The Police Forces in Scotland

The structure is similar to the one of the local police forces in England and Wales. The Scottish Office employs a Special Inspector for the around fifty Scottish police forces.

The largest police authority after the Metropolitan Police is the City of Glasgow Police which is led by the well-known

Chief Constable Sillitoe. The Glasgow police has seven divisions and includes about 2,300 men, with its headquarters at 21 St Andrew's Street.

Grades of uniformed police are: Assistant Chief Constable (1), Superintendents (8), Lieutenants (14) (a rank unique to the Scottish police and equivalent to English Chief Inspector), Inspectors (73), Sergeants (180), Constables (1,900).

Criminal Police: Assistant Chief Constable (1), Superintendents (2), Lieutenants (9), Inspectors (19), Sergeants (31), Constables (87).

The City of Glasgow Police may be regarded as the unofficial centre for Scottish forces, since it is the collection point for all fingerprints taken in Scotland, publishes the *Scottish Police Gazette* and runs the radio installations.

IV. Special Police Forces

a) The Railway Police: Through special legislation the four large railway companies – the London, Midland and Scottish Railway; Great Western Railway; the Southern Railway; London and North-Eastern Railway – are permitted to employ special police, both uniformed and CID officers, within their areas of business. The Railway Police are divided into four different forces, each under its own Chief Constable, and have existed since 1921. If necessary, they work hand in hand with the local police forces and the Metropolitan Police. Their organisation is equivalent to the other police forces, as is the structure of their criminal departments.

b) The Ports Police: The Port of London Authority Police has to be specially mentioned because it is a separate force with a total strength of about 800 men and its own criminal department of nearly 30 men.

c) Police Reserves and Auxiliaries: Civilians of irreproachable character may be recruited into the police's auxiliary service to support them in strikes, at demonstrations, exhibitions, etc. These Special Constables are uniformed but wear other rank insignia; they have been specifically sworn in and have full powers of arrest. In general, they are honorary members of the police, but receive a certain indemnity whenever they have to make an arrest. In 1937 there were about 150,000 men enrolled as Special Constables.

B. Criminal Police

The English CID is closely linked to the uniformed branch in organisation, so there has never been a neat separation of the areas of responsibility of the two branches. Uniformed police relieve the criminal police of some of their duties. Both specialist groups work together and stay in close touch. The new generation of the CID is recruited exclusively from the uniformed police. The following explanations shall be limited to the structure of the Greater London CID, which in a sense is regarded as the central criminal bureau for the whole of England.

The Greater London criminal police, the Criminal Investigation Department (CID) is structured into: a) the crime officers at headquarters (C Department); b) the local crime officers, who form part of the police apparatus of the divisions; and c) the political department (Special Branch), which is a sub-section of C Department.

About 400 CID officers are employed at headquarters and the political department. Heading the CID is Assistant Commissioner Sir Norman Kendal, Great Britain's representative in the International Criminal Police Commission. He is an Englishman through and through, who speaks French and understands some German. He was awarded a knighthood on merit in 1937 and his representative is Chief Constable J.E. Horwell who, in contrast, is an experienced, practical man who has worked his way up from a simple detective. He has

behaved in a pro-German manner and has always been helpful
without any obvious political interest.

I. The C Department

This consists of groups C1 to C5.

1. C1: Central Office is responsible for all domestic and inter-
    national searches, for all foreign requests, for extradition
    and deportation, crimes of local and international charac-
    ter, and special investigations for government authorities.
    The specialists are mostly at Central Office, but speciali-
    sation does mean that from their recruitment particular
    officers are appointed to certain types of crime. The offi-
    cers of Central Office are older, experienced officers
    (inspectors and sergeants) who are also sent to the
    provinces to lead investigations. Normally, murder
    prompts the local force to call for Scotland Yard's assis-
    tance. An officer is assigned to the respective local police
    for the time of the investigation, but remains under the
    direct control of Scotland Yard.

    Central Office itself is also strictly structured into
    departments. There are for example five inspectors (First
    Class) (approximately corresponding to a German
    Kriminalkommissar) who are more active in handling big
    cases than in supervision.

    The head of the women's criminal police is also affili-
    ated to Central Office (in a supervisory capacity).

    The Map Room is where different flags pinned on large
    maps of Greater London indicate particular unsolved
    offences. The Map Room is often visited by local divi-
    sional CID officers in order to determine links between
    individual special offences.

    Finally, the Flying Squad is also part of Central Office.
    Many cars and disguised vans, which are not identifiable
    as police cars but are driven by CID officers, patrol the

urban area day and night. Each of these cars is equipped
with wireless telegraphic transmissions (Morse) and is in
constant wireless contact with the Information Room at
Scotland Yard. The Flying Squad is specifically concerned with car thieves and robberies, and watches the
movements of professional and habitual criminals. It
works in close contact with the local divisional CID
offices. Reception in the cars is good and radio messages
can be received from across the country.

The radio exchange centre, or Information Room, is
located in the main building and is dependent on D
Department, since not only motorised CID patrols but a
large number of the uniformed police of the four districts
and of traffic control are travelling the streets. The positions of the traffic police are always known to the
Information Room. Some of the radio cars are also
equipped with transmitters. As soon as an incident is
detected, corresponding radio messages are sent to the
cars if it is sufficiently serious. An important role is also
played by the web of blue-and-white painted police telephone boxes which are for everyone's use. There are about
500 in the Metropolitan Police area, and they also hold
first-aid equipment and medicine.

2. The C2 group is (among other things) concerned with
registration, surveillance and deportation of foreigners.
The central registry for foreigners is located in Bow Street
Police Station, 28 Bow Street, London WC2. Every foreigner living in the police district of Greater London is
registered in this central registry with his exact personal
and residence details. For English nationals there is no
obligation to register, so there is no residents' registration
office.

The central registry for England and Wales is the so-
called Passenger Register in the Home Office.

The collection of fingerprints is located on the third
floor at Bow Street. The collection of ten-digit

fingerprints, classified according to the Henry system, is the central collection for Great Britain and contains the prints of more than 600,000 people. The collection of single fingerprints is relatively insignificant. The prints are secured with argenturate and photography. The photographic workshop is located on the ground floor and has very little modern equipment.

3. The Criminal Record Office (CRO) is also located at New Scotland Yard (ground and third floors). It contains complete reports on all criminals convicted in Great Britain and distributes information to all the country's police authorities. The CRO's collection is the most important apart from the ten-digit fingerprints, since there is no criminal register as such. Very important too are the CRO's 'Records of Criminals': detailed reports about individual lawbreakers which also record previous convictions, arrests and releases from detention, and the Crime Index, which contains a Method Index (record of unlawful conduct), Nominal Index (names of convicted persons), Wanted Index (register of wanted persons) with around 90–100,000 notations, and a photo collection of criminals. The CRO also publishes the *Police Gazette* and its bulletins are distributed to all police forces in Great Britain and Ireland.

4. The C4 group corresponds more or less to our administrative office.

5. The Forensic Science Institute also depends on C Department. It is located at the Police College in Hendon and has very modern equipment.

II. The Crime Police in the Divisions

The crime officers working in the divisions form this part of the departmental organisation. Each Superintendent is subordinate to a Divisional Detective (DDI) who is assisted by one or two Detective Inspectors and a number of Detective-

Sergeants and Detectives according to the size of the district. The Superintendent is the superior of all crime officers working within his division. In spite of their simultaneous subordination to the CID, they are answerable to him so as to assure co-operation between uniformed and crime officers, whose reports are checked by the Superintendent so that he always knows about their activities. When these officers deal with cases, they are supervised and led by the officers of the CID. The Divisional Detective Inspector, who has his office in the division's main station, is responsible for the activities of the crime officers in his division. The criminal police in the divisions deal with all crimes and offences within their district, even murders, if the Central Office does not intervene.

The CID in the sub-divisions usually consists of only one to three rooms, one of which is reserved for the senior officer. All CID officers (sergeants and detectives) are accommodated most of the time in one or two very big but generally unfriendly rooms (with sometimes up to twelve people in a room). Long interrogations and detailed analysis of the records is largely unknown to the English CID officer; as he is mainly on duty outside. Suspects can be interrogated only with their unconstrained consent. Witnesses are usually only questioned. After the solving of a case, the records are immediately handed over to the court where the accused will appear.

To ensure a constant exchange of CID information and experience, and a clear overview of the activities of the divisions, CID Inspectors meet once a week for a conference at Scotland Yard. The Divisional Superintendents also have to send off four detailed reports to Scotland Yard every morning, of which the Morning Crime Report gives details about each punishable offence reported during the past twenty-four hours.

III. The Special Branch

Special Branch, or political police, is a sub-division of C

Department. It is also located at New Scotland Yard and is under the responsibility of the Assistant Commissioner of Department C. Its main duties are the protection of the royal family, ministers and important foreign dignitaries; dealing with crimes against the security of the state, and those involving weapons and explosives. It helps in cases of naturalisation and passport matters; surveillance of foreigners; observation of organisations hostile to the state and of the opposition. It is the department responsible for any police action taken in the interests of national security, and its responsibilities therefore extend throughout Great Britain. It also co-operates closely with Military Intelligence. Special Branch officers are stationed in almost all of the ports and larger airports for surveillance of people entering and leaving the country, where they work discreetly, hand in hand, with the immigration staff. Special Branch officers can give orders to local Chief Constables. Its officers are required to speak at least one foreign language. (It was noticed that by 1936–7 many of London's police officers showed an interest in studying German.) (The MIS equates with 'British Intelligence'.)

Of particular value to secure in London are:

1. The ten-digit fingerprint collection, 3rd Floor, New Scotland Yard.
2. The collection of the Criminal Record Office, ground floor:
    a) Records of Criminals;
    b) Nominal Index;
    c) Wanted Index.
3. The Forensic Science Institute at the Police College in Hendon.
4. The records of the Special Branch, main building (New Scotland Yard).
5. The register of the Aliens Department at 28 Bow Street.
6. The Information Room (supervising radio patrols) in the main building, 4th floor.

7. The files of the ICPC, located with Sir Norman Kendal, on the 1st floor, main building.

The Intelligence Service

In reply to a parliamentary question from a member of the Commons concerning the budget of the British Intelligence Service, a member of government explained: 'It is the nature of the Secret Service to be secret. Therefore it cannot be talked about. Any discussion would contribute to endangering secrecy.'

This principle has been applied to all areas relevant to the British Secret Service. Indeed, the secrecy begins with its official description, which nobody seems to understand in detail. Novels, films and articles by authorised outsiders and specialists have combined to cause more confusion than clarity about British Intelligence on our side, probably with the enemy's silent acquiescence. Sometimes we talk of the 'Secret Service', sometimes of the 'Intelligence Service'. Captain Best and Major Stevens, who were captured by the German Service, have declared that there is not any comprehensive organisation called the 'Intelligence Service', but that a 'Secret Service' in our sense of the expression did not exist either. At best one could speak of 'SIS', the Secret Intelligence Service. Nevertheless they called their boss, Admiral Sinclair, the 'CSS', the Chief of the Secret Service.

This lack of precision is as characteristic as the deliberate decentralisation of the service's organisation which does not need to be disguised for technical reasons: these are the offices of the central authorities and the Passport Control Offices (PCOs) of the legations and consulate-generals. Many of its aspects are not disguised because they distract the attention of an enemy from the effective agencies.

Accordingly, we note at the beginning that we have to free

ourselves from conventional ideas of strict organisation, from the particularly German need for precise detail, separation and definition, if we really want to understand the structural essence of British Intelligence. Hitherto we have been prevented from examining the machinery, the central nervous system of all the service's channels, which provides the impulse for operations. Nobody can truthfully say the service is organised in such and such a way, is located here or there, or employs this or that person who does this or that task. If any details about the British Intelligence Service are ever made known or published by the English, one can be sure that only those authorities and offices whose existence cannot be hidden in the long term will be highlighted. The head and hands of the entity called the Secret Service, first outlet of command and the last executive channel, remain secret. Publications about it should be regarded with suspicion, as should reports on its failures. In general, these are probably tactics of diversion, with the real errors kept secret so that lessons can be learned from them quietly.

The contradictory and arbitrary characteristics of the British, of which their language structure is an example, are also conspicuous in this area, where the English have achieved mastery through tradition and experience, favoured by certain attributes of their national character – unscrupulousness, self-discipline, cool calculation and ruthless action.

Two definitions have now become universally popular across the globe: 'Secret Service' and 'Intelligence Service', and from time to time an author uses both in the same sentence. It usually designates what we call the *Nachrichtendienst*, without anyone having precisely defined the term. One has been limited to repeating what has been published and putting together mutually contradictory statements, only to admit in the end that nothing is known for certain. Official or private publications, for example the extract in *Encyclopaedia Britannica*, have no value of proof for these reasons.

This advance observation is probably a measure of the value

for what follows – an outline of what has been learned so far.
On the issue of names, two main sections can be recognised:

a)   the military Secret Service (ND); the non-military ND of
     political and economic nature.
b)   the active secret service, including propaganda, sabotage;
     the analytical and the leading service.

The *Encyclopaedia Britannica* says that 'Secret Service' and
'Military Intelligence' originally meant any kind of intelligence
service. 'Secret Service' then slowly became the term for the
activity, while 'Military Intelligence' remained the name of
the organisation. In practice this is not so. Military
Intelligence is a special term, but it does not designate anything comprehensive. If one was to call the Service by one
name, it would be Secret Service. This was what the British
dailies called it when they reported the budget discussions in
the House of Commons.

Besides this, the term 'Intelligence' is found in several combinations: Intelligence Department, Intelligence Division,
Intelligence Section and Intelligence Branch, according to the
authorities or commands they belong to. It may be the safest
way to translate 'Intelligence' simply as *'Nachricht'*. In
Germany there were once Intelligence Bulletins which were
the predecessors of our newspapers. They did not require a
particular degree of intelligence to read; they simply published the day's news for its readership. But here too the
English are contradictory. An Englishman is not consistent, so
when   he   designates   the   intelligence   departments
(*Nachrichtenabteilungen*, not in the sense of telecommunica-
tions) of the Admiralty and the War Office as, for example,
Intelligence Division or respectively Intelligence Department,
he gives the same appellation to the army's intelligence staff in
the field, possibly calling it Intelligence Section. The English
are not disturbed by the fact that these two groups have completely different tasks: while the Intelligence Department

mainly undertakes analysis at its headquarters, makes plans
and edits handbooks, and does not run an active service in the
sense of espionage or counter-intelligence. The intelligence
officer of military units, or those in continual service, such as
with the Indian Army, are masters of both branches of activity. They hold in their hands the decision, the execution of an
attack, defence and the analysis of the results.

Stevens and Best may have told the truth, at least subjec-
tively, when they claimed that there was an SIS but not a Secret
Service, or an Intelligence Service, or both as independent
organisations. If one is to give a name, this definition seems to
be appropriate for a body which will appear to be amorphous
and non-organic in the area of duties and liaison – as long as
we demand to see something invisible. Even for someone
working in the service it resembles the Freemasons' lodges in
their presumed shapelessness, their false mysticism and
anonymity which gave them such power. Like the Freemason
who often knows only his direct superior, the individual in
the Service only knows those instructing him. In the bureau-
cratically constructed Military Intelligence, for example, if
one cares to name it that way, he knows only his direct superior, his relatively small organisation and the limits of this
framework, his authorities and command. He knows of an
integral organisation, and he may imagine that the results of
his work may be collated with those of another agent's, may be
compared and analysed; but he does not know where or by
whom. What he does not know he cannot give away, neither in
a fever nor under hypnosis. He is an instrument on which,
and with whom, mysterious people can play.

Having said all this it cannot be wrong to speak of the
Secret Intelligence Service, when talking of British
Intelligence in general or even the Secret Service. Perhaps
there is an aftertaste of powder and poison when it is said, just
as the expression 'Intelligence Service' contains a notion of
intelligence as insight, here mainly passivity and study, over
action and execution. There has been so much fuss made

about the secrets of the Intelligence Service that the terms seem to flow into one another and melt together.

In accordance with this effort to hide what one is up to, nothing is denied, not even the statement that the service mainly supports itself. Zischka claims that the main shareholder of the Service is the AIOC, the Anglo-Iranian Oil Company. Others accuse it of subscribing to barter methods by selling secrets to its own country. Truth and exaggeration confront each other, but there is certainly some truth in it. A centralised direction, even if just in the hands of a few men, perhaps even of one man alone, has to exist. If not, nobody would be in a position to handle efficiently the funds approved by Parliament. The island population has never willingly invested its capital in ambiguous business, or wasted it.

It is commonly believed that one can understand the Service once one has taken a look behind the scenes of one of its organisations. This is a mistake which is certainly encouraged by the Service. Even if one gets in touch with only the lowest levels of the Service, whence one could advance towards the top, the question remains: who directs it?

It could be a fact that in the political life of Britain those men who are least prominent play the main part. For example Lord Hankey is mentioned only marginally, a small humble man, who is a member of the Cabinet but does not have a defined responsibility, has no portfolio. From time to time a note appears to say that this discreet man is member of the Committee of Imperial Defence, an entity which meets only when the Empire is in imminent danger, and which has been in existence continually since 1907.

Lord Maurice Hankey, now 63 years of age, used to be a colonel. From 1902 to 1906 he was assigned to the Naval Intelligence Department (now 'Division') at the Admiralty in London. In 1907 he served as an intelligence officer to the commander-in-chief of the British Mediterranean squadron. When Lloyd George formed the so-called War Cabinet in 1916 for 'fighting the war better', Hankey became its

Secretary while remaining Secretary of the Committee of Imperial Defence. When the War Cabinet was dissolved at the end of 1918, Lloyd George took on Hankey as his Cabinet Secretary and also named him Secretary of the British delegation at the Peace Conference in Paris, where Hankey dealt personally with President Wilson and Clémenceau. Hankey has sharply opposed the tendency of different conservative statesmen to come to 'an understanding with Japan's imperial court on the basis of a division of Asia'. He has always been committed to a merger of the USA and the British Empire.

Sir Robert Gilbert Vansittart has become better known due to his dispute with Cadogan, his successor as Speaker of the Commons, and through his office as adviser to the government. He is 49 years of age and lives in London at 44 Park Street, Grosvenor Square, telephone: Mayfair 1144. There is proof that Vansittart maintained his own information service, employing agents who reported only to him. These informers were selected because of their status, their access to information, and their willingness to indulge in treachery. It is possible that Vansittart and/or Hankey are two of the men where all the threads would come together, but it is not certain.

The sources which are the catalyst for the organisation's decisions are multiple. They are as many as there are methods used by the agencies to collect and distribute information. From time to time the attentive observer can catch a glimpse, thanks to the brief highlighting of a misfortune, as happened when the British envoy in Christiania wanted to get rid of Sir Roger Casement. Such an example, with negative results, is in many senses instructive and proves that even Britons are only human and make blunders. It shows the extent to which the service is devoid of scruples, it reveals that British diplomatic representatives are part of the machinery of the Service – apart from military, naval and airforce attachés who, with their reports and this or that 'reasoning' carry out their duties in the same manner as their colleagues from other nations.

This clumsy envoy, Mr M. de C. Findlay, His Britannic Majesty's Minister, reported directly to his superior, Sir Edward Grey. This is probably not the case most of the time.

The Foreign Office (FO = Auswärtiges Amt), the War Office (WO = Kriegsministerium), the Admiralty (= Marineministerium), the Air Ministry (= Luftfahrtministerium), the Secretary of State for the Colonies, the Board of Trade (= Handelsministerium) and the Board of Overseas Trade all have their own sources of information and their own Intelligence departments and divisions. As central authorities, they use their subordinate offices which include the diplomatic missions and consular services. Even if their interest is in their own subject, it can be assumed that other information would be channelled into the appropriate departments.

Before other sources are dealt with, the account given by Stevens and Best of their services will be set out, but it still remains to be seen whether they are speaking the truth, whether they have invented anything or whether they have left anything out of their account. Certainly, some of their evidence has proved to be correct; however, it must not be forgotten that they are only small cogs or, in the previously mentioned example, 'freemasons of a minor order'.

Stevens is known to have run the Passport Control Office in The Hague. Still a serving officer in the army, he came into contact with the Secret Service in India and Persia. As a linguist, he took over a position which was officially part of the consulate-general and therefore the embassy, although geographically it was separate. Its official description covered only a small part of its activities. Stevens and his staff were mainly concerned with the acquisition of military intelligence from and about Germany. They also accepted any other information which came their way and were, according to Stevens, 'interested in simply everything'. He claims that they were on their own, and that the staffing of the other PCOs abroad remained as vague to the head of the office as the detail of SIS's organisation and methods.

Stevens reported either to his boss, Admiral Hugh Paget Sinclair, or to the Admiral's headquarters housed at 54 Broadway Buildings, near St James's Park Station. According to Stevens, the Admiral had retired from active service when appointed head of the Secret Service, and was known as 'CSS'. His deputy was Colonel Stuart Menzies, a Scotsman who succeeded his boss on Sinclair's death on 4 November 1939. His ADCs were Captain Howard RN, Captain Russell and Hatton-Hall. Stevens seems to believe that Sinclair alone was responsible to the Cabinet via the Foreign Office.

Sinclair was reputed to have his offices on the fourth floor of the same building that housed the chancellery and registry. On the occasions when Stevens visited the building, he noticed that departments had been moved around within the building, but the second and fourth floors contained offices of private firms which were nothing to do with the service. On the first floor were the offices of the London PCO, which overlooked numbers 21, 23 and 25 of Queen Anne's Gate, the road running parallel to the Broadway.

The following sections were said to be Admiral Sinclair's responsibility: Administration, Military, Naval, Air, Communications, Political, Cipher, Financial, Press and Industrial.

Departmental Duties

1. Administration Section: Head of Department: Captain Howard (RN); under him Commanders Slocum and Bowlbey (uncertain spelling). Duties: Vetting of personnel, officers as well as civilian employees and agents as identified by PCOs, which the department accepts or rejects. The organisation of the entire service lies with Section 1, which distributes incoming intelligence.

Location: Fifth floor of Broadway Buildings.

2. Military Section: Head of Department: Major Hatton-Hall. No other officers. Duties: All intelligence received is forwarded to him if it concerns the army. Stevens gives the following example: 'I inform the department of an impending attack by the Germans. Section 1 passes the information on to Section 2, where the intelligence is compared with information received from PCOs. Taking its own position, the section then transmits the information to the War Office, probably the Intelligence Branch.'
    Location: Fifth floor.

3. Naval Section: Head of Department: Captain Russell. No other officers. Duties: As in Section 2, but for naval issues. Information is passed to the Admiralty, Naval Intelligence Division.
    Location: Sixth floor.

4. Air Section: Head of Department: Wing-Commander (?) Winter-Bottom, assisted by two officers, Adams and [?]. Duties: As in Section 2 and 3, but adapted to the needs of the RAF. Information is sent to the Air Ministry, Intelligence Section.
    Location: Sixth floor.

The Sections 2, 3 and 4 are concerned mainly with evaluation of information. They also give orders, that is, express wishes, ask questions, etc., which are then sent to the PCOs. This is either done on their own initiative or as middlemen for the demands of the three intelligence divisions.

5. Communication Section: Head of Department: Gambier Perry, calls himself Colonel but this seems to be untrue. Stevens claims to know nothing about the department. It is reputed to have moved to Bletchley. Duties: Wireless/radio communications, telephone, pigeon-post, etc.
    Location: until recently in the Broadway building, floor unknown.

6. Political Section: Head of Department: Major Vivien, assisted by Police Officer Mills. (Vivien calls himself Major, but he is also a police officer.) Duties: 'Counter-intelligence' (see below) in connection with MI5 (see below). The handling of subversive movements, communists, fascists, etc. Control of enemies of the state in England.

    Stevens and Best do not differentiate between counter-intelligence and espionage.

    Stevens says 'they overlap so much, there can be no division'. The department keeps in contact with all political organisations for intelligence purposes. Stevens claims that he does not know the title of this sub-section of Section 6. The information by '101 B' (Agent von Hendricks in Antwerp, opponent of Pötzsch) was given by Section 1 to Section 6.
    Location: Fifth floor.

7. Cipher Section (Cipher and Decipher Section): Head of Department: Not known. A retired colonel by the name of Geffreys used to work there. Duties: Code breaking, preparation of own codes and codes for PCOs.
    Location: Stevens does not know.

8. Financial Section: Head of Department: Commander Sykes. Duties: Allocation of funds for intelligence work, salaries, etc., for PCOs and the Central Office.
    Location: Fourth floor.

9. Press Section: Head of Department: probably Hennecker-Heaton. No other officers. Duties: Reading, supervision of insertions, liaison with the press as necessary.
    Location: Fourth floor.

10. Industrial Section (economic intelligence): Head of Department: Admiral Limpenny, retired. Duties: Collection of information on the economic situation abroad, on how many planes have been manufactured, on coal production, supplies of raw materials. Processed

information possibly sent to the Board of Trade.
Location: unknown.

There was one more office situated on the ground floor
which, according to Stevens, belonged to the propaganda
department. It was said to have been in existence by April
1938 when Stevens returned from India. Actually its true
function was that of sabotage, both in the planning and executive stages. The head of department was Colonel Grand, and
his assistant Lieutenant Colonel M.R. Chidson (formerly the
PCO in The Hague). The duties and position of a certain
Clively remain obscure. This department is reputed to have
been separated from the 'Service' and has not been located in
Broadway Buildings since June 1939. With the outbreak of
war several of the above departments are alleged to have been
transferred to Bletchley. However, the Propaganda and
Sabotage Departments are not among these. Apparently
Sinclair, although recognising the need for sabotage, wished to
have nothing to do with it. Stevens says that to his knowledge
the department was still subject to the CSS even after its separation. It prepared plans for acts of sabotage which were then
sent via Sinclair to the appropriate PCOs. SIS did not carry
out these acts of sabotage; it was only the executive organ.

The PCOs are said to have code numbers, Stevens' being
33000. The PCOs in all countries are subject to Sinclair's
office.

Best was apparently head of the Dutch section of yet
another organisation known as 'Z', which was also controlled
by Sinclair. Best's office was situated next to the PCO which
was so well known that it was frequently pointed out by children as the British Intelligence office. Sinclair had complained
that the PCOs in general – and the Dutch office in particular –
did not collect enough information. The Z organisation was
headed by Colonel Claude Dansey, who had been selected by
Sinclair. He, in turn, had employed Best whom he had known
from the First World War. Z kept a small office in Bush

House, Aldwych, London WC2. Best's colleagues were Kenneth Cohan, codenames Cowan, Keith Crane and Robert Craig. At the outbreak of war Best's office had been amalgamated with Stevens' PCO. According to Best, Z, at least in Holland, was dissolved after his arrest.

Best sent his information to Sinclair by post and he used the firm Menoline Ltd as cover, whose address was 24 Maple Street, London W1. Best was a director of the Dutch firm N.V. Menoline in The Hague. The directors in The Hague included John P. Richards and one of Best's colleagues in Z, Pieter Nikolaas van der Willik.

On 19 February 1937 *The Times* (issue no. 47 613) printed an article on a speech made by the Minister for the Co-ordination of Defence the previous day in the House of Commons. The speech went as follows:

Recently a Joint Intelligence Committee has been formed from representatives of the three Services which works under the Chiefs of Staff, and we have formed a Committee of Industrial Intelligence in foreign countries. It is impossible for me to disclose the nature of the report we receive (!) and the information the Joint Intelligence Committee prepares for the Chiefs of Staff. I can only give assurance they are an immense and indispensable (!) aid to the right planning, which continues from today in connection with these questions.

It remains undisclosed whether Admiral Sinclair's so-called SIS was the main British Secret Service organisation or just one of its branches. It is possible that it worked for the Joint Intelligence Committee or was attached to a part of it. The article makes it clear that in 1937 the three services of the armed forces had their own intelligence sections. Both Stevens and Best confirmed that the Admiralty, the Air Force and the Imperial General Staff had their own intelligence departments or divisions, but as in the First World War they deny having an independent intelligence service which includes sabotage. Therefore one can accept that they are still working in the same manner as in the other branches, especially, according to Stevens, the British Indian General Staff.

The organisation under Admiral Sinclair was not purely military. It had subdivisions for the Army, the Navy and the RAF, but it also worked for the Foreign Office and the Ministry of Economic Affairs. The Foreign Office inquired as to the effect of the leaflet campaigns in Germany, and the Ministry of Economic Affairs demanded information relating to Germany's money supply.

According to Stevens, the Military Intelligence Service (MIS) had nothing to do with the SIS. The Director of Military Operations is a departmental head of the General Staff and the Intelligence Service. Subordinate to him is the Deputy Director of Military Operations (DDMO) and the Deputy Director of Military Intelligence (DDMI). The latter gathers information, for example on communications systems, about countries in which military operations are about to take place. The sub-division does not extend to intelligence work undertaken by agents. Whenever the secondment of military intelligence officers is discussed in Intelligence or at the Intelligence Branch, it is meant to be in the service of the DDMI. For all other branches or military activities the expression military intelligence does not apply.

Best is of a different opinion from Stevens, and unlike Stevens is not a professional soldier, but he is superior as far as experience in the intelligence service is concerned, and as a result his understanding is more penetrating. He combines these qualities with considerable character defects and a total lack of scruples. He is not a British officer like Stevens, but a civilian who loves to live well and acts as a successful businessman. He may therefore see things in a clearer light in spite of a pretended lack of significance, or he may say more than Stevens. He has stated that the Foreign Office, the Admiralty and other departments have their own espionage centres which exchange information. Navy, Army and Air Attachés give their reports to department I5 (meaning Intelligence 5) of the General Staff's headquarters. For the army in the field that department is called Ib, being an active branch of the Intelligence Service, of espionage. NI, AI and MI (meaning Naval Intelligence, Military Intelligence, and Air Intelligence Department) are the departments which process information, which is then transmitted to the headquarters of the Navy, Army and RAF respectively.

Special mention must be made of the Department of Military Intelligence of the Imperial General Staff, MI5, which is concerned with counter-intelligence and holds an ambiguous position. (The duties of the departments MI1–4 are unknown; MI3 is concerned with Germany.) In this context one has to discuss once more what the British mean by counter-espionage. Stevens and Best both speak of counter-espionage, and called it either this or counter-intelligence, but they refused to distinguish between the two. They considered any differentiation illogical. Best defined it this way: 'Counter-espionage includes all security and police action which is taken to avert events that may become the source of national or political danger.' During the First World War counter-espionage was, according to Best, the responsibility of MI5, a department of the War Office. It worked closely with Scotland Yard detectives, who would come to Department 1b at headquarters in France with the same brief. They were combined into a larger organisation with a massive staff of intelligence officers and civil servants. This development perhaps explains that the modern MI5 is under the authority of the Minister of Home Affairs and is a part of Scotland Yard, even though its headquarters, at Thames House, Millbank, London, is quite separate from Scotland Yard. Before the outbreak of war about seventy-five officers worked for MI5 and occupied the building's entire top floor.

It is MI5's duty to perform counter-espionage tasks and to observe communists and other 'subversive movements', which also included fascist and national socialist foreign organisations, with the intelligence and investigation activities linked to these. MI5 also employs agents and correspondents abroad who are concerned with local surveillance to build a base of experience and monitor developments. The head of department was up to very recently Sir Vernon Kell. His best-known colleague is Lieutenant-Colonel Hinchley-Cook who was repeatedly named in espionage trials. He is not mentioned in any official list so it is therefore assumed that he is a police officer. Other collaborators were G. Liddel and a Mr. Curry, who devoted special attention to German national socialists.

Apparently MI5 finances itself through funds of the individual branches of the Secret Service and the budget which is passed annually.

The *Picture Post* of 26 November 1938 published an article, 'The Secret Service'. It says that MI5 has an 'executive' arm, Scotland Yard's Special Branch. This in turn is claimed to be a 'department of the Secret Service'. MI5 was said to be unable to arrest people. The Special Branch carried out surveillance operations on unwanted foreigners and was working in association with the Secret Police which specialises in the detection of subversive activity in the Army, Navy and Air Force. MI5, Special Branch, Foreign Office and the Intelligence Departments of Navy and Airforce worked closely together.

Certainly Hinchley-Cook has himself, together with officers from Scotland Yard, made arrests, searches and interrogations of unwanted people and had them deported by his officers. The article probably deliberately mixes up several things. 'Secret Police' is either the Special Branch or the entire Metropolitan CID. We also often wrongly call Scotland Yard, London's criminal police, the 'Secret Police', since a crime officer was and is commonly known as a Secret Agent. This explains the frequent confusion of Scotland Yard with the Secret Service. In addition, the Special Branch could well be working so closely with MI5 that the two are not easily distinguished. It is probably correct that MI5 at Thames House is the link between the Special Branch and Intelligence – even if to a certain degree they work independently. This would guarantee that the 'Service' remains secret, and the larger world gets to know special agents only through their official duties. The Special Branch has its headquarters at New Scotland Yard at Victoria Embankment (see 'Structure of British Police', IIIB).

Stevens declared that MI5 was working in close connection with the political Section 6 of Major Vivien (see above).

Hinchley-Cook wears glasses, is robust, fresh-faced, appears to be good-natured and speaks German fluently in a mix of dialects from Saxony and Hamburg.

Captain King's office is in 308 Hood House, Dolphin Square, using the name Coplestone which is a cover for MI5. It is here that MI5 briefs and debriefs its contacts. Captain King lived at Whitehall Mansions and his official office was located at the War Office.

Sources of the British Intelligence Service

To the question whether he also collected information on German oil and fuel supplies, Stevens answered: 'No. I did not think that was necessary, whatever is known to Shell is also known to the SIS.' This is a question already posed about British Intelligence's sources of information. Its answer also explains, to some degree, British Intelligence's methods of operation.

The conditions and circumstances are very favourable to the British, or at least they were until not too long ago. International capitalist networking, the vast scale of the British Empire, national character and a centuries-old tradition and practice are the ideal foundation for the Intelligence Service. The Service has access to information regarding the economy, trade and industry, finance, supply of raw materials, and everything connected with them, and can therefore draw

conclusions about military or political matters. The Service
thus possesses a cheap and reliable multi-faceted apparatus
which spares it from employing agents or informers of dubious reliability. The big oil conglomerates whose reports to
their parent companies in Great Britain and the USA are disguised as internal communications, always give a precise
outline about an adversary's situation (seen from the English
perspective) and therefore enhances military decision-making.
It is the same in the other areas of the economy such as trade
and finance, where the conglomerates play vital roles, and
where management or main board directors are not only
nationals of the country being spied on but also British
nationals or individuals serving Britain. The implications are
clear from the importance given to this 'Economic
Intelligence' in Britain. Major Stevens spelled this out as far as
he could understand it from his viewpoint. Blacklists were of
minor economic significance in the last war when they were
written up by Laming, the Trade Attaché in The Hague, but
as they were constantly published in the Dutch papers they
were not very secret.

Stevens made this comment about the real 'economic issue'
and its value: 'If I know how many workers are employed by,
for example, an aircraft factory, and how many shifts they are
working, I can draw conclusions on the company's production
capacity.'

The British obtained a not insignificant advantage from
social connections with important, well-informed circles in
the Reich. 'Social Espionage' is not a strictly correct description, since it rarely required any espionage activity.
Talkativeness, intimacy instead of distrust and reserve, and a
false need to be candid with others, have done a lot of damage.
Even if such talk seemed inconsequential, remarks found a
ready listener and often fitted into the bigger picture.
Credulousness, admiration of the foreigner and megalomania
are all characteristics used by the British. They found a fertile
environment, especially in circles where people held double

and triple nationalities, thus making them ideal tools to be manipulated into committing treachery without the public ever knowing anything about it – often unintentionally, out of sheer negligence.

Another reliable and free source are the big British daily newspapers, with their correspondents deployed across the world. The East German commentator Posen highlighted this fact in an article published in August 1940. A former Reuter's correspondent in Prague named Rudl has also written extensively on this subject. According to him, all the Reuter's bureaux in the entire world have dual tasks: their journalistic daily routines and technical duties, taken care of by the specialised journalists, and the so-called grand service, performed exclusively by British nationals who were often former military officers. These so-called Reuter's correspondents did not have any journalistic duties and only communicated important political information, even though they appeared to be legitimately accredited newspapermen. Their information is passed on with the assistance of the Consulates and the Passport Control Offices and they fulfil other duties which serve the same purpose, such as making discreet contact with representatives of the host country's press, either for propaganda purposes or, as in Prague, to influence the country's politics through corruption. The Reuter's correspondents F.I. Ferguson and W.E. Cross attracted attention during the Czech crisis because they were so clumsy. Cross was recalled and Ferguson was sent to the Reuter's bureau in Budapest with special orders. It is a proven fact that the Berlin representative of the *Daily Express* was engaged in espionage of a military nature before the war. The correspondent was Selkira Panton, and at the moment he is in Denmark.

The British also like to use so-called official study commissions or what appear to be scientific expeditions. The highly controversial Colonel Lawrence was able to undertake his reconnaissance for the subsequent Arab raid using an archaeological expedition as cover. Bilateral associations, international correspondence, and exchange organisations of all kinds, including pacifist groups were carefully cultivated as means to an end. Unusually, the British developed a system of clubs which had offensive and defensive purposes. Access to the top echelons of English society has required membership of one or more clubs, which has facilitated surveillance and in some cases allowed exposure.

However, of the greatest importance has been information volunteered by private, financially independent individuals. It has been said that every British expatriate is an agent for his country, and each expatriate German a traitor by negligence, and this may have been true to a certain extent. The causes lie in national character, a knowledge the British have had and exploited for a long time. The last British Ambassador in Berlin, Sir Nevile Henderson, gave an example of a British value judgement about us in his final report. It is the Briton's mistake that he takes his arrogance too far and underestimates his adversary. But equally it is true that the German in his misunderstood objectivity always tended to presume only the best qualities in his partner, and to criticise openly the institutions and situation of his own country. The British also have a high opinion of their Intelligence Service whereas there were Germans who, out of some misconstrued or obsolescent belief, saw the German Intelligence Service as detestable and inferior, seeing the men who devote themselves to it as shady characters and adventurers leading ruinous lives, and with whom no decent person would want to associate. For them espionage is something an honourable man should not be concerned with, a dirty business for gamblers, gangsters and desperadoes. Popular culture throws the spy, informer and traitor into the same pot, together with explorer, paid informant and agent driven by ideals, who fights for his country like any other soldier, but under far more dangerous conditions. What Lody did for Germany has been forgotten.

The British consider it entirely natural to serve their country, not objecting to the methodology involved, which might seem ethically repellent or reprehensible to a foreigner. The word agent in English does not have the negative connotations it has here. The so-called counsel to the Indian princes and Arab sheiks have the official title of agent, and there is no implication which would put agent on the same level as an informer or paid traitor. It does not matter whether it is a junior clerk of a branch office in the middle of the jungle who tells his consul what he has observed, or whether it is a rich globe-trotting lord who reports what he has seen on his journey around the world. It is safe to assume that these reports, like those from companies, newspapers, travel agencies and shipping companies, end up at a central office. In recent times the Royal Institute of International Affairs, located at London's Chatham House, has been suspected (see the Special Wanted List). The Institute houses a considerable library which is open only to its membership.

The Service does use traitors and paid informants, but only to a very limited extent. The reason for this, apart from what has been remarked on, is that, contrary to current assumptions the Service receives only minimal funds in peacetime. Minimal, that is, in comparison with the enormous responsibilities and scale of organisation which the Service, perhaps with the exception of India with its own Service, has to undertake.

Paid junior agents were used only when it was not considered worthwhile to deploy a large-scale operation. However (and this would also correspond to British unscrupulousness), it was sometimes their intention to distract attention to such informers and pass them off as the sole representatives of British Intelligence. They even placed a different value on the report of a volunteer in comparison with those supplied by a paid informer. The fact that before and immediately prior to the war it has been possible to detect and arrest some of the so-called agents of the British suggests that conditions within the British Service must have deteriorated considerably. When Best claims his boss was unhappy with the Service's performance, it is entirely credible, but it is only an argument if

Stevens and Best had to compensate informers whom they despised.

It would be wrong to underestimate the enemy, but it would be equally wrong to admire him and to think of him as infallible. The British Service has a tradition of about three hundred years. In spite of its contradictions, the English national character has a flaw of putting tradition above all, retaining for as long as possible what might have been all right some decades before. It is possible that in an emergency the British would be capable of letting everything go and becoming surprisingly modern. It is also possible that it could be too late to change. With almost cynical candour, Best complained contemptuously of the Intelligence Service's bureaucracy, greed and sheer heavy-handedness, but he added that the British are capable of a complete transformation when thinking that their country was in imminent danger, and that they are at their most formidable in that situation. However, it seems as though it is all too late for the British Intelligence Service, for it was only in February 1940 that the press reported that the British Service had increased its budget from £400,000 to £1,100,000. Even if this tells nothing fundamental, it is symptomatic, and in this respect an article dated 13 August 1940, published by a paper in Toulon, under the heading: 'Bankruptcy of the Intelligence Service', is most interesting. It concludes that the British Service had become disorientated because Germany had decided to restrict information about future intentions until they were ready for execution. It claims that the Intelligence Service's omnipotence has evaporated and asserts – with a degree of probability – that the British Service had failed diplomatically and militarily, and had been bound to do so because people like Eden and Chamberlain relied upon it for missions intended to bring about Europe's economic suffocation. In addition, it was said to be indisputable that the British Service's personnel had been devalued. The previously dominant colonial and Irish elements had been replaced, for

economic reasons, not with men of substance but with financially motivated agents. (Special Branch employs mainly Irish
nationals.) Well-informed people were listened to no longer,
ignoring the fact that Germany did not depend on paid agents
of dubious reliability because its ideology attracted sufficient
support among those who serve their country selflessly, like
soldiers in a real army.

As an island Empire, England relies upon the sea, and its
fleet has a special importance, which may also have been man-
ifested in the considerable influence exercised by the Navy
over the Intelligence Service. However, this seems to have
changed in favour of politicians and their circles, and what
remains is the Admiralty's sole privilege to be permitted to call
their Intelligence Service the 'Naval Intelligence Division'.

The Passport Control Offices have been mentioned already
as the official, even if disguised, channels of intelligence for
Britain's top authorities. Apparently their usefulness has been
in doubt for some time and their competence considered
insufficient, which was why Best's Z organisation came into
existence. The official intention was to maintain the PCOs,
but to pass their clandestine role to local groups of the British
Legion or other apparently harmless organisations yet to be
developed. But at least in the West this has not happened.

It is unnecessary to mention that this outline does not claim to
be comprehensive, and it is impossible to enumerate and discuss all the many ways, channels and means at the British
Service's disposal. There is too much complexity to expect a
clear profile of the Service, so attempts of this kind remain
incomplete. Chapters on Freemasons, interrogation debrief-
ings, and issues relating to the state and to ideology would
each fill an entire volume. An account appropriate for a card
file is probably not as important as the knowledge that the
adversary should not be underestimated, but nor should it be
overestimated either. The principle is to acquire from him
what is good, and bear in mind what can weaken him; to study

his methods in order to counter and exploit them, and that, by concentrating on valuable details, totality is not overlooked.

It would be going too far to delve into the detail of their methods, especially as there is insufficient authentic comparative material upon which to draw final conclusions. Stevens, for example, insisted that he was forbidden to deal with agents himself, but it could have been different elsewhere. Apparently the small contribution made by the Passport Control Offices went unrecognised. Equipment, training and selection seem to have been surprisingly primitive, but this says little about the main Service, whose large-scale espionage operations have been described above. The methodology was certainly adapted to circumstances and it says nothing about the question of what the Service is capable of in the execution of its duties and what degree of voluntary effort could be relied upon. The involvement of 'civilians' of independent means, even heads of state, are significant clues; so-called 'accidents', murders, wars and revolutions demonstrate the methods the Service is capable of, and shows that it uses means which can hardly be distinguished from those of a common criminal.

Nevertheless, it is certain that the Service has helped significantly to construct and support the Empire. The motto: 'My country, right or wrong' does not have to be a British monopoly and, having been adapted to suit our ideology, it can and should be transferred to Germany.

PART 2

Special Wanted List GB

Introduction

Described by William Shirer in *The Rise and Fall of the Third Reich: A History of Nazi Germany* (London, Secker & Warburg, 1961) as 'among the more amusing "invasion" documents', the *Sonderfahndungsliste GB* (literally translated as the Special Search List GB, but known to history as *The Black Book*) was compiled 'hurriedly and carelessly' by Walter Schellenberg, Chief of *AMT* (Bureau) *IVE* of the RSHA (*Reichssicherheitshauptamt*), the Bureau responsible for counter-espionage, in May 1940.

The list contains the names of 2,820 persons, British subjects and European exiles, who were to be arrested or 'taken into protective custody' in the event of a successful German invasion. Against the name of each is the RSHA section in whose file particulars of the individual were to be found. Also included is a directory of establishments and institutions (embassies, universities, newspaper offices and Freemasons' Lodges) in which the Nazis were interested.

The list contains obvious arrestees such as Churchill, Eden and Duff Cooper, but also authors like H. G. Wells, Virginia Woolf, Vera Brittain, E. M. Forster, Aldous Huxley (who had emigrated to the USA in 1936), J. B. Priestley, C. P. Snow and Stephen Spender. Rebecca West is on the list as is Noël Coward, who had made no attempt to disguise his disgust with the pre-war appeasement policy. In his war memoirs *Future Indefinite* (London, Heineman, 1954) Coward wrote:

> If anyone had told me at that time that I was high up on the Nazi black list, I should have laughed and told him not to talk nonsense. In this, however, I should have been wrong, for, as it ultimately transpired, I was. In 1945,

when the Nazi list of people marked down for immediate
liquidation was unearthed and published in the press
there was my name; I remember that Rebecca West, who
was one of the many who shared this honour with me,
sent me a telegram which read: 'My dear – the people we
should have been seen dead with'.

In their post-war memoirs others were as equally proud of
inclusion as Coward. Denis Sefton Delmer, who as *Daily
Express* Berlin correspondent had accompanied Hitler on pre-
war election rallies, broadcast immediately after the *Führer*'s
19 July 1940 *Reichstag* speech, 'A last appeal to reason', a fierce
rejection of the Nazi 'peace offer'. In *Black Boomerang*
(London, Secker & Warburg, 1962) Delmer recalled:

But there was still another sequel to my unauthorized
rejection of Hitler's offer. At least I like to think of it as
a sequel. In these days of July 1940 the special commando of Himmler's Security Service, which was
intended to take charge of occupied Britain in the wake of
the Wehrmacht's invasion, was putting the finishing
touches to a list of personalities who were to be immediately arrested and handed over to the Gestapo. 'This
list . . . was among the many secret documents captured
by the Allies in Germany in 1945. Number 33 on the list
was a certain Sefton Delmer, Paris representative of the
Daily Express. He was to be handed over, said the list, to
Dept IV B4 of the Central Reich Security Office. Maybe
I would have been on that list in any case . . . . But, as I
said, I like to think it was my maiden broadcast that put
me there.

It should be noted at this stage that the names are listed alphabetically, and not in order of importance to the Nazis, as many
believed. A typical claim was that of Victor Gollancz, the left-
wing publisher and founder of the Left Book Club:

I was very high on Hitler's list of people to be dealt with in England. I think as a matter of fact I was number seven, out of about 2,000.

In fact, Gollancz was number 75, followed by Golssenau, Arnold von, better known as the writer Ludwig Renii, at number 76.

Many individuals were fully aware that should the German invasion succeed they would be immediate targets. Harold Nicolson, Parliamentary Secretary to the Ministry of Information, wrote to his wife, the writer Vita Sackville-West, on 26 May 1940:

> I don't think that even if the Germans occupied Sissinghurst they would harm you, in spite of the horrified dislike which they feel for me. But to be quite sure that you are not put to any humiliation, I think you really ought to have a 'bare bodkin' [a poison pill] handy so that you can take your quietus when necessary. I shall have one also. I am not in the least afraid of such sudden and honourable death. What I dread is being tortured and humiliated. But how can we find a bodkin which will give us quietus quickly and which is easily portable. I shall ask my doctor friends.

On 19 June he wrote again:

> I have got the bare bodkin. I shall bring down your half on Sunday. It all looks very simple.

In fact, death had already claimed some of those listed in *The Black Book*. Sigmund Freud had died on 23 September 1939, and Lytton Strachey as far back as 21 January 1932. Included on the list were two former personal friends of Hitler's, Ernst 'Putzi' Hanfstaengl, former Foreign Press Chief of the Nazi Party, who had fled abroad in 1937, and

Hermann Rauschning, ex-President of the Danzig Senate and author of the 1940 bestseller *Hitler Speaks*. Other foreign dignitaries included President Eduard Benes of Czechoslovakia and his Foreign Minister, Jan Masaryk, Chaim Weizmann and Ignace Paderewski, the Polish statesman and pianist. Neutral Americans were also included, mainly newspaper correspondents who the Nazis considered hostile in their reporting: John Gunther, author of *Inside Europe*, M. W. Fodor and Louis Fischer. The Jewish Wall Street financier and personal friend of both Churchill and Roosevelt, Bernard Baruch, is listed as is Paul Robeson, the American negro singer, actor and left-wing sympathiser. An interesting omission from the writers included on the list is George Bernard Shaw. He was one of the few eminent English-language writers to be published and performed in Nazi Germany, and in the 7 October 1939 issue of the *New Statesman* had written of Hitler:

Our business is to make peace with him and with all the world instead of making more mischief and ruining our people in the process.

Also absent is Britain's First World War prime minister, David Lloyd George, who had said of Hitler in 1936:

He is indeed a great man. Führer is the proper name for him, for he is a born leader – yes, a statesman.

Further, the former premier had, in the House of Commons on 3 October 1939, made a veiled proposal that Britain and France make peace with Hitler. Ironically, Lloyd George's daughter Megan is on the list (number 111).

Although *The Black Book* abounds with howlers and obvious inaccuracies – Colonel Kenneth Strong, who in 1940 was head of MI14 at the War Office, and had served as Assistant Military Attaché in Berlin immediately before the war, is shown as a naval officer – the fate of those arrested might have been far from pleasant. How unpleasant could perhaps be gauged from the later career of the man who was to have headed the SS arrest operations in Britain, SS Colonel Professor Dr Frank Six. Six was responsible for wholesale massacres in the Soviet Union, where, according to Shirer, 'one of the professor's specialities ... [was] to ferret out captured Soviet political commissars for execution'. Six, whose headquarters were to have been in London, and who was to command six *Einsatzkommandos* (Action commandos – in London, Bristol, Birmingham, Liverpool, Manchester and Edinburgh), was sentenced in 1948 at Nuremberg as a war criminal to twenty years in prison, but was released in 1952.

The Reichssicherheitshauptamt (RSHA)

On 17 September 1939, Hitler signed the decree creating an overall directorate of Reich Security, the RSHA (*Reichssicherheitshauptamt*), with SS *Obergruppenführer* Reinhard Heydrich at its head. The RSHA comprised six, later seven, main offices or bureaux (*Amt*):

1. *AMT I* '*Personalabteilung, Ausbildung, Organisierung*'. This bureau was concerned with the entire RSHA personnel and its training. The first section chief was Dr Werner Best (1939–40), who also had responsibility for counter-espionage. He was succeeded by Bruno Streckenbach (1940–3), Erwin Schulz (1943–4) and Erich Erlinger (1944–5).

2. *AMT II* '*Haushalt und Wirtschaft*'. 'This office was in charge of administrative, economic and judicial arrangements for the entire RSHA. It too was headed by Dr Werner Best until 1940; his successors were Dr Nockmann (1940–3), Dr Preitzel (1943–4) and Dr Spacil (1944–5). The assistant chief from 1939 until 1941 was Professor Dr Franz Six, the man

appointed by Heydrich on 17 August 1940 to head RSHA
activities in conquered Britain:

> Your task is to combat, with the requisite means, all anti-
> German organizations, instructions, and opposition
> groups which can be seized in England, to prevent the
> removal of all available material and to centralize and
> safegard it for future exploitation. I designate London as
> the location of your headquarters . . . and I authorize
> you to set up small Einsatzgruppen in other parts of
> Great Britain as the situation dictates and necessity arises.

Six had previously been the Dean of the Economic Faculty at
Berlin University before joining the SD.

3. *AMT III* '*Deutsche Lebensgebiete: Sicherheitsdienst* – Inland
(SD Inland)'. This bureau dealt with the internal security
information service, a Nazi Party organism entirely under the
control of the SS. Its active information service within
Germany was divided into five sections and many sub-sections, and dealt with such topics as public opinion (it was also
responsible for the compilation of the Nazi equivalent of
opinion polls, *Meldungen aus dem Reich*) ethnic minorities,
race, public health and cultural, artistic and scientific matters. Willy Seibert's Sector IIID, for example, was responsible
for dealing with economic matters, the supervision of industry
and industrialists, manpower, commerce and provisioning.
AMT III's director was the early Nazi Party member
(number 6531) and SS man (number 880) Otto Ohlendorf.
Ohlendorf later achieved notoriety as the leader of
Einsatzgruppe D in Russia, and was responsible for the murder
of 90,000 Jews and other Soviet citizens between June 1941
and July 1942. Sentenced to death at Nuremberg on 10 April
1948, he was executed on 8 .June 1951.

4. *AMT IV* '*Gegnererforschung und Gegner bekamfung*'

(Investigation and combating of opposition). This bureau was better known as the Gestapo (Secret State Police – *Geheim Staats Polizei*). The Gestapo was headed from 1939 until the end of the war by the Bavarian Heinrich Müller, born in 1900 and last seen in the Führerbunker, Berlin, on 29 April 1945. His ultimate fate remains unknown. *AMT IV* comprised six sections, and in the five and a half years of its existence underwent many internal transformations while its organisation and specific powers remained the same (directors' names in parentheses):

a. IVA (Panziniger) dealt with opponents of the regime, acts of sabotage, and provided a protection service to Nazi notables.

b. IVB (Hartl, Roth) covered the churches, religious sects, Freemasons, Jews and Gypsies. The most important sub-section was *IV-B4*, which dealt with Jewish affairs, evacuations, recovery of goods held by 'enemies of the people and of the Reich', and forfeiture of German nationality, and was directed by Adolf Eichmann, described as the 'technician of the Holocaust'. He escaped to Argentina after the war, was kidnapped by Israeli agents on 11 May 1960, tried in Jerusalem from 11 April to 14 August 1961, found guilty of war crimes and hanged on 31 May 1962.

c. IVC (Rang, Berndorff) dealt with records, preventive detention, Nazi Party and Press matters.

d. IVD (Weinmann, Rang) dealt with the sphere of influence of Greater Germany – Slovakia, the Protectorate, etc.

e. IVE, which dealt with counter-espionage, was directed from 1939 to 1942 by Walter Schellenberg, the man responsible for the compilation of *The Black Book* in May 1940, and from 1942-5 by Walter Huppenkothen (though still under Schellenberg's control). Sub-section *IV-EI* was concerned with counter-espionage administration and the delivery of agents' papers, passports, etc. Other subsections dealt with economic affairs in general and economic and political counter-espionage, which was divided into regions: West (*IV-E3*), East (*IV-E5*), North (*IV-E4*) and South (*IV-E6*).

f. IVF (Krause) dealt with passports and the aliens' police.

5. AMT V *'Verbrechensbekampfung'* – (Combating crime, the *Krimminalpolizei* or Kripo). Like the Gestapo the *Krimminalpolizei* was a department of state rather than of the Nazi Party, and it had the executive power of right of arrest in criminal matters. It was headed by Artur Nebe, who, like Ohlendorf, left his desk to command an *Einsatzgruppe* (B) in Russia, where he was responsible for the murder of 46,000 Jews and other Russians from June to November 1941. Supposedly having a change of heart, he joined in the 20 July 1944 bomb plot against Hitler and was purportedly executed on 21 March 1945 in Berlin, although rumours persisted that he survived the war.

6. AMT VI *'Sicherheitsdienst-Ausland'*, *'SD Ausland'* or *'Auslandsnachtrichtendienst'* (The Security Service abroad). As with *AMT III*, this was a Nazi Party organism, entirely under the control of the SS; from 1939 to 1941 it was directed by Heinz Jost, and until the end of the war by Walter Schellenberg. In 1944 the military intelligence organisation, the *Abwehr*, was absorbed into the RSHA, and a section *VI-Mil* was specially created with Schellenberg as its chief. In 1939 *AMT VI* was divided into six sub- sections:
a. VI-A was directed by Dr Gerhard Filbert (1939-43), and Herbert Müller (1943-5) and was concerned with the general organisation of the SD, missions abroad, the security of couriers and the supervision of sections. Within *VI-A* there were further geographical sub-divisions: West, North, East, South and Centre.
b. VI-B was responsible for espionage in Western Europe, under the direction of Eugen Steimle and his assistant Dr Wilhelm Hottl, who postwar wrote *The Secret Front* and *Hitler's Paper Weapon*. *VI-B* was divided into six sub-sections:
    VI-B1 dealt with France, Belgium, the Netherlands and Luxembourg

VI-B2 with Italy and the Vatican
VI-B3 with North Africa
VI-B4 with Spain, Portugal and South America
VI-B5 with the Balkans
VI-B6 with Switzerland.

c. *VI-C* was responsible for espionage activities in Russia and Japan including their 'zones of influence' – Manchuria, Iran, etc.

d. *VI-D* dealt with espionage against the 'Anglo-Saxon' powers – Britain, the USA and the British Empire.

e. *VI-E* was responsible from 1939 until 1943 for locating opponents of the Nazi regime abroad. From 1943 it dealt with espionage activities in the Balkans, Italy and the Vatican.

f. *VI-F* was directed by Alfred Naujocks, 'the man who started the war' – he staged the fake 'Polish' attack on the German wireless transmitter at Gleiwitz on 31 August 1939 which gave Hitler a *casus belli*. This sub-section dealt with the technical requirements of the entire SD. It was also responsible for the forging of millions of British five pound notes in Operation 'Bernhard", named after Naujocks' successor, Bernhard Kruger.

In 1942 subsection *IV-G* was added by Schellenberg to deal with scientific research, and also sub-section *IV-S*, which carried out 'physical, moral and political sabotage'. This included such exploits as the rescue of Mussolini from the Gran Sasso on 12 September 1943, and the kidnapping of the Regent of Hungary, Admiral Horthy's son Miklos, on 15 October 1944. *IV-S* was directed by Otto Skorzeny, who told of his exploits in *Skorzeny's Secret Missions* and was also the subject of Charles Foley's *Commando Extraordinary*.

7. AMT VIII *'Welktanschauliche Forschung'*. This bureau was the written documentation service created in July 1940 by Professor Dr Franz Six.
Sentenced at Nuremberg in 1948 to twenty years' imprisonment, Dr Six Was released in 1952 under a general amnesty.

Soon after he joined General Gehlen's West German intelligence service, which included many of Six's former SS and Gestapo colleagues. His particular task involved setting up groups of agents recruited from among former Soviet prisoners-of-war or displaced persons who would be infiltrated back into Russia. At the same time he acted as publicity manager for Porsche-Diesel, a subsidiary of the Mannesmann group. At his trial in Jerusalem in 1961 Adolf Eichmann described Six as the man who had descended lowest from the pedestal of a self-professed 'intellectual' to the depravity of mass murder, only to 'bounce back after the war as the confidant and advisor of both the American and [West] German governments'.

Terry Charman
Department of Printed Books
Imperial War Museum, 1989

Please note!

The Special Wanted List GB consists of 3 parts:*

1. register of persons,
2. subject index,
3. register of locality.

1. The register of persons is ordered purely alphabetically. The identification character is on top of each right-hand page. Within the separate id. characters individual persons are listed by successive numbers. The abbreviated designation for each person is composed of the identification character and the serial number. Example: A. 1 is the designation for Aalten, J.
2. The subject index contains objects of interest, e.g. authorities, companies, motor vehicles, lodges, associations and newspapers.
3. The register of locality is structured into the registers of places of findings and of persons.

Places of findings designate all known addresses, banks, authorities, cover addresses, companies, news agencies, special courts of justice and associations of one place, where there is presumably important material.

All the persons to be arrested living in one place are listed separately in the register of locality under their identification character and serial number.

Only those persons are listed in the register of locality whose presence is certain in the respective city. The places of residence are listed according to the spelling advised by the departments.

* See footnote to p.xxvii.

All the people listed in the Special Wanted List GB are to be arrested.

Comments

The Special Wanted List GB is ordered alphabetically. Sch, Sp, and St are listed after Sz.

The letter combinations of ai, ay, ei, and ey in a name are always under 'ai' in alphabetical order after the given name. Example: Alfred Mayer, Samuel Meier, Victor Maier, Zacharias Meyer.

The departments enlisted right behind the search information give evidence of the original events. Duplicate copies are to be included for any further enlisted departments.

Slides of persons to arrest*

The people to arrest enlisted under A. 48, A. 82, B. 102, B. 142, B. 208, B. 264, E. 67, F. 80, F. 85, F. 103, F. 106, F. 124, G. 32, G. 103, H. 50, H. 102, H. 103, H. 111, H. 134, K. 84, K. 125, M. 120, M. 173, N. 5, S. 40, S. 99, S. 112, T. 33, V. 49 are depicted at the end of the Information Book GB.

---

*N.B. These slides are of such poor quality in the original that they have been omitted from this edition.

I   Registry of Persons (white paper)
Letters A-Z

1. **Aalten, J.,** zuletzt: Holland, vermutl. England (Täterkreis: Brijnen), RSHA IV E 4.
2. **Abbassi, Mohamed Oma,** 21.9.94 Junagort/Indien, London, RSHA IV E 4.
3. **Abbotte, Maude,** 19.7.06 Liverpool, RSHA IV E 4.
4. **Abercrombie, Lascelles,** 9.1.81, Prof. u. Dichter, wohnh. Oxford, Merton College, RSHA VI G 1.
5. **Abrahamczijk, Louis Markus Heinz,** 15.4.00 Berlin, zuletzt: Holland, vermutl. England, RSHA IV E 4.
6. **Abrahamer, Isidor,** 18.5.01 Mährisch-Ostrau, Kaufm., Arzt, zuletzt: Teschen, vermutl. Engl., RSHA IV E 5.
7. **Abrahams,** brit. ND-Offizier, vermutl. England, RSHA IV E 4.
8. **Abramowicz, Bruno,** 2.6.95 Berlin, Redakteur, RSHA IV E 5.
9. **Abramowitz, Simon,** 23.6.87 Ruß, Kr. Heydekrug, früher Min.-Rat, Wohng.: London, RSHA IV A 1.
10. **Abrasimos, Irma** geb. **Michelson,** 12.9.01 Riga, Kontoristin, Bardame. Deckn.: Michalowski, RSHA IV E 5, Stapo Königsberg.
11. **Abt, Gottfried,** 10.5.92 Heinzberg, (Täterkreis: Christian van Houdt), RSHA IV E 4.
12. **Ackermann, Ernst,** 25.5.95 Gnarrenberg, Gewerkschaftsangestellter, RSHA IV A 1.
13. **Ackermann, Manfred,** 1.11.98 Nikolsburg, ehem. Gewerkschaftssekretär, Deckn.: „Mandl" u. „Martin", RSHA IV A 1 b.
14. **Acland, Richard,** Antifaschist, liberaler Abgeordneter, RSHA VI G 1.
15. **Adams, David,** 23.2.75, Labour-Abgeordneter, Wohng.: London, 8 Southill Street Poplar E. C. 4, RSHA VI G 1.
16. **Adams, R. A.,** Major, Gehilfe d. Luftattaché, RSHA IV E 4.
17. **Adams, Vyvyan Samuel,** 22.4.00, konsul. Abgeordn., Wohng.: London, 3. Gloucester Gate, U. W. 1, RSHA VI G 1.
18. **Adamski, Stanislaus, Dr. phil.,** Gymnasialprof., 5.4.99 Wezerow i. Polen, RSHA IV E 5, Stapo Danzig.
19. **Adamson, Jennie,** Vertreterin d. 2. Internationale, RSHA VI G 1.
20. **Addison, Christopher,** 19.6.69 Hogsthorpe, Wohng.: Bucks bei Great Missenden, Peterley Farm. RSHA VI G 1.
21. **Adler, Friedrich, Dr.,** 9.7.79 Wien, Schriftsteller, Sekr. d. II. Internationale, RSHA IV A 1.
22. **Adler, Leonhard, Dr.,** 1882 geb., Dozent, Emigrant, RSHA III A 1.
23. **Adler, Max, Dr.,** 1907 geb., Assistent, Emigrant, RSHA III A 1.
24. **Adler, Nettie,** London W. 14, 121 A, Sinclair Rd. Edison Gardens, RSHA II B 2.
25. **Adolf, Alfred Fritz Berthold Adolf,** 30.7.95 Sommerfeld, Dreher (Am-Apparat), RSHA IV A 2.
26. **Adolph, Alfred,** 30.7.95 Sommerfeld, Dreher (Am-Apparat), RSHA IV A 2.
27. **Aenderl, Franz Xaver,** 25.11.83 Steinweg, Versicherungs-Insp., Wohng.: London, RSHA IV A 1, Stapo Nürnberg.
28. **Alaeddin, Jusuf,** brit. Agent, zuletzt: Ankara, vermutl. England, RSHA IV E 4.
29. **Agnew, Andrew,** Verw.-Dir., Wohng.: London E C 2, St. Helen's Court, Leadenhall Street, RSHA IV E 2.
30. **Albarda, Johann Willem,** 5.6.77 Leeuwarden, chem. holl. Minister, zuletzt: Holland, vermutl. England, RSHA III B.
31. **Albot, H., Frl.,** zuletzt: Brüssel, vermutl. Engl. (Täterkreis: Karel Machacek), RSHA IV E 4.

32. **Albrecht, Alfred,** 2.7.04 München, Vertr., zuletzt: Zagreb/Laibach, vermutl. Engl. (Täterkreis: I. E. Roos), RSHA IV E 4.
33. **Albrecht, Otto,** 19.3.05 Dirschau, Mechaniker, poln. Provokateur, RSHA IV E 5.
34. **Alecander, Kurt,** Deckname: Freeman, Schriftsteller, Emigrant, London N 2, 38 Vivian Way, RSHA II B 5.
35. **Alexander, Albert Victor,** 1.5.85 Weston-Super-Mare, Minister, Wohnung: London, 1 Viktoria Street, RSHA VI G 1.
36. **Alexander, John Alexis,** engl. Konsul, Wohng.: London (Täterkreis: Eric Eissler). RSHA IV E 4.
37. **Alletrino** (Täterkreis: Werner Mikkelsen), RSHA IV E 4.
38. **Allina, Heinrich,** 24.11.78 Schaffa/CSR, Nationalrat, RSHA IV A 1 b
39. **Mac-Alpine, Charles B.,** RSHA VI G 1.
40. **Altmann, Viktor, Dr.,** 7.3.00 Wien, Schriftst., Kompon. (Österr. Legitimist), RSHA IV A 3.
41. **d'Alton,** Leiter d. Intellig. Serv. i. Rotterdam (Täterkreis: Egon Rohr), RSHA IV E 4.
42. **Ambridge, Miß,** Wohng.: Dawigdor-rand-Hove, RSHA IV E 4, Stapol. München.
43. **Amery, Leopold,** 22.11.73 Gorakhpur (Indien), Minister, Wohng.: London S. W. 1, 112 Laton Square, RSHA VI G 1 II D 5.
44. **Ammer, Karl,** 5.5.98 Pettenbach, Schlossergehilfe, Wohng.: Jersey, RSHA IV A 1.
45. **Amsling,** Emigrant, evgl. Geistlicher (Vikar), London (Täterkreis: Hildebrand-Boeckheler-Rieger-Freudenberg), RSHA II B 32, VI II 3.
46. **Anders, Friedrich,** 19.3.99 Barmen (Am-Apparat), RSHA IV A 2.
47. **Anderson, Fargus,** 9.2.09 Vallington, Rennfahrer, Wohng.: London SW 1, Viktoria-Street 36, RSHA IV E 4.
48. **Anderson-Foster, G. Herbert,** 30.5.90 Liverpool, brit. Agent, zuletzt: Riga, vermutl. Engl. (Täterkreis: Maundry Gregory), RSHA IV E 4, VI C 2.
49. **Anderson, William Albert,** 4.3.83 Spezia/Italien, zuletzt: Rom, vermutl. Engl., RSHA IV E 4.
50. **Andriessen,** Mitinh. d. Bankfirma Pierson u. Co., Amsterdam, vermutl. jetzt in England (Täterkreis: Stevens/Best), RSHA IV E 4.
51. **Angell, Normann,** 26.12.74, Präs. d. Weltkomitees gegen Krieg u. Faschism., Wohng.: London, Temple L. C., 4, King's Bench Walk, RSHA VI G 1.
52. **van Angeren, Mr. Dr.,** J. R. M., Generalsekr. im Justizmin., zuletzt: Holland, vermutl. Engl., RSHA III D Holl.
53. **Antal, Friedrich, Dr.,** 1882 geb., Dozent, Wohng.: London, Universität, Emigrant, RSHA III A 1.
54. **Antonczyk, Erich,** 5.10.99 Bielschowitz, Kaufm., poln. N-Agent, RSHA IV E 5, Stapo Oppeln.
55. **Appel, Herbert, Dr.,** Assistent, H. K. A., 1907 geb., Wohng.: Birmingham, Universität, Emigrant, RSHA III A 1.
56. **Appel, Karl,** 29.1.92 Hamburg, Seemann, in Engl. intern. (Schiffssabotage), RSHA IV A 2, IV A 1.
57. **Arcy-Cooper, F. D.,** Wohng.: London, Unilever Haus, Blackfriars, RSHA IV E 2.
58. **Arenz, Heinrich,** 3.9.01 Köln, ehem. Straßenb.-Schaffner (Am-Apparat), RSHA IV A 2.
59. **Arian, Alexander,** 28.4.96 Warschau, poln. Offizier, RSHA IV E 5.
60. **Arijs, Franz,** RSHA VI G 1.

61. **Aris, Reinhold,** 1904 geb., Dr., Wohng.: Cambridge, Univers., Emigrant, RSHA III A 1.
62. **Armann, Josef,** Wohng.: High Cross, Castle Windemen, Westmorland, RSHA IV A 1 b.
63. **Armann, Otto,** 6.8.10 Elisenthal, Arbeiter, Wohng.: High Cross, Castle Windemen, Westmorland, RSHA IV A 1 b.
64. **Armbruster, Theodor,** 2.2.06 'Gnibel, Krs. Tübingen, Schuhmacher (Am-Apparat), RSHA IV A 2.
65. **Arnold, Fritz,** richtig **Kleine, Fritz,** 7.3.01 Apolda, RSHA IV E 4, Stapo Prag.
66. **Arnold, Robert,** Wohng.: London?, richtig **Narr, Adolf Paul** RSHA VI G 1.
67. **Arnold-Forster, William Edward,** polit. Schriftsteller, RSHA IV G 1.
68. **Arnold,** Oberst, Chef d. Nachr.-Abt. d. engl. Gen.-Stabes, RSHA IV E 4.
69. **Arnthal, Eduard,** 3.2.93 Hamburg, Kunstmaler, zuletzt: Zagreb, vermutl. Engl., RSHA IV E 4, Stapo Graz.
70. **Artischewski, August,** 23.4.15 Rundfließ, Krs. Lyck, Reichsw.-Angeh., RSHA IV E 5, Stapo Allenstein.
71. **Artner, Mary,** 2.7.14 Hamburg-Gr. Flottbeck (Am-Apparat), RSHA IV A 2.
72. **Arton, Henry Rolf,** 28.10.12, brit. Leutn., RSHA IV E 4, Stapo Frankf./O.
73. **Aschaffenburg, Rudolf,** Dr., 1902 geb., Wohng.: Edinburgh, Universität, Emigrant, RSHA III A 1.
74. **Corbett-Ashby,** Frau, Führerin d. lib. Partei, RSHA VI G 1.
75. **van Asselt, A. J.,** zuletzt: Rotterdam-Arnheim, vermutl. England, RSHA IV E 4, Stapol Hamburg.
76. **Astbury, Herbert Purcel,** 13.11.07 Leeds, Ingenieur, Wohng.: London W 4, The Lodge Bedfort Park (Täterkreis: Rudolf Köppel), RSHA IV E 4.
77. **Astor, John,** 20.5.86, Abgeordn., Wohng.: London SW 1, 18, Carlton House Terrace, RSHA VI G 1.
77a **Astor, Lady,** London, deutschfeindlich, RSHA IV E 4.
78. **Atherton-Smith, Aline Sybil,** 13.11.75 Ryde, Wohng.: Chantrya, RSHA IV A 1.
79. **Atholl, Duchess of, Katharine,** Wohng.: London SW 10, Elm-Park Gardens u. Blair Castle, Blair Atholl, Perthshire, RSHA VI G 1.
80. **Attlee, Clement Richard,** 3.1.83, Major, Wohng.: Heywood, Stanmore (Middlesex), RSHA VI G 1, II D 5.
81. **Attlee, Clemens,** Führer d. Labour-Party, Wohng.: London SW 1, Smith Square, Transport House, RSHA II B 4.
82. **Aue, Werner Karl Rudolf,** 8.1.98 Albion Villas, brit. Vize-Konsul, zuletzt: Antwerpen, vermutl. Engl., RSHA IV E 4, Stapol. Hannover.
83. **Auerbach, Walter,** 22.7.05 Hamburg, Archivleiter, Deckn.: **Dirksen** (Am-Apparat), RSHA IV A 2, IV A 1 b.
84. **Avigdor, Rifat** (Jude), 9.8.95 Konstantinopel, Konstruktionsleiter (286), RSHA IV B 3.
85. **d'Avigdor-Goldsmith, Henry Joseph,** 1909 geb., Wohng.: London E C 2, 7, Throgmorton Ave., RSHA II B 2.
86. **d'Avignor-Goldsmith, Sir Osmond Elim,** zuletzt: London SW 1, Sommerhill, Tonbridge, 47 Hans Place, RSHA II B 2.
87. **Aziria, Alfonso,** zuletzt: Brüssel, vermutl. Engl. (Täterkreis: Hendrik Peter Kreuzenkamp), RSHA IV E 4.

1. **Baalen, Bernhard Franz**, richtig: **Donkers, Bernhard Franz**, 21.5.05 in Duisburg geb., Arbeiter, 1938 Nymwegen, Kroonestr. 18, vermutl. England (Täterkreis: Pfaffhausen.) RSHA IV E 4 P. 2091.
2. **Baat, M. G.**, London, Unilever House, Blackfriars, IV E 2 — 130/40.
3. **Babel, Kurt**, 10.10.97 in Liegnitz, Kreis-Sekretär der KPC. England, RSHA IV A 1.
4. **Bach, Stefan, Dr.**, geb. 1897, Assistent (Emigrant), Cambridge, III A 1.
5. **Backhouse, Geoffrey**, 1939 in Green, Garden-Birmingham, Stettin III A 4380/39, RSHA IV E 4 B. 4506.
5a **Badmann, Ludwig**, Mitarb. d. Merton, London RSHA III D.
6. **Baden-Powell, Lord**, RSHA IV E 4, Gründer der Boy-Scout-Bewegung.
7. **Baer, F.**, Schriftsteller/Emigrant, London E. C. 3, 7 Gracechurch Street, RSHA II B 5.
7a **Bär, Karl**, Mitarb. d. Merton, London, RSHA III D.
8. **Baginski, Oberst**, Mitglied der poln. Regierung, RSHA IV D 2.
9. **Bagnay, Guillaume Edouard**, geb. 17.4.83, wohnh. zuletzt Holland, jetzt vermutl. England (Täterkreis Stevens-Best), RSHA IV E 4 — B. 4936, Stapoleit Münster.
10. **Bahnik, Wilhelm**, 15.5.00 in Gnesen, Decknamen: **Martin, Dicker, Nasenhermann** (Am-Apparat), RSHA IV A 2.
11. **Baier, Adolf**, 30.9.07 in Oberkirch/B., Schlosser (Am-Apparat), RSHA IV A 2.
12. **Baier, Dora**, 6.6.04 in Berlin (Am-Apparat), RSHA IV A 2.
13. **Baier, Josef**, 24.1.79 in Atschau, Bez. Kaaden, Konsumbeamter, Manchester 20, Palatine Road 4 a, RSHA IV A 1.
14. **Bayer, Aloys**, 21.6.04 in Wittlich, Schriftsteller (Am-Apparat), RSHA IV A 2.
15. **Baker, G. H.**, britischer Vizekonsul, vermutlich England, RSHA IV E 4.
16. **Baker-Noel, Philipp, J.**, 1889 geb., Abgeordneter, Professor, London SW 1, 43 South Latou Place, RSHA VI G 1.
17. **Baker**, britischer N.-D.-Offizier, Colonel (Britisch Legion), London (Täterkreis: White Baker), RSHA IV E 4 450/2 W, 1820/72. 34.
18. **Bakken, D.**, richtig **Helmut Kern**, 3.6.05 in Magdeburg, Redakteur, vermutl. England (Täterkreis: Kern-Kreis), RSHA IV A 1.
19. **Bakken, geborene Bauer, Margot**, 27.12.08 in Hamburg, 1940: Oslo, Hansteengate 5, vermutlich England (Täterkreis: Hugo Bentscher), RSHA IV E 4 — B. 5210.
20. **Ballantyne, Horatio**, London, Unilever House, Blackfriars, RSHA IV E 2 — 130/10.
21. **Balley, Eva Lewis**, brit. Journalistin, 1939: Portugal, vermutl. England, RSHA IV E 4.
22. **Barbé, Gaston**, richtig **Dickwell**, britischer N.-Agent, 1939: Brüssel, rue de Houbloniere 64 (Täterkreis: Kurt Felsenthal), vermutl. England, RSHA IV E 4.
23. **Bardt, Johann**, 18.7.90 Hochweiler, Chemiker, 1939 in England, RSHA IV E 4 B.
24. **Barion, Hans**, 19.12.97, Decknamen: **Hans Ober, Karl Mertens, Dr. Westhoff, Kaulbach, Adolf Steinemann**, Großbüllesheim, Oberstadtsekretär, (Am-Apparat), RSHA IV A 2.
25. **Barker, Ernest**, 23.9.74, Professor in Cambridge, 17, Cranmer Road, RSHA VI G 1.
26. **Barkley**, britischer Militärattaché, Budapest, vermutl. England (Täterkreis: Berkeley), RSHA IV E 4.

27. **Barnes, George Nicoll,** 2.1.59 Delegierter bei der Friedenskonferenz London E. C., 76 Herne Hill, RSHA VI G 1.
28. **Barnes, Hugh S.,** Direktor, London E. O. 2, Britannic House, Anglo-Iranian-Oil Co., RSHA IV E 2.
29. **Barnett, Lawrence,** Beamter des brit. Konsulates in Panama, vermutl. England, RSHA IV E 4 31 165, Auswärtiges Amt Pol. IX 658/40.
30. **Barnisch, C. W.,** London, Unilever House, Blackfriars, RSHA IV E 2.
31. **Baron, B.** (Antifaschistische Liga), RSHA VI G 1.
32. **Baron, Hans, Dr.,** 1900, Privatdozent, London (Emigrant), RSHA III A 1.
33. **Barry, Gerald,** 20.11.98, Journalist (Direktor bei „News Chronicle"), London S. W. 7, 43 Cheval Place, RSHA VI G 1.
34. **Barry,** britischer N.-Agent, vermutl. England, RSHA IV E 4.
35. **Barski, Franciszek (Franz),** 18.6.91 Jablone, Krs. Wollstein, polnischer Kreissekretär, RSHA IV E 5, Stapostelle Schneidemühl.
36. **Barstow, George N.,** Vertreter der Britischen Regierung, London E. C. 2, Britannic House, Anglo-Iranian-Oil Co., RSHA IV E 2.
37. **Barth, Willi,** 25.9.99 Ingersleben, Tischler, vermutl. Sowjetrußland, RSHA IV A 1, Stapostelle Weimar.
38. **Barthel, Alfred,** 4.12.07 Berlin, Deckname: **Friedrich Förstel,** 19.2.99 geboren, Elektromonteur, vermutl. England (Am-Apparat), RSHA IV A 2.
39. **Bartholdy - Mendelsohn, Albrecht,** Oxford, Balliol College, RSHA VI G 1.
40. **Bartik, Josef,** 8.6.97 Stachau, Deckname: **Josef Baranek, Beta,** London 53, Lexham, Gardens Kensington W 8, RSHA IV E 4.
41. **Bartik, Josef,** 30.6.97 Stachny-Suice, ehem. tschechischer Major, London (Täterkreis: Frantisek Moravec), RSHA IV E 6.
42. **Bartlakowski, Leonhardt,** 31.8.16 Berlin, Uffz., RSHA IV E 5, Stapostelle Breslau.
43. **Bartlett, Vernon Werner,** 30.4.94 Westbury, Dipl. Korrespondent v. „News Chronicle", Abgeordneter, Llotead Sure, The old Farm House, RSHA IV B 4 2019/E u. VI G 1.
* 44. **Baruch, Bernhard,** London S. W. 1, 1, Carlton Gardens, RSHA II B 2.
45. **Basch, Anton, Dr.,** 5.6.96 Deutsch-Brod, Direktor, RSHA IV E 4 31238, Stapostelle Prag.
46. **Bashford, R. F. O. N.,** Presseattaché, England, RSHA IV E 4.
47. **Bates-Jones, Reginald,** vermutl. England, RSHA IV E 4.
48. **Bauer, Margarete,** 12.11.01 Königswarth, Lagerhalterin, Ashbourne-Derby, Ham-Hall, RSHA IV A 1 b, Stapostelle Karlsbad.
49. **Bauer,** verh. **Bakken, Margot,** 27.12.08 Hamburg, 1940: Oslo, Hansteengate 5, jetzt: vermutl. England (Täterkreis: Hugo Bentscher), RSHA IV E 4 B. 5210.
50. **Bauer, Dr.,** Beauftragter d. Petschek-Gruppe, London, 458/9 Salisbury House, RSHA IV E 4.
51. **Bauerfeind, Adolf,** 24.5.04 Eibenberg, Deckname: **Kornähre, David,** Maurer, England, Attentäter, RSHA IV A 2 — 02141/39 g.
52. **Bauerfeind, Robert,** 11,5.13 Markhausen, England, RSHA IV A 1.
53. **Baukart, Johann,** Schuldirektor, 1940: Luttenberg/Jugosl., vermutlich England, RSHA IV E 4, Stapostelle Graz.
54. **Baumeister, Alfred Ottomar,** 16.11.07 Plauen, Deckname: **Reichenberger, Erich,** Bäcker (Am-Apparat), RSHA IV A 2.
55. **Baumgärtel, Elise, Dr.,** 1892, London (Emigrantin), RSHA III A 1.

*See notes on pages 266–272

56. **Baumgardt, David. Dr.,** 1880, a. o. Professor, Birmingham (Universität), (Emigrant), RSHA III A 1.
57. **Baumgartner, Rupert,** 20.5.10 München, Former (Am-Apparat), RSHA IV A 2.
58. **Baxa, Paul, Dr.,** tschechischer Rundfunksprecher, London (Täterkreis: Benesch), RSHA IV D 1 a.
59. **Baylis, L. G.,** britischer Vizekonsul, vermutlich England, RSHA IV E 4, Stapoleitstelle Hamburg.
60. **Bearsted, Viscount,** Präsident, London E. C. 3, St. Helen's Court 22, Shell Transport und Trading Co., RSHA IV E 2.
61. **Bearsted, Viscount Walter Horace Samuel,** 13.3.82, Industrieller, London, Carlton House Gardens, und Banbury, Upton House, RSHA VI G 1
62. **Beaton, Grace N.,** London, Sekretärin des Internat. Rates der Internat. Kriegsdienstgegner, RSHA VI G 1.
63. **Beaumont,** geborene **Vanek, Emilie,** 20.3.94 Wien, Agentin, Prag, vermutl. England, RSHA IV E 4 — B. 684.
64. **Beaumont, Frank,** 10.5.96, britischer N.-Offizier, London, RSHA IV E 4 — B. 3998.
* 65. **Beaverbrock, Lord,** 25.5.79, Zeitungsmagnat, Minister, Cherkley, Leatherhead (Surrey), RSHA VI G 1.
66. **Bebensee, Hans Heinrich,** 11.2.17 Kiel, Schütze, RSHA IV E 5, Stapostelle Allenstein.
67. **Bech,** Redakteur, vermutlich England (Täterkreis: Jens Dons), RSHA IV E 4, Stapostelle Kiel.
68. **Bechholt, Peter,** 2.7.73 Gelsenkirchen (Am-Apparat), RSHA IV A 2.
69. **Beck, Adolf, Dr.,** 1905, Assistent, Greenwich (Emigrant), RSHA III A 1.
70. **Beck, Eugen,** 29.3.07 Stuttgart, Kaufmann (Am-Apparat), RSHA IV A 2.
71. **Beck, Francis,** Schriftsteller (Emigrant), Paignton (Devon), Shorton Coottage, RSHA II B 5.
72. **Beck, Stephan, Dr.,** 1895, Assistent, Glasgow (Emigrant), RSHA III A 1.
73. **Beck, Walter, Dr.,** Direktor, Boston (Universität), (Emigrant), RSHA III A 1.
74. **Becke, Jan** (Emigrant), London, RSHA II B 5.
75. **Becker, Jerome Sidney,** 20.8.81 New York, Korrespondent, angebl. England, RSHA IV E 4 u. II A 5.
76. **Becker, Karl,** 19.11.94 Hannover, Deckname: **Karin,** Schriftsteller, zuletzt Prag, jetzt vermutlich England, RSHA IV A 1.
77. **Beckert, Friedrich,** 22.11.97 Giengen, wohnh. in England, RSHA V C 2 c — St. A. Berlin 1 Mu. 52/38.
78. **Becko, Johann Jan,** 16.11.89 Jasemek, ehem. sozialdemokratischer Abgeordneter, 1940: London, RSHA IV E 4, IV D 1 a — Stapoleitstelle Prag.
79. **Becvar, Gustaf,** 13.9.94 Neu-Jetschin, Privatbeamter, London, RSHA IV E 4, Stapoleitstelle Prag.
80. **Beekhorst,** britischer Agent, 1939: Rotterdam, vermutlich England, RSHA IV E 4.
81. **Graf Beenstorff** (Täterkreis: Siegfried Franke), RSHA IV E 4.
82. **Beer, Arthur, Dr.,** 1900, wohnh. Cambridge, Physikalisches Observatorium, Universität (Emigrant), RSHA III A 1.

*See notes on pages 266–272

83. **Beer, Friedrich (Fritz),** 15.8.00 Schweinfurt, Deckname: Heinrich Grunov, Schriftsteller, vermutl. England (Schwarze Front), RSHA IV A 3.
84. **Beer, ehem.** britischer Konsul in Preßburg, vermutl. England, RSHA IV E 4.
85. **Begoll, Siegfried,** 5.2.98 Lusow/Polen, poln. Zollkomm., RSHA IV E 5, Stapo Schneidemühl.
86. **Behrens verh. Spiegel, Annemarie,** 25.7.01 Altona, England, RSHA IV A 1.
87. **Behretz, Max,** 22.1.13 Roermond, Radiohändler, zuletzt: Holland, vermutl. England (Täterkreis: Theo Heespers), RSHA IV E 4.
88. **Beiles, Normann John,** britischer Agent, vermutlich England, RSHA IV E 4.
89. **Beiner, Rudolf,** 6.11.08 München (Jude), 1939: Brüssel, vermutlich England (Täterkreis: Leo Heymann), RSHA IV E 4.
90. **Belchambers, Harald,** Agrarprofessor, Oxford, RSHA IV A 1.
91. **Hore-Belisha, Leslie,** London S. W. 14, The Close Sheen Connwon, RSHA VI G 1.
92. **Belisha, Albert I.,** London E. C. 3, 15, St. Helens Place, RSHA II B 2.
93. **Belkot, Ludwig,** 24.8.13 Ruda, Krs. Schwientochlowitz, Grubenarbeiter, polnischer Deserteur, RSHA IV E 5, Stapostelle Oppeln.
94. **Bell, Nancy,** Völkerbundsbewegung, RSHA VI G 1.
95. **Bell,** britischer Agent, zuletzt: Belgrad, vermutl. England, RSHA IV E 4.
96. **Benda, Clemens Ernst, Dr.,** 1898, Assistent, Universität Cambridge (Emigrant), RSHA III A 1.
97. **Bender, Josef Theo,** 25.8.06 Wuppertal-Elberfeld, Arbeiter (Am-Apparat), RSHA IV A 2.
* 98. **Benes, Eduard, Dr. phil.,** 28.5.84 (83?) Kozlanech, Expräsident der CSR., RSHA VI G 1, IV D 1 a, IV E 4, Stapoleitstelle Prag.
99. **Benes, geb. Vlcek, Hanna,** 16.7.85 Deutzendorff, vermutlich London, RSHA IV E 4, Stapoleitstelle Prag.
100. **Benesch, Edward,** Emigrant, Vorsitzender d. tschech. Nationalkomitees in Frankreich und England, London S. W. 15, Gwendole Ave. 27, RSHA II B 5.
101. **Bengen, Davis,** 23.7.01 in London, vermutl. London, RSHA IV E 3 — Stapoleitstelle München.
102. **Benninghaus, Walter,** 25 1.98 in Kirpse (SPD-Funktionär), England, RSHA IV A 1 b.
103. **Benscher, Hugo Israel,** 17.6.03 in Hamburg, vermutlich England, RSHA IV E 4, Stapostelle Kiel.
104. **Bentley, J. W.,** RSHA VI G 1.
105. **Bentwich, Norman,** 1883, Rechtsanwalt und Schriftsteller, Professor, Hollycot, Vale of Health, N. W. 3., VI G 1.
106. **Benz, Theodor,** 19.7.80 Köln-Mühlheim, Arbeiter (Am-Apparat), RSHA IV A 2.
106a **Berendson, Helene,** Mitarb. d. Merton, London, RSHA III D.
107. **Bergh, van den, Clive,** Kaufmann, London NW 3, Eton Avenue, Eton Court 50, Unilever Konzern, RSHA III D 2.
108. **Bergh, van den, Albert,** 1875 in London, London W. 1, Alderbrook Park, Cranleigh, Surrey, Flat 54, 20 Grosvenor Square, RSHA II B 2.
109. **Bergh, van den, James Paul,** London, Unilever House, Blackfriars, RSHA IV E 2.

*See notes on pages 266–272

110. **Berg, van den, Jakob Hermann,** 1l.9.00 Viersen, 1939, Blerick, Holland, Spoorstr. 26, vermutlich England (Täterkreis: Gerrit Spruijtenburg), RSHA IV E 4.
111. **Berg, van den, Matthias,** 22.8.05 in Viersen, 1939: Blerick/Holland, Spoorstr. 26 (Täterkreis: Gerrit Spruijtenburg), RSH IV E 4.
112. **Bergh, van den, Sidney** (Jude), Kaufmann. Ostlands Merc, Weybridge Surrey (Unilever-Konzern), RSHA III D 2.
113. **Bergh, van den, Sam,** London, Unilever House, Blackfriars, RSHA IV E 2.
114. **Bergh, van den,** Kapitän d. niederl. Armee, Margarinefabrikant, zuletzt Holland, vermutl. England, RSHA III B.
115. **Berg geborene Schmidt, Martha,** 4.7.97 in Fiel/Süderdithmarschen, Fabrikarbeiterin (Am-Apparat), RSHA IV A 2.
116. **Berg, Wolfgang, Dr.,** 1908, Assistent (Emigrant), London, RSHA III A 1.
117. **Bergel, Franz, Dr.,** geb. 1900, Privatdozent, Edinburgh, Universität (Emigrant), RSHA III A 1.
118. **Berger, Max Bernhard,** 2.8.95 Wüstenbrand-Nadelrichter, RSHA IV A 1. Stapo Chemnitz.
119. **Berger, Richard,** britischer Polizeiagent, Deckname: **C. Siemens, Simmons,** und **James Upson,** London SW, Brixton Stockwall Road 83, RSHA IV E 4.
120. **Berkeley,** britischer Oberst u. Militärattaché, Budapest, vermutlich England, RSHA IV E 4.
121. **Berkenheim,** London, RSHA IV E 4.
122. **Berlin, Paul Wilhelm Karl,** 2.4.14 Petersdorf, Dienstpflichtiger, London E. C. 1, 29 Barbican, RSHA V D 2 f, und Gericht der Kommandantur Berlin v. 28.3.39.
123. **Bernal, John, D.** Professor (Einkreisungspolitiker), RSHA VI G 1.
124. **Bernegau, Wilhelm,** 27.2.03 Werdohl, Arbeiter, Deckname: **„Der rote Graf"** (Am-Apparat) RSHA IV A 2.
125. **Bernstein, Alex** (Einkreisungspolitiker), RSHA VI G 1.
126. **Berry, George William,** 25.8.95 Jelgava/Lettland, Chef der Paßabtlg. im brit. Kons. Wien, vermutlich England, RSHA IV E 4, Stapoleit Wien.
127. **Berthoud,** Angestellter d. AJOC, London E. C. 2, Britannic-House, RSHA IV E 2.
128. **Bertl, Georg,** 12.12.01 Prag, Journalist, 1939: Bukarest (Täterkreis: Bretlislav Kika), RSHA IV E 4.
129. **Best, geborene van Rees, Maria Margareta,** 9.1.92 Hellevoentssluis, London NW. 3, Hampstead 3, Holford Road (Täterkreis: Stevens-Best), RSHA IV E 4.
130. **Beuer, Otto,** 25.9.98 Reichenberg, Geschäftsführer, Putney bei London SW. 15, 24, Egliston Road, RSHA IV A 1.
131. **Bevin, Ernest,** Minister (Einkreisungspolitiker), Gewerkschaftler, RSHA VI G 1.
132. **Beyer, Martha,** 2.11.06 Hamburg, Schneiderin (Am-Apparat), RSHA IV A 2.
133. **Beyll,** britischer Agent, Belgrad, vermutl. England, RSHA IV E 4.
134. **Bharu, James,** britischer Agent, vermutlich England, RSHA IV E 4.
135. **Bieberstein, von, Hans Bodo,** vermutlich England (Täterkreis: Siegfried Franke), RSHA IV E 4.
136. **Biedermann, Lorenz,** 17.7.10 Haslau, Ashbourne-Derby, Ilam Hall, RSHA IV A 1 b.

137. **Biesemann, Leo,** 17.3.93 Emmerich, Kapitän a. D., Deckname: **Jupp Leo** (Am-Apparat), RSHA IV A 2.
138. **Biesterfeld, Bernhard,** holländischer Prinz, RSHA IV E 4.
139. **Bikerman, J. J., Dr.,** 1898 Manchester Universität (Emigrant), RSHA III A 1.
140. **Bileckl, Dr. jur, Tadeusz,** Mitglied des polnischen Nationalrates, RSHA IV D 2.
141. **Bing, Gertrud, Dr.,** 1892, Assistent, London, Emigrantin, RSHA III A 1.
142. **Birch, Julius Guthlac,** 8.4.84 London, britischer Oberst und ND-Offizier, vermutlich England. RSHA IV E 4.
143. **Birch, Natan** (Antifaschistische Liga), RSHA VI G 1.
144. **Birkenmayer, Alfred,** 28.5.92 Krakau, poln. Konsulatsbeamter, Leiter des poln. ND., RSHA IV E 5, Stapoleit Danzig.
145. **Birkett, W. E.,** 11.1.82 Blaeckbura, Botschaftssekretär, 1939: Den Haag, vermutl. England, RSHA IV E 4.
146. **Birnbaum, Gerhard,** britischer Agent, 1938 Warschau, vermutlich England, RSHA IV E 4.
147. **Blaazer, J.,** N.-Agent, vermutlich England (Täterkreis: Waldemar Pötsch), RSHA IV E 4.
148. **Black,** Deckname: **Simpson,** 45 Jahre alt, britischer Agent, England, RSHA IV E 4.
149. **Blackett, P. M. S.,** 18.11.97, Professor, London E. C. 4, Birchbeck Colledge, Breams, Buildings, Felber Lane, RSHA VI G 1.
150. **Blackwood,** Angestellter der AJOC., London E. C. 2, Britannic House, RSHA IV E 2.
151. **Blaikie, E. R.,** London, 32 Fleet Lane E. C. 4, (Jude, Emigrant), RSHA VI G 1.
152. **Blanche-Koelensmid, Gerardus Adrianus Everhard,** 8.4.84, 1939: Amsterdam, vermutl. England (Täterkreis: Snatager), RSHA IV E 4.
153. **Blank, Robert, Dr.,** 25.9.88 London, Leiter der Kreditanstalt „Bernia" in Buchs/Schweiz, London, Folkestone 18, Grinston-Gardens, RSHA IV E 3, IV A 1, Stopoleit München.
154. **Blankenhagen,** 50 bis 60 Jahre alt, Doorn/Holland, vermutl. England (Täterkreis: Stevens-Best), RSHA IV E 4.
155. **Blankenstein, van, Markus,** 3.6.80 Oderkark, Redakteur (Nieuwe Rotterdamsche Courant), vermutl. England (Täterkreis: Karl Nihom), RSHA IV E 4.
156. **Blaschko, Hermann, Dr.,** 1900, Assistent, Cambridge Universität (Emigrant), RSHA III A 1.
157. **Bloca, Alfred M. Sc., Dr.,** 1904, Assistent, London (Emigrant), RSHA III A 1.
158. **Bloch, Berthold,** 5.7.00 Randegg bei Konstanz, Kaufmann, Gibraltar, IV A 1, RSHA IV A 1.
159. **Bloch, Max,** richtig **Katzenellenbogen,** 1.2.06 Leipzig, Chemiker, vermutl. England (Am-Apparat), RSHA IV A 2.
160. **Bloch, Robert, Dr.** Professor, 1898, Leeds, Universität (Emigrant), RSHA III A 1.
161. **Blochmann, Elisabeth, Dr.,** Prof., 1892, Oxford, (Emigrant), RSHA III A 1.
162. **Blohm, Edgar Georgs,** Kaufmann, 1936 London, Cromwell Road 168, RSHA IV E 3, Stapoleit Berlin.
163. **Bloss, Christian,** 24.5.98 Asch, Laborant, England, RSHA IV A 1, Stapostelle Karlsbad.

164. **Blume, Franz,** Deckname: **Michel,** 26.9.05 Hamburg, Tischler (Am-Apparat), RSHA IV A 2.
165. **Blumenberg, Werner,** 21.12.00 Hülsede, Redakteur, vermutlich England, RSHA IV A 1.
166. **Blumenfeld, Ralph D.,** 1864 USA., Muscombs, Little Easton Dunmow, RSHA III B 2.
167. **Bodenheimer, Wolf, Dr.,** 1905 geb., London (Emigrant), RSHA III A 1.
168. **Bodenstein,** verh. Masur, **Annemarie,** 18.11.09 Gronau, RSHA IV A 1, Stapoleit Hamburg.
169. **Böhm, Dr. ing.,** 2.7.84 Zaborze (Hindenburg), London, RSHA IV A 1.
170. **Boeckheler,** evg. Pfarrer, London S. E. 23, 23 Manor Mount Forest Hill (Täterkreis: Amsling-Hildebrand-Freudenberg), RSHA III B 32, VI H 3
171. **Boeijen von, Hendrik,** 23.5.89 Putten, ehem. holl. Innenminister, England, RSHA III B.
172. **Boekelman,** britischer Agent, 1939: Den Haag, vermutlich England, RSHA IV E 4.
173. **Boersma, August,** vermutl. England (Täterkreis: August de Fremery), RSHA IV E 4.
174. **Bogard, van den,** holl. Autovermieter, Bergen-Daal/Holland (Täterkreis: Wilhelm Willemse, RSHA IV E 4.
175. **Bogdoll, Karol,** 4.11.95 Zawadzki, Gr. Strehlitz, ehem. poln. Insurgentenführer, ND.-Agent, RSHA IV E 5, Stapo Oppeln.
176. **Bogomoletz, Viktor, Dr.,** 8.5.95 Kiew, Journalist, London, RSHA IV A 1.
177. **Bohn, Jane,** 1939: Kopenhagen, vermutl. England (Täterkreis: Brijnen), RSHA IV E 4.
178. **Boland, H.,** britischer Agent, 1939: Den Haaag, vermutlich England, RSHA IV E 4.
179. **Boland,** kath. Schwester, 1940 vermutlich England, RSHA IV E 4.
180. **Bolkestein, Gerrit,** 9.10.71, Amsterdam, ehem. holl. Unterrichtsminister, vermutlich England, RSHA III B.
181. **Boller, Robert,** Büro-Inhaber. 1940: Yokohama/Japan, vermutlich England. RSHA IV E 4, IV D 5.
182. **Bonham-Carter, Lady, Violet,** London W. 2, 40 Gloucester Square (Einkreisungspolitikerin), RSHA VI G 1.
183. **Bonk, Wladislaus,** 24.11.06 Sokohowo, Kurzwarenhändler, RSHA IV E 5, Stapoleit Schneidemühl.
184. **Bonn, Moritz, Dr.,** 1873 geb., Professor, London, Emigrant, RSHA III A 1.
185. **Bonneau, Madelene,** 1939: Paris, vermutl. England (Täterkreis: Albert Albseit), RSHA IV E 4, Stapoleit Wien.
186. **Bonneau, Susanne,** 1939: Paris, vermutl. England (Täterkreis: Albert Albseit), RSHA IV E 4, Stapoleit Wien.
187. **Boon,** Kammerabgeordneter, Rechtsanwalt, 1939: Den Haag, vermutlich England (Täterkreis: Prins), RSHA IV E 4.
188. **Boothby, Robert,** 1900, Sekretär von Winston Churchill, London S. W. 1, 17. Tall Male, RSHA VI G 1.
189. **Borinski, Friedrich, Dr.,** 17.6.03 Berlin, London, 44. Lemsford-Lane, Welwyn Garden, City 1 Blakomer Road, Schwarze Front, RSHA IV A 3.
190. **Borkenau-Pollak, Franz, Dr.,** 1900, London, RSHA III A 1.
191. **Borlinski, Ludwig, Dr.,** 1910, Cambridge, Emigrant, RSHA III A 1.

* 192. **Boronowski, Georg**, 2.9.12 Schwientochlowitz, Wehrpflichtiger, zuletzt: Südafrika, RSHA V—D 2 f., Reichskriegsgericht St. P. L. (RKA.).
193. **Bottländer, Theodor,** 18.11.04 Schwartau, Kesselschmied, Deckn.. **Josef Fiebig, Kurt Richter, Arthur, Kurt,** vermutl. England, (Am.Apparat), RSHA IV A 2.
194. **Bouvard, Hugo,** Hauptmann, London, RSHA IV A 3.
195. **Bove, Charles,** London WS. 14 Paterstreet, RSHA IV E 4.
196. **Bower, Philipp George,** England, RSHA IV E 4.
197. **Boyce, Ernest,** Beamter, zuletzt Reval, vermutl. England, brit. ND.-Agent, RSHA VI C 2.
198. **Bozek, Arka,** Mitgl. d. poln. Nationalrates, vermutl. England, RSHA IV D 2.
199. **Bracken, Brendan,** 1901 Direktor, Abgeordneter, London SW 1, 8 North Street, RSHA VI G 1.
200. **Bracker, Frl.,** zuletzt Kopenhagen, vermutl. England (Täterkreis: Jens Dons), RSHA IV E 4, Stapo Kiel.
201. **Bradby, Robert A.,** Prof., 13.5.01, London, RSHA IV A 1.
202. **Bragg, William, Sir,** Prof., 31.3.90 Australien, Windy House Alderley Ledge Cheshire, RSHA VI G 1.
203. **Braginski, Borris,** Deckn.: **Jubanski,** zuletzt: Antwerpen, vermutl. England (Täterkreis: Waldemar Pötsch), RSHA IV E 4.
204. **Brailsford, Henry Noel,** geb. 1873, Journalist, London N. W. 3, Belsize Park Gardens, RSHA VI G 1.
205. **Brakensiek, Leo,** 28 Jahre alt, zuletzt: Amsterdam, vermutl. England (Täterkreis: Prins), RSHA IV E 4.
206. **Bramley, Ted,** Organisator, vermutl. England, RSHA VI G 1.
207. **Brandl, Franz,** 24.12.98 Tachau, Cefn Cöed bei Merthyr Tydfil, 28 Field Street South Wales, RSHA IV A 1 b.
208. **Brandon, Albert Ernest** Acton, 18.9.89 London, brit. Cpt., zuletzt: Genf, vermutl. England (Täterkreis: Burnell), RSHA IV E 4.
209. **Brandt, Arthur, Dr. med.,** Jude, 26.3.69 Posen, London (Abtreibung), RSHA IV B 1 c.
210. **Brandt, Johann,** 17.7.93 Geestemünde, brit. Agent, vermutl. England, RSHA IV E 4.
211. **Branys, Jan,** Mitgl. d. poln. Regierung, zuletzt: Chorzow, vermutl. England, RSHA IV D 2.
212. **Brauers, Leon,** zuletzt: Holland, vermutl. England (Täterkreis: J. Hermans), RSHA IV E 4.
213. **Braun, Hans,** 24.1.06 München, Deckn.: **Peter, Georg,** Angestellter, vermutl. London (Am-Apparat), RSHA IV A 2.
214. **Braun, Hugo,** 12.2.01 Johanngeorgenstadt, vermutl. England, RSHA IV A 1.
215. **Braun, Matthias,** 13.8.92 Neuß/Rhein, Deckn.: **Matz,** Schriftsteller, vermutl. England, RSHA IV A 1.
216. **Brautferger, Anton,** 15.8.94 Falkenau, England, RSHA IV A 1 b.
217. **von Bredow, Hans,** vermutl. England (Täterkreis: Siegfried Franke), RSHA IV E 4.
218. **Breijnen, Pieter,** Journalist, zuletzt: Holland, vermutl. England, RSHA IV E 4.
219. **Breine,** Agent, zuletzt: Soest, vermutl. England (Täterkreis: Prins), RSHA IV E 4.
220. **Breitscheid, Rudolf, Dr.,** Emigrant, 2.11.74 Köln, Schriftsteller, RSHA II B 5.

*See notes on pages 266–272

221. **Brems, Helmut,** 28 Jahre alt, zuletzt: Riga, vermutl. England, RSHA IV E 4, Stapo Tilsit.
222. **Brendel, Otto, Dr.,** geb. 1901, vermutl. England, Emigrant, RSHA III A 1.
223. **Brewer,** 35 Jahre alt, brit. Agent, zuletzt: Den Haag, vermutl. England, (Täterkreis: Stevens/Best), RSHA IV E 4.
224. **Brieger, Ernst, Dr.,** Cambridge, Emigrant, RSHA III A 1.
225. **Brinkhof,** brit. Agent, zuletzt: Holland, vermutl. England (Täterkreis: Arends), RSHA IV E—4, Stplt. Düsseldorf.
227. **Brittain, Vera,** verh. **Catlin,** Journalistin, London SW 3, 19 Glebe Palace, RSHA VI G 1.
228. **Brock, Werner, Dr.,** 1901, Cambridge, Emigrant, RSHA III A 1.
229. **Brockway, Archibald, Fenner,** 1888 Calcutta, The Spinney Londwater, Rickmansworth Herts, RSHA VI G 1.
230. **Brod, Luise,** verh. **Öhl,** 29.10.07 München, Deckn.: **Erna Christel,** Hausangestellte, vermutl. England (Am-Apparat), RSHA IV A 2.
231. **Brodetsky, Selig,** 10.2.88 Rußld., Prof., Headlingley (Leeds), 3 Grosvenor Road, RSHA VI G 1.
232. **Brodniewicz, Stanislaus,** ehem. pol. Komm., vermutl. England, RSHA IV E 5.
233. **Brönstein, Walter, Dr.,** geb. 1890, vermutl. England, RSHA III A 1.
234. **Brond, Max, Dr.,** 1882, Prof., Edinburgh, RSHA III A 1.
235. **Broumer, Theodor,** 22.6.92 Münster/W., richtig **Theodor Franssen,** Ing., zuletzt Amsterdam, vermutl. England, RSHA IV E 4.
236. **Brousson, R. P.,** Aufsichtsratmitgl., London EC 3, St. Helens Court, Shell-Max and B. P. Ltd., RSHA IV E 2.
237. **Brown, H. Runhan,** Gen.-Sekretär, vermutl. England, RSHA VI G 1.
238. **Brown, J.,** Schriftsteller, vermutl. England, RSHA IV B 4.
239. **ten Brucker** richtig **Harry Richter,** zuletzt: Den Haag, vermutl. England (Täterkreis: Karl Nihom), RSHA IV E 4, StPLt: Münster.
240. **Brücker, Erna,** verh. **Owen,** 21.12.04 Oberhausen, vermutl. England, RSHA IV A 1.
241. **v. d. Brug, J. J. H.,** zuletzt: Utrecht/Holland, vermutl. England (Täterkreis: Brijnen, RSHA IV E 4.
242. **Flesch-Brun, Hans,** vermutl. England, RSHA VI G 1.
243. **Brunert, Helene Elisabeth,** verh. **Robinson,** 27.2.97 Martenan/Frankr., vermutl. England, RSHA IV E 4.
244. **Bruss, Josef,** 8.5.08 Herne/W., Arbeiter, vermutl. England, RSHA IV E 5, Stapoleit. Breslau.
245. **Brussowansky, Viktor,** 27.7.15 Charinopol, Student, vermutl. England, RSHA IV E 4, Stapoleit Prag.
246. **Bryan, Carter Roy,** Korrespondent, vermutl. England (Täterkreis: Sigrid Schulz), RSHA IV E 4.
247. **Brzezinski, Franziszek,** 14.9.95 Gardschau Krs. Dirschau, Nachrichtenoffizier, vermutl. England, RSHA IV E 5, Stapo Schneidemühl.
248. **Buchardt, Fritz, Dr.,** geb. 1902, Oxford, Emigrant, RSHA III A 1.
249. **Budberg, Maria,** geb. **Sakrewska,** Baronin, Deckn: **Mura,** London, brit. ND.-Agentin, RSHA VI C 2.
250. **Budzislawski, Hermann,** 11.2.01 Berlin, Emigrant, Jude, RSHA II B 5.
251. **von Bülow, Horst,** 3.3.02 Berlin, vermutl. England (Täterkreis: Siegfried Franke), RSHA IV E 4.
252. **Bürger, Hans,** Schriftst., Emigrant, London W. C. 1, 8 Mecklenburgh Square, RSHA II B 5.

253. **Büttner, Gottfried,** 23.5.14 Offenbach, Wehrpflichtiger, England, Moosley, RSHA V D 2 f, Ger. d. Kommandantur Berlin.
254. **Bullock, Harry,** brit. Vizekonsul, vermutl. England, RSHA IV E 4.
255. **Bunzel, Robert,** 15.3.82, vermutl. England, RSHA VI G 1, II B 5.
256. **Burawoy, Onissim, Dr.,** geb. 1899, Emigrant, RSHA III A 1.
257. **Burch, William Isaak,** London, RSHA IV E 4.
258. **Burckert, Egon Kurt,** 4.6.10 Setzingen, Krs. Aalen, Lehrer, vermutl. England, RSHA IV A 1, Stl. Stuttgart.
259. **Burde, Friedrich,** 20.9.01 Bln.-Schöneberg, Deckn.: **Adolf Edgar Schwarz, Dr.,** Schlosser (Am-Apparat), RSHA IV A 2.
260. **Burge, M. R. H.,** London, RSHA VI G 1.
261. **Burghley, Lord,** London, St. James Court, Buckingham Gate, RSHA VI G 1.
262. **Burianek, A.,** London (Täterkreis: H. Sneevliet), RSHA IV E 4.
263. **Burn, Erika,** geb. **Korsetz,** 9.4.14 Berlin, London, 4 Alrington Gardens Chiswick, RSHA IV A 1.
264. **Burnell, Albert Ernest Acton,** 18.9.89 London, brit. Cpt., Deckn.: Brandon, zuletzt Genf, vermutl. England, Kraftw. GE 21351 GB, RSHA IV E 4.
265. **Burnham, William Lawson, Lord,** 19.3.64 Barton Court Kintbury, Berkes, RSHA VI G 1.
266. **Burt, Ronald,** 27.10.20 Leichester, Ringstead, Knigton, RSHA IV E 4, Stapo Frankfurt/M.
267. **Burton,** brit. Major, vermutl. England, RSHA IV E 4.
268. **Butcher,** brit. Cpt., zuletzt Riga, vermutl. England, RSHA IV E 4.
269. **Buttinger, Josef,** 30.4.06 Reichenbrunn, Deckn.: **Hubert, Gustav Richter,** Handelsangestellter, vermutl. England, RSHA IV A 1.
270. **Buxton, Kenneth Ernest,** 16.9.16 London, Pilot, England, RSHA IV E 4, Stapo Köln.
271. **Byron,** brit. ND-Agent, England, (Täterkreis: Jens Dons), RSHA IV E 4, Stapo Kiel.
272. **Bytel, Simon,** York, 5 South View, Acomb Road, RSHA VI G 1, II B 5.
273. **Bzdyl, Piotr,** 13.6.98 Polen, Geistlicher, zuletzt Holland, vermutl. England, RSHA IV E 4, Stapo Aachen.

1. **Cable, Eric,** 1897 Helsingfors, brit. Konsul, vermutl. England, RSHA IV E 4.
2. **Cadbury, Elizabeth,** RSHA VI G 1.
* 2a **Sir Cadogan,** Leiter des brit. ND., vermutl. England, RSHA IV E 4.
3. **Calderwood, James,** 13.10.11 Glasgow, vermutl. England, RSHA IV E 4.
4. **Calerghi-Coudenhove, Richard,** 17.11.94 Tokio, Schriftsteller, vermutlich England, Österr. Legitimist, RSHA IV A 3.
5. **Camber, Theodor,** 28.11.94 Kowno, brit. ND.-Agent, zuletzt Wilna, vermutl. England, RSHA IV E 4, Stapo Tilsit III E 4.
6. **Cameron, Marian Eilene Mabel,** 15.9.96 London, England, RSHA IV A 1, IV E 4.
7. **Campbell, Angus,** 6.8.01 London, Beamter d. brit. Passport-Office Berlin, zuletzt Oslo, vermutl. England, RSHA IV E 4.
8. **Campbell, Anjus,** 10.2.61 Sorel/Canada, Rentier, England, Deckn. Finkelstein, Steen, RSHA IV E 4, Stapoleit Berlin.
9. **Camrose, Lord, William E. Berry,** 23.6.79, Eigentümer d. „Daily Telegraph Morning Post", Barrow Hills Long Crose, Surrey, London, 25 St. Dames Place, RSHA VI G 1.
10. **Mc. Cann, Mr.,** zuletzt Wallasey (Chesbire), 4 Meddoecroft Road (Täterkreis: Ignatz Petschek, RSHA III D 4.
11. **Gordon-Canning, Robert,** England, RSHA IV E 4.
12. **Capper, David.** 2.3.01 London, Lehrer, London, RSHA IV A 1.
13. **Cargill, John T.,** Direktor, London E. C. 2, Britannic House, Anglo-Iranian Oil Co., RSHA IV E 2.
14. **Carlton, W. J.,** London, RSHA VI G 1.
15. **Carner-Cohen, Mosco, Dr.,** geb. 1904, Dozent, London, RSHA III A 1.
16. **Caro, Walter Heinz Bubi Anton, Dr. phil.,** 19.6.09 Berlin, Deckn.: **Dr. Kurt Glanz,** Chemiker, vermutl. England (Am-Apparat), RSHA IV A 2.
17. **Carstens, Friedrich.** 25.8.03 Erfde, Geschäftsführer d. Firma Page Wate Farrer, London, vermutl. London, RSHA IV E 3, Stl. Karlsruhe.
18. **Carter, Henry,** Geistlicher, RSHA VI G 1.
19. **Carter-Bonham,** geb. **Asquith, Violet,** London W. 2, Glouchester Square, RSHA VI G 1.
20. **Mc. Carthy, G. M.,** Mittarb. d. „Sunday Referee Ld.", RSHA VI B 4.
21. **Carton, Maxwell,** Deckname: **Rogersen,** London, Vauxhall Bredge 173, RSHA IV E 4.
22. **Carvell, J. E. M.,** brit. Generalkonsul, England, RSHA IV E 4.
23. **Caslavka, Alois,** 9.9.99 Bömisch-Skalitz, Deckname: **Cizek,** ehem. Stabskapt. d. tschech. Heeres (ND.-Offizier), zuletzt: Prag-Device, Vevarska 49, vermutl. England, RSHA IV E 4, Stapoleit Prag.
24. **Caslavsky, Karl,** Deckname: **Rotenstein,** zuletzt: Olmütz, vermutl. England, RSHA IV E 4.
25. **Caspari, Johann, Dr.,** 10.2.88 Berlin, Landeshauptmann, vermutl. England, Deckname: **Weiß, Pick, Dr. Jakobi** (Schwarze Front), RSHA IV A 3.
26. **Cassau, Theodor,** 1884, Direktor, London, RSHA III A 1.
27. **de Castejar, Conde,** zuletzt: Lissabon, vermutl. England, RSHA IV E 4.
28. **Castelchomond, Graf de, O. Brien,** brit. Cpt., zuletzt: Kitzbühl, vermutl. England (Täterkreis: O.-Brien French), RSHA IV E 4.
29. **Catlin, George Edward Cordon,** 29.7.96, Politiker, London S. W 3, 19 Glebe Place, RSHA VI G 1.

*See notes on pages 266–272

30. **Catlin, geb. Brittain, Vera,** Journalistin, London SW 3, 19 Glove Place, RSHA VI G 1.
31. **Cazalet, Victor Alexander,** 27.12.96, Offizier, London W 1, 66 Grosvenor Street, RSHA VI G 1.
32. **Cebular, Alfred,** zuletzt: Novi Sad, vermutl. England, RSHA IV E 4.
33. **Cecil, Lord, Robert,** geb. 1864, London, 16 South Eaton Place, RSHA VI G 1.
34. **Le Cerep, Frederik,** 22.3.96 New York, Advokat, England (Kraftw.: AMO 269 GB), RSHA IV E 4.
35. **Chain, Ernst, Dr.,** 1906, zuletzt Oxford, RSHA III A 1.
36. **Chaloner, Thomas,** 18.8.99 Wiltshire, brit. Cpt., England, RSHA IV E 4.
* 37. **Chamberlain (Arthur) Neville,** 18.3.69, Politiker, ehemaliger Ministerpräsident, London S. W. 1, 10 Downing-Street, Westbourne, Edgbaston, Birmingham, RSHA II D 5 — VI G 1.
38. **Chamier, Fred William,** 8.4.76 Stanmore b. Syney, Dr. d. Staatswissenschaft, England, RSHA IV E 4.
39. **Chapman, Sir, Sidney John,** 29.1.88, Prof., London S. W. 7, The Imperial College, RSHA VI G 1.
40. **Charles, B.,** brit. Agentin, zuletzt: Brüssel, vermutl. England (Täterkreis: Josef Menneken), RSHA IV E 4.
41. **Charoux geborene Treibl, Margarete,** 25.5.95, Wien, Reisende, London, RSHA IV A 1.
42. **Charroux, Siegfried,** 15.10.96 Wien, Bildhauer, London W. 4, Riverside 51, British Grove, RSHA IV A 1, III A.
43. **Chidson, M. Reamy,** 13.4.93 London, Militärattaché, brit. Oberstleutn., zuletzt: Den Haag, vermutl. England (Kraftw.: HZ 36 927 GB.), RSHA IV E 4.
43a **China, John, Edwin,** 21.1.01 Bradlington, zuletzt: Kopenhagen, vermutl. England, RSHA IV E 4.
44. **Chingford, Charles,** Vertreter, London W. 1, Cambridge 119, RSHA IV E 4.
45. **Chountzarias, Andreas,** Arzt, zuletzt Athen, vermutl. England (Täterkreis: Crawford), RSHA IV E 4.
46. **Choiseul-Gouffier, Louis,** zuletzt: Kowno, vermutl. England (Täterkreis: Th. Camber), RSHA IV E 4, Stapo Tilsit.
47. **Chrisoston, Segrue John,** 7.1.84, Liverpool, Journalist, England, RSHA IV E 4.
47a **Christie,** brit. Nachrichtenoffizier, London, RSHA IV E 4.
48. **Church, Archibald George,** 1886 London, Major, Rostrevor, Seledon-Road, Sanderstreet, RSHA VI G 1.
49. **Churchill, Winston Spencer,** Ministerpräsident, Westerham/Kent, Chartwell Manor, RSHA VI A 1.
50. **Chwatal, Johann,** 16.8.92 Suchenthal, vermutl. England, RSHA IV A 1.
51. **Chwatal, Silvester,** 21.11.94 Suchenthal, vermutl. England, RSHA IV A 1.
52. **Cibulski, Gerhard,** 12.11.08 Barnim, London N. W. 2, 47 Blenheim Gardens, RSHA IV A 1.
53. **Cichy, Georg,** 30.9.14 Scharley/Ostoberschlesien, Obergefreiter, vermutl. England, RSHA IV E 5, Stapo Oppeln.
54. **Cigna, Vladimir,** 3.6.98 Olmütz, ehem. tschech. Stabscpt., London 59 Lexan Gardens, Kensington W. 8 (Täterkreis: Frantisek-Moravec), RSHA IV E 4, IV E 6.

*See notes on pages 266–272

55. **Citrine,** Sir, **Walter,** geb. 1887, Gèneralsekretär, London S.W.1, Smith Square, RSHA VI G 1.
56. **Cizek,** richtig **Caslavka,** RSHA IV E 4, Stapoleit Prag.
57. **Clark, Charles,** brit. Agent, zuletzt: Lüttich, vermutl. England (Täterkreis: Kurt Felsenthal), RSHA IV E 4.
58. **Clark, Herta,** geb. **Braunthal,** 1.2.87 Wien, vermutl. England, RSHA IV A 1.
59. **Clark, Hilda, Dr.,** RSHA VI G 1.
60. **Clark, John,** Sekretär, London E. C. 2, Britannic-House, Anglo-Iranian Oil Co., RSHA IV E 2.
61. **Clark, R. T.,** Schriftsteller, RSHA III A 5.
62. **Clark, William,** 13.8.85 London, Redakteur, London, RSHA IV A 1.
63. **Clarke, Eric Allan,** brit. Hauptmann, England, RSHA IV E 4.
64. **Clavering,** Sir, **Albert,** Deckname: **Closenburg,** Reklameagent, vermutl. England, RSHA VI G 1.
65. **Cleyg, Charles,** brit. Leutnant, zuletzt: Dänemark, vermutl. London (Täterkreis: John Hugill), RSHA IV E 4.
66. **Clutterbuk,** geb. **Kant, Lina,** 15.8.98 Pforzheim, London, Übersetzerin der ITF., RSHA IV A 1 b.
67. **Cnockaert, Martha,** verh. **Mckenna,** England, RSHA IV E 4.
68. **Coatts, W. P.,** Schriftsteller, vermutl. England, RSHA VI G 1.
69. **Corbett-Ashby,** Frau, Führerin der liberalen Partei, RSHA VI G 1.
* 70. **Cockburn, Claude,** 56 Jahre alt, Korrespondent, London S. W. 1, 34 Victoria Street, Deckname: **Frank Pitcain,** RSHA IV A 1, VI G 1.
71. **Cockerill, John,** brit. General, zuletzt: Antwerpen, vermutl. England, RSHA IV E 4.
72. **Cocks, Seymour,** 1882, Politiker, RSHA VI G 1.
73. **Coenen, Peter,** 6.3.88 Stettin, Gewerkschaftssekretär, vermutl. England, RSHA IV A 1.
74. **Cohen, Abraham, Dr.,** Rev., Wohnung: Birmingham 15, 2, Highfield Rd. Edg. Baston, RSHA II B 2.
75. **Cohen, Chapman,** Journalist, vermutl. England, RSHA VI G 1.
76. **Cohen, Israel,** Politiker, vermutl. England, London N. W. 2, 29 Pattison Road Child's Hill, RSHA VI G 1.
77. **Cohen-Carner, Mosco, Dr.,** 1904, Dozent. London, RSHA III A 1.
78. **Cohen, Lionel Leonard,** 1888 geb., Bankier, Wohnung: London W. 2, Orme Sq., 3, RSHA II B 2.
79. **Mac Cohen,** richtig **Makohim,** vermutl. England, RSHA IV D 3 a.
80. **Cohen, Reuss Emanuel,** 30.1.76 Langenberg, vermutl. England, RSHA IV A 1.
81. **Cohen, Robert Waley,** Verw.-Direktor, London E. C. 3, 22. St. Helen's Court, Shell Transport u. Trading Co., RSHA IV E 2.
82. **Cohn, Ernst, Prof.,** vermutl. London, RSHA III A 1.
83. **Cohn, Walter,** 5.9.01 Chemnitz, Kaufmann, England, RSHA IV A 1.
84. **Cole, George,** Lektor, Univ. Oxford, RSHA VI G 1.
85. **Collins, Norman,** Direktor, RSHA VI G 1.
86. **Collins,** brit. Agent, vermutl. England, RSHA IV E 4.
87. **Conze, Edward, Dr.,** 1869, Prof., London, RSHA III A. 1.
* 87a **Hinchley-Cook,** Colonel u. Leiter v. M. I. 5 (Military-Intelligence), London, RSHA IV E 4.
88. **Cooper, Alfred Duff,** Informationsminister, London S. W. 1, Chapel Street 34, RSHA II D 5, VI G 1.
89. **Cooper, F. D'Arcy,** Kaufmann, Westbridge Reigate Surrey, Unilever House, Blackfriars, RSHA IV E 2, III D 2.

*See notes on pages 266–272

90. **Cooper, Ivor,** Mitgl. d. brit. Rüstungsausschussses, London, The Old School House, Rudgewick (Sussex), RSHA III D 2.
91. **Copeland, Fred,** RSHA VI G 1.
92. **Coralfleet, Pierre,** richtig: **Frank Davison,** vermutl. England, RSHA IV E 4.
93. **Cormack, Georges,** Direktor, zuletzt Riga, vermutl. England, RSHA IV E 4.
94. **Coudenhove-Calerghi, Richard,** 17.11.94 Tokio, Schriftsteller, vermutl. England (Österr. Legitimist), RSHA IV A 3.
95. **Courboin,** brit. Agent, zuletzt Brüssel, vermutl. England, RSHA IV E 4.
* 96. **Coward, Noel,** vermutl. London, RSHA VI G 1.
97. **Mc. Cracken, C.,** 18.7.80 London, brit. Oberleutn., zuletzt Brüssel, vermutl. England, RSHA IV E 4.
97a **Craig, Noel,** 11.11.86, zuletzt Kopenhagen, vermutl. England, RSHA IV E 4.
98. **Cranborne, R.,** Unterstaatssekretär, England, RSHA VI G 1.
99. **Crawford, Janet,** 14.4.77, zuletzt Bukarest, vermutl. England, RSHA IV E 4.
100. **Crawford,** Leiter d. brit. ND., zuletzt Athen, vermutl. England, RSHA IV E 4.
101. **Creighton, T. M.,** vermutl. England (Täterkreis: Algernon Slade), RSHA IV E 4.
102. **Crick, Siegfried,** 40 Jahre alt, England, Deckname: **Krik,** RSHA IV E. 4.
103. **Cripps, Sir Stafford,** Botschafter in Moskau, London E. C. 4, 3 Elm Court, Temple, RSHA II B 4, VI G 1.
104. **Cromwell, William,** England, RSHA IV E 4.
105. **Crook,** Angehöriger des brit. ND., England, RSHA IV E 4.
106. **Crossfield, B. F.,** 1882, Direktor der New Chronicle, RSHA VI G 1.
107. **Crossman, R. H. S.,** RSHA VI G 1.
108. **Crowther, Goffrey,** 1907, Direktor, England, RSHA VI G 1.
109. **Crozier, W. P.,** Hauptschriftleiter, England, RSHA VI G 1.
110. **Cummings, A. J.,** Mitarb. d. News Chronicle, RSHA IV B 4, VI G 1.
111. **Cunard, Nancy,** England, RSHA VI G 1.
112. **Curitz, David Nathaniel,** Wohnung: Cardiff, Four Winds Pensisely Rd, RSHA II B 2.
113. **Curnbull, John,** England (Täterkreis: Stevens/Best), RSHA IV E 4.
114. **Curtis, Frederick F. C., Dr.,** Privatdozent, vermutl. England, RSHA III A 1.
115. **Czogalla, Stanislaus, Dr.,** 23.4.98 Zawade b. Ratibor, Vertreter, vermutl. England, RSHA IV E 5, Stapo Oppeln.
116. **Czoska, August,** 1.4.85 Soppischin, poln. Zollinspektor, vermutl. England, RSHA IV E 5, Stapo Graudenz.

*See notes on pages 266–272

1. **Dabrowski**, verh. **Runge, Maria**, 18.7.96 Zoznitzere, ehem. Sekretär i. ehem. poln. Konsulat, RSHA IV E 5.
2. **Dahlmann, Johann**, 2.8.94 Thorn, Bergmann, poln. ND-Agent, RSHA IV E 5.
3. **Dallas, George**, 1878, Labour-Abgeordneter, RSHA VI G 1.
4. **Dale-Herbst**, richtig **Dale-Long**, zuletzt: Brüssel, jetzt: vermutl. England, RSHA IV E 4.
5. **Dale-Long, Herbert**, Deckname: **Long, Lessing, Lane, Lennox**, 15.12.75 London, brit. Agent, vermutl. England, RSHA IV E 4.
6. **Dalton, Hugh**, Wirtschaftler (Universität London), RSHA VI G 1.
7. **Daly**, brit. Oberst, zuletzt: Lissabon, vermutl. England, RSHA IV E 4.
8. **Daly, T. D.**, Oberst. Mil.-Attaché, vermutl. England, RSHA IV E. 4.
9. **van Damm**, vermutl. England (Täterkreis: Albert Albseit), RSHA IV E 4.
10. **Damm**, Deserteur, brit. Agent, vermutl. England, RSHA IV E 4.
11. **Daniel, de Luce**, 8.6.11 USA, Journalist, vermutl. England (Täterkreis: Segrue Chrisoston), RSHA IV E 4.
12. **Danckwerts**, brit. Captain, Leiter d. Sp.-Abteilung, vermutl. England, RSHA IV E 4.
* 12a **Dansey, Claude**, brit. Oberstleutnant a. D., brit. Hauptagent, London, RSHA IV E 4.
13. **Darwin**, vermutl. England, RSHA IV E 4.
14. **Dassau, Robert**, Deckname: **Munki, Max**, 1.5.03 Hamburg, Arbeiter (Am-Apparat), RSHA IV A 2.
15. **Daube, David, Dr.**, geb. 1909, Assistent, Cambridge (Universität), Emigrant, RSHA III A 1.
16. **Davidson**, geb. **Boday, Käthe**, 25.8.05 Fürstenwalde, Sekretärin, vermutl. London, RSHA II A 1.
17. **Davidson, R.**, Verleger d. „News Chronicle", RSHA VI G.
18. **Davidson, Theodora**, vermutl. England (Täterkreis: Algernon Sladen), RSHA IV E 4.
19. **Davies, C. E.**, vermutl. London, Unilever House, Blackfriars, RSHA IV E 2.
20. **Davies, David, Lord**, Bank- u. Eisenbahndirektor (Völkerbundsbewegung, Einkreisungsfront gegen Deutschland), RSHA VI G 1.
21. **Davies, Randolph S.**, Schriftsteller, Verfasser d. Buches „Hitler's Spy Ring", RSHA IV B 4.
22. **Davies, Stephan**, 1886, Labourabgeordneter, Förderer der Einkreisungsfront, RSHA VI G 1.
23. **Davies**, brit. Captain u. N.-Agent, London NW 2, 54 Crewys Road Childs Hill, Golden Green, RSHA IV E 4.
24. **Davis**, zuletzt Riga, jetzt vermutl. England, brit. ND. Lettland, RSHA VI C 2.
25. **Davisohn-Spencer, Frank Ch.**, 10.8.89 Montabu, Rechtsanwalt, vermutlich England, RSHA IV E 4.
26. **Dawson, Horace Cortland**, 11.11.01 London, Ingenieur, zuletzt Berlin-Grunewald, vermutl. England, RSHA IV E 4, Stapoleit Berlin.
27. **Dawson of Penn, Lord**, Mitunterzeichner der engl. Rundfunkbotschaft an das deutsche Volk im Jahre 1939, RSHA VII G 1.
28. **Day, Donald**, USA-Staatsangehöriger, Vertreter der „Chicago Tribune", zuletzt Riga, brit. ND. Lettland, RSHA VII C 2.
29. **Day**, zuletzt Den Haag, vermutl. England (Täterkreis: Vyth), RSHA IV E 4.

30. **van Deep, brit.** Oberleutnant, vermutl. England, RSHA IV E 4.
31. **Deichmüller, Karl,** 3.11.79 Lichow, Musiker, Southampton, RSHA IV E 4.
32. **Delahaya, J. V.,** Führer der Labour-Party, RSHA VI G 1.
33. **Delmer, Sefton,** Pariser Vertreter d. „Daily Express", London, RSHA IV B 4.
34. **Demikowski, Stanislaus, Dr.,** brit. Agent, vermutl. England (Täterkreis: Fray Strong), RSHA IV E 4.
35. **Demmer, Aneta,** 1940: 24 Jahre, Journalistin, zuletzt Den Haag, vermutlich England (Täterkreis: Stevens/Best), RSHA IV E 4.
36. **Dengel, Georg,** 17.9.08 Marktheidenfeld, Seemann, zuletzt: Antwerpen, vermutl. England (Täterkreis: Waldemar Pötzsch), RSHA IV E 4.
37. **Dennys, Rodney,** zuletzt Den Haag, vermutl. England (Täterkreis: zu Putlitz), RSHA IV E 4.
38. **Derby (Lord Derby),** Mitunterzeichner der engl. Rundfunkbotschaft 1939, London, RSHA VII G 1.
39. **Derkow, Willi,** 17.11.06 Charlottenburg, Bankangestellter, vermutl. England, RSHA IV A 1.
40. **Dessauer, Marie, Dr.,** geb. 1901, Ass., London, Emigrant, RSHA III A 1.
41. **Detraz-Schweitzer, Alfred,** Bankprokurist, zuletzt Basel, vermutl. England, RSHA IV E 4, Stapoleit Karlsruhe.
42. **Deutsch, Adam, Dr.,** 1907, Ass., Edinburgh, Emigrant, RSHA III A 1.
43. **Deutsch, Julius, Dr.,** 2.2.84 Lackenbach, ehem. österr. Staatssekretär, vermutl. England (Arbeiter-Sport-Internationale), RSHA IV A 1.
44. **Deutsch, Oscar,** Birmingham 15, 5, Baston, Augustus Rd. Edg. RSHA II B 2.
45. **Deutsch, Walter, Dr.,** 1894, Privatdozent, vermutl. Universität Manchester, Emigrant, RSHA III A 1.
46. **Devereux, Roy,** vermutl. England (Täterkreis: Algernon Sladen), RSHA IV E 4.
46a **Dewald, Walter,** ehem. Pförtner d. brit. Gen.-Konsulats Rotterdam, zuletzt Rotterdam, vermutl. England (Täterkreis: Walter Ewald), RSHA IV E 4.
47. **Dewhurst, Norman,** 29.9.87 Southport, brit. ND.-Offizier, Schriftsteller, zuletzt Riga, jetzt London, RSHA IV E 4, VI C 2.
48. **Dey, W.,** brit. Agent, zuletzt Stockholm, vermutl. England, RSHA IV E 4.
49. **Diamond, A. S.,** London E. C. 4, 1 Temple Gardens, Temple, RSHA II B 2.
50. **Dible, brit.** Konsul, zuletzt: Amsterdam, vermutl. England (Täterkreis: Theo Hespers), RSHA IV E 4.
51. **Dick, Albin,** 24.4.13 Tiss, vermutl. England, RSHA IV A 1.
52. **Dick,** geb. **Horn, Lina,** 19.6.12 St. Joachimsthal, vermutl. England, RSHA IV A 1 b.
53. **Dick, Rudolf,** richtig: **Baron von Gerlach,** vermutl. England (Täterkreis: Stevens/Best), RSHA IV E 4.
54. **Dicken, Ellen,** ca. 29 Jahre, Krefeld, Kunstgewerbelehrerin, früher in Düsseldorf, vermutl. England, RSHA IV E 4.
55. **Dickinson, Baron,** 1859 geboren, Pazifist, RSHA VI G.
56. **Dickson, Alec,** Journalist, London SW, Struan-Wimbledon-Park, RSHA IV E 4, III 2, Stapo Reichenberg.

57. **Dickwell**, Deckn.: **Gaston Barbé**, brit. Agent, zuletzt Brüssel, vermutlich England (Täterkreis: Kurt Felsentahl), RSHA IV E 4.
58. **Spiegel-Diesenberg, Graf von, Felix**, 19.1.91 Iglau/Mähren, zuletzt Mißlitz, vermutl. England (Täterkreis: von Gerlach), RSHA IV E 4.
59. **Dietzschold, Kurt**, 9.1.88 Leipzig, Sägemüller, Bristol 8, Pembrok Road Clifton, RSHA IV A 1.
60. **Dijxhoorn, A. Q. H.**, früherer holl. Verteidigungsminister, zuletzt Den Haag, vermutl. England, RSHA III B.
61. **Dill, Erhard**, 28.4.10 Selb, Student, vermutl. England, RSHA IV A 1.
62. **Dill, Johann**, 25.6.87 Brand, Parteisekretär, RSHA IV A 1 b.
63. **van Dillen, H.**, brit. Agent, vermutl. England (Täterkreis: Waldemar Pötzsch), RSHA IV E 4.
64. **Dimanski, Hermann**, 16.11.10 Berlin, zuletzt Antwerpen, vermutl. England, RSHA IV E 4.
65. **Dinhorn, Ruth**, 1908 geb., vermutl. England (Täterkreis: Lukapello), RSHA IV E 4.
66. **Dirksen, Walter**, richtig: **Auerbach, Walter**, vermutl. England, RSHA IV A 1 b.
67. **van Dittmar**, zuletzt Rotterdam, vermutl. England, RSHA IV E 4.
68. **Dittmar**, ehem. russ. Leutnant, zuletzt Amerika, vermutl. England, RSHA IV E 4.
69. **Divish, Anna**, 3.5.02 Pilsen, Ehefrau des Alfred Frank, vermutl. England, RSHA IV E 4.
70. **Dix**, brit. Captain, früher Kopenhagen, vermutl. England, RSHA IV E 4.
71. **Dixen**, brit. Agent, vermutl. England, RSHA IV E 4.
72. **Dixey, Neville**, Antifaschist, Vorsitzender von Lloyds, Mitglied d. IPC u. Lib. P., RSHA VI G.
73. **Djordjewic, Dragi**, Holzhändler, zuletzt: Zagreb, vermutl. England (Täterkreis: Lukapello), RSHA IV E 4.
74. **Dlouhy, Dominik**, Großkaufmann, zuletzt: Zagreb, vermutl. England, RSHA IV E 4, III A, Stapo Graz.
75. **Doberer, Kurt**, 11.9.04 Nürnberg, Ingenieur, vermutl. England, RSHA IV A 1 b.
76. **Doberlet**, Radiohändler, brit. ND-Agent, zuletzt: Laibach, vermutl. England (Täterkreis: J. C. Ross), RSHA IV E 4.
77. **Doby**, brit. Captain, vermutl. England, RSHA IV E 4.
78. **Docharly**, London, White Hall (Täterkreis: Allan Graves), RSHA IV E 4.
79. **Dodds, Eric Robertson**, Professor, Oxford, Propagandist gegen Franco, Einkreisungsfront gegen Deutschland, RSHA VI G.
80. **Dörfler, Franz**, 13.4.03 Schwaderbach, vermutl. England, RSHA IV A 1 b.
81. **Dörin, F. P.**, Emigrant, RSHA VI G 1, II B 5.
82. **Döring, Friedrich**, 4.3.82 Tobertitz, Lehrer, vermutl. London, RSHA IV A 1.
83. **Dohrn, Nikolaus**, 28.6.06 Dresden, Schriftsteller, vermutl. England, österr. Legitimist, RSHA IV A 3.
84. **Dolivo, Myra (Irma)**, Musiklehrerin, zuletzt: Bukarest, vermutl. England (Täterkreis: Janet Crawford), RSHA IV E 4.
85. **Dolphin**, Major, Leiter brit. Mil. Sp. in Wiesbaden, vermutl. England, RSHA IV E 4.

85a Donald, Mac, James Richards, 21.1.81, brit. N.-Agent, zuletzt: Kopenhagen, vermutl. England, RSHA IV E 4.
86. Donaldson, richtig: Clement Arnold de Haas, zuletzt: Den Haag, vermutl. England, RSHA IV E 4.
87. van der Donk, Hector, brit. Leutnant, zuletzt: Brüssel, vermutl. England, RSHA IV E 4.
88. Donkers, Bernhard Franz, Deckname: Baalen,- 21.5.05 Duisburg, Arbeiter, zuletzt: Nymwegen, vermutl. England (Täterkreis: Pfaffhausen), RSHA IV E 4.
89. Donkers, Franz, 11.7.10 Duisburg, Händler/Arbeiter, zuletzt: Nymwegen, vermutl. England (Täterkreis: Pfaffhausen), RSHA IV E 4.
90. Donkers, Johanna Sofia, geb. Schleess, 18.6.06 Büderich, zuletzt: Nymwegen, vermutl. England (Täterkreis: Wilhelm Willemse), RSHA IV E 4.
91. Donkers, Kornelius, 5.10.75 Horsen, zuletzt: Duisburg-Wanheimerort, vermutl. England (Täterkreis: Wilhelm Willemse), RSHA IV E 4.
92. Donkers, Wilhelm, 2.4.12 Duisburg, zuletzt: Nymwegen, vermutl. England (Täterkreis: Wilhelm Willemse), RSHA IV E 4.
93. Donoghue, J. K., ehem. Mitglied der brit. Botschaft in Berlin, vermutl. England, RSHA IV E 4.
94. Doric, Vlado, Dr., brit. Agent, vermutl. England (Täterkreis: Lukapello), RSHA IV E 4.
95. Dostali-Möller, Rudolf, London W. C. 1, Bedford-Place 12, RSHA VI G 1.
96. Douglas, J., Journalist, Herausgeber kommunistischer Schriften, RSHA VI G.
97. Dowden, A. E., früherer brit. Vizekonsul, RSHA IV E 4.
98. Drage, Sir, Benjamin, London N. W. 3, 28 Eton Ave., RSHA II B 2.
99. Draper, B., vermutl. England, RSHA IV E 4.
100. Dresel, Karl, 18.2.87 Reitendorf, kommunistischer Senator, England, RSHA IV A 1.
101. Dresen, J. J. K., 19.3.92 Maastricht, Portier, zuletzt: Den Haag, vermutl. England (Täterkreis: Arthur Bastin), RSHA IV E 4.
102. Drobnik, Jerzy, Pole, Mitarbeiter der Schrift „Free Europe", vermutl. London, RSHA VI G 1.
103. Drtina, Prokop, Dr., Referent in der Kanzlei des Expräsidenten Benes, RSHA IV D 1 a.
104. Drucker, Peter, 1909, Prof., Dr., vermutl. London, Emigrant, RSHA III A 1.
105. Drummond, Lord, Deckname: Grove Spiro, vermutl. England, RSHA IV E 4.
106. Drummond, R. I. D. Alex, 12.3.79, brit. Fliegeroffizier, vermutl. England, RSHA IV E 4.
107. Dubicz, Charles, 2.6.92 Warschau, Major, poln. N.-Offizier, RSHA IV E 5, Stapo Danzig.
108. Dubie, vermutl. England, RSHA IV E 4.
109. Dubinski, D., vermutl. England (Täterkreis: H. Sneevliet), RSHA IV E 4.
110. Duchazek, Ivo, Dr., 27.2.13 Proßnitz, Redakteur, vermutl. England, RSHA IV E 4, Stapoleit Prag.
111. Rosenbaum-Ducomun, Vladimir, Rechtsanwalt, vermutl. England, RSHA IV E 4.
112. Noble-Dudley, Henry, 11.10.01 London, Direktor, vermutl. England, RSHA IV E 4.

113. **Duff, Charles,** Schriftleiter, vermutl. England, betrieb rotspanische Propaganda in England, RSHA VI G.
114. **Duff-Cooper, Alfred,** Informationsminister, England, RSHA VI G 1.
115. **Dukker, D.,** zuletzt: Antwerpen, vermutl. England (Täterkreis: Hermann Knüfken), RSHA IV E 4.
116. **Dulkeit, Erwin,** brit. Agent, zuletzt: Riga, vermutl. England, RSHA IV E 4, Stapoleit Hannover.
117. **Dumas,** brit. Agent, zuletzt: Brüssel, vermutl. England, RSHA IV E 4.
118. **Dumont,** Angehöriger des brit. N.-D., vermutl. England, RSHA IV E 4.
119. **Dumphy, Peddy,** brit. Offizier, vermutl. England, RSHA IV E 4.
120. **Dumpi,** Leiter eines brit. N.-Büros, vermutl. England, RSHA IV E 4.
121. **Duncan, Oliver,** Sir, London E. C. 2, 7/8 Princes Street (Täterkreis: Ignatz Petschek), RSHA III D 4.
* 122. **Dunkan-Sendys,** Abgeordneter, Schwiegersohn von Winston Churchill, RSHA VI G.
123. **Dunker, Karl, Dr.,** 1903, Ass., vermutl. London, Emigrant, RSHA III A 1.
124. **Dunderdale,** brit. Leutnant, vermutl. England (Täterkreis: Stevens/ Best.), RSHA IV E 4.
125. **Dunhan, A. P. R.,** brit. Agent, zuletzt Riga (brit. N.-D. Lettland), vermutl. England, RSHA IV E 4, VI C 2.
126. **Dunk, Edgar,** Direktor des Linksbuch-Clubs, Antifaschist, RSHA VI G.
127. **Dunstan, Mary,** Schriftstellerin, RSHA IV B 4.
128. **Durban, Edward Charles,** 27.3.91 Berningham, brit. Oberst, vermutl. England (Täterkreis: Lew Trofimow), RSHA IV E 4.
129. **Durward,** richtig **Porter,** Leiter d. sowj.-russ. Sp.-Abteilung, vermutl. England, RSHA IV E 4.
130. **Dutsh,** brit. Captain, vermutl. England, RSHA IV E 4.
131. **Dutt, Eric,** brit. Major, Leiter d. IS in Valencia, zuletzt: Valencia, vermutl. England, RSHA IV E 4.
132. **Dutt, Palme R.,** 15.4.93 (96) Cambridge, Journalist, London, Antifaschist, RSHA IVA 1, VI G.
133. **Dyks, Paul,** Deckn.: **Pavel Pawlowitsch,** brit. Oberst, vermutl. England, RSHA IV E 4.

*See notes on pages 266–272

1. **Eastermann, Alexander Levvey,** Journalist, London N.W.1, 15 Regent's Court, Hanover Gate, RSHA II B 2.
2. **Ebbutt, Norman,** Berl. Korresp. der Times, RSHA IV B 4 b.
3. **Ebeling, Hans, Dr.,** 2.9.97 Krefeld, Kaufmann, London (Täterkreis: Stevens/Best), RSHA IV E 4, IV B 1.
4. **van Eck, Baron,** Direktor, London E.C.5, St. Helens Court, RSHA IV E 2.
5. **Ecker, Fritz,** 5.3.92 Fürth i. W., England, RSHA IV A 1 b.
6. **Eden, Robert Anthony,** 12.6.97, Kriegsminister, London W.1, Fitzhardinge Str. 17, RSHA II D 5, VI G.
7. **Eden,** Chef d. Fa. Einkaufshaus für Kanada in Zürich, vermutl. England, RSHA IV E 4.
8. **Ederheimer A., Dr.,** Mitarbeiter d. „Merton", London, RSHA III D.
9. **Edmonds,** brit. Oberst, England, RSHA IV E 4.
10. **Edmondson,** brit. Vizekonsul, Dairen/Ostasien, vermutl. England (Täterkreis: Klingmüller), RSHA IV E 4, Stapo Köln.
11. **Edwards, Sir Charles,** Labour-Abgeordneter, RSHA VI G.
12. **Edwards, Hendrik,** richtiger Name: **Stein, Kurt,** 20.2.00 London, England, RSHA IV E 4.
13. **Edwards,** richtig **Moscow,** Leiter d. brit. ND. in Amsterdam, zuletzt: Amsterdam, vermutl. England, RSHA IV E 4.
14. **Eeman, Harald,** richtig **Watson,** dipl. Beamter, vermutl. England, brit. ND. in Lettland, RSHA VI C 2.
15. **Egemeier, Frieda,** Kent, RSHA IV E 4, Stapoleit Prag.
16. **Ehm, Franz,** 21.1.01 Zwodau, England, RSHA IV A 1.
17. **Ehrenfried, Daniel,** 3.9.81 (6.10.83) Gotzdowo/Mühle, Rennstallbesitzer, Prag, vermutl. England (Täterkreis: von Einem, Gerta, Luise), RSHA IV E 4.
18. **Eichelberg, L.,** Schriftsteller, Emigrant, Oxford, 159 Woodstock Road, RSHA II B 5.
19. **Eichler, Wilhelm,** 7.1.96 Berlin, Leiter des ISK., London, RSHA IV A 1 b.
20. **Eigler, Josef,** 22.8.04 Bärringen, Hope Wiew, Castleton, Derbyshire, RSHA IV A 1 b.
21. **op't'Einde,** Deckname: **van der Heide,** vermutl. England RSHA IV E 4.
22. **Einsenschitz, Robert, Dr.,** 1898, Emigrant, London, RSHA III A 1.
23. **Einstein, Alfred, Dr.,** 1880, Emigrant, London, RSHA III A 1.
24. **Einzig, Paul, Dr.,** Redakteur, RSHA III A 5, VI G.
25. **Merling-Eisenberg, Kurt,** 1899, Priv.-Doz., London, RSHA III A 1.
26. **Eisenberg, Margarethe,** verh. **Nußbaum,** 23.2.06 Wien, Den Haag, vermutl. England, RSHA IV E 4.
27. **Ekblom, Gustav,** 50—55 Jahre alt, Seemann, Stockholm, Köpmangaten 18, vermutl. England, RSHA IV E 4, III A 1, Stapo Hamburg.
28. **Ekrosher,** zuletzt: Kopenhagen, vermutl. England, RSHA IV E 4, Stapo Kiel.
29. **Eliot,** brit. N.-Agent, England, RSHA IV E 4.
30. **Elissen,** brit. Major, England, RSHA IV E 4.
31. **Ellermann, Sir, John Reeves,** 21.12.09, London W.1, South Audley Str., RSHA II B 2.
32. **Ellinger, Arthur,** Mitarb. d. „Merton", London, RSHA III D.
33. **Ellinger, Philipp, Dr.,** 1887, o. Prof., Emigrant, London, RSHA III A 1.
34. **Ellinger, Walter,** Mitarb. d. „Merton", vermutl. England, RSHA III D.

35. **Ellis, Eunice (Enris)**, 22.9.89 Cheffleld, brit. od. franz. Agentin, England, RSHA IV E 4.
36. **Ellis**, brit. Journalist, England, RSHA IV E 4.
37. **Ellwood, M.**, brit. Beamtin, England, RSHA IV E 4.
38. **Elsas, M. J.**, 1881, Dozent, Emigrant, London, RSHA III A 1.
39. **Eltrop, Rudolf**, 1.1.04 Hamm, Umwalzer, England, RSHA II A, Stapo Potsdam.
40. **Elvin, Herbert Henry**, RSHA VI G.
41. **van Emden, Fritz**, 1898, Kurator im Brit. Museum, Emigrant, London, RSHA III A 1.
42. **Emmering, A.**, richtig: **Vrinten**, 13.11.93 Loon op Zand, brit. N.-Agent, zuletzt: Rotterdam, vermutl. England (Täterkreis: Stevens-Best), RSHA IV E 4, Stapo Köln.
43. **Emonts, Karl**, 14.10.89 Eupen, Gewerkschaftssekretär, vermutl. England, RSHA IV A 1.
44. **Endt, Aloisia**, verh. **Meixner**, 14.3.05 Bärringen, Norfolk Falkenhamm, Thorpland Hall b. Miss Savnry, RSHA IV A 1 b.
45. **Enfreas**, brit. Hauptmann u. ND.-Offizier, England, RSHA IV E 4.
46. **Engel, Stefan, Dr.**, 1878, a. o. Prof., Emigrant, London, Great Ormonde Street, RSHA III A 1.
47. **Engelmann, Ludwig**, 24.3.03 Iserlohn, Heizer, England, Internierungslager, RSHA IV A 1.
48. **Engemann, Herbert**, 16.7.01 Berlin, Dipl.-Ing., vermutl. England, RSHA IV E 4.
49. **English**, brit. Cpt., vermutl. England, RSHA IV E 4.
50. **Enoc**, Mitarb. d. Chefs des brit. Nachrichtendienstes, vermutl. England (Täterkreis: Walter Oehme), RSHA IV E 4.
51. **Epstein, Fritz, Dr.**, 1898, Assistent, Emigrant, London, Univ., RSHA III A 1.
52. **Epstein, Jacob**, 1880 New York, Bildhauer, London S. W. 7, 18 Hydepark Gate, RSHA II B 2.
53. **Erban**, früh. Presseattaché d. tschech. Gesandtschaft, vermutl. England (Täterkreis: Stevens/Best), RSHA IV E 4.
54. **Erchmann, Erich**, vermutl. England (Täterkreis: Wilhelm Willemse), RSHA IV E 4.
55. **Erlanger, Richard**, Mitarb. d. Merton, London, RSHA III D.
56. **Ermi**, brit. Vizekonsul, zuletzt: Zagreb, vermutl. England, RSHA IV E 4, Stapo Graz.
57. **Ernst, Alois, Dr.**, Deckname: **Schwarz**, 8.11.01 Neurode, Schriftsteller, London, evtl. nach Schottland verzogen, RSHA IV A 3.
58. **Eschka, Hermann**, 3.3.88, Voigtsgrün, England, RSHA IV A 1 b.
59. **Eschka, Karl**, 15.7.82 Voigtsgrün, Leeds, RSHA IV A 1 b.
60. **Esser, Eugenie**, brit. Agentin, zuletzt: Riga, vermutl. England, RSHA IV E 4.
61. **Etherington-Smith, R. G. A.**, Botsch.-Sekr., England, RSHA IV E 4.
62. **Everett**, Motoreningenieur, London E. C. 2, Britannic House, RSHA IV E 2.
63. **Eves, H. B. Heath**, Direktor, London E. C. 2, Britannic House, RSHA IV E 2.
64. **Eving, Alfred**, England, RSHA IV E 4.
65. **Evingham**, brit. Captain, England, RSHA IV E 4.
66. **Ewert**, brit. General, England, RSHA IV E 4.
67. **Ewinger, Margarete**, geb. **Schenk**, Dr. phil., 23.3.81 Gotha, Sekretärin, England, RSHA IV E 4, Stapo Nürnberg.

68. **Ewings, Elisabeth,** 31.7.90 Brüssel, Konzertpianistin u. Sprachlehrerin, vermutl. England, RSHA IV E 4, S V 7, Stapoleit München.
69. **Ewoldt, Walter,** 20.11.05 Kiel, Deckname: **Papageien-Walter,** England (Südengland interniert), (Insel), RSHA IV A 1.
70. **Eyre,** chemaliger brit. Konsul in Holland, Revisor, London, Unilever Haus, RSHA IV E 4, IV E 2.

1. **Fabian, Dora,** geb. **Heinemann, Dr. phil.,** 28.5.01 Berlin, RSHA IV A 1 b.
1a **Fabius, H. A. C.,** General, Leiter d. holl. ND., vermutl. England, RSHA IV E 4.
2. **Fachreddin, Osman,** brit. Agent, vermutl. England, RSHA IV E 4.
3. **Fairholme, W. E.,** brit. Brigadegeneral, England, RSHA IV E 4.
4. **Fajans, Edgar, Dr.,** geb. 1911, Bristol (Univers.), Emigrant, RSHA III A 1.
5. **Falk, Werner, Dr.,** Dozent, geb. 1906 Oxford (Univers.), Emigrant, RSHA III A 1.
6. **Falk, Deserteur,** brit. Agent, vermutl. England, RSHA IV E 4.
7. **Fallowfield, Allgernon Gordon,** Vizekonsul, England, RSHA IV E 4.
8. **Falter, Alfred,** 25.7.80 Ropa b. Gorlice, Industrieller, Mitglied der poln. Emigrantenregierung in England, RSHA III B 15.
9. **Falter,** Mitglied d. poln. Nationalr., Stellvertr. d. Finanzmin., RSHA IV D 2.
10. **Fanshawe,** brit. Kommandeur, vermutl. England, RSHA IV E 4.
11. **Farell, John,** England (Täterkreis: Engemann), RSHA IV E 4.
12. **Farkas, Adalbert,** geb. 1906 Cambridge (Univers.), Emigrant, RSHA III A 1.
13. **Farlane, F. N. Mason Mac,** ehemaliger brit. Militärattaché in Berlin, vermutl. England, RSHA IV E 4.
14. **Featherton,** brit. Capitain, vermutl. in England, RSHA IV E 4.
15. **Fechner, Max,** 3.10.05 Charlottenburg, Gemälderestaurator (Am-Apparat), RSHA IV A 2.
16. **Feddersen, Fritz,** Deckname: **Fred Karlssen,** 10.9.14 Hamburg, Matrose, Emigrant, zuletzt Stockholm, vermutl. England, RSHA IV E 4, Stapoleit Hamburg.
17. **Feierabend, Ladislaus, Dr.,** 14.6.99 Kostelec, Staatsmin. d. csl. Auslandsregierung, Emigrant, RSHA IV D 1 a.
18. **Feilding, R. C.,** Oberst, London, Stoke House bei Slough (Täterkreis: Julius Petschek), RSHA III D 4.
19. **Feiler, Erich,** geb. 1882, a. o. Prof., Emigrant, London, RSHA III A 1.
20. **Feldmann, Egon,** 21.7.09 Hamburg, zuletzt Amsterdam, vermutl. England (Täterkreis: Karl Nihom), RSHA IV E 4, Stapoleit Münster.
21. **Felstead, S. Theodore,** Schriftsteller, RSHA IV B 4.
22. **Fenston, Joe,** 40 J. alt, brit. ND.-Agent, London 77, Ourtney-Court Maida Vale W. 9, RSHA IV E 4.
23. **Ferguson, C. H.,** London, Unilever Haus, Blackfriars, RSHA IV E 2.
24. **Fergusson, Mary,** Journalistin, RSHA VI G.
25. **Ferl, Gustav,** Deckn.: **Rachel Clerk,** 23.12.90 Gr. Ottersleben, ehem. SPD.-Parteisekr., vermutl. England (Sopade), RSHA IV A 1 b.
26. **Fern, Rose,** Hotelangestellte, Yokohama/Japan, vermutl. England, RSHA IV E 4.
27. **Feuchtwanger, Franz,** Deckname: **Hugo Boenecke,** 6.6.08 München, Student (Am-Apparat), RSHA IV A 2.
28. **Feuchtwanger, Lion,** 7.7.84 München, Schriftsteller, Emigrant, London W. C. 6, Henriette Street, RSHA VI G 1, II B 5.
29. **Feuermann, Emanuel,** Emigrant, London, RSHA III A 1.
30. **Fewster Arnold,** 6.3.12 Newcastle, Student, RSHA IV E 4, Stapoleit Stettin.
31. **Fichter, Oskar,** Deckname: **Oskar,** 30.1.98 Furtwangen/Baden, Steindrucker (Am-Apparat), RSHA IV A 2.
32. **Ficker, Hermann,** 4.10.93 Friedrichsreuth, RSHA IV A 1 b.
33. **Fildes, J. V.,** London, Unilever House, Blackfriars, RSHA IV E 2.

34. **Filipowlcz, Tytus,** Mitgl. d. poln. Nationalrates, RSHA IV D 2.
35. **Fillter, D. F. S.,** brit. Gen.-Konsul, vermutl. England (Täterkreis: Werner Aue), RSHA IV E 4.
36. **Fimmen, Edo (Edu),** 18.6.81 Amsterdam, Generalsekr. d. ITF., London (Täterkreis: Stevens/Best), RSHA IV E 4, IV A 1 b, IV A 5.
37. **Findley,** brit. ND.-Agent, RSHA IV E 4.
38. **Fink-Trier, Troels,** Zeitungsangestellter, zuletzt: Apenrade, vermutl. England (Täterkreis: Jens Dons), RSHA IV E 4, Stapo Kiel.
39. **Finkelstein, Anjus,** richtig **Campbell,** 10.2.61 Sorel/Kanada, Rentier, vermutl. England, RSHA IV E 4, Stapoleit Berlin.
40. **Firla, Gustav,** 1.7.00 Opama, Konsulatssekr., Pressereferent, RSHA IV E 5, Stapo Leipzig.
41. **Fischbach, Anton,** 14.7.99 Rotau, Osmondthorpe (Leedsg.), bei Rev. A. A. Hoskings, St. Philips, Vicarage, RSHA IV A 1.
42. **Fischer, Louis,** Mitarbeiter d. „Union d. demokratischen Kontrolle", RSHA VI G.
43. **Fischer, Marie,** 23.5.98 Elbogen, Barry (Glan), 17. Castel Street, RSHA IV A 1 b, Stapo Karlsbad.
44. **Fischer,** Mitarbeiter d. Militärattachés Kala, Emigrant, Jude, London, RSHA II B 5.
45. **Fischer,** RSHA VI G 1.
46. **Fischer,** brit. Feldwebel, vermutl. England, RSHA IV E 4.
47. **Fisher, William,** 14.8.96 Lodz, vermutl. England, RSHA IV E 4.
48. **Fisher,** Sergeant bei Scotland-Yard, vermutl. England, RSHA IV E 4.
49. **Fisher-Sarasin,** brit. Major, Leiter d. brit. Spionagebüros in Bern, vermutl. England, RSHA IV E 4.
50. **Fischgold, Harry, Dr.,** geb. 1903, Emigrant, Ass. am City Mental Hospital in Nottingham, RSHA III A 1.
50a **Fjedlgaar,** brit. N.-Agent, vermutl. England, RSHA IV E 4.
51. **Flack, Josef,** geb. 1901, vermutl. England, RSHA IV E 4, Stapo Brünn.
52. **Fleck, Karl,** 5.11.90 Sinbitz, vermutl. England, RSHA IV A 1 b.
53. **Fleck, Karl,** 5.12.90 Seibitz b. Teplitz, Sekr. d. Keramarbeiterverbandes, vermutl. England, RSHA II A, Stapo Karlsbad.
54. **Fleischhacker, Hans, Dr.,** geb. 1898, Ass., Emigrant, London, Maudsley Hospital, RSHA III A 1.
55. **Fleischmann, Karl,** 15.6.90 Wassersuppen, vermutl. England RSHA IV A 1 b.
56. **Fleischmann, Paul, Dr.,** geb. 1879, a. o. Prof., Emigrant, London, RSHA III A 1.
57. **Flening, Edward L.,** RSHA IV D 4.
58. **Flemming, Edward L.,** Schriftsteller, RSHA III A 5.
59. **Flesch-Brun, Hans,** Vorstandsmitglied d. „Freien deutschen Kulturliga in England", Emigrant, RSHA VI G 1, II B 5.
60. **Fletcher, Reginald,** geb. 1885, Offizier, Abgeordneter, RSHA VI G.
61. **Floid, Marguerite,** vermutl. England, RSHA IV E 4.
62. **Florent,** brit. Auftraggeber, vermutl. England (Täterkreis: Franzius Janssens), RSHA IV E 4.
63. **Flower, Clement,** 14.9.78 England, vermutl. England, RSHA IV E 4.
64. **Fodor, M. W.,** Schriftsteller, RSHA IV B 4, VI G 1.
65. **Förstel, Friedrich,** 19.2.99 Elektromonteur, richtig **Barthel, Alfred,** vermutl. England, RSHA IV A 2.
66. **Förster, Max, Dr.,** geb. 1869, o. Prof., Emigrant, New Haven, Yale Universität, RSHA III A 1.

67. **Fohrmann,** Nikolaus, Johannes, Präsident d. lux. Gewerkschaften, früher Luxemburg, vermutl. London, RSHA IV A 1 b.
68. **Follen, William J.,** Beamter d. brit. Konsulats in Panama, vermutl. England, RSHA IV E 4.
69. **Folley, Frank Edward,** Kapitän, ehemaliger Leiter d. brit. Paßbüros in Berlin, vermutl. England, RSHA IV E. 4.
70. **Fomferra, Heinrich,** 19.11.95 Essen-Schonnebeck, Deckname: **Franz,** Maurer (Am-Apparat), RSHA IV A 2.
71. **Foot, Dingle,** geb. 1905, Abgeordneter d. liberalen Partei, RSHA VI G 1.
72. **Footman, David,** London, 25 Collingham Place, RSHA IV E 4.
73. **Forbarth, A.,** Schriftsteller, RSHA IV B 4.
74. **Forbes, Dita,** 27.10.05 Düsseldorf, Erzieherin, vermutl. England (Täterkreis: Gustav Weber), RSHA IV E 4.
75. **Forbes, Ogilvie George,** 47 Jahre alt, Botschaftsrat, vermutl. England, RSHA IV E 4.
76. **Forbes,** Agent im brit. ND., vermutl. England (Täterkreis: Gustav Weber), RSHA IV E 4.
77. **Ford, Josef Alfred,** 26.7.64 Darlington, brit. Journalist, England, RSHA IV E 4.
78. **Foréne,** brit. Agent, England, RSHA IV E 4.
79. **Forester, W. B. C. W.,** brit. Vizekonsul, vermutl. England, RSHA IV E 4.
80. **Forst, Josef,** 01.7.95 Prag, ehem. tschech. Oberleutnant, London (Täterkreis: Frantisek Moravec), RSHA IV E 6.
81. **Forster, Edward Morgan,** geb. 1879, Schriftsteller, RSHA VI G 1.
82. **Forster, G.,** brit. Agent (Täterkreis: James Haymes), RSHA IV E 4.
83. **Forster-Arnold, William Edward,** politischer Schriftsteller, RSHA VI G 1.
84. **Fort (Forst), Josef,** 21.7.95 Ziskow, ehem. tschech. Stabskapitän, London, 53 Lexham Gardens Kensington W. 8, RSHA IV E 4.
85. **Foster-Anderson, G. Herbert,** 30.5.90 Liverpool, brit. Agent, zuletzt: Kaunas, vermutl. England (Täterkreis: Gregory Maundry), RSHA IV E 4.
86. **Foulds,** brit. Konsul i. Ostasien, vermutl. England (Täterkreis: Klingmüller), RSHA IV E 4.
87. **Fraenkel, Eduard, Dr.,** geb. 1888, o. Prof., Oxford (Universität), Emigrant, RSHA III A 1.
88. **Fraenkel, Ernst,** geb. 1886, a. Prof., Emigrant, London, RSHA III A 1.
89. **Fraenkel, Gottfried, Dr.,** geb. 1901, Priv.-Doz. u. Prof. d. Zoologie, Universität London, RSHA III A 1.
90. **Fränkel, Hermann, Dr.,** geb. 1888, a.-o. Prof. a. d. Stanford-Universität, Emigrant, RSHA III A 1.
91. **Franco,** brit. Konsul, zuletzt: Den Haag, vermutl. England, RSHA IV E 4.
92. **Frank, Alfred,** 3.6.97 Brüssel, ehemaliger Beamter d. British Paßport-Controll-Office, vermutl. England, RSHA IV E 4.
93. **Frank, Alois,** 3.6.97 Sobekurech, ehem. tschech. Major, London (Täterkreis: Frantisek Moravec), RSHA IV E 6.
94. **Frank, Karl, Dr.,** 01.5.93 Wien, Schriftsteller, Deckname: **Willi Müller,** vermutl. England, RSHA IV A 1.
95. **Frank, Kurt,** Angestellter, zuletzt: Den Haag, vermutl. England (Täterkreis: Stevens/Best), RSHA IV E 4.

96. **Frank, Steven,** 20.9.03 London, Sekretär i. brit. Paßbüro, zuletzt: Kopenhagen, vermutl. England, RSHA IV E 4, Stapo Kiel.
97. **Frank,** ehem. tschech. Major, London, 53 Lexham Gardens, Kensington W. 8, RSHA IV E 4.
98. **Franke, Ludwig,** richtig: **Kleine, Fritz,** 7.3.01 Apolda, RSHA IV E 4, Stapoleit Prag.
99. **Franke, Otto,** 15.9.77 Berlin-Neukölln, London, RSHA IV A 1.
100. **Frankel, Dau,** Abgeordneter der Labour Party, Jude, RSHA VI G 1.
101. **Frankenstein, George (Georg),** Schriftsteller, RSHA IV B 4.
102. **Frankenstein, Georg,** Baron, 18.3.78 Wien, London, RSHA VI G 1, II B 5.
103. **Franssen,** geb. **Gentsch, Elisabeth,** 1.9.91 Ruhla/Thür., zuletzt: Amsterdam, vermutl. England, RSHA IV E 4.
104. **Franssen, Gerhard,** 21.8.86 Bysen/Holland, zuletzt: Amsterdam, vermutl. England, RSHA IV E 4.
105. **Franssen, Leo,** zuletzt: Amsterdam, vermutl. England, RSHA IV E 4, Stapo Osnabrück.
106. **Franssen, Ruth,** 6.3.20 Dortmund, zuletzt: Amsterdam, vermutl. England, RSHA IV E 4, Stapo Lüneburg.
107. **Franssen, Theodor,** 22.6.92 Münster/W., Ing., Deckname: **de Jong, de Friessen, Broumer,** zuletzt: Amsterdam, vermutl. England, RSHA IV E 4.
108. **Fraser, Harold Dareton,** Deckname: **Geoffrey,** 8.10.89 Chicago, Berichterstatter d. Chicago Tribune, vermutl. England, RSHA IV E 4.
109. **Fraser, William,** stellvertretender Präsident, London, E. C. 2, Britannic House Anglo-Iranian Oil Co., RSHA IV E 2.
110. **Freemann-Horn,** Leiter der brit. Aluminium-Comp., London, RSHA IV E 4.
111. **de Fremery, August,** Deckname: **John,** 7.5.95 's Gravenhage, zuletzt: 's Gravenhage, vermutl. England (Täterkreis: Steven/Best), RSHA IV E 4.
112. **French, Marquis de Castelchomond,** O'Brien, brit. Agent, Kapitän, vermutl. England, RSHA IV E 4, Stapoleit München.
113. **French,** brit. Nachrichtenoffizier, vermutl. England (Täterkreis: Stevens/Best), RSHA IV E 4,
114. **Freud, Sigmund, Dr.,** Jude, 6.5.56 Freiburg (Mähren), London, RSHA II B 5.
115. **Freudenberg, Alexander,** 11.1.93 Colombo auf Ceylon, Kaufmann, vermutl. England, RSHA IV E 4.
116. **Freudenberg, Dr.,** ehem. Legationssekr., Emigrant, zuletzt: Berlin, jetzt: London, W. C. 1, 26, Bedford Way, RSHA VI G 1, II B 3, II B 5, VI H 3.
117. **Freudenberg, Frau,** London, W. C. 1, 26 Bedford Way, Jüdin, RSHA III 3, VI H 3.
118. **Freudenthal, Walter,** geb. 1893, Priv.-Doz., Emigrant, London, RSHA III A 1.
119. **Freund, Ernst, Dr.,** Prof., zuletzt: Wien, jetzt: London, RSHA VI G 1.
120. **Freund-Kahn, Otto,** Schriftsteller/Emigrant, London N. W. 6, 1 Fawley Road, RSHA II B 5.
121. **Freund, Richard,** Schriftsteller, RSHA III A 5.
122. **Freundlich, Herbert, Dr.,** geb. 1880, o. Prof., Emigrant, London (Universität), RSHA III A 1.

123. **Freyhan, Robert, Dr.,** geb. 1901, Prof., Emigrant, London (Universität), RSHA III A 1.
124. **Fricer, Alexander,** 3.5.94 Pilsen, ehem. tschech. Major, RSHA IV E 4, Stapoleit Prag.
125. **Fricke, Otto,** London, E. C. 6., Broadstreet Place, RSHA IV E 4.
126. **Friedberg, Curt,** geb. 1904, Assistent, Emigrant, vermutl. London, HSHA III A 1.
127. **Friediger, Karl,** 21.5.06 München, vermutl. England, RSHA IV A 3.
128. **Friedl, Karl,** 3.4.84 Auschowitz, England, RSHA IV A 1 b,
129. **Friedländer, Erich, Dr.,** geb. 1897, Assistent, Emigrant, zuletzt Berlin, vermutl. England, RSHA III A 1.
130. **Friedländer, Ernst,** 15.8.08 Posen, Ing., London. (Am-Apparat), RSHA IV A 2.
131. **Friedmann, Ernst Joseph, Dr.,** geb. 1877, a. Prof., Emigrant, Cambridge (Universität), RSHA III A 1.
132. **Friedmann, Hans,** 26.6.94 Berlin, Kaufmann, London, RSHA IV A 1.
133. **Friedmann, Dr.,** früherer tschech. Minister, Jude, zuletzt Prag, jetzt tschech. Gesandtsch. in London, RSHA VI G 1, II B 5.
134. **Friedrich, Gerhard,** 4.2.16 Graudenz, Dienstpflichtiger, London, RSHA V D 2 f.
135. **Friedrich, Josef,** 25.8.95 Orpur/Sudetengau, Tischler, Liverpool, RSHA IV A 1.
136. **Fries, Reeltje,** Vertr. d. brit. Fa. Royal Mail Steamship Comp., vermutl. England, RSHA IV E 4.
137. **Friess, Herbert Friedrich,** 30.6.09 Markneukirchen, Bekenntnispfarrer, St. Leonards-On Sea, Sussex/England, RSHA IV A 5 b.
138. **Friess** geb. **Volz, Hildegard Wilhelmine Elsa Margarete,** 3.7.07 Wüstegiersdorf/Schl., St. Leonards-On Sea Suxex/England, RSHA IV A 5 b.
139. **de Friessen, Theodor,** richtig **Theodor Franssen,** 22.6.92 Münster/ Westf., Ing.. zuletzt Amsterdam, vermutl. England, RSHA IV E 4.
140. **Frings, Josef,** Deckname: **Taxi-Frings,** 24.9.95 Vaals/Holland, Taxiunternehmer. zuletzt Vaals/Holland, vermutl. England (Täterkreis: Stevens/Best), RSHA IV E 4.
141. **Frinten, Adrianus Johannes Josephus,** richtig **Vrinten,** 13.11.93 Loon op Zand, brit. N.-Agent, zuletzt Rotterdam, vermutl. England (Täterkreis: Stevens/Best), RSHA IV E 4.
142. **Frischauer, Willi,** Schriftsteller, österr. Emigrant, vermutl. London, RSHA VI G 1, II B 5.
143. **Fritsch (Fryc), Franz.** 23.12.95 Prag, ehem. tschech. Stabskapitän, London 53. Lexham Gardens. Kensington W. 8, RSHA IV E 4.
144. **von Fritz, Kurt, Dr.,** geb. 1900, Priv.-Doz., Emigrant, Portland, Reed College, RSHA III A 1.
145. **Fröhlich, Hans,** 10.3.99 Johannisburg/Transvaal, vermutl. England, RSHA IV E 4.
146. **Fröhlich, Herbert, Dr.,** geb. 1905, Priv.-Doz., Emigrant, Bristol (Universität), RSHA III A 1.
147. **Frölich, Paul,** 7.8.84 Neusellerhausen, Redakteur, vermutl. England, RSHA IV A 1.
148. **Frommer, Leopold, Dr.,** geb. 1894, Assistent, Emigrant, London, RSHA III A 1.
149. **Fry, A. Ruth,** Schatzmeisterin d. Intern. Rates der Internationale der Kriegsdienstgegner, London, RSHA VI G 1.

150. **Fry, Magery Sarah,** geb. 1874, Direktorin d. Rundfunkgesellschaft, RSHA VI G 1.
151. **Fryč, Franz,** 23.12.95 Prag, ehem. tschech. Stabskap., London (Täterkreis: Frantisek Moravec), RSHA IV E 6.
152. **Fuchs, Hans J., Dr.,** geb. 1897, Assistent, Emigrant, London, RSHA III A 1.
153. **Fuchs, Martin, Dr.,** 26.9.03 Wien, franz. dipl. Beamter, vermutl. England (österr. Legitimisten), RSHA IV A 3.
154. **Fulham, Frank,** brit. Vizekonsul, RSHA IV E 4.
155. **Fullham, Francis,** 18.1.95 Crewe-Chechere, engl. Vizekonsul, vermutl. England (Täterkreis: C. E. King), RSHA IV E 4.
156. **Furmanek, Joseph,** 23.8.95 Betsche, Krs. Meseritz, Angestellter, poln. Offizier, RSHA IV E 5, Stapo Schneidemühl.

1 **Gaihede, Janus,** Kaufmann (Fischexportgeschäft), vermutl. England, RSHA IV E 4.
2. **Gainer, St. Clair D.,** 18.10.91 Thrapston, ehem. Brit. Gen.-Konsul in Wien, vermutl. England, RSHA IV E 4.
3. **de Gay,** verh. Rozier, London, RSHA IV E 4.
4. **Gallacher, William,** Dez. 1891 Paislay, Metallarbeiter, England, RSHA IV A 1, IV C 1.
5. **Gallienne, Wilfred Hansford,** brit. Gesandter in Estland, zuletzt: Reval, vermutl. England, RSHA VI C 2.
6. **Gamma-Stocker, Gustav,** 23.10.04 Zürich, Hotel-Sekretär, zuletzt: Zürich, vermutl. England, RSHA IV E 4, Stapoleit Karlsruhe.
7. **Gaposchkin, S. Till, Dr.,** Emigrant, Cambridge, RSHA III A 1.
8 **Garbutt, Reginald,** Schriftsteller, RSHA IV B 4.
9. **Garratt, Geoffrey, Theodor,** Journalist (Ztg. „Manchester Guardian"), RSHA VI G 1.
10. **Garston, Lancelot Cyril Brewster, Dr.,** 6.9.08 Bramley, England (Kraftw. GB. EYH. 270), RSHA IV E 4, Stapo Kiel.
11. **Gartner, Josef,** 17.7.88 Tachau, Süd-England, RSHA IV A 1.
12. **Garvin, James Louis,** 12.4.68, Dir. der Ztg. „Observer", London, RSHA IV B 4.
13. **de Gaulle,** ehemaliger französischer General, London RSHA VI G 1.
14. **Gawlina, Josef,** Bischof, Mitgl. d. poln. National-Rat, RSHA IV D 2..
15. **Gawronski, Sigismund (Zygmunt), Dr.,** Deckname: **Dr. Rawita-Gawronski,** 9.12.86 Genf, Handelsrat, Poln. Botsch. Berlin, RSHA IV E 5.
16. **de Gay** verh. gew. Rozier, Angestellte d. Fa. General Trading u. Shipping Co., London, RSHA IV E 4.
17. **de Geer, D. J.,** 14.12.70 Groningen, ehem. holl. Ministerpräsident, zuletzt: Den Haag, vermutl. England, RSHA III B.
18. **Geijsendorfer,** Flieger, England, RSHA III B.
19. **Gellert, Ernst,** 7.1.00 Hannover, vermutl. England, RSHA IV A 1.
20. **Gellert, Grete,** Ashot-Berks/London, RSHA III D.
21. **Gellert, Mitzi,** Mitarbeiterin d. Petscheks, Ashot-Berks, bei London, RSHA III D.
22. **Gellert, Oswald, Dr.,** Askot Berks b. London (Täterkreis: Julius Petschek), RSHA III D 4.
23. **Gemant, Andreas, Dr.,** 1895, Privatdozent, Emigrant, Oxford (Universität), RSHA III A 1.
24. **Gembalczyk, Anton,** 4.4.94 Wittkowitz, Büroangestellter, RSHA IV E 5, Stapo Troppau.
25. **Gems, Adolf,** 11.10.06 Eibenberg, Wilmslow, Provinz Cheshire, High. Bank-Fulschaw Park, RSHA IV A 1.
26. **Gentsch, Elisabeth,** verh. Franssen, 1.9.91 Ruhla/Thür., zuletzt: Amsterdam, vermutl. England, RSHA IV E 4.
27. **Gérard, Roger,** Deckname: **Leather, Henri Jean,** ND.-Agent, England, RSHA IV E 4.
28. **Gerards, Eugenie,** geb. **Meuter,** verw. **Lösch,** Ehefrau, früher Sittart/ Holl., vermutl. England (Täterkreis: Stovens/Best), RSHA E 4.
29. **Gerards, Josef Heinrich Arnold,** 19.3.89 Haarlem, holl. Oberleutn. d. R., zuletzt: Sittart/Holl., vermutl. England (Täterkreis: Stovens/ Best), RSHA IV E 4.
30. **Gerasimov, Georg,** 15.7.00 Odessa, vermutl. England, RSHA IV E 4.
31. **Gerbrandy, Pieter, Sjoerds,** 13.4.85 Goengamiedon, ehem. holl. Justizminister, England, RSHA III B.

32. von Gerlach, Baron, Rudolf, 13.7.86 Baden-Baden, Privatmann, Deckname: „Dick", vermutl. England (Täterkreis: Best/Stevens), RSHA
IV E 4.
33. Germens, brit. Major, England, RSHA IV E 4.
34. Gessner, Rudolf, Emigrant, London, RSHA VI G 1.
35. Geurts, Jakob, brit. Agent, zuletzt: Basel, vermutl. England, RSHA
IV E 4.
36. Gewlitsch, Serge, 9.11.92 Nikiforowka, ehem. russ. Rittmeister, vermutl. England, RSHA IV E 4.
37. Geyer, Kurt, Dr. phil., 19.11.91 Leipzig, vermutl. England, RSHA
IV A 1.
38. Geyer, Richard, 29.10.98 St. Joachimsthal, England, RSHA IV A 1.
39. Gibb, C., brit. Agent d. Secr. Service, zuletzt: Shanghai, vermutl.
England, RSHA IV E 4.
40. Gibbs, Philipp, Schriftsteller, RSHA IV B 4.
41. Gibbson, Harold C. L., 13.5.97 London, brit. Hauptmann, Major,
zuletzt: Prag, vermutl. England, RSHA IV E 4.
42. Gibson, Harald, brit. Agent, vermutl. England (Täterkreis: Borris
Sobinoff), RSHA IV E 4.
43. Gibson, England, Major, zuletzt: Libau, RSHA VI C 2.
44. Gibson, Korrespondent der Ztg. „Times", zuletzt: Bukarest, vermutl.
England, RSHA IV E 4.
45. Giddings, brit. Cpt., vermutl. England, RSHA IV E 4.
46. Giersch, Willi (Wilhelm), 14.7.01 Berlin, Maurer, RSHA IV A 2.
47. Giffey, England, Major, Sekr. an engl. Gesandtsch. in Reval, Chef
des Passport-Office, ND.-Agent, Freimaurer, zuletzt: Reval/Estl.,
vermutl. England RSHA IV E 4, VI C 2.
48. Gilbert, Simon, London EC 2, 47 Moorlane, RSHA II B 2.
49. Giles, G. C. T., Sekretär, RSHA VI G 1.
50. Gilewicz, Waclaw, 10.1.09 Maciegiew, Poln. Konsulatssekretär,
RSHA IV E 5.
51. Gillies, William, Mitgl. d. Unters.-Komm. London SW 1; Transport
House, Smith Square RSHA II B 4.
52. Gillies, Sekretär d. Labour-Party, London, Smith Square Transport
House, Trade Union, RSHA IV E 5.
53. Ginsberg, Morris, Prof., London WC 2, Houghton Street, RSHA II B 2.
54. Gintrowski, Waclaw, 26.9.94 Czempin, Elektromonteur, poln.-N. Agent,
RSHA IV E 5, Stapo Schneidemühl.
55. Girling, Charles John, brit. Vizekonsul, vermutl. England,
RSHA IV E 4.
56. Gittner, Franz, 4.11.97 Staab/Bez. Mies, Maurer, London, RSHA IV A 1.
57. Gladstone, Dorothy, Viscountess, Präsidentin, RSHA VI G 1.
58. Glanz, Kurt, Dr., richtig: Walter Caro, 19.6.09 Berlin, Dr. phil.,
Chemiker, vermutl. England. RSHA IV A 2.
59. Glaser, Ludwig, 4.3.93 Elm, Kreis Karlsbad, Bergmann, Neat-Inverness-
Schottland, RSHA IV A 1 b, Stapo Karlsbad.
60. Glenvil, Vizekonsul, vermutl. England, RSHA IV E 4.
61. Glöckner, Anton, 18.2.00 Trinksaifen, Edinburgh, RSHA IV A 1.
62. Glückauf, Eugen, Dr., 1906, Emigrant, London (Univers.), RSHA III A 1.
63. Glücksmann, Alfred, Dr., 1904, Assistent, Emigrant, Cambridge,
RSHA III A 1.
64. Glückstein, L. H., konservativer Abgeordneter, RSHA VI G 1.
65. Glückstein, Morris, Stadtrat, RSHA VI G 1.

66. **Godber, Frederick,** Verw.-Direktor, London E. C. 3, 22 St. Helens Court, Great St. Helen's (Shell Transport u. Trading Co.), RSHA IV E 2.
67. **Goder,** Fritz, 2.7.08 Grünberg, Schlosser, RSHA IV A 2.
68. **Godfrey,** verh. **Stevens, Moya,** 16.2.95 London, Schriftstellerin, London (Täterkreis: Stevens/Best), RSHA IV E 4.
69. **Götz, Martin, Dr. phil.,** 13.9.03 Nürnberg, Emigrant, London, RSHA IV A 1, III A 1.
70. **Götze, Albrecht, Dr.,** 1897, o. Prof., Emigrant, New Haven, Yale Universität, RSHA III A 1.
71. **Gold, Barbara,** RSHA VI G 1.
72. **Goldsmith, Cecil C.,** chem. Lehrer, London, RSHA IV E 4.
73. **Goldsmith,** engl. Major, Direktor, vermutl. England (Täterkreis: Hans Schönfeld), RSHA IV E 4.
74. **Gollancz, Ruth,** Leiterin des Linksbuch-Clubs, London, 14 Henrietta Street, RSHA VI G 1.
75. **Gollancz, Viktor,** 1893, Verleger, London, 14 Henrietta Street, RSHA VI G 1, IV B 4.
76. **von Goissenau Arnold, Vieth,** Deckname: **Ludwig Renn,** 22.4.89 Dresden, Polizeioberleutnant a. D., RSHA IV A 2.
77. **Golton, Mary,** vermutl. Agentin d. brit.N.-D., Liverpool, RSHA IV E 4.
78. **Gomolla, Karl,** 7.11.16 Burghof, Flieger, RSHA IV E 5.
79. **Gooch, George Peabody,** geboren 1873, Historiker, London W. 8, 76 Campden Hill Road, RSHA VI G 1.
80. **Goodall, Dora,** London, S. W. 4, The Old Corner House, Paradies Road, RSHA IV A 1.
81. **Goodmann, Paul,** London N. W. 11, Hatikvah The Rich Way, RSHA II B 2.
82. **Goossenaerts, Miel,** zuletzt: Brüssel, vermutl. England, RSHA IV E 4.
83. **Gordon-Canning, Robert,** RSHA IV E 4.
84. **Gostynski, Erich, Dr.,** 1904, Emigrant, Manchester, RSHA III A 1.
85. **Gotelee, Emily,** 1.8.14 Medstead/England, Sprachlehrerin, vermutl. England, RSHA IV E 4.
86. **Gottfried, Nelly Katharina,** 7.7.02 Stolberg, zuletzt Holland, vermutl. England, RSHA IV E 4.
87. **Gottfurcht, Fritz,** Emigrant, London, RSHA VI G 1.
88. **Gottfurcht, Hans,** 7.2.96 Berlin, Handlungsgehilfe, RSHA IV A 1 b.
89. **Gotthelf, Herta,** Schriftstellerin, Emigrantin, London W. 2, 120 Sussex Gardens, RSHA II B 5.
90. **Gouffier-Choiseul, Louis,** zuletzt: Kowno, vermutl. England (Täterkreis: Th. Camber), RSHA IV E 4, Stapo Tilsit.
91. **Gough, Fritz Herbert Charles Gerald,** 20.12.99 London, brit. Kolonialbeamter, Nevin, Northwales, Gosse Chliff/Engl., Kraftw. CHU 64 GB, RSHA IV E 4.
92. **Gount, Reginald Gye,** brit. Admiral a. D., Mitarbeiter d. Intelligence Service, RSHA IV E 4.
93. **Grabowski, Felix,** 19.11.05 Culmsee, Poln. Deserteur, RSHA IV E 5, Stapo Schneidemühl.
94. **Grabowski, Jan (Johann),** Deckname: **Lamkowski,** 26.1.88 Lessen, Kr. Graudenz, Poln. N.-Offz., RSHA IV E 5, Stapo Graudenz.
95. **Gräf, Hugo,** 10.10.92 Rehstädt, Schlosser, Sekretär, London, RSHA II A 1.
96. **Graetzer, Rosa,** 23.5.99 Berlin, Angestellte, London, RSHA IV A 1.
97. **Graffy, J. A.,** chem. Kriegsgefangener, Essex/Engld., 95 Devon Road Barking, RSHA IV E 4.

98. **Graham, A.,** Lord, Beauftragter der Petschek-Gruppe, Woodbridge Suffolk, RSHA III D.
99. **Graham, Ronald,** Priv.-Detektiv, London, RSHA IV E 4.
100. **Gralinsky, Justizm.,** Mitgl. d. poln. Nation.-Rates, RSHA IV D 2.
101. **Grant, Leiter der Sabot.** Abtlg. des S. I. S. i. London, (Täterkreis: Stevens/Best), RSHA IV E 4.
102. **Grant, Leslin Remvik,** 8.1.93, brit. Cpt., vermutl. England, RSHA IV E 4.
103. **Graves, Allan,** 19.8.91 New Ross/Engl., Attaché d. brit. Botsch., Dublin, 44 Sluphens Green, RSHA IV E 4.
104. **Gray, Margarete,** Gesellschafterin, zuletzt: Paris, vermutl. England, RSHA IV E 4.
105. **Grecgor,** Übersetzer, zuletzt: Yokohama/Jap., vermutl. England, RSHA IV E 4.
106. **Green,** etwa 57 Jahre alt, brit. ND.-Agentin, RSHA IV E 4.
107. **Greenberg, Ivan Marion,** London E. C. 2, 47/49 Moor Lane, RSHA II B 2.
108. **Greenhalgh, H. R.,** London, Unilever House, Blackfriars, RSHA IV E 2.
109. **Greenwood, Arthur,** 1880, Minister, London S. W. 1, 28 Old Queen Street, RSHA VI G 1.
110. **Gregory, J. D.,** Schriftsteller, RSHA IV B 4.
111. **Greif, Walter,** 30.6.11 Wien, Ingenieur, RSHA IV A 2.
112. **Grenfeld, A. D. Thomas,** 14.6.69 St. Ives, engl. Major, England, RSHA IV A 1.
113. **Grenson, William,** brit. ND.-Offizier, vermutl. England, RSHA IV E 4.
114. **Grigg, Edward,** RSHA VI G 1.
115. **Gronenberg, Elsa,** 4.1.09 Königsberg, Stenotypistin, vermutl. England, RSHA IV A 1.
116. **Gross, Fabius, Dr.,** 1906, Assistent, Emigrant, Plymouth, RSHA III A 1.
117. **Gross, Fritz,** Schriftsteller, Emigrant, London W. C. 1, 3 Regent Square, RSHA II B 5.
118. **Gross, Emil,** 6.8.04 Bielefeld, vermutl. England, RSHA IV A 1.
119. **Gross-Mayer, Willy, Dr.,** 1889, a. o. Prof., Emigrant, London, Maudsley Hospital, RSHA III A 1.
120. **Gross, Wilhelm, Dr.,** 1883, o. Prof., Emigrant, zuletzt: Breslau, RSHA III A 1.
121. **Großheim, Emil,** 24.5.80 Essen-Borbeck, Zeitungshändler, England, RSHA IV A 3.
122. **Grossmann, Henryk, Dr.,** a. o. Professor, 1881, Emigrant, London, RSHA III A 1.
123. **Grossmann, Kurt,** 21.5.97 Berlin, Präsident der deutschen Liga für Menschenrechte, vermutl. England, RSHA IV A 1.
124. **Grove-Spiro, Stanley,** Deckname: **Lord Drumond, George Saville,** 18.1.00 Cap Town/S.-Afrika, ehemaliger engl. Fliegerleutnant, Kaufmann, Bankier, Makler, London-Kensington, W. 8, Cottes more Gardens 18, Büro: London V., Suffolk-Street, Pall-Mall S. W. 1, RSHA IV E 4.
125. **Grüneberg, Hans, Dr.,** 1907, Assistent, Emigrant, London, RSHA III A 1.
126. **Grüner, H. E.,** 1916: 28 Jahre alt, brit. Agent, vermutl. England, RSHA IV E 4.
127. **Grünfeld, Hans,** 25.5.99 Neudorf, Student, RSHA IV A 2.

128. **Grunov, Heinrich,** 15.8.00 Schweinfurt, richtig: **Friedrich Beer,** Schriftsteller, England, RSHA IV A 3.
129. **Grunwald, Heinz,** 3.1.03 Friedenau, London 170, Goswell-Road C. 1, RSHA IV A 1.
130. **Gruschwitz, Max,** 9.10.92 Breslau, Redakteur, England, RSHA IV A 3.
131. **Grynling, James,** 27.11.99 Stammvove/Engl., Privatier, vermutl. England, RSHA IV E 4.
132. **Grzonka, Maria,** Deckname: **Keiwitz, Helene,** 6.11.97 Heydebreck O. S., RSHA IV E 5, Stapo Oppeln.
133. **Guedalla, Herbert,** RSHA VI G 1.
134. **Günther, August,** vermutl. England, RSHA IV E 4.
135. **Gunther, John,** Schriftsteller, RSHA IV B 4.
136. **Gupta, Dilip Kumar,** 9.7.07 Kalkutta, Sekretär, England, RSHA IV A 1.
137. **Gutkind, Curt Sigmar, Dr.,** 1896, a. o. Prof., Emigrant, London, Bedfort College, RSHA III A 1.
138. **Gutmann,** vermutl. England (Täterkreis: Stevens/Best), RSHA IV E 4.
139. **Guttmann, Bernhard,** Schriftsteller, Emigrant, Hindhead (Surrey), Windwhistle Grayshott, RSHA II B 5.
140. **Guttmann, Erich, Dr.,** 7.2.80 Berlin, Arzt, England, RSHA V C 3 c.
141. **Guttmann, Erich, Dr.,** 1896, Priv.-Dozent, Emigrant, London, Maudsley Hospital, RSHA III A 1.

1. **de Haas, Clement Arnold,** zuletzt: Den Haag, vermutl. England, RSHA IV E 4.
2. **de Haas,** 5.6.11 Uckel, zuletzt: Den Haag, vermutl. England, RSHA IV E 4.
3. **Habsburg, Erzherzog von, Robert,** 1915 geb., London, RSHA VI G 1, II B 5.
4. **Hadke,** brit. Agent, RSHA IV E 4.
5. **Haefner, Victor,** 18.5.96 Brenden, Bez. Waldshut, Oberltn. a. D., Flugzeugf., London W. 2, 24 Norfolk-Square, RSHA IV E 3, Stapoleit Stuttgart.
6. **Hahn, Karl,** 27.3.09 Hannover, früh. KPD-Funktionär, zuletzt: Amsterdam, vermutl. Engl., RSHA IV E 4.
7. **Haide, Paul,** 3.10.79 Hohenstein-Ernsttbal, kaufm. Angest., RSHA IV A 1 b.
8. **Hakin, Wally,** j., brit. Agentin, RSHA IV E 4.
9. **Haldane, Charlotte,** RSHA VI G 1.
10. **Haldane, John B. S.,** Prof., geb. 5.11.92, RSHA VI G 1.
11. **Halder, richtig Strauß, Berthold, Dr.,** brit. Agent, zuletzt: Den Haag, vermutl. England, RSHA IV E 4.
12. **Halevy, Elazar,** London E. W. 2, 32 Sarre Road, RSHA II B 2.
13. **Halford, F. L.,** Generalmanager, Wohng.: London E. O. 3, St. Helens Court, Shell-Mex and B. P. Ltd., RSHA IV E 2.
14. **Halifax, Viscount Edwart Frederick,** Lindley Wood, 16.4.81, Politiker, London SW 1, 88 Eaton Square, u. Garrowby York u. Hickleton Hall, Doncaster, RSHA II D 5.
15. **Hall, King,** Schriftsteller, RSHA IV B 4.
16. **Sir Hall, Reginald,** ehem. Leiter d. ND. d. engl. Admiralität (Täterkreis: Rintelen), RSHA IV E 4.
17. **Hall, Hatton,** brit. Major, brit. ND.-Offizier, RSHA IV E 4.
18. **Hall, Lady,** RSHA VI G 1.
19. **Haller,** polit. Org. u. Prop., Mitgl. d. poln. Reg., RSHA IV D 2.
20. **Hamacher, Hermann,** 28.1.86 Süchteln, RSHA IV A 1.
21. **Hamburger, Richard, Dr.,** a. o. Prof., 1884 geb., Priv.-Praxis in London, Emigrant, RSHA III A 1.
22. **Hamer, Fritz,** 10.10.00 Klenzau, Masch.-Schlosser (Am-Apparat), RSHA IV A 2.
23. **Hamilton, Gerald,** 1.11.90 Schanghai, RSHA IV A 1.
24. **von Hammerstein, Abraham Chaim,** 1.10.95 Lodz, N-Agent, Deckname: **Margullis,** RSHA IV E 5, Stapoleit Danzig.
25. **Hammerstein, Reeder,** zuletzt Holland, vermutl. England, RSHA III B.
26. **Hammon, John,** 31.12.01 London, Angestellter, RSHA IV A 1 b.
27. **Hampel, Franz,** 12.2.07 Karbitz, Redakteur, RSHA IV A 1.
28. **Hampl, Marie,** 27.4.95 Tachau, Wohng.: Margate/Kent, RSHA IV A 1 b.
29. **Hänsel, Jude,** Mitinh. d. Fa. Hänsel u. Schmitt, London SW. 1, 13 Viktoria-Street, RSHA IV E 4.
30. **Hanfstaengl, Ernst, Dr.,** 11.2.87 München, Wohng.: London, 28. Gunterstone Road W. 14, West Kensington, RSHA IV C 5.
31. **Hanisch, Franz,** 9.7.99 Klösterle, Wohng.: New Field-Hall, Bels-Bust bei Kipton/York, RSHA IV A 1 b
* 31a **Hankey, Sir,** brit. ND.-Agent, England, RSHA IV E 4.
32. **Hans, Heinrich,** 25.4.15 Zerbau/Schles., ehem. Schütze I. R. 87, zuletzt: Belgien, vermutl. England, RSHA IV E 4, Stapo Aachen.
33. **Harand, Irene,** Schriftstellerin, Wohng.: London, RSHA VI G 1, II B 5.

*See notes on pages 266–272

34. **Harewood, Earl of, Henry George Ch.** (Loscelles), 9.9.82, Wohng.: London, 32 Green Street, RSHA VI G 1.
35. **Harford, Lionel Wilfred,** zuletzt: Riga, vermutl. England, engl. ND.-Lettland), RSHA VI C 2.
36. **Harke, Hermann,** 29.6.86 Leopoldshall, ehem. Gewerkschaftssekr., RSHA IV A 1.
37. **Harle, Edwin,** brit. Vizekonsul (Täterkreis: Renald Panton), RSHA IV E 4.
38. **Harmann, Kathleen,** Wohng.: London, 22 Lauderdale (Täterkreis: Siegfried Wreszynsky), RSHA IV E 4.
39. **Harmar, Leslie,** Inh. d. Fa. Binder Hamlin, zuletzt: Belgrad, vermutl. England, RSHA IV E 4.
40. **Harms, Otto Gustav Ernst,** 17.11.92 Hamburg, brit. Agent, zuletzt: Amsterdam, vermutl. England (Täterkreis: Theodor Franssen), RSHA IV E 4.
41. **Harnier, Maria,** verh. **Roweck,** 23.10.90 Maasmünster, zuletzt: Holland, vermutl. England, RSHA IV E 4.
42. **Harper, Mac,** 21.9.94 Gloucester, brit. Major, RSHA IV E 4, Stapo Kiel.
43. **Harris,** Sir, **Percy, Alfred,** geb. 1876, RSHA VI G 1.
44. **Harris, Pincus,** London N. W. 2, 149 Anson Road, RSHA II B 2.
45. **Harrison, G. W.,** Botschaftssekr. d. brit. Botschaft in Berlin, RSHA IV E 4.
46. **Harrison, Hubert,** 28.11.98 Walsall, Journalist, RSHA IV E 4, Stapo Graz.
47. **Harting, A.,** Wohng.: London, Unilever House, Blackfriars, RSHA IV E 2.
48. **Hartland, L. H.,** Wohng.: London, Unilever House, Blackfriars, RSHA IV E 2.
49. **Hartmann, Erna,** 23.4.96 Hamburg, Redaktionssekr., RSHA IV A 1 b.
50. **Hartmann, Hans,** 17.2.07 Biederitz, Brauer, London, S. W. 1, Cramer, Court Sloane, Avenue Chelsea, RSHA IV E 4, Stapoleit Magdeburg.
51. **Hartner, Willy, Dr.,** 1905 geb., Dozent, Cambridge, Harvard-Universität, Emigrant, RSHA III A 1.
52. **Harvey, John,** 2.7.10 Vindes, zuletzt: Preßburg, vermutl. England, RSHA IV E 4.
53. **Harwood,** Kaufmann, zuletzt: Reval, vermutl. England, (engl. ND.-Estland), RSHA VI C 2.
54. **Hasselbring, Heinrich,** 14.3.99 Holdenstedt, Forstarb. (Am-Apparat), RSHA IV A 2.
55. **Hasting,** Diener des Stevens (Täterkreis: Stevens/Best), RSHA IV E 4.
56. **Hatton-Hall,** brit. Major, brit. ND.-Offizier, RSHA IV E 4.
57. **Hauck, Walter,** 5.6.88 Steinau, Vertreter, London W. 2, Park West, Etgwareroad (Schwarze Front), RSHA IV A 3.
58. **Haunzwickel, C.** (Täterkreis: H. Sneevliet), RSHA IV E 4.
59. **Hauptmann Eduard (Edward),** 7.2.04 Zgier, poln. N.-Offizier, RSHA IV E 5, Stapoleit Danzig.
60. **van Haute, J.,** brit. Konsul, zuletzt: Amsterdam, vermutl. England, RSHA IV E 4.
61. **Hawkins,** ehem. Poln. Kapitän, Mitarbeiter im brit. ND., zuletzt: Windhuk/Südwestafrika, vermutl. England, RSHA IV E 4.
62. **Hay, August,** 12.5.97 Dudweiler/Saar, Bergarbeiter (Am-Apparat), RSHA IV A 2.
63. **Hay, Howard, Georges,** brit. Oberstl. i. Gen.-Stab, RSHA IV E 4.

64. **Hay, Dr.,** brit. Militärattaché, RSHA IV E 4.
65. **Hayday, Arthur,** 1869 geb., RSHA VI G 1.
66. **Haywood,** Colonel, brit. Botschafter, RSHA IV E 4.
67. **Head, Georges,** 17.10.10, Bergbauing., RSHA IV E 4.
68. **Hearn, A. C.,** Direktor, Wohng.: London E. C. 2, Britannic House, Anglo-Iranian-Oil-Co., RSHA IV E 2.
69. **Hearson, Glynn,** 31.10.02 Shanghai, Commander d. brit. Armee, RSHA IV E 4.
70. **Heartfield, John,** 1891 geb., Karikaturist, richtig **Herzfeld, Helmut,** RSHA VI G 1, III A 5.
71. **Heatcote-Quechterlone, Tomas Alexander,** brit. Kapit., zuletzt: Esbjerg/Dänemark, vermutl. Engl. (Täterkreis: John Hugill), RSHA IV E 4, Stapo Kiel.
72. **Heaton-Armstrong, William Duncan Francis,** 29.9.86 Veldes/Jugosl., London, Pall Mall (C. o. Lloyds Bank), RSHA IV E 4.
73. **Hecht,** Hauptmann, Wohng.: London, RSHA IV A 3 a.
74. **Heckmann, Gustav,** 22.4.98 Voerde-Niederrhein, Studienassessor, RSHA IV A 1.
75. **Hedley, Snowden,** Inh. einer Autorep.-Werkst., zuletzt: Sofia, vermutl. Engl., RSHA IV E 4.
76. **Heger, Josef,** 21.7.07 Weipert, Wohnort: Goldsborough, Yorkshire, RSHA IV A 1 b.
77. **Heichelheim, Fritz, Dr.,** 1901 geb., Privatdozent, Wohng.: Cambridge, Emigrant, RSHA III A 1.
78. **van der Heide,** richtig: op't'Einde, (holl. St.-A.), RSHA IV E 4.
79. **Heidelberger, Rudolf,** 6.5.01 Trinksaifen, Wohng.: Beech Mount, Selattyn Oswestry Salop, RSHA IV A 1 b.
80. **Heidler, Johann,** 29.12.03 Neudeck, RSHA IV A 1 b.
81. **Heilbronn, Hans-L., Dr.,** 1908 geb., Assistent, Cambridge (Univers.), Emigrant, RSHA III A 1.
82. **Heilbuth, George Henry,** London SW 1, 20 Suffolk-Street, RSHA II B 2.
83. **Heilfort, Dora Magdalene,** 9.12.03 Chemnitz, Sekretärin, Wohng.: verm. Short Hills, Sandy Lodge, Road Moor-Park Herts, RSHA II A, Stapo Chemnitz.
84. **Heimann, Betty, Dr.,** 1888 geb., a. o. Prof., London (Universität), Emigrant, RSHA III A 1.
85. **Heimann, Fritz, Dr.,** 3.2.09 Schöneberg, Jurist (Schwarze Front), RSHA IV A 3.
86. **Heiman, Paula Gertrud,** geb. **Klatzko, Dr. med.,** 3.2.99 Danzig, RSHA IV A 1.
87. **Hein, Josef,** 9.12.03 Ottowitz, Wohng.: Brook, Guildford-Surrey, RSHA IV A 1 b.
88. **Heine, Friedrich (Fritz),** 6.12.04 Hannover, RSHA IV A 1.
89. **Heinemann, Fritz, Dr.,** 1889 geb., a. o. Prof., Privatdozent, Emigrant, RSHA III A 1.
90. **Heinrich, Günther Eberhard,** 30.10.14 Berlin, Dienstpfl., London W. 1, 63 Grafton Way, RSHA IV E 4, V-D 2 f.
91. **Heinsdorf-Lewinson, Helene,** geb. **Heinsdorf,** 18.2.99 Gora-Calwarja, Journalistin, RSHA IV E 5.
92. **Heintze, Joseph,** etwa 43 J., Grenzw.-Beamter, RSHA IV E 5, Stapo Liegnitz.
93. **Heiser, Herbert,** 20.1.18 Eppendorf, Arbeitsmann, RSHA IV E 5, Stapoleit Königsberg.

94. **Heitler, Walter, Dr.,** 1904 geb., Privatdozent, Bristol (Universität), Emigrant, RSHA III A 1.
95. **Hellmann, Reinhard,** 1909 geb., Assistent, Emigrant, RSHA III A 1.
96. **Hellmers, Arno,** 11.1.02 Oberhausen-Sterkrade, zuletzt Rotterdam, vermutl. England, RSHA IV E 4, Stapo Kiel.
97. **Helmer-Hirschberg, Olaf, Dr.,** 1910 geb., London (Universität), Emigrant, RSHA III A 1.
98. **Helmers, Anton,** 11.1.02 Sterkrade, zuletzt: Rotterdam, vermutl. Engl., Deckname: Hellmers, Jan Smits, RSHA IV E 4, Stapoleit Kiel.
99. **Henderson, Arthur,** 1893 geb., RSHA VI G 1.
100. **Henderson, A.,** Journalist, RSHA IV B 4 b.
101. **Henderson, Neville Meyrick,** 1882 geb., ehem. brit. Botschafter in Berlin, RSHA IV E 4.
102. **Hendriks, Henry Augustus,** 20.5.90 Lebbeke, brit. Agent, London Südwest 7, Rolandsgardens, RSHA IV E 4.
103. **Hendrika, Harry (Henry),** 22.6.78 Oss/Holland, zuletzt: Den Haag, vermutl. England (Täterkreis: Aloisius Porta), RSHA IV E 4.
104. **Hendricks, Jan,** Deckname des de Fremery, RSHA IV E 4.
105. **Hennemann, Karl,** 17.9.98 Köln, Tischler (Am-Apparat), RSHA IV A 2.
106. **Hennig, Elisabeth,** 16.9.00 Düsseldorf, RSHA IV A 1.
107. **Henri, Ernst,** Schriftsteller, RSHA IV B 4 b.
108. **Henriques, Cyril,** London W. 8, 4 Capden Hill Square, RSHA II B 2.
109. **Mitschell-Henry, Mauriel,** 28.8.93 Bradford/England, Reklameleiterin (Täterkreis: Julius Guthlac Birch), RSHA IV E 4.
110. **Hensen, Franz,** 28.9.96 Vaalnyk, Kurier, brit. Agent, zuletzt: Utrecht/Holland, vermutl. England (Täterkreis: Wilhelm Willemse), RSHA IV E 4, Stapoleit Düsseldorf.
111. **Hepper, Montaen Goffry Alarig,** 22.10.06 Basingstole/London, brit. Armeekpt., London 10, Warrington Crecent, RSHA IV E 4, Stapo Lüneburg.
112. **Herb, Max,** Schriftsteller, Emigrant, London N. W. 3, 3—4 Thurlow Road, RSHA II B 5.
113. **Herbert, Alfred, Sir,** zuletzt: Coventry, RSHA IV E 4.
114. **Herbert, Godfrey,** brit. Commander, RSHA IV E 4.
115. **Herbschild, Moritz,** Mitarbeiter d. Merton, London, RSHA III D.
116. **Hering, Franz Paul Felix, Dr. phil.,** 23.4.02 Webgelsdorf, RSHA IV A 1.
117. **Hermans, Johannes,** 20.7.98 Venlo, zuletzt: Amsterdam, vermutl. England, Deckname: „Bank" (Stevens/Best), RSHA IV E 4.
118. **Herrmann, Max,** 25.5.86 Neisse, Schriftsteller, London, Bryanston Court Flat, 82 Upper George Street, RSHA IV A 1, II B 5.
119. **Hertog, Edgar,** Mitarbeiter d. Merton, London, RSHA III D
120. **Hertz, Friedrich, Prof.,** Schriftsteller, London N. W. 11, 37 Corringham Road, RSHA VI G 1.
121. **Hertz, Joseph Hermann,** 25.9.72, Hauptrabbiner, Wohng.: a) London 4, St. Jame Place, b) London N W. 8, 103 Hamilton Terr, c) London E C. 3, 4 Creechurch Pl. Aldgate, RSHA VI G 1, II B 2.
122. **Hertz, Mathilde, Dr.,** Privatdozent, 1891 geb., Cambridge (Universität), Emigrant, RSHA III A 1.
123. **Herzfeld, Helmut,** 1891 geb., Karikaturist, richtig: Heartfield, John, RSHA VI G 1.
124. **Herzfeld, John,** richtig: Heartfield, John, RSHA VI G 1.
125. **Herzheimer, Rudolf,** Mitarbeiter d. Merton, London, RSHA III D.

126. **Herzstein, Anna,** verb. **Neubeck,** 20.6.00 Witten/Ruhr (Am-Apparat), RSHA IV A 2.
127. **Hespers, Theo (Theodor),** 12.12.03 München-Gladbach, kath. Jugendführer (Täterkreis: Stevens/Best), RSHA IV E 4.
128. **Tiltman-Hessell,** Hubert, 2.2.97 Birmingham, brit. Journalist, RSHA IV E 4.
129. **Heusden, van, H.,** Sekretär, zuletzt: Leiden/Holland, vermutl. England, RSHA IV E 4.
130. **Heussen, J. H.,** zuletzt: Heerlcbaan/Holland, vermutl. England (Täterkreis: Céline Joosten), RSHA IV E 4, Stapo Aachen.
131. **Hevliger, W.,** Sekretär, zuletzt: Middelburg/Holland, vermutl.: England (Täterkreis: Brijnen), RSHA IV E 4.
132. **Hexmann, Friedrich,** 28.4.00 Brünn, Journalist, Deckname: **Franz Walter** (Am-Apparat), RSHA IV A 2.
133. **Heymann, Gertrud Elisabeth Sarah,** 16.9.22 Hamburg, RSHA IV E 4, Stapoleit Hamburg.
134. **Heymann, Leo,** 24.11.10 Altenstadt, Vertreter, Kaufm., zuletzt: Brüssel, vermutl. England, RSHA IV E 4.
135. **Heywards, J.,** 2.3.99 Summrey/England, brit. Cpt., London (Täterkreis: Pacey), RSHA IV E 4, Stapoleit Berlin.
136. **Heyworth, Geoffrey,** Wohng.: London, Unilever House Blackfriars, RSHA IV E 2.
137. **Hicks, George,** 1879 geb., Wohng.: London S. W. 4, RSHA VI G. 1.
138. **Hicks, George,** 2.1.96 London, Abgeordneter (Täterkreis: H. Sneevliet), RSHA IV E 4.
139. **Hieke, Emil,** 16.4.94 Böhmisch-Wiesenthal, RSHA IV A 1 b.
140. **Hildebrand,** Geistlicher, vermutl. London, (illegaler ND. der Bekenntnisfront), RSHA II B 3, VI H 3.
141. **Hiller, Kurt,** 17.8.85 Berlin, Schriftsteller, Wohng.: London S. W. 2, 126 Fordwich Road London N. W. 6, 7. St. Lawrence Mansions, Priory Park Road (Täterkreis: Schwarze Front), RSHA IV A 6, II B 5.
142. **Hillmann, Hermann Christian M. A.,** 1910 geb., Assistent, Dundee, Emigrant, RSHA III A 1.
143. **Himmelweit, F., Dr.,** 1903 geb., Assistent, London, Emigrant, RSHA III A 1.
143a **Hinchley-Cook,** Colonel u. Leiter von M. I. 5 (Military-Intelligence), London, RSHA IV E 4.
144. **Hinderks, Hermann,** 19.12.07 Hamburg, Student (Am-Apparat), RSHA IV A 2.
145. **Hintze, Karl,** 13.8.84 Puttbus/M., zuletzt: USA, vermutl. England, RSHA IV E 4, Stapo Schwerin.
146. **Hinze, Gerhard,** Wohng.: London, Emigrant, RSHA VI G 1, II B 5.
147. **Hirsch, Adolf,** 21.3.87 Mandel, RSHA IV E 4, Stapo Koblenz.
148. **Hirsch, Emil,** 24.12.76 Berlin, London N. W. 4, Elliot-Road Hendon, Deckname: **Schwarz, Erich,** London N. W. 11, Golderes Green Bo, Poste Restante, RSHA IV A 1.
149. **Hirsch, Kurt A., Dr.,** 1906 geb., Cambridge (Universität), Emigrant, RSHA III A 1.
150. **Hirsch, Max,** 4.2.03 Gleiwitz, Arbeiter, Wohng.: Margate-Kent, Montros 100/2 — Northdown Road Park, Gliftonville, RSHA IV A 1, Stapo Karlsbad.
151. **Hirschfeld, Hans,** 26.11.94 Hamburg, RSHA IV A 1.
152. **Hirschlaff, Ernst, Dr.,** 1908 geb., Cambridge (Universität), Emigrant, RSHA III A 1.

153. **Hitzemann, Johannes,** 29.11.05 Glückstadt, Wehrpfl., Okt. 39 in d.
Südafr. Union festgen., RSHA V—D 2 f.
154. **Hoblyn, G. E. J.,** brit. Vizekonsul, RSHA IV E 4.
155. **Hobson, John Atkinson,** 1858 geb., RSHA VI G 1.
156. **Graf Hochberg,** Mitgl. d. poln. Reg., RSHA IV D 2.
157. **Hodgkins, Tommy,** brit. Pol.-Beamter, Sunderland/Engl., Alexander
Road 5, Holm Gardens (Täterkreis: Norits), RSHA IV E 4, Stapo
Königsberg.
158. **Höfer, Johann,** 6.9.15 Frauenberg, Bez. Bruck a. d. Mur, Kraftfahrer,
Wohng.: London, RSHA IV A 2, Stapo Graz.
159. **Höft, Otto,** 31.3.07 Plagow, RSHA IV A 1.
160. **Höltermann, Karl,** 20.3.94 Pirmasens, Schriftsteller, Emigrant,
London, RSHA IV A 1, IV E 4, VI G 1, II B 5, IV A 5.
161. **Hölzel, Camillo,** 6.12.08 Sobnitz, London (Attentäter), RSHA IV A 2.
162. **Hoffmann, Simon,** 8.8.76 Wien, Generaldir., RSHA IV E 4.
163. **Hofmann, Lothar,** 16.2.03 Leipzig, Techniker, Deckname: **Richter,**
Hans (Am-Apparat), RSHA IV A 2.
164. **Hofmann, Max,** 1.3.91 Mülhausen, RSHA IV A 1.
165. **Hofmann, Walter,** 25.7.07 Pirmasens, Modelleur, Verkäufer, RSHA
IV A 1.
166. **Fürstin von Hohenberg, Maria,** Wohng.: London, Emigrantin,
RSHA VI G 1, II B 5.
167. **Holler,** Emigrant, London, RSHA II B 5.
168. **Holman, A.,** ehem. 1. Sekr. d. Botschaft in Berlin, RSHA IV E 4.
169. **Holzinger, Arthur,** 13.11.98 Gängerhof, RSHA IV A 1.
170. **Honigmann, Hans, Dr.,** 1891 geb., Direktor, London (Zoolog. Gesellschaft), Emigrant, RSHA III A 1.
171. **Honnebecke, Jan Harms,** 1.5.80 Hoogesand, Arbeiter, RSHA IV E 4.
172. **Hoogesand,** Angestellter, zuletzt: Den Haag, vermutl. England
(Täterkreis: I. A. Rietveld), RSHA IV E 4.
173. **Hooper, William John,** 23.4.05 Rotterdam, brit. Agent, zuletzt:
Scheveningen/Holland, vermutl. England (Täterkreis: Stevens/
Best), Deckname: **Konrad,** RSHA IV E 4.
174. **Hope, W. P.,** 26.3.05 London, Ing., zuletzt: Overschie b. Rotterdam,
vermutl. England (Täterkreis: James Haynes), RSHA IV E 4.
175. **Hopf, Fritz,** 23.7.02 Neudorf, RSHA IV A 1 b.
176. **Hopmans, M. J.,** Sekr., zuletzt: Zwolle/Holland, vermutl. England
(Täterkreis: Brijnen), RSHA IV E 4.
177. **Hore-Belisha, Leslie,** Wohng.: London S. W. 14, The Close, Sheen
Common, London S. W. 1, Reform Club, London S. W. 1, 104 Pall
Mall, RSHA II B 2, VI G 1.
178. **Horn, Wenzl,** 17.9.94 Simmer, RSHA IV A 1 b.
179. **Freemann-Horn,** Leiter d. brit. Alumin.-Comp., London, RSHA
IV E 1.
180. **Horner, Arthur,** Präsident d. Bergarb.-Gewerksch., RSHA VI G 1.
181. **Horning, Eric,** Chemiker, London N. W. L., Dorset Square 33, RSHA
IV E 4.
182. **Horowitz, Phineas,** London N. W. 2, 9 Großvenor Garden, RSHA
II B 2.
183. **Horrabin, James Francis,** 1884 geb., Abgeordnete d. lib. Partei,
RSHA VI G 1.
184. **Horsemann, Dorothy,** Direktorin vom „Linksbuch-Club", RSHA
VI G 1.

185. **Horstmann, Hermann,** 12.3.93 Osnabrück, Rechtsanw. (Am-Apparat), RSHA IV A 2.
185. a. **Houser,** brit. ND.-Agent, früh. Kopenhagen, vermutl. England, RSHA IV E 4.
186. **Houtermann, Fritz, Dr.,** 12.3.03 Danzig, Assistent, RSHA IV A 1.
187. **Howard, Elisabeth,** 6.3.73 London, Leiterin d. engl. Quäker, RSHA IV A 1.
188. **Howard, Stanley,** brit. Cpt., Wohng.: Aston Clinton, Park-Hotel, RSHA IV E 4, Stapoleit Hamburg.
189. **Howard,** brit. Cpt., London S. W. 1, Sloane Street 144, Deckname: Hughes, auch S. C. Tavlor, RSHA IV E 4.
190. **Howe, Robert,** Diplomat, zuletzt: Riga, vermutl. England (engl. ND-Lettland), RSHA VI C 2.
191. **Hubmann, Josef,** 13.11.10 Pernegg, Schlosser (Am-Apparat), Deckname: Josef Lustig, RSHA IV A 2.
192. **Hudson,** brit. ND-Offizier (Täterkreis: Jens Dons), RSHA IV E 4, Stapo Kiel.
193. **Hüller, Johann,** 20.1.11 Pechbach, London, RSHA IV A 1 b.
194. **Hüsgen, Ernst Hugo,** 3.3.14 Wiescheid, zuletzt: Rotterdam, vermutl. England (Täterkreis: Julius Rogosch), RSHA IV E 4.
195. **Huetting, L.,** Sekr., zuletzt: Holland, vermutl. England (Täterkreis: Brijnen), RSHA IV E 4.
196. **Hütgens, Louis,** 9.11.85 Venlo/Holland, Gärtner (Täterkreis: Stevens/Best), RSHA IV E 4.
197. **Hütter, Helmut,** 15.89 Krems, Nachr.-Agent (Österr. Legitimist), RSHA IV A 3.
198. **Hugh, Isabell,** 28.4.04 Dublin, London, Clampham Park, 72 Rodenhurst Road, RSHA IV E 4.
199. **Hughes, James Mogurk,** richtig: **Howard,** brit. Cpt., London S. W. 1, Sloane Street 144, RSHA IV E 4.
200. **Hughes, W. R.,** Wohng.: Herts Welwyn Garden City (Täterkreis: von der Ropp), RSHA IV E 4.
201. **Hugill, John Michael,** 6.11.15 (17) Sanderstead, Student, Wohng.: Treford-Purley (Kraftw.: „HPH" 231 GB), RSHA IV E 4, Stapo Kiel.
202. **Hummel, Georges,** Mitgründ. d. Investment Comp. Luxemburg, einer Petschek'schen Holding-Ges., London (Täterkreis: Ignatz Petschek), RSHA III D 4.
203. **Hummel, Sidney,** Mitgründ. d. Investment Comp. S. A. Luxemburg, einer Petschek'schen Holding-Ges., London (Täterkreis: Ignatz Petschek), RSHA III D 4.
204. **Humphrey,** brit. Major, Abt.-Leiter im brit. N.-D., London (Täterkreis: M. King), RSHA IV E 4.
205. **Hurwitz, Max,** Leeds 7, 56 Harehills Avenue, RSHA II B 2.
206. **Husband, Patrick,** Bücherrevisor, Angest. d. brit. N.-D., Middleton-Sea (Sussex), Yapton Road, RSHA IV E 4.
207. **Huston,** brit. Major, zuletzt: Bukarest, vermutl. England (Täterkreis: Elbing), RSHA IV E 4.
208. **Hut, S.,** Sekr., zuletzt: Veendam/Holland, vermutl. England (Täterkreis: Brijnen), RSHA IV E 4.
209. **Huxley, Aldous,** 26.7.94, Schriftsteller, RSHA VI G 1.
210. **Huxley, Julian Sorell,** 22.6.87 Prof., London N. W. 8, Regents Park (Zoologial Society), RSHA VI G 1.
211. **Graf v. Huyn, Hans,** Schriftsteller, London, Emigr., RSHA VI G 1, II B 5.

212. **Hyamson, Albert,** London N.W. 2, 82 Teigmourth Road, RSHA II B 2.
213. **Hymans, Marulce,** brit. Agent, Deckname: **de Leenw** u. **Dr. Haas,**
     RSHA IV E 4.

1. **Ide, W. H.,** Agent, zuletzt: Amsterdam, Toldwaarstr. 8, vermutl. England, brit. ND-Agent, (Täterkreis: Prins), RSHA IV E 4.
2. **Iedema, J.,** Sekretär, zuletzt: Holland, Laan 1, brit. ND.-Agent, vermutl. England, (Täterkreis: Breijnen, RSHA IV E 4.
3. **Ignatief, A.,** Angeh. d. brit. ND, London, Shell Max House, Strand, RSHA IV E 4.
4. **Iltis, Lucian,** Deckn. **Fritz Theo Otto,** 15.5.03 Mannheim, Redakteur, RSHA IV A 2.
5. **Ingr, Sergey,** 1894, Div.-General, Minister für nat. Verteidigung der tschech. Regierung in London, RSHA IV D 1 a.
6. **Ingrams, Leonhard,** London, (Täterkreis: Julius Petschek), RSHA III D 4.
7. **Ingres, Sergej,** tschech. Minister f. nationale Verteidigung, RSHA II B 5.
8. **Inkpin, Albert,** Zeitungsverleger, RSHA VI G 1.
9. **Intosk, Max,** Deckn.: **Macintoch,** Café-Besitzer, zuletzt: Rotterdam, vermutl. England, RSHA IV E 4.
10. **Iravor, Keith,** Major, zuletzt: Reval (Estland), RSHA VI C 2.
11. **Irmer, Eduard,** 9.9.89 Dottmannsdorf, Direktor der niederl. Handelsgesellschaft, zuletzt: Amsterdam, vermutl. England, RSHA IV E 4, Stapoleit Berlin.
12. **Irmer, Erich,** 26.3.08 Berlin, Vertreter, London, RSHA IV A 1, Stapoleit Berlin.
13. **Isaac, Gerald Rufas,** richtig: **Reading,** Lord, RSHA VI G 1.
14. **Isaaks, George Alfred,** 1883, Sekr. d. Nationalunion d. Drucker, RSHA VI G 1.
15. **Isaacs, Morris,** RSHA VI G 1.
16. **Isherwood, Henry,** 23.10.98 Wimborne, Beamter d. brit. Luftfahrtmin., London W. C. 1, Russel Square, Hotel Royal, RSHA IV E 4, Stapoleit Berlin.
17. **Israel, Wilhelm James, Dr.,** 1881, Privatdozent, Emigrant, London (seit 1933 Privatpraxis), RSHA III A 1.
18. **Isrealski, Martin, Dr.,** 1901, Emigrant, seit 1936 in Glasgow, RSHA III A 1.

1. **Jablonski, Robert,** 29.4.09 Paris, vermutl. England, RSHA IV A 1.
2. **Jabotinsky, Vladimir,** London N. W. 8, 47 Finchley Road, RSHA II B 2.
3. **Jacks (Jaksch), Eissi,** 16.7.91 London, Schiffssabotage, RSHA IV A 2.
4. **Jacobi,** gesch. Honig, **Johanna,** 17.8.96 Thorn, Photographin, London, RSHA IV A 1, IV A 2.
5. **Jacobs, von, G. H.,** richtig: **Jacabos,** 17.9.96 Hettin/Rum., Direktor, London, RSHA IV E 4.
6. **Jacobs, Norman Myer,** Manchester 7, 86 Upper Park Road, RSHA II B 2.
7. **Jacobson, Werner, Dr.,** 1906, Assistent, Emigrant, Cambridge, RSHA III A 1.
8. **Jacobsthal, Paul, Dr.,** 1880, o. Prof., Emigrant, Oxford (Univ.), RSHA III A 1.
9. **Jacobus, M. H.,** London N. W. 8, 22. Abercon Place (Täterkreis: Longstaff-Jakobus), RSHA IV E 4, Stapoleit München.
10. **Jacoby, Fritz, Dr.,** 1902, Ass., Emigrant, Birmingham (Universität — Physiologisches Institut), RSHA III A 1.
11. **Jacomb, William,** 29.8.03 (96), Brighton, brit. Offizier, London, Pall Mall 116, RSHA IV E 4.
12. **Jäckh, Ernst,** 22.2.75 Urach, Direktor, Emigrant, RSHA II B 5, III A 1, VI G 1.
13. **Jäger, Hans Ferdinand Heinrich,** Deckname: **Kohout,** 10.2.99 Berlin-Friedenau, Redakteur, London N. 7, 21 Anson Hoad bei Mrs. Greening, Schwarze Front, RSHA IV A 3, IV E 6.
14. **Jaffe, Gerda Josephine,** 21.6.10 Berlin-Charlottenburg, RSHA IV A 1.
15. **Jagger, John,** Jude, Labour-Abgeordneter, RSHA VI G 1.
16. **Jakabos, G. I. (G. H.),** 17.9.96 Hettin/Rumänien, Direktor, London, RSHA IV E 4.
17. **Jakubczik, Jerzy,** 19.12.10 Strzemieszyl, Student, RSHA IV E 5, Stapo Danzig.
18. **Jaksch, Wenzel,** 25.9.96 Langstrobnitz, Maurer, London N. W. 3, 35. Park Gardens im Hause Miß Warninger bei Belsize, RSHA IV A 1, IV A 1 b.
19. **Janczak, Johann (Jan),** 8.5.11 Hamborn, Arbeiter, RSHA IV E 5, Stapoleit Breslau.
20. **Janner, Barnett,** London W. 2, 3 Lancaster Terr., RSHA II B 2.
21. **Jansen, Cornelius,** 4.8.83 Made in Drimmelen, Leutn. d. Nachr.-Abteil. in Roermond, zuletzt: Roermond, vermutl. England (Täterkreis: Stobben), RSHA IV E 4.
22. **Jansen,** zuletzt: Rotterdam, vermutl. England (Täterkreis: J. A. Rietveld), RSHA IV E 4.
23. **Jansens, H. J. H.,** Kunstmaler, zuletzt: Amsterdam, Lijnbaangracht 302, vermutl. England (Täterkreis: J. W. Lousing), RSHA IV E 4.
24. **Jaworski, Antoni,** 15.5.04, RSHA IV E 5.
25. **Jaworski, Jan, Dr.,** Mitgl. d. poln. Nationalrats, RSHA IV D 2.
26. **Jelic, Branimir, Dr.,** 28.2.05 Dolac/Jugoslawien, Arzt, vermutl. im engl. Internierungslager oder Gefängnis, RSHA IV D 3.
27. **Jellinek, Frank,** 9.1.08 London, Schriftsteller, vermutl. England, RSHA IV E 4.
28. **Jenkins, Muriel,** London S. E. 26, 20 Dukesthorpe Road, Sydenham, RSHA IV A 1.

29. **Jequier, Richard Adrien,** Prokurist der Swiss Bank Corp., London E. C. 2, Gresham Street 99 (Täterkreis: Ignatz Petschek), RSHA III D 4.
30. **Jerry, Gregoire,** zuletzt: Bayonne, vermutl. England, RSHA IV E 4.
31. **Jewelowski, Julius,** 6.5.74 Willimpol, Emigrant, London, RSHA II B 5.
32. **Jirris, Gerhard,** etwa 23 Jahre alt, Student, zuletzt: Treebeek, Treebeekstraat 25, vermutl. England (Täterkreis: Erwin Stroschein), RSHA IV E 4.
33. **Joachim, Willy,** 17.10.92 Walfischbay/Südwest-Afrika, Steuermann, vermutl. England, RSHA IV E 4.
34. **Joad, Cyril Edwin,** 12.8.91, Prof. u. Schriftsteller, London N. W. 3, 4 East Heath Road, RSHA VI G 1.
35. **John, Fritz, Dr.,** 1910, Assistent, Emigrant, Lexington, RSHA III A 1.
36. **Johnson, Fran W.,** etwa 42 Jahre, 1934, brit. ND.-Agent, ehem. brit. Offizier, vermutl. England, RSHA IV E 4.
37. **Johnson,** Leiter des brit. ND. in Jugosl., vermutl. England, RSHA IV E 4.
38. **Johnston, Ellen,** vermutl. England, RSHA IV E 4.
39. **De Jong, Theodor,** richtig **Theodor Franssen,** 22.6.92 Münster/W., Ing., zuletzt: Amsterdam, vermutl. England, RSHA IV E 4.
40. **Johnstone, Harcourt,** 1895, Leiter d. Publikationsabteilung, RSHA VI G 1.
41. **Price-Jones, Alan,** London (Täterkreis: Ignatz Petschek), RSHA III D 4.
42. **Jones, Edith,** 16.2.10 London, Sekr. i. d. brit. Paßabteilung Kopenhagen, vermutl. England (Täterkreis: Steven/Frank), RSHA IV E 4.
43. **Jones, Evelyn,** RSHA VI G 1.
44. **Jones, Frederick Elwyn,** Schriftsteller, RSHA III A 5.
45. **Jones-Bates, Reginald,** vermutl. England, RSHA IV E 4.
46. **Jones, Oscar Philipp,** 15.10.98 Beckenham/England, Master-Pilot (Aircraft), London, RSHA IV E 4, Stapo Köln.
47. **Joseph, Walter,** Mitarbeiter d. Merton, London, RSHA III D.
48. **Jowett, William Frederick,** Abg. der Labour-Party, RSHA VI G 1.
49. **Joye, Harold Cornellé,** Direktor, vermutl. England, RSHA IV E 4.
50. **Jozwiak, Stanislaw,** Mitgl. d. poln. Nat.-Rates, RSHA IV D 2.
51. **Jubanski, Boris,** richtig **Braginski,** zuletzt: Antwerpen, vermutl. England (Täterkreis: Fritz W. Eger), RSHA IV E 4.
52. **Juliusburger, Franz, Dr.,** 1906, London, Emigrant, RSHA III A 1.
53. **Jurasch, Felix Franz,** 5.10.12 Tirschtiegel, RSHA IV E 5, Stapo Schneidemühl.

1. **Kabel, E. G.,** brit. Generalkonsul, England (Täterkreis: E. G. Cable), RSHA IV E 4.
2. **Kabelik, Dr.,** Vorsitzender d. britisch.-tschech.-slow. Zentrums in London, London W. 9, 3 Clifton Gardens (Täterkreis: Benesch VI G 1, Telef.: Abercon 6232), RSHA IV D 1 a.
3. **Kaczmarczyk, Josef,** 2.5.1900 Siemianowitz, poln. Agent, RSHA IV E 5, Stapoleit Breslau.
4. **Kadega, Kurt,** brit. Offizier, England, RSHA IV—II O 2.
5. **Kadi, Abdul,** brit. Agent, zuletzt: Kabul, vermutl. England, RSHA IV E 4.
6. **Kahn, Ludwig W., Dr.,** 1910, Assistent, London, RSHA III A 1.
7. **Kahn-Freund, Otto,** Schriftsteller, Emigrant, London N. W. 6, 1 Fawley Road, RSHA II B 5.
8. **Kaiser, Ch.,** Jude, zuletzt: Kowno, vermutl. England, brit. ND.-Litauen, RSHA VI C 2.
9. **Kaiser, Walter,** 22.11.09 Barmen, Stukkateur (Am-Apparat), RSHA IV A 2.
10. **Kaizer, Arnold Meer,** Journalist, London N. 3, 37 North Crescent, RSHA II B 2.
11. **Kala,** Oberst, London, RSHA VI G 1.
12. **Kallin, Anna,** 55 Jahre, ehem. Tänzerin, zuletzt: Bukarest, vermutl. England, RSHA IV E 4.
13. **Kamnitzer, Bernhard, Dr.,** 25.10.90 Dirschau, London, RSHA IV A 1.
14. **Kant, Lina,** 15.8.98 Pforzheim, Übersetzerin der ITF, London, RSHA IV A 1 b.
15. **Kantorowicz, Hermann,** 1877, Prof., England, RSHA III A 1.
16. **Kantorowitsch, Miron, Dr.,** 1895, London, RSHA III A 1.
17. **Kantorowicz, Otto, Dr.,** 1906, London, RSHA III A 1.
18. **Karin,** richtig: **Karl-Becker,** vermutl. England, RSHA IV A 1.
19. **Karpinski, Marian Vladimir,** 1.8.91 Lemberg, poln. Nachrichtenoffizier, RSHA IV E 5, Stapoleit Danzig.
20. **Karplus, Kurt,** 1907, Assistent, vermutl. England, Emigrant, RSHA III A 1.
21. **Kaspar, Jaroslav,** 22.03 Alt Paka, ehem. tschech. Stabscpt., vermutl. England, RSHA IV E 4, Stapoleit Prag.
22. **Kasper, Wilhelm,** 8.8.92 Neustadt b. Freiburg, Kaufmann (Am Apparat), RSHA IV A 2.
23. **van Kasteel, Piet A., Dr.,** Journalist, zuletzt: Den Haag, vermutl. England, RSHA III B.
24. **Kastner, Rudolf,** Schriftsteller, Emigrant, London N. W. 8, South Lodge Grove End Road, RSHA II B 5.
25. **Katas, Alada,** Journalist, Budapest, vermutl. England (Täterkreis: Lukapello), RSHA IV E 4, Stapo Köln.
26. **Katz, David,** 1884, Prof., London, Emigrant, RSHA III A 1.
27. **Katzenellenbogen, Max,** 1.2.06 Leipzig, Deckname: **Bloch,** Chemiker (Am-Apparat), RSHA IV A 2.
28. **Kaufmann, Boris, Dr.,** 1904, London, Emigrant, RSHA III A 1.
29. **Kaufmann, Fritz, Dr.,** 1891, Emigrant, Privatdozent, Oxford, RSHA III A 1.
30. **Kauffmann, Robert, Dr.,** Jude, London, RSHA VI G 1.
31. **Kaulbach,** 19.12.97 Großbüllesheim, richtig: **Hans Barison,** Oberstadtsekretär, vermutl. England (Am-Apparat), RSHA IV A 2..
32. **Kay, G. R.,** Schriftsteller, RSHA IV B 4.

33. **Kaye, G., Führor d. Union d. demokr. Kontrollen, vermutl. England,** RSHA VI G 1.
34. **Keenan,** brit. Major, London, RSHA IV E 4.
35. **Keenan,** Offizier, England, brit. ND.-Estland, RSHA VI C 2.
36. **Keilwerth, Ernst,** 29.7.09 Graslitz, vermutl. England, RSHA IV A 1 b.
37. **Keizer, I. A.,** Sekretär, zuletzt: Holland, vermutl. England, RSHA IV E 4.
38. **Kellner, Lotte, Dr.,** 1904, vermutl. London, Emigrant, RSHA III A 1.
39. **Kemmerling, Jacob,** 23.8.95 Kerkrade, vermutl. England, RSHA IV E 4.
40. **Kempf, Johann,** 12.3.93 St.Joachimsthal, Winsgombe, Cleusield, Road EXT., Leichester, RSHA IV A 1 b.
41. **Kendrick, Thomas,** 26.11.81 Cape Town (Capstadt), brit. Cpt., England, RSHA IV E 4.
42. **Kennard,** brit. Major, zuletzt: Windhuk/Südwestafrika, vermutl. England, RSHA IV E 4.
42a **Kenney, Rowland,** brit. N.-Agent, zuletzt: Kopenhagen, vermutl. England, RSHA IV E 4.
43. **Kenny, Francis,** 6.2.00 Kongston/England, Beamter, Hull, 72 Langstoft Grave Cottinghan Road, RSHA IV A 1.
44. **Kenny,** brit. Cpt., England, RSHA IV E 4.
45. **van Kerkhoff, Christian,** 31.1.83 Leiden, Zigarrenfabrikant, zuletzt: Holland, vermutl. England (Täterkreis: Albert Steigers), RSHA IV E 4.
46. **Kern, Alfred,** richtig **Helmut Kern,** 3.6.05 Magdeburg, Redakteur, vermutl. England (Täterkreis: Kern-Kreis), RSHA IV A 1.
47. **Kern, Helmut,** 3.6.05 Magdeburg, Redakteur, vermutl. England (Täterkreis: Kern-Kreis), Deckname: **Alfred Kern** und **D. Bakker,** RSHA IV A 1.
48. **Kernroy,** brit. Pol.-Beamter, Deckname: **Bromdoy,** RSHA IV E 4.
49. **Kerr, Alfred,** Berichterstatter d. Pariser Tageszeitung, vermutl. England, RSHA IV B 4.
50. **Kerran, Ferdinand Louis,** 18.8.83 Framere/England, Parlamentsmitgl., London W. C. 1, First Avenue House, 45 High-Holborn, RSHA IV E 4, Stapoleit Wien.
51. **Kessler, J. B. A.,** Direktor, London E. C. 3, 22 St. Helens Court, Shell Transport u. Trading Co., RSHA IV E 2.
52. **Keyser, Edward G.,** Angestellter, zuletzt: Brüssel, vermutl. England (Täterkreis: Waldemar Pötsch), RSHA IV E 4.
53. **Kibble, Miß, K.,** Manchester (Täterkreis: Walter Becker), 12 Newton Street, RSHA IV E 4.
54. **Kich, Egon Erwin** (Jude), Emigrant, Schriftsteller, RSHA II B 5.
55. **Kidd, Ronald,** vermutl. England, RSHA VI G 1.
56. **Kiewitz, Helene,** 6.11.97 Heydebreck/OS., Deckname: **Maria Grzonka,** RSHA IV E 5, Stapo Oppeln.
57. **Kika, Bretislav,** 25.11.09 Zablate, ehem. tschech. Militärattaché, vermutl. England, RSHA IV E 4.
58. **Killby, Kannath,** 24.4.89 London, brit. Cpt., zuletzt: Kopenhagen, vermutl. England, RSHA IV E 4, Stapo Kiel.
58a **Killey, Kenneth,** 24.4.89, brit. N.-Agent, zuletzt: Kopenhagen, vermutl. England, RSHA IV E 4.
59. **King, M.,** brit. Cpt., London, White-Hall, RSHA IV E 4.
60. **King-Hall, Stephan,** 21.3.93, Herausgeber der „K.-H.-Briefe", London, Headfield House, Headley Hants, RSHA VI G 1.

61. **Kinghorn, R.,** Kaufmann, zuletzt: Reval, vermutl. England, brit. ND. Estland, RSHA VI C 2.
62. **Kinlay, K. G.,** London, RSHA VI G 1.
63. **Kinsey, George William Ernest,** 8.9.01 London, Elektriker, London, 53 Revelstokera, RSHA IV E 4, Stapo Köln.
64. **Kirchner, Wilhelm,** 6.1.20 Düsseldorf, Arbeitsdienstmann, RSHA IV E 5, Stapoleit Breslau.
65. **Kirkpatrik, Leonard,** 6.11.90 Woodhidge, Commender d. Royal Nay Admiralty, London (Täterkreis: George Campbel), RSHA IV E 4, Stapo Kiel.
66. **Kirsch, Hans,** Ingenieur, London, RSHA IV E 4.
67. **Kirschmann, Emil,** 13.11.88 Oberstein/Nahe, vermutl. England, RSHA IV A 1 b.
68. **Kirschneck, Christof,** 29.11.12 Haslau, Handlungsgehilfe, vermutl. England, RSHA IV A 1, Stapo Karlsbad.
69. **Kiss, Paul Alfred,** 1.8.94 Greiz-Dölau, London N. 14, 62 The Woodland, RSHA IV A 1, Stapoleit Dresden.
70. **Klaas, Rudolf Jesse,** 19.2.15 Beddington/England, Dienstpflichtiger, Beddington Croydon, The First Hilliers Lame, RSHA V D 2 f.
71. **Klausmann, Robert,** 15.5.96 Essen, ehem. komm. Landtagsabgeordneter (Am-Apparat), RSHA IV A 2.
72. **Klee-Rawidowicz, Esther E., Dr.,** geb. 1900, Assistent, London, RSHA III A 1.
73. **van Kleffens, Mr., E. N.,** chem. holländ. Außenmin., zuletzt: Den Haag, vermutl. England, RSHA III D.
74. **Klein, Heinz** (Jude), Emigrant, zuletzt: Brüssel, vermutl. England (Täterkreis: Karl Machacek), RSHA IV E 4.
75. **Klein, Steffan,** vermutl. England (Täterkreis: Albert Albseit), RSHA IV E 4, Stapoleit Wien.
76. **Kleine, Fritz,** 7.3.01 Apolda, Maschinenmeister (Am-Apparat), RSHA IV A 2.
77. **Kleine, Fritz,** 7.3.01 Apolda, Werkmeister, Decknamen: **Fritz Arnol, Rudolf Ludwig Franke, Wagner,** vermutl. England, RSHA IV E 4, Stapoleit Prag.
78. **von Kleist,** richtig: **Franz Rintelen,** 19.8.78 Frankfurt/O., deutscher Korvettenkapitän, England, RSHA IV E 4.
79. **Klepper, Otto,** 17.8.88 Brotterode, Deckname: **Charles Reber,** Rechtsanwalt, vermutl. England (Deutsche Freiheitspartei), RSHA IV A 1.
80. **Klibansky, Raymond, Dr.,** 1905, Privatdozent, Oxford, Emigrant, RSHA III A 1.
81. **Klienberger, Emma, Dr.,** 1892, Priv.-Dozent, London, RSHA III A 1.
82. **Klimpl, Resie,** 3.4.09 Fischern, vermutl. London, RSHA IV A 1 b.
83. **Klinger, Eugen,** 30.5.06 Rosenberg, Redakteur, London, 14. Kingsroad Rugboy Mansions Flat 13, RSHA IV E 4, Stapoleit Prag.
84. **Klvana, Franz,** 30.1.00 Drahotus, chem. tschech. Stabshpt., vermutl. England, RSHA IV E 4, Stapoleit Prag.
85. **Kniefke, Hans,** Deckname: **Hans,** brit. Agent, zuletzt Antwerpen, vermutl. England (Täterkreis: Waldemar Pötsch), RSHA IV E 4.
86. **Kniefke, Karl,** Deckname: **Wagner, Fritz,** brit. Agent, zuletzt: Holland, vermutl. England, RSHA IV E 4, Stapo Wilhelmshaven.
87. **Knight, Jaspar,** führend i. Unilever-Konzern, Wohng.: Oxon, Bolney Court, RSHA III D.
88. **Knoblauch, Louis,** Leith, Baltic Street 18, RSHA IV E 3, Stapo Trier.

89. **von Knörringen, Waldemar, 6.10.06** Rechtesberg, vermutl. England, RSHA IV A 1.
90. **Knop, Werner, 29.12.11** Cuxhaven, Journalist, London E. 1, Pine Cottage Foyebell Hall 28, Comercialstr., RSHA IV E 4.
91. **Knowles, James Metcalfe, 3.9.11,** Halifax, Architekt, London S. W. 7, 150 Cromwell Road, RSHA IV E 4, Stapoleit München.
92. **Knowles, M., 25.11.81** Askern, brit. Cpt., London, (Täterkreis: Werner Pohl), RSHA IV E 4.
93. **Koc, Adam, 31.8.91** Suwalken, polnischer Minister, vermutl. England, Decknamen: **Witold, Krajewski, Warminski, Adam,** RSHA III B u. IV D 2.
94. **Kochanski, Theodor, 29.5.00** Makowarsk, poln. Sergeant, vermutl. England, RSHA IV E 5, Stapoleit Danzig.
95. **Koebel, Eberhard, 22.6.07** Stuttgart, Schriftsteller, Deckname: **Tusk,** London S. W. 20, 224 Coombe Lane (bündische Jugend), RSHA IV B 1 b.
96. **Köhler, Franz, 12.9.97** Silberbach, England, RSHA IV A 1 b.
97. **Koehler, Hans Jürgen, 21.3.05** Frankfurt/M., richtig **Pfeiffer, Heinrich,** Schriftsteller, vermutl. England, RSHA IV B 4.
98. **Koek, Joh. M.,** Sekretär, zuletzt: Amsterdam, vermutl. England (Täterkreis: Brijnen), RSHA IV E 4.
99. **Blanche-Koelensmid, G. A. E.,** zuletzt: Amsterdam, vermutl. England (Täterkreis: Prins), RSHA IV E 4.
100. **Koenen-Wenzel, Wilhelm, 7.4.86** Hamburg, Redakteur, vermutl. England, RSHA IV A 1, Stapo Halle.
101. **König, Ernst, 20.6.97** Halle (Am-Apparat), RSHA IV A 2.
102. **Körbel, Josef, Dr. jur., 20.9.09** Geiersberg, Leg. Attaché, vermutl. England, RSHA IV E 4, Stapoleit. Prag.
103. **Körner, Tito, 26.4.89** Santiago/Chile, Journalist, zuletzt: Den Haag, vermutl. England, RSHA IV E 4.
104. **Köwer, Anton, 3.6.16** Altrolau, England, RSHA IV A 1 b.
105. **Mac Kogen,** richtig **Makohin,** vermutl. England, RSHA IV D 3 a.
106. **Mac Kohen,** richtig **Makohin,** vermutl. England, RSHA IV D 3.
107. **Kohl, Marie,** verh. **Wagner, 1.8.08** Haslau, Strickerin, vermutl. England, RSHA IV A 1.
108. **Kohn, Hans, Dr., 1891,** Prof., Northampton, RSAH III A 1.
109. **Kohout, Hans, 10.2.99** Berlin-Friedenau, richtig **Jäger, Hans,** Redakteur, London N. 7, 21 Anson Road (Schwarze Front), RSHA IV A 3.
110. **de Kok, J. E. F.,** Direktor, zuletzt: 's Gravenhage, vermutl. England, RSHA IV E 2.
111. **Kokoschka, Oskar, 8.10.68** Pöschlarn, Emigrant, Vorstandsmitgl. d. freien dtsch. Kulturliga i. England, London, RSHA VI G 1, II B 5.
112. **Kolbe, F.,** Bankier, London W. 1, Velbeckstreet 17 (Schwarze Front), RSHA IV A 3.
113. **Kollibac, Mate, 45** Jahre alt, Dobrownik, Konsulatssekretär, zuletzt: Zagreb, vermutl. England, RSHA IV E 4, Stapo Graz.
114. **Kolodziejczyk, Julian, 46** Jahre alt, poln. Kpt., Deckname: **Kolodziejczak,** vermutl. England, RSHA IV E 5, Stapo Oppeln.
115. **Kolodziejczak, Julian, 54** Jahre alt, poln. Kpt., Deckname: **Krzysowski, Kolodziejczyk,** vermutl. England, RSHA IV E 5, Stapo Oppeln.
116. **Konrad, Josef, 18.9.91** Schönwald, Oxford, RSHA IV A 1 b.
117. **Kooning, H. G.,** Sekretär, zuletzt: Amsterdam, vermutl. England (Täterkreis: Brijnen), RSHA IV E 4.

118. **Kopetz, Josef,** 19.2.92 Mies, Farlay Hall, Aakomowo Staffardsh, RSHA IV A 1.
* 119. **Korda, Alexander,** 16.9.93 Turkeve, Ungarn, Direktor d. Korda Film-Productions Ltd., London N. W. 81, Avenue Road, St. John's Wood, RSHA II D 5.
120. **Koren, Ludwig,** 4.2.96 St. Martin-OSR., vermutl. England, RSHA IV E 5, Stapoleit Wien.
121. **Kornaszewski, Wladislav,** 2.7.99 Strelno, Krs. Mogilno, Kaufmann, vermutl. England, RSHA IV E 5, Stapo Graudenz.
122. **Kosmack, Imogen,** 12.4.13 Glasgow, richtig: **Veit,** Sprachlehrerin, London, RSHA IV E 4.
123. **Kossak, Ling,** richtig: **Hermann Peveling,** vermutl. England, RSHA IV E 4, Stapoleit Prag.
124. **Koster, van Gross Ir. M. H.,** Sekretär, zuletzt: Holland, vermutl. England (Täterkreis: Brijnen), RSHA IV E 4.
125. **Koster, Paul,** 17.1.96 Helder/Holland, Decknamen: **K. Bakker, Paul Kalter, Peter Ballin,** Nachrichtenagent, zuletzt: Paris, vermutl. England, RSHA IV E 4.
126. **Kot, Stanislav,** 22.10.85 Ruda, O. Schles., Prof., poln. Emigrant, vermutl. England, RSHA III B 15.
127. **Kotas, Josef,** 12.8.91 Schles. Ostrau, Sekretär, vermutl. England, RSHA IV A 1.
128. **Kotting, Gerardus Cornelius,** 18.7.80 Rotterdam, Deckname: **Klings,** brit. Agent, zuletzt: Rotterdam, vermutl. England, RSHA IV E 4.
129. **Roney-Kougal, Jan,** 1914 Paigton/England, brit. Offizier, Old Rectory Codforf, Wilts, England (Täterkreis: David Peter), RSHA IV E 4, Stapo Innsbruck.
130. **Kowalski, Josef,** 14.3.04 Laar-Duisburg, Pächter, vermutl. England, RSHA IV E 5, Stapo Oppeln.
131. **Kowoll, Johann Jan** 27.12.90 Siemianowitz, Redakteur, London, RSHA IV A 1 b.
132. **Kraemer, Wilhelm,** 11.2.99 Duisburg, Decknamen: **Kraenel, Kroenel, Kroel,** Lagerist, zuletzt: Holland, vermutl. England (Täterkreis: Wilhelm Willemse), RSHA IV E 4, Stapoleit Düsseldorf.
133. **Krafft, Jerzy,** Grenzwachtkommissar, vermutl. England, RSHA IV E 5, Stapo Schneidemühl.
134. **Krajewski,** richtig: **Koc, Minister,** vermutl. England, RSHA III B 15.
135. **Kraus, Otto.** 1.1.83 Platten, Krs. Neudeck, Leichester, 67 Sparkenhoe Street, RSHA IV A 1.
136. **Kraus, Wolfgang,** geb. 1905, Assistent, Cambridge, RSHA III A 1.
137. **Krause,** brit. Agent, London S. W. 5, Black Friars Road, RSHA IV E 4.
138. **Kraushaar,** geb. **Szepanski, Luise,** Deckname: **Trude,** 13.2.05 Berlin, Stenotypistin (Am-Apparat), RSHA IV A 2.
139. **Krauss, Max,** Mitarbeiter des Merton, London, RSHA III D.
140. **Krautter, Kurt,** 27.11.04 Neukölln, Arbeiter, vermutl. England (Am-Apparat), RSHA IV A 2.
141. **Krayer, Otto, Dr.,** 1899, Privatdozent, vermutl. England, RSHA III A 1.
142. **Krebs, Hans Adolf,** 1900, Privatdozent, Sheffield, RSHA III A 1.
143. **Kregloh,** brit. Agent, zuletzt: Rotterdam, vermutl. England, RSHA IV E 4.
144. **Kreibich, Karl,** 14.2.83 Ooikov, vermutl. England, RSHA IV A 1.

145. **Krejcl, Ludwig**, 17.8.90 Brünn, chem. tschech. General, vermutl. England, RSHA IV E 4, Stapoleit Prag.
146. **Kreißl, Johann**, 18.6.98 Christophhammer, Eisendreher, Leichester/ England, RSHA IV E 4, Stapo Chemnitz.
147. **Kressmann, Willi**, 6.10.07 Berlin, vermutl. England, RSHA IV A 1 b.
148. **Kreissl, Werner**, 18.6.22 Christophhammer, vermutl. Leichester, RSHA IV A 1.
149. **Kretkowski, Franzisek**, 5.2.97 Jaksice, Kpt., vermutl. England, RSHA IV E 5, Stapo Oppeln.
150. **Kreuziger, geb. Babic, Maria**, 21.11.03 Pivola/Jugosl., zuletzt: Belgrad, vermutl. England, RSHA IV E 4.
151. **Kreyssig, Gerhard**, 25.12.99 Krossen, Gewerkschaftsfunktionär, London, RSHA IV A 1 b.
152. **Kriazek, Jan**, 8.3.98 Cicie, Krs. Warschau, Landwirt, vermutl. England, RSHA IV E 5.
153. **Krier, geb. Becker, Lily**, Ehefrau, London, RSHA IV A 1 b.
154. **Krier, Peter (Pierre)**, 4.3.85 Bonneweg, Luxemb., Minister, London, RSHA IV A 1 b.
155. **Kriz, Karl, Dr.**, 28.10.03 Bilin, techn. Beamter, London S. W. 5, Trebovir Road, RSHA IV E 4, Stapoleit Prag.
156. **Kröpke, Jan**, 42 Jahre, Grenzwachtbeamter, vermutl. England, RSHA IV E 5, Stapo Frankfurt/O.
157. **Kroll, Josef**, 16.11.05 Laszow, Krs. Kalisch, Arbeiter, vermutl. England, RSHA IV E 5, Stapoleit Breslau.
158. **Krnadnasky, Wenzel**, 5.6.76 Prag, Redakteur, London, RSHA IV E 4, Stapoleit Prag.
159. **Krüger, Emil**, 19.11.02 Braunschweig, vermutl. England, RSHA IV A 1.
160. **Krzysowski, Julian**, Deckname: **Kolodziejczak**, 54 Jahre alt, poln. Kpt., vermutl. England, RSHA IV E 5, Stapo Oppeln.
161. **Krzyzanowski, Winfried**, Deckname: **Lüdecke**, 14.5.86 Neustettin, Schriftsteller, vermutl. England, RSHA IV E 5, Stapo Innsbruck.
162. **Ksiazek**, brit. Agent, zuletzt: Ungvar, vermutl. England (Täterkreis: R. Kukiz), RSHA IV E 4.
163. **Kubis, Paul**, 22.3.12 Rünthe, Krs. Hamm, Melker, vermutl. England, RSHA IV E 5, Stapo Allenstein.
164. **Kuczinski, geb. Gradenwitz, Berta**, 30.6.79 Kottbus, London, RSHA IV A 1.
165. **Kuczynski, Robert**, 1876, Direktor, London, Emigrant, RSHA III A 1, IV A 1.
166. **Kugler, Josef**, 22.1.87 Schönfeld, Bez. Ellbogen, Arbeiter, Inverness/ Nord-Scotland, Culloden House, RSHA IV A 1, Stapoleit Karlsbad.
167. **Kühndorf, Karl-August**, Emigrant, zuletzt: Riga, vermutl. England, brit. ND. in Lettland, RSHA VI C 2.
168. **Kühnl, Franz**, 13.11.91 Saaz, Albury/England, RSHA IV A 1 b.
169. **Künzl, Oskar**, 18.3.13 Rothau, Margate/Kent, 25 Northdown Road, RSHA IV A 1 b.
170. **Kürtl, Nicholas, Dr.**, 1908, Assistent, Oxford/England, Emigrant, RSHA III A 1.
171. **Kuhn, Heinrich, Dr.**, 1904, Privatdozent, Oxford, Emigrant, RSHA III A 1.
* 172. **Kukel, Mitgl. d. poln. Regierung**, vermutl. England, RSHA IV D 2.
173. **Kukiz, Rudolf**, 23.6.09 Bukowsko/Krs. Sanok, brit. Agent, vermutl. England, RSHA IV E 4.

*See notes on pages 266–272

174. **Kumpost,** Prokop, 18.7.94 Hnevkovize, ehem. tschech. Oberst, England, RSHA IV E 4, Stapoleit Prag.
175. **Kunzlik, Anton,** 14.4.00 Staab, vermutl. England, RSHA IV A 1 b.
176. **Kupfer-Sachs, Rudolf,** 22.5.97 Berlin, richtig: **Sachs,** Graphiker, vermutl. England, RSHA V-C 3 a, Stapoleit Berlin.
177. **Kupka, Franz,** 2.1.01 Rosenberg/O.-Schles., Kellner, vermutl. England, RSHA IV E 5, Stapo Oppeln.
178. **Kuplent, Wenzl,** 22.6.97 Eleonorenhain, vermutl. England, RSHA IV A 1 b.
179. **Kurz, Jaroslav,** 7.4.99 Klattau, ehem. tschech. Major, vermutl. England, RSHA IV E 4, Stapoleit Prag.
180. **Kurz, Otto, Dr.,** 1908, London, Warburg-Institut, RSHA III A 1.
181. **Kutschker, Franz,** 26.11.16 Groß Endersdorf, Dienstpflichtiger, Manchester, 14 Wisnistay Grove 3, RSHA V D 2 f, Ger. d. 22. Div.
182. **Kuttner, Erich,** 27.5.87 Berlin-Schöneberg, Redakteur, vermutl. England, IV A 1 b.
183. **Kysilewskyj, Wladimir, Dr.,** Schriftsteller, vermutl. England, RSHA IV D 3 a.

1. **Labarthe, André,** London, Mitglied der illeg. französ. Regierung, RSHA VI G 1.
2. **Laborski, Karl,** ca. 45 Jahre, Fellhändler, vermutl. England (Täterkreis: Fred Schidloff), RSHA IV E 4.
3. **Lagarde, Leo,** 25.11.92 Znaim, vermutl. England, RSHA IV A 1 b.
4. **Lambert, Charles Albert,** 14.10.00 London, Berichterstatter, RSHA IV A 1.
5. **Lambert, Charles A.,** ehemaliger Berliner Korrespondent d. „Manchester Gardian", vermutl. England, RSHA IV B 4.
6. **Lamkowski, Jan (Johann),** Deckname: Grabowski, 26.1.88 Lessen, poln. N.-Offizier, RSHA IV E 5, Stapo Graudenz.
7. **Lamm, Arnold,** brit. N.-Agent, zuletzt: Antwerpen, vermutl. England, RSHA IV E 4.
8. **Lampersberger, Josef,** 16.9.12 Degerndorf, Kellner, vermutl. England, RSHA IV A 1, Stapoleit München.
9. **Landau, Hans, Dr.,** 1892, a. o. Professor, London, Emigrant, RSHA III A 1.
10. **Landau, Josef,** Dr. phil., 29.4.77 Litzmannstadt, Bankier, vermutl. England, poln. Emigrantenregierung, RSHA III B.
11. **Landau, Max (Jude),** Bankbeamter, London (Täterkreis: Ignatz Petschek), RSHA III D 4.
12. **Landshoff, F. H., Dr.,** vermutl. London, RSHA II B 5.
13. **Lane,** brit. Captain, London, RSHA IV E 4.
14. **Lange, Gerhard,** 2.7.92 Rhede, Werftzeichner, vermutl. England (Täterkreis: Aloisius Porta), RSHA IV E 4.
15. **Lange, Robert,** 21.5.82 Magdeburg, Werkmeister, vermutl. England, RSHA IV E 4.
16. **Lange, Willy,** 20.5.99 Öderan, vermutl. England, RSHA IV A 1 b.
17. **Langer, Felix, Dr.,** Schriftsteller, Emigrant, London N. W. 3, 16. Kemplay Road, RSHA II B 5.
18. **Langhammer, Karl,** 25.3.85 Schwaderbach, vermutl. England, RSHA IV A 1 b.
19. **Langsner, Adolphe Maximilian, Dr. Dr.,** 14.7.93 Woronienka, Agent, vermutl. England, RSHA IV E 4.
20. **Langstädt, Erich, Dr.,** geb. 1910, Prof., Cambridge, Emigrant, RSHA III A 1.
21. **Lanner, V.,** „Internationaler Friedensfeldzug", RSHA VI G 1.
22. **Lansbury, George,** 1859, London E. 3, 39 Bow Road, fördert deutsche Emigranten und Einkreisungspolitik, RSHA VI G 1.
23. **Lareida, Jean,** Deckname: Victor, Vaucher, 17.4.03 Zürich, ND.-Agent, RSHA IV E 4, Stapo Bremen.
24. **Lasalle, Raffael,** 10.5.87 Köln, brit. ND.-Agent, vermutl. England, RSHA IV E 4.
25. **Laser, Hans, Dr.,** 1899, Privatdozent, Cambridge, Molteno-Institut, Emigrant, RSHA III A 1.
26. **Laski, Harold J.,** 30.6.93 Prof., London W. 14, Devon Lodge, Addison Bridge Place, Antifaschistische Liga, RSHA VI G 1.
27. **Laski, Nathan,** Manchester, Antifaschist, RSHA VI G 1.
28. **Laski, Neville, Jonas,** Rechtsanwalt, London N. W. 3, 10, Wedderburn Rd., jüdische Abgeordneten-Kammer, Völkerbundsanhänger, RSHA VI G 1, II B 2.
29. **Laskowski, Ludyga,** 15.3.94 Rosenberg, poln. Major, Kaufmann, RSHA IV E 5, Stapo Oppeln.

30. **Lasnitzki, Arthur, Dr.**, geb. 1896, Ass., Manchester Universität, Emigrant, RSHA III A 1.
31. **Last, Samuel, Dr.**, 1902, Ass., Northampton, Mental-Hospital, Emigrant, RSHA III A 1.
32. **Lathan, George,** 1875, Abgeordneter, Gewerkschaftler, RSHA VI G 1.
33. **Lauber, Heinrich, Dr.**, 1899, Privatdozent, Emigrant, London, RSHA III A 1.
34. **Lauber,** geb. Zettl, Marie, 1.10.84 Neuhammer, RSHA IV A 1.
35. **Laurence, Martin,** richtig: Adolf Paul Narr, London, RSHA VI G 1.
36. **Laurence, Robert,** richtig: Adolf Paul Narr, London, RSHA VI G 1.
37. **Lauthew,** verh. Webb, geb. Sellheim, Magda Antonowna, Russin, zuletzt: Reval, vermutl. England, brit. ND.-Estland, RSHA VI C 2.
38. **Peethick-Lawrence, Frederic William,** 1871, Abgeordneter, RSHA VI G 1.
39. **Lawrence, George,** Reverend, Prediger, vermutl. England, RSHA IV E 4.
40. **Lawrenson,** brit. Agent, zuletzt: Petrinja, vermutl. England, RSHA IV E 4, III A, Stapo Graz.
41. **Lawson, E. F.,** Jude, brit. Hauptmann, RSHA VI G 1.
42. **Lawther, Will,** Rotspanienpropagandist, RSHA VI G 1.
43. **Layton, Dorothey,** London, Anhänger der Harand-Bewegung, RSHA VI G 1.
44. **Layton, Walter Thomas,** Sir, 15.3.84, Vorsitzender „News Chronicle", London S. W. 15, 198 West Hill, Putney, Antifaschist, RSHA VI G 1.
45. **Lazarus, Abraham,** Kommunistenführer, Jude, RSHA VI G 1.
46. **Lazarsfeld-Jahoda, Marie, Dr.**, 26.1.07 Wien, Schriftstellerin, Jüdin (Täterkreis: SPÖ.-Auslandszweigstelle), London N. W. 1, 10 Regents Park Perrace, RSHA II B 5, IV A 1 b, VI G 1.
46 a. **O'Leary,** brit. N.-Agent, zuletzt: Kopenhagen, vermutl. England, RSHA IV E 4.
47. **Leather, Henryk,** vermutl. England (Täterkreis: Fisher), RSHA IV E 4.
48. **Leather, Henry Jean,** Deckname: Roger Gerard, 45 Jahre, brit. Offizier, vermutl. England, RSHA IV E 4.
49. **Leatry,** Leiter d. brit. Pass. Office, zuletzt: Kopenhagen, vermutl. England (Täterkreis: C. M. Bjerring), RSHA IV E 4, Stapo Kiel.
50. **Lecwicz, Zygmunt,** 25.3.86 Warschau, Kunstreiter (ehem. poln. Oberst), RSHA IV E 5, Stapo Schneidemühl.
51. **Lederer, Richard,** 6.3.05 Asch, RSHA IV A 1.
52. **Leeb, Rudolf,** 7.5.02 Berlin, vermutl. England, RSHA IV A 1.
53. **de Leeuw, Maurice,** Deckname: Heymann, brit. ND.-Agent, vermutl. England (Täterkreis: Tinsley), RSHA IV E 4.
54. **Lefontaine, Dick (Edward),** brit. Konsulatsbeamter, N.-Offizier, zuletzt: Istanbul, vermutl. England, RSHA IV E 4.
55. **Leftwich, Joseph,** Journalist, London N. 6, 24 Shepherds Hill High Gate, RSHA II B 5.
56. **Legh-Jones, George,** Direktor, London E. C. 3, 22. St. Helens Court, Shell Transport u. Trading Co., RSHA IV E 2.
57. **Lehmann, Hans Leo, Dr.**, 1907, Ass., London (Universität), Emigrant, RSHA III A 1.
58. **Lehmann, Kurt,** 20.8.06 Barmen, Seemann, RSHA IV A 1, Stapoleit Hamburg.
59. **Lehmann-Rüßbüldt, Otto,** 1.1.71 Berlin, London, RSHA II B 5.

60. **Lehmann, Werner,** 22.5.04 Bochum, Seemann, vermutl. London, RSHA IV A 1.
61. **Leichentritt, Bruno, Dr.,** 1888, a. o. Prof., vermutl. London, Emigrant, RSHA III A 1.
62. **Leichter, Otto, Dr. jur.,** Deckname: **Konrad Huber,** 22.2.97, vermutl. England, RSHA IV A 1.
63. **Leiper, Henry, Dr.,** Methodistenpfarrer, vermutl. England, Anhänger der „Friends of Europe", RSHA VI G 1.
64. **Leiser, Arthur,** brit. N.-Agent, vermutl. England (Täterkreis: Fray Strong), RSHA IV E 4.
65. **Leißler, Rudolf,** 20.3.11 Nieder-Ramstedt, Heizer, Internierungslager, RSHA IV A 1, Stapoleit Hamburg.
66. **Lengborne,** brit. Oberstleutnant, vermutl. England, RSHA IV E 4.
67. **Lengyel, Emil,** Schriftsteller, vermutl. England, RSHA IV B 4.
68. **Lennox, John Robert,** 12.10.96 London, Architekt, London, S. E., 14 Courtside, RSHA IV E 4.
69. **Lennox, V. C. H. Gordon,** Korrespondent d. „Daily Telegrafe", vermutl. England, RSHA IV B 4.
70. **Lenz, Friedrich,** 14.10.02 Saarbrücken, Installateur (Am-Apparat), RSHA IV A 2.
71. **Leonhard, Leo,** 21.1.16 Frankfurt/M., Dienstpflichtiger, London N. W. 8, 230 Finchley Road oder 70 Westend Lane, RSHA Amt V D 2 f.
72. **Leslie, I. E. P.,** Kaufmann, zuletzt: Reval, vermutl. England (Brit. ND.-Estland), RSHA VI C 2.
73. **Lesser, J., Dr.,** Schriftsteller, Emigrant, London N. W. 6, 56 Fairhazel Gardens, RSHA II B 5.
74. **Lessig, Herbert,** Deckname: **Bert, Ping-Pong, Tilly,** 5.7.02 Dresden, Buchdrucker (Am-Apparat), RSHA IV A 2.
75. **Leubuscher, Charlotte, Dr.,** a. o. Prof., 1888, Oxford, Emigrant, RSHA III A 1.
76. **Leubuscher, Walter,** 9.1.09 Marburg, Techniker, vermutl. England, Schwarze Front, RSHA IV A 3.
77. **v. Reichenau-Leuchtmar, Ernst,** 23.5.93 Berlin, Privatlehrer, vermutl. England (Am-Apparat), RSHA IV A 2.
78. **von Leusden, D. M.,** Holländer, Sekretär, zuletzt: Holland, vermutl. England (Täterkreis: Brijnen), RSHA IV E 4.
79. **Leusing, I. W.,** 22.5.02 Mettmann, brit. Agent, zuletzt: Rotterdam, vermutl. England, RSHA IV E 4.
80. **Leverhulme, Viscount,** London, Unilever-House, Blackfriars, RSHA IV E 2.
81. **Levi, Adolf,** Mitarbeiter d. Merton, London, RSHA III D.
82. **Levinthal, Walter, Dr.,** Assistent, 1886 Bath, Emigrant, RSHA III A 1.
83. **Levisohn, Ida, Dr.,** Prof., 1901, London, Emigrant, RSHA IV A 1.
84. **Levy, Hermann,** a. o. Prof., 1881 London, Emigrant, RSHA III A 1.
85. **Levy, Hyman,** Prof., Einkreisungsfront - Anhänger, Jude, RSHA VI G 1.
86. **Lewandowski, Leon,** 2.2.99 Lissa, Radiohändler, RSHA IV E 5, Stapo Liegnitz.
87. **Lichfield, Jack,** 10.9.84 London, Kaufmann, vermutl. England, RSHA IV E 4.
88. **Lichtenstaedter, Ilse, Dr.,** 1901 geb. Oxford (Universität), Emigrant, RSHA III A 1.

89. **Liebermann, Hermann,** 3.1.70 Drohodycz, Rechtsanw., Jude, politischer Sejm-Abgeordneter, RSHA III B, IV D 2.
90. **Liebmann, Gerhard,** Deckname: **Meier, Werner,** 29.6.06 Charlottenburg, Konstrukteur, Cambridge (Am-Apparat), RSHA IV A 1, IV A 2.
91. **Liebmann, Hermann, Dr.,** 1907, Edingburgh (Universität), Emigrant, RSHA III A 1.
92. **Liepmann, Heinrich, Dr.,** 1904, Dozent, vermutl. London, Emigrant, RSHA III A 1.
93. **Liepmann, Leo, Dr.,** 1900 geb., Privatdozent, vermutl. London, Emigrant, RSHA III A 1.
94. **Lincoln, Ashe,** Jude, vermutl. London, Anglo-Ukrainisches Komitee, London 1, Essex Court Temple E. C. 4, RSHA D 3 a.
95. **Lindsay, Alexander,** Dunlop, 1871, Oxford (Universität), Volksfrontanhänger, RSHA VI G 1.
96. **Lindsay-Scott,** vermutl. England, Angehöriger des Nationalrats d. Arbeiterbewegung, RSHA VI G 1.
97. **Lindstädt, Erich,** 5.11.06 Rixdorf, vermutl. England, RSHA IV A 1 b.
98. **Lionell, Wiette,** vermutl. England (Täterkreis: Fisher), RSHA IV E 4.
99. **Lis, Josef,** Major, N.-Offz., vermutl. England, RSHA IV E 5, Stapo Graudenz.
100. **Lisbeths,** brit. Hauptmann, N.-Offz., vermutl. England, RSHA IV E 4.
101. **Lisicki,** vermutl. London (Free Europe), Emigrant, RSHA VI G 1, II B 5.
102. **Lissmann, Hans, Werner, Dr.,** 1909, Cambridge (Universität), Emigrant, RSHA III A 1.
103. **Listerwell,** brit. Journalist, vermutl. England, RSHA IV E 4.
104. **Listowel, William,** London-Kensington S. W. 7, 36. Onslowgardens, Anhänger gegen Deutschland gerichteter Organisationen, RSHA VI G 1, IV A 5.
105. **Lisycky, Karl,** 28.3.93 Holleschau, ehem. Sekr. d. tschech. Außenministeriums, vermutl. London, RSHA IV E 4, Stapoleit Prag.
106. **Litgeber, Boleslaw,** vermutl. London (Free Europe), RSHA VI G 1.
107. **Liticky, Karl, Dr.,** 23.3.93 Holleschau, CSR.-Legationsrat, RSHA IV D 1 a.
108. **Liverman, Maurice Gordon,** geb. 1892, London N. W. 2, 13 Coverdale Rd., RSHA II B 2.
109. **Livingstone, Adelheid,** Leiterin d. brit. Gräberkommission, N.-Agentin, vermutl. England, RSHA IV E 4.
110. **Lloyd, J. B.,** Direktor, London E. C. 2, Britannic House, Anglo-Iranian-Oil Co., RSHA IV E 2.
111. **Lloyd, George Megan,** 1902, lib. Abgeordneter, London, (Völkerbundsbewegung), RSHA VI G 1.
112. **Lord Lloyd,** Chef d. British Council, London, RSHA IV E 4.
113. **Lobkowicz, Max Erwin,** 29.12.88 Bilin, Gutsbesitzer, London, tschech. Emigrant, RSHA IV E 4, Stapoleit Prag.
114. **Lobkowicz, Max Ernst,** Fürst, CSR.-Attaché, vermutl. London, RSHA IV D 1 a.
 * 115. **Lockhart, Bruce,** 2.8.87, Journalist, London, RSHA IV E 4.
116. **Loeb, Otto, Dr.,** 30.5.98 Trier, London N. W. 3, 6 Eton Rise, RSHA IV E 4, Stapo Koblenz.
117. **Loeser, Alfred, Dr.,** vermutl. London (Privatpraxis), Emigrant, RSHA III A 1.
118. **Löwe, Adolfo,** 1893, Professor, Emigrant, Manchester, RSHA III A 1.

*See notes on pages 266–272

119. **Löwe, Eberhard,** 24.12.90 Berlin, Major, vermutl. England, RSHA IV E 5, Stapo Tilsit.
120. **Loewe, Lionell,** brit. ND.-Offizier, zuletzt: Den Haag, vermutl. England (Täterkreis: Stevens/Best), RSHA IV E 4.
121. **Löwenbach, Jan, Dr.,** Emigrant, Welwyn Garden City (Hertfordshire), 36 Digswellroad, RSHA II B 5.
122. **Loewenson, Leo,** 1884, Assistent, London, Emigrant, RSHA III A 1.
123. **Löwenstein, Otto, Dr.,** 1906, Assistent, Birmingham (Universität), Emigrant, RSHA III A 1.
124. **Loewenthal, Hans, Dr.,** 1899, Assistent, London, Emigrant, RSHA III A 1.
125. **Löwi, Siegmund,** 5.4.83 Barnsdorf, Gewerkschaftssekretär, vermutl. London, RSHA IV A 1 b.
126. **Löwy, Siegmund,** 5.4.83 Warnsdorf, vermutl. England, RSHA IV A 1, Stapol Dresden.
127. **Loggin, Estelle,** vermutl. England (Emigrantenzeitschrift „Die Zukunft"), RSHA VI G 1.
128. **London, Heinz, Dr.,** 1907, Bristol (Universität), Emigrant, RSHA III A 1.
129. **Lorenz, Charlotte Elisabeth,** geb. Heide, 6.11.04 Dresden, RSHA IV A 1, Stapoleit Dresden.
130. **Lorenz, Ludwig,** 6.3.17 Altrohlau, vermutl. England, RSHA IV A 1 b.
131. **Lorentz, Roman,** 20.7.10 Troppau, ehem. estn. Offizier, vermutl. England, RSHA IV E 4, III E 4, Stapo Tilsit.
132. **Lorimer, Emily,** Overend, Schriftstellerin, vermutl. England, RSHA III A 5.
133. **Loscelles, Henry George Ch.,** richtig: **Harewood, Earl of, Henry George Ch.,** RSHA VI G 1.
134. **Losch, Johann,** 26.12.09, Anstreicher, RSHA IV A 1, Stapoleit Karlsbad.
135. **Lothar, Hans,** Mitinh. d. Fa. „Secker u. Warburg", Emigrant, London W. C. 2, 22, Essex Street, RSHA II B 5.
136. **Loudon, Direktor,** zuletzt: Wassenaar, vermutl. England, RSHA IV E 2.
137. **Low, David,** 7.4.91, Karikaturist des „Evening Standart", London N. W. 11, 3 Rodborough Road, RSHA IV B 4, VI G 1.
138. **Lubszynski, Gerhard Hans,** 31.8.04 Berlin, Ingenieur, vermutl. London, RSHA IV A 1.
139. **Lucas, F. L.,** Prof., Cambridge (Universität), (Emigrantenzeitschrift: „Die Zukunft"), RSHA VI G 1.
140. **Ludwig, A. H.,** brit. N.-Agent, zuletzt: Den Haag, vermutl. England, RSHA IV E 4.
141. **Lübeck, Hans,** 12.7.08 Bremen, Handlungsgehilfe, vermutl. England, RSHA IV A 1.
142. **Lüdecke, Winfried,** Deckname: **Krzyzanowski,** 14.5.86 Neustettin, Schriftsteller, RSHA IV E 5, Stapo Innsbruck.
143. **Lukapello, Ljubomir, Dr.,** brit. N.-Agent, vermutl. England, RSHA IV E 4.
144. **Lund, F. W.,** Direktor, London E. C. 2, Britannic House, Anglo-Iranian-Oil-Co., RSHA IV E 2.
145. **Lund, R. T.,** Secretary des Boy-Scout I. B., London S. W. 1, 25 Buckingham Palace Road, Internationales Büro der Boy-Scouts, RSHA IV B 1 b.

146. **Luyten, Mey (Frau),** Sekretärin, vermutl. England (Täterkreis: Brijnen), RSHA IV E 4.
147. **Lyall, George,** brit. Generalkonsul, vermutl. England, RSHA IV E 4.
148. **Lyon, George Ernest,** 24.4.88 London, Ingenieur, vermutl. London (Täterkreis: Henry Noble-Dudley), RSHA IV E 4, Stapoleit Königsberg.
149. **Lyttelton, Oliver,** Captain, vermutl. London, Personenkreis: Merton, RSHA III D 5.

1. **v. Maanen, Mej. C.,** zuletzt: Breda/Holl., vermutl. England (Täterkreis: Brijnen), RSHA IV E 4, Stapo Osnabrück.
2. **Maars, P.,** zuletzt Bergen-Schoorl, Laanweg C 156 Schoorl, vermutl. England (Täterkreis: Brijnen), RSHA IV E 4, Stapo Osnabrück.
3. **Macadam, Frl.,** RSHA VI G 1.
4. **Mac-Alpine, Charles B.,** RSHA VI G 1.
5. **Macaullay, Rose,** Schriftstellerin, RSHA VI G 1.
6. **Mac-Cann, Mr.,** Wallasey (Chesbire), 4 Meddoecroft Road (Täterkreis: Ignatz Petschek), RSHA III D 4.
7. **Max-Carthy, G. M.,** Mitarb. v. „Sunday Referee Ltd.", RSHA IV B 4.
8. **Macoene, Alexander,** Deckname: **Masume, Masmoe, Mazome,** 5.12.85 Petersburg, Prof. d. Chemie, England, RSHA IV A 2.
9. **Mac-Cohen,** richtig: **Makohin,** vermutl. England, RSHA IV D 3 a.
10. **Mac-Cracken, C.,** 18.7.80 London, brit. O.-Leutnant, zuletzt: Brüssel, vermutl. England, RSHA IV E 4.
11. **Mac-Kogen,** richtig: **Makohin,** vermutl. England, RSHA IV D 3 a.
12. **Mc-Mahon,** Direktor, London S. W. 1, 5 Wilton Place, RSHA IV E 2.
13. **Mackiewicz, Stanislaw,** Mitgl. d. poln. Nat.-Rates, RSHA IV D 2.
14. **Macleay, Ronald,** RSHA VI G 1.
15. **Mc-Mahon, Henry,** Direktor, London S. W. 1, 5 Wilton Place, RSHA IV E 2.
16. **Macmillan, Harold,** 1894, Politiker u. Verleger, Haywards Heath/ Sussex, Chelwood Gate, RSHA VI G 1.
17. **Macmillan, Lord,** RSHA VI G 1.
18. **Macmurray, Major, N. J.,** Cttee-Sckre., RSHA VI G 1.
19. **Macohon,** richtig: **Makohin,** vermutl. England, RSHA IV D 3 a.
20. **Macuarie, Eduard Henri,** 6.6.11 London, Steward (Fluggesellsch. „Imperial Airways"), London, RSHA IV E 4.
21. **Mager, Hans,** 13.8.16 Berlin, fahnenfl. Soldat, England, RSHA V D 2 f.
22. **Magowan, J. H.,** Handelsrat b. einer Botschaft, England, RSHA IV E 4.
23. **Maier (Maier-Hultschin), Johannes,** Redakteur, Emigrant, London N. W. 3, Belsize Park Gardens, RSHA II B 5, IV A 3.
24. **Maier-Hultschin, I. G.,** Schriftsteller, Emigrant, London N. W. 3, 22 Belsize Park Gardens, RSHA II B 5.
25. **Mayer, Gustav, Dr.,** 1871, a. o. Prof., Emigrant, London, RSHA III A 1.
26. **Mayer, Peter,** Schriftsteller, Emigrant, London W. 9, 34 Lanhill Road (Maida Hill), RSHA II B 5.
27. **Mayer-Groß, Willy, Dr.,** 1889, a. o. Prof., London, Maudsley Hospital, Emigrant, RSHA III A 1.
28. **Meier, Johannes C.,** 2.5.01 Ostrog, Krs. Ratibor, Chefredakteur, RSHA IV E 5.
29. **Meier, Karl,** 25.5.87 Königstein, Krs. Pirna, Schlosser, Liverpool, RSHA IV A 1.
30. **Meyer, Alfred, Dr.,** 1895, a. o. Prof., Emigrant, London, Maudsley Hospital, RSHA III A 1.
31. **Meyer, E. H.,** Emigrant, London, RSHA VI G 1.
32. **Meyer, Ernst-Wilhelm,** 2.4.92 Leobschütz, RSHA IV A 1 b.
33. **Meyer, Gerhard, Dr.,** 1904, Emigrant, Manchester, RSHA III A 1.
34. **Meyer, Herbert,** 1911, Ass., Emigrant, London, RSHA III A 1.
35. **Meyer, Martin,** London, RSHA III D.
36. **Meyer, Otto,** Deckname: **Otto,** 17.11.08 Peine (Am-Apparat), RSHA IV A 2.
37. **Meyer,** 20.5.01 Leyden, zuletzt: Den Haag, vermutl. England (Täterkreis: de Haas), RSHA IV E 4, Stapo Aachen.

38. **Maine, W.,** Abtleiter b. brit. ND., London, RSHA IV E 4.
39. **Mainz, Martin,** 13.11.15 Frankfurt/M., Kaufmann, zuletzt: Den Haag, vermutl. England (Täterkreis: Meijer, Arnold), RSHA IV E 4, Stapoleit Münster.
40. **Mais, Anton,** Redakteur, London, RSHA II B 5.
41. **Maisner, Joe,** brit. Agent, zuletzt: Brüssel, vermutl. England (Täterkreis: Kurt Felsenthal), RSHA IV E 4.
42. **Makant, Anna,** 30.3.81 Waterford/England, Witwe, Sevenolks-Kent, Hazelbourne/England (Täterkreis: Holden Hill Makant), RSHA IV E 4, Stapo Neustadt/W.
43. **Makant, Holden Hill,** 22.7.09 Broadstairs, Student, Sevenolks-Kent, Hazelbourne/England, RSHA IV E 4, Stapo Neustadt/W.
44. **Makohin, Jakob,** Decknamen: **Mac-Cohen, Mac-Kohen, Razumowsky, Macohon, Mac-Kogen, Mokriwsky, Masepa-Razumowsky,** 27.9.80 Wicza oder Wien, vermutl. England, RSHA IV D 3 a.
45. **Malcolm, H. W.,** Direktor, London E. C. 3, 22 Great St. Helen's (Shell Transport u. Trading Co.), RSHA IV E 2.
46. **Malcolm, S.,** Angestellter d. Fa. Harries Scarfe Limited, London, — 4 Lloyd's Av. Fenchurch Street, RSHA IV E 3, Stapo Karlsruhe.
47. **Malech, Lord,** 11.4.85, RSHA VI G 1.
48. **Mallon, James Joseph,** 1880, Soziologe, Fab.-Soc., RSHA VI G 1.
49. **Malone, Cecil,** L'Estrange, Oberst, Mitgl. d. Parlaments, London, RSHA IV D 3 a.
50. **Mandelbaum, Kurt, Dr.,** 13.11.04 Schweinfurt, London, RSHA IV A 1.
51. **Mander, Geoffrey,** geb. 1882, Politiker, Abgeordneter, London S. W. 1, 4. Barton Street, RSHA VI G 1.
52. **Manheim, Ernst, Dr.,** 1900, Ass., Emigrant, London, RSHA III A 1.
53. **Mannheim, Karl, Dr.,** 1893, o. Prof., Emigrant, London, RSHA III A 1.
54. **Mannheim, Dr.,** 1889, a.-o. Prof., Emigrant, London, RSHA III A 1.
55. **Mann, Heinrich,** 27.3.71 Lübeck, Schriftsteller, Emigrant, RSHA II B 5.
56. **Mann, Jakob,** 11.11.14 Bobrka/Polen, Student, RSHA IV E 5, Stapo Köslin.
57. **Mannet, Josef,** 27.2.12 Karlsbad, Bad Bari, RSHA IV A 1 b.
58. **Mannin, Ethel,** 1900, Journalistin, RSHA VI G 1.
59. **Manning, Leah,** Politikerin, RSHA VI G 1.
60. **Mannton,** 1886, Arbeiterführer, RSHA VI G 1.
61. **Manschinger,** geb. Hartwig, Stenotypistin, RSHA IV A 1 b.
62. **Manthey, Stanislaus,** poln. Krim.-Beamter, RSHA IV E 5, Stapo Liegnitz.
63. **de la Mar, A.,** Leiter des Büro Reuter in Amsterdam, zuletzt: Amsterdam, vermutl. England, RSHA IV E 4, Stapo Münster.
64. **Marchbank, John,** Generalsekr. d. engl. Eisenbahnerverb., vermutl. England, RSHA IV A 1 b.
65. **Marchbank, John,** 1883, Gewerkschaftler, vermutl. England, RSHA VI G 1.
66. **Margies, Rudolf,** Decknamen: **Stacho, Stach** u. **Stachud,** 25.2.84 Parchau, Fabrikarbeiter, vermutl. England (Am-Apparat), RSHA IV A 2.
67. **Margullis, Abraham Chaim,** Deckname: **von Hammerstein,** 1.10.95 Lodz, poln. N.-Agent, RSHA IV E 5, Stapo Danzig.

68. **de Marich, A. H. (Agoston)**, 19.1.82, Grenzpolizeimajor a. D., zuletzt: Utrecht, vermutl. England (Täterkreis: Verheuwen), RSHA IV E 4, Stapo Aachen.
69. **Marks, Simon**, London S. W. 7, 42 Hyde Park Gate, South-Kemington, RSHA II B 2.
70. **Markscheffel, Günther**, 16.11.08 Gleiwitz, vermutl. England, RSHA IV A 1.
71. **Marley, Lord**, 16.4.84, Fab.-Soc., Toronto, 417 Bloor Street West, RSHA VI G 1, IV A 5.
72. **Marmorek-Schiller, Dr.**, 10.11.78 Wien, Redakteur, vermutl. England, RSHA IV A 1.
73. **Marochetti, Baron**, 22.7.94 Vouse, angebl. engl. Offizier, London, 13. Emperorsgate, RSHA IV E 4.
74. **Marrack, Prof.**, London. RSHA VI G 1.
75. **Mars, Hans**, 1898, Dozent, Emigrant, Birmingham, RSHA III A 1.
76. **Marschak, Jacob**, 1898, Priv.-Dozent, Emigrant, Oxford, RSHA III A 1.
77. **Martin, Hans**, Direktor d. holl. Luftf.-Ges. K. L. M., Den Haag, zuletzt: Den Haag, vermutl. England, RSHA IV E 4.
78. **Martin, Kingsley**, 28.7.97, Journalist, London W. C. 1, 16. Great James Street, RSHA VI G 1.
79. **Martin, Robert**, richtig: **Narr, Adolf Paul**, vermutl. London, RSHA VI G. 1.
80. **Martin**, Leiter d. Intern. Büros d. intern. Pfadfinderbewegung in London, vermutl. London, Emigrant, RSHA IV E 4.
81. **Marx, A.**, Bankdirektor, zuletzt: Amsterdam, vermutl. England, RSHA IV E 4.
82. **Marx, Fritz M., Dr.**, 1900, Ass., Emigrant, Cambridge (Universität), RSHA III A 1.
* 83. **Masaryk, Jan**, fr. tschech. Gesandter in London, Außenmin. d. csl. Regierung in London, Emigrant, RSHA IV D 1 a II B 5.
84. **Masaryk, Johann**, Emigrant, London, RSHA VI G 1.
85. **Maschler, Kurt**, Schriftsteller, Emigrant, Stanmore b. London, 7 Woodcroft Avenue, RSHA II B 5.
86. **Masepa-Razumowsky, Jakob**, richtig: **Makohin (Prinz)**, vermutl. England, RSHA IV D 3 a.
87. **Masmoe, Alexander**, Deckname: **Macoene, Alexander**, 5.12.85 Petersburg, Prof. d. Chemie, RSHA IV A 2.
88. **Mason-MacFarlane, F. N.**, Oberst, Attaché f. Luftfahrt, England, RSHA IV E 4.
89. **Mastel, Frau**, vermutl. England, RSHA VI G 1.
90. **Masterson**, brit. Capt. u. Generaldirektor d. Phönix Oil in London, London/Bukarest (Täterkreis: Dr. Fritz Rauth), RSHA IV E. 4.
91. **Masume, Alexander**, richtig: **Macoene**, 5.12.85 Petersburg, Prof. d. Chemie, England, RSHA IV A 2.
92. **Masur, Erwin**, 20.1.99, Friedrichstadt, Prokurist, vermutl. England, RSHA IV A 1, Stapoleit Hamburg.
92a **Masur**, geb. **Bodenstein, Annemarie**, 18.11.09 Gronau, vermutl. England, RSHA IV A 1, Stapoleit Hamburg.
93. **Mathieu**, Kommandant, zuletzt: Brüssel, vermutl. England, RSHA IV E 4, Stapoleit Münster.
94. **Mattes, Richard**, 20.12.96 Neuwied, Metzger, London, Hendon Parc Mansion Flat 24, RSHA IV A 1.

*See notes on pages 266–272

95. **Mattuck, Israel,** Goistlicher, vermutl. England, RSHA IV G 1.
96. **Matuschek, Josef,** 19.2.97 Radwanitz, Redakteur, vermutl. England, RSHA IV A 1.
97. **Maude, Charles R.,** 27.2.82 England, Leiter d. Berl. Spionageabteil. d. engl. Mission, Colonel, vermutl. England, RSHA IV E 4.
98. **Maxse, Ernst G. B.,** Sir, engl. Generalkonsul i. Rotterdam, zuletzt: Rotterdam, vermutl. England, RSHA IV E 4.
99. **Maxton, James,** 22.6.85, Politiker, Abgeordneter, Geechwood Barhead, Renfrewshire, RSHA VI G 1.
100. **May, Edward, Dr.,** 1903, London, Privatpraxis, Emigrant, RSHA III A 1.
101. **May, J. Henry,** 1867, Wirtschaftler, RSHA VI G 1.
102. **Maynard, John,** Sir, vermutl. England, RSHA VI G 1.
103. **Mazome, Alexander,** Deckname: **Alexander Macoene,** 5.12.85 Petersburg, Prof. d. Chemie, England, RSHA IV A 2.
104. **McKenna, Martha,** vermutl. England, RSHA IV E 4.
105. **Meisel, Hans,** Emigrant, Princeton, 65 Stockton Street, RSHA II B 5.
106. **Meißner, Ferdinand, Dr.,** 28.3.96 Olmütz, fr. Hauptschriftleiter des Preßburger „Grenzboten", London S. W. 7, 8 Mason Place, RSHA IV E 4.
107. **Meixner,** geb. Endt, **Aloisia,** 14.3.05 Bärringen, b. Miß Savvnry Thorpland Hall, Norfolk Falkenham, RSHA IV A 1 b.
108. **Melchert, Willi,** Schriftsteller, vermutl. England, RSHA III A 5.
109. **Melchett, Henry,** 10.5.98 London, Bankdirektor, London S. W. 3, 8 Chelsea Embankment, RSHA II B 2.
110. **Mellor, William,** 1888, Journalist, RSHA VI G 1.
111. **Mellors, Taddy,** engl. Rennfahrer, vermutl. England (Täterkreis: Kurt Felsenthal), RSHA IV E 4.
112. **Mendelsohn-Bartholdy, Albrecht, Dr.,** 1874, o. Prof., Emigrant, Univers. Oxford, RSHA III A 1, VI G 1.
113. **Menne, Bernhard,** Schriftsteller, London W. 9, 67. Warrington Crescent, Emigrant, RSHA III A 5, II B 5.
114. **Mennicke, Carl, Dr.,** 1887, Prof., Emigrant, Amersfoort, RSHA III A 1.
115. **Menzies, Frederick,** London, RSHA IV E 4, Stapo Darmstadt.
116. **Merling-Eisenberg, Kurt,** 1899, Priv.-Dozent, Emigrant, London, RSHA III A 1.
117. **Merry, A. F.,** Handelssekr., RSHA IV E 4.
118. **Mertens, Karl,** richtig: **Hans Barison,** 19.12.97 Großbüllesheim, Oberstadtsekr., vermutl. England (Am-Apparat), RSHA IV A 2.
119. **Merton, Alfred, Dr.,** London, RSHA III D.
120. **Merton, Israel Richard,** 1.12.81 Frankfurt/M., Kaufmann, Emigrant, Jude, London (Brit. Metallcorporation Ltd.), RSHA IV E 4, III D 5, Stapo Frankfurt/M.
121. **Merz, Josef,** 12.2.14 Rotenfels, Eisendreher, zuletzt: Utrecht/Holland, vermutl. England, RSHA IV E 4, Stapoleit Karlsruhe.
122. **Merzbach, Hilde,** 2.2.09 Frankfurt/M., London, RSHA IV A 1.
123. **Meses, L.,** Worthing-Susex, 25. Bulkinington Cunte, RSHA IV E 4.
124. **Meston, Lord,** 12.6.65, Präs. d. lib. Part. Hurst Place, Cookham Dene Berks., RSHA VI G 1.
125. **Metal, Julio,** 23.5.79, Jarow, Bankier, London, RSHA IV A 1.
126. **Meusel, Alfred, Dr.,** 1896, a. o. Prof., Emigrant, London, RSHA III A 1.

127. **Meyenberg, Friedrich, Dr.,** 1875, a. o. Prof., Emigrant, Sheffield, RSHA III A 1.
127a. **Meyer, Martin,** Mitarbeiter d. Merton, London, RSHA III D.
128. **Meynen, Hermann,** Deckname: **Meynen-Sellerbeck,** 7.5.95 Mülheim, fr. Wirtschafts-Schriftsteller, vermutl. England (Schwarze Front), RSHA IV A 3.
129. **Meyrowitz, Paul,** 22.11.88, Frankfurt/M., Bankier, London (Täterkreis: Frank Beaumont), RSHA IV E 4, Stapolt Berlin.
130. **Mevering, B.,** zuletzt: Hilversum/Holl., vermutl. England (Täterkreis: Breijnen), RSHA IV E 4.
131. **Michael, Siegfried E., Dr.,** 1898, Birmingham, Emigrant, RSHA III A 1.
132. **Michalowski, Günther Isidor,** Deckname: **Joachim,** 7.8.11 Düsseldorf, Student, vermutl. England (Am-Apparat), RSHA IV A 2.
133. **Michalowski, Irma,** richtig: **Abrasimos, Irma,** geb. **Michelson,** 12.9.01 Riga, Kontoristin, Bardame, vermutl. England, RSHA IV E 5, Stapolt Königsberg/Pr.
134. **Michealis, Lorenz, Dr.,** 1902, Ass., Emigrant, Glasgow, RSHA III A 1.
135. **Michelson,** verheiratete **Abrasimos, Irma,** Deckname: **Michalowski,** 12.9.01 Riga, Kontoristin, Bardame, RSHA IV E 5, Stapolt Königsberg.
* 136. **Middelton-Peddelton,** richtig: **Ustinov,** London, RSHA IV E 4.
137. **Middleton, James Smith,** 1878, Politiker, vermutl. England, RSHA VI G 1.
138. **Migawa, Anton,** Arbeiter, vermutl. England, RSHA IV E 5, Stapo Schneidemühl.
139. **Mijer,** brit. Agent, vermutl. England (Täterkreis: Oberst Gibson), RSHA IV E 4.
140. **Mikolajczyk, Stanislaw,** Mitgl. d. poln. Nat.-Rat., vermutl. England, RSHA IV D 2.
141. **Miles, Dr.,** vermutl. England, RSHA VI G 1.
142. **Miller, Cyrill.** Lehrer, zuletzt: Riga, vermutl. England, engl. ND.-Lettland, RSHA VI C 2.
143. **Mills, David,** Abteilungsleiter d. Völkerbundsliga u. IS.-Mann, London, RSHA IV E 4.
144. **Mills, John Kanneth,** 1908: etwa 26 Jahre, Kensington geb., Reisender, London, RSHA IV E 3.
145. **Mitchell, John George,** 19.11.06 Blekchley, Arzt, Biddonkam bei Bedfort (Kraftw. BPO 450 GB), RSHA IV E 4.
146. **Mitchell, Peter Chalmers, Sir,** 23.11.64, Wissenschaftler, vermutl. England, RSHA VI G 1.
147. **Mitchell, William Foot,** Direktor, Essex, Quendon Hall, RSHA IV E 2.
148. **Mitchell,** Angestellter der AJOC, London E. C. 2, Britannic House, RSHA IV E 2.
149. **Mitchison, G. R.,** vermutl. England, RSHA VI G 1.
150. **Mitchison, Naomi,** 1.11.97, Novellistin, River Court, Hammersmith Mall, RSHA VI G 1.
151. **Mitschell-Henry, Muriel,** 28.8.93 Bradford, Reklameleiterin, vermutl. England, (Täterkreis: Julius Guthlac Birch), RSHA IV E 4.
152. **Modrze, Annelise, Dr.,** geb. 1901, Emigrantin, Oxford (Universität), RSHA III A 1.
153. **Möckel, Wilhelm,** 20.2.96 Asch, Scherer, London N. 8, SS-Prince 40, Church Linei, RSHA IV A 1, Stapo Karlsbad.

*See notes on pages 266–272

154. **Möller-Dostali, Rudolf,** Journalist, Emigrant, London W.C.1, Bedford-Place 12, RSHA VI C 1, II B 5.
155. **Möser, Hertha,** 26.9.11 Berlin, Schneiderin, vermutl. England, Am-Apparat, RSHA IV A 2.
156. **Mohrer, Rose,** 11.6.12 Frankfurt/M., stud. med., London, RSHA IV A 1.
157. **Mokriwsky,** richtig: **Makohin,** vermutl. England, RSHA IV D 3 a.
158. **Molitor, Willi,** 25.5.02 Essen, Schlosser, London, RSHA II A 1, · Stapoleit Düsseldorf.
159. **Moncrieff, A., Dr.,** vermutl. England, RSHA VI G 1.
160. **Monk, Herbert,** brit. Vizekonsul, vermutl. England, RSHA IV E 4.
161. **Monks, Noel,** Korresp. des „Daily Express", vermutl. England, RSHA VI G 1.
162. **Monolovisi, Sandu,** zuletzt: Bukarest, vermutl, England, RSHA IV E 4.
163. **Montagu, Lionel Samuel,** geb. 1889, Bankier, London W.1, 5 Saville Row, RSHA II B 2.
164. **Montague, Frederick,** geb. 1876, Politiker, vermutl. England, RSHA VI G 1.
165. **Montague, Soor,** Schriftsteller, vermutl. England, RSHA VI G 1.
166. **Montefiori, L. G.,** London W.1, 37 Weymouth St., RSHA VI G 1, II B 2.
167. **Montresor, John,** 1912 Captown/Südafrika, angebl. engl. Offizier, Borthmouth, Gun House (Täterkreis: David Peter), RSHA IV E 4, Stapo Innsbruck.
168. **Monzer, Ferdinand,** 12.7.98 Mlady-Smoliwec, ehem. tschech. Oberstleutnant, vermutl. England, RSHA IV E 4, Stapoleit Prag.
169. **Moore, Taddy,** engl. Motorradrennfahrer (Täterkreis: Felsenthal), RSHA IV E 4.
170. **Moos, Siegfried,** 19.9.04 München, Bankangestellter, London, RSHA IV A 1.
171. **Moosberg, Fritz,** 16.5.02 Lippstadt, Kaufmann, zuletzt: Holland, vermutl. England, RSHA IV E 4, Stapo Dortmund.
172. **Moravec, Franz,** 23.7.95 Caslau, ehem. tschech. Oberst, London W.8. 53 Lexham Gardens, Kensington, RSHA IV E 4, Stapoleit Prag.
* 173. **Moravec, Frantisek,** 23.7.95 Tschaslau, ehem. tschech. Oberst, London, RSHA IV E 6.
174. **Morgan, David,** Herausgeber des „Youth at Work", RSAH VI G 1.
175. **Morris,** Angestellter der AJOC, London E.C.2, Britannic House, RSHA IV E 2.
176. **Morton,** zuletzt: Libau, vermutl. England (engl. ND.), RSHA VI C 2.
177. **Morton,** brit. Major, vermutl. England (Täterkreis: Oberst Gibson), RSHA IV E 4.
178. **Morrison, Herbert,** Stadtpräsident v. London, London (Täterkreis: Treviranus), RSHA IV E 4.
179. **Morrison, Herbert Stanley,** 3.1.88, Minister, London S. E. 9, 55 Archery Road, RSHA VI G 1.
180. **Morisson, R. M. S.,** West Lychelt, East Lane, engl. ND., RSHA VI C 2.
181. **Morrison, Stanley,** Direktor d. Londoner Rundfunkges., London, RSHA VI G 1.
182. **Morton, S. Guy (Stanley), Dr.-Ing.,** 2.1.85 London, Journalist, RSHA IV E 4, Stapoleit Prag.

*See notes on pages 266–272

183. **Moscow, Eduard,** 1939 etwa 40 Jahre, Leiter des brit. ND. in Amsterdam, zuletzt: Amsterdam, vermutl. England, Kraftw. G 34887, RSHA IV E 4.
184. **Mosenthal, Ellen,** 28.1.20 Berlin, London S. W. 15, Putney Lane, RSHA IV E 4, Stapoleit Hamburg.
185. **Moses, Artur,** Verkäufer, zuletzt: Heerlen/Holl., vermutl. England, RSHA IV E 4, Stapo Aachen.
186. **Mozer, Alfred,** 15.3.05 München, Schriftleiter, RSHA IV A 1.
187. **Mrozowski, Felix,** 18.5.96 Krakau, poln. Hptm. N.-Offizier, RSHA IV E 5, Stapo Graudenz.
188. **Müller, Josef,** 22.8.08 Zuflucht, England, RSHA IV A 1 b.
189. **Müller, Stephan,** 6.1.13 Schwaderbach, London, RSHA IV A 1 b.
190. **Münter, Heinrich,** 1883, a. o. Professor, Emigrant, Oxford, RSHA RSHA III D.
191. **Münzenberg, Wilhelm,** Emigrant, 14.8.89 Erfurt, Schriftsteller, RSHA II B 5.
192. **Muir, Ramsey,** 1872, Historiker u. Politiker, RSHA VI G 1.
193. **Muir, R. H.,** führend i. Unilever-Konzern, Bracknell, Pop's House, RSHA III D
194. **Munnik, J. H. D.,** zuletzt: Enschede/Holland, jetzt vermutl. England (Täterkreis: Breijnen), RSHA IV E 4.
195. **Mura,** richtig **Budberg,** geb. **Baronin Sakrewska,** engl. ND. Estland, RSHA VI C 2, B 249.
196. **Murphie, John Thomas,** 9.12.88 Manchester, Journalist, London 5, Crossroad Highbury, New Park 145, RSHA IV A 1.
197. **Murray, Barbara,** London, RSHA VI G 1.
198. **Murray, Gilbert,** geb. 1866, Prof. der Univers. Oxford, Oxford, RSHA VI G 1.
199. **Murray, Rodney Margarethe,** 18.9.94 Gramond/Schottland, zuletzt: Buchschlag/Hessen, vermutl. England, RSHA IV E 4, Stapo Darmstadt.
200. **Murry, Mary,** vermutl. England, RSHA VI G 1.
201. **Musil, Josef,** London, Rosendaal Road, RSHA IV E 4.
202. **Myer, Morris,** Journalist, London N. W. 11, 63 Ashbourn-Avenue, RSHA II B 2.
203. **Mykura, Franz,** 9.9.96 Trnovan, England, RSHA IV A 1 b.

1. **Nabakowski, Josef,** 27.1.10 Broeswnow/Krs. Stargard, Arbeiter, poln. N.-Agent, RSHA IV E 5.
2. **Nagelschmidt, Franz, Dr.,** 1875, Manchester, Emigrant, RSHA III A 1.
3. **Nagelschmidt, Günther, Dr.,** 1908, ledig, Ass., Emigrant, London, RSHA III A 1.
4. **Najdowski, Zygmunt Stanislaus,** 22.2.10, Hamborn, Student, poln. N.-Agent, RSHA IV E 5.
5. **Napp, Agnes,** 13.6.04 Andernach, zuletzt: Brüssel, jetzt vermutl. England (Täterkreis: Leo Heymann), RSHA IV E 4, III A, Stapo Aachen.
6. **Narr, Adolf Paul,** 18.3.92, Kunstmaler, Schriftsteller, Deckname: **Arnold, Robert, Laurenze, Robert, Martin, Robert, Laurence, Martin,** London, RSHA VI G 1.
7. **Nathan, Harry Louis,** geb. 1889, Rechtsanw. u. Politiker, RSHA VI G 1.
8. **Naumann, Hans, Dr.,** geb. 1901, Emigrant, Greenwich, Hospital, RSHA III A 1.
9. **Necas, Jaromir,** 17.9.88 Neustadt, ehem. Minister d. CSR., London, RSHA IV D 1, II B 5.
10. **Nemec, Min. d. ehem. CSR.,** Emigrant, London, RSHA II B 5.
11. **Neubeck, Anna,** geb. Herzstein, 20.6.00 Witten/Ruhr' (Am-Apparat), RSHA IV A 2.
12. **Neubeck, Hans,** 20.6.97 Essen/Ruhr (Am-Apparat), RSHA IV A 2.
13. **Neuberger, Albert, Dr.,** 1908, Emigrant, London, RSHA III A 1.
14. **Neudert, Franz,** 28.11.12 Eibenberg, England, RSHA IV A 1.
15. **Neudert, Franz,** 18.3.20 Poschetzau, Kaufmann, England, RSHA IV A 1.
16. **Neudert, Josef,** 10.8.02 Eibenberg, England, RSHA IV A 1.
17. **Neugroschel, Dr.,** Rechtsanwalt, London (Täterkreis: Alabert Albseit), RSHA IV E 4, Stapoleit Wien.
18. **Neumann, Bernhard Herrmann, Dr.,** geb. 1909, Cambridge, Univers., Emigrant, RSHA III A 1.
19. **Neumann, Ernst,** 1.5.08 Breslau, Kaufmann, RSHA IV E 5, Stapoleit Breslau.
20. **Neumann, Franz, Dr.,** Mitarbeiter i. d. Labour Party, London W.C. 1, 52 Dorthy Street, Telefon: Holborn 0747, RSHA IV A 1-IV A 5.
21. **Neumann, Otto Reinhold Gustav,** 4.4.02 Saabor, Kr. Grünberg, Arbeiter, komm. Funktionär u. brit. N.-Agent, RSHA IV E 4.
22. **Nevinson, Henry Woodd,** Journalist, RSHA VI G 1.
23. **Newbiggin,** RSHA VI G 1.
24. **Newby, Kennth.,** 11.9.08 Bradford, RSHA IV A 1 b.
25. **Newhouse, Peter Henry,** 14.3.14 Barrackpore/Indien, England, RSHA IV E 4.
26. **Nichel, Mac.,** führend im Unilever Konzern, London E.C. 4, Unilever-House, Blackfriars, RSHA III D.
27. **Nichhols, H. W.,** Mitarb. des „Manchester Guardian", London, RSHA IV B 4.
28. **Nicholson, England,** dipl. Beamter (engl. ND.-Lettland), zuletzt: Riga, RSHA VI C 2.
29. **Nichtson, Arthur George,** Flieger, London, RSHA IV E 4, Stapo Köln.
30. **Nickel, Wilhelm,** 24.12.91 Schwerte, Schauspieler, England, RSHA IV A 1.
31. **Nicolson, Harold,** geb. 1886 Teheran, Schriftsteller u. Politiker, London S. E. 1, 4 King's Bench-Walk, RSHA VI G 1.

32. **Niebergall, Otto,** 5.1.04 Kusel, Sekretär (Am-Apparat), RSHA IV A 2.
33. **Nihom, Karel,** 6.10.00 Winterswijk, zuletzt: Holland, jetzt vermutl. England, RSHA IV E 4, Stapoleit Münster.
34. **de Nijs, H.,** zuletzt: Schagen/Holland, vermutl. jetzt England (Täterkreis: Breijnen), RSHA IV E 4.
35. **Nitkewitsch, Otto,** 30 Jahre alt, vermutl. England, RSHA IV E 4, Stapoleit Stuttgart.
36. **Noble-Dudley, Henry,** 11.10.01 London, Direktor, London (Kraftwg.: „DDU 469" GB), RSHA IV E 4, Stapoleit Königsberg.
37. **Noel-Baker, Philipp J.,** geb. 1889, Abgeordneter, Professor, London S. W. 1, 43 South Eaton Place, RSHA VI G 1.
38. **Norbeck,** geb. Norbeck, **Hannie Marie,** 14.11.99 Budin/Norw., poln. Agentin, RSHA IV E 5.
39. **Norreys,** früher **Newton,** London W. 1, 41 Hertford Street Mayfair, RSHA IV E 3, Stapoleit Wien.
40. **Norris, F. B. V. (Francis Benedikt),** 6.6.83 London?, engl. Lt. Col. (S. L.), J. M. K. K., London, RSHA IV E 4, Stapo Kiel.
41. **Norris, Francisco,** Oberst a. d. d. engl. Armee, RSHA VI G 1.
42. **Norten, Michael,** London, RSHA IV E 4, Stapo Innsbruck.
42a. **North, Harald,** früher Kopenhagen, vermutl. England, brit. ND.-Agent, RSHA IV E 4.
43. **Novotny, Anton,** 13.7.91 Wrschowitz, Arbeiter, Maurer, RSHA IV A 1.
44. **Novy, Wilhelm,** 20.2.92 Zuckmantel, Parteisekretär, RSHA IV A 1.
45. **Nowack, Gerda,** 22.1.15 Schmiedeberg i. Hirschberg, Stenotypistin, Grove-Meadow b. Beaconsfield, RSHA IV A 1.
46. **Nowak, Peter,** 29.6.16 London, Dienstpflichtiger, RSHA V — D 2 f —, A. G. Hamburg.
47. **Nowakowski-Tempka, Siegmund, Dr.,** 1891 Krakau, Journalist, Schriftsteller, Mitglied der poln. Emigrantenregierung i. England, RSHA III B.
48. **Nowakowski, Zygmunt, Dr.,** Mitgl. d. poln. Nat.-Rates, RSHA IV D 2.
49. **Nuding, Hermann,** 3.7.02 Oberurbach, Fabrikarbeiter, Deckname: Klaus Hermann Degen (Am-Apparat), RSHA IV A 2.
50. **Nußbaum,** geb. Eisenberg, **Margarethe,** 23.2.06 Wien, 1938: Den Haag, jetzt: vermutl. England, RSHA IV E 4.
51. **Nußbaumer, A. C.,** London E. C. 2, 99. Gresham Street (Täterkreis: Ignatz Petschek (Banksachverständiger der Petscheks), RSHA III D 4.
52. **Nygryn, B. H. S.,** Agent des brit. ND., London, RSHA IV E 4.

1. **Ober, Hans** (richtig: **Hans Barison**), 19.12.97 Großbüllesheim, Ober-stadtsekretär, vermutl. England (Am-Apparat), RSHA IV A 2.
2. **Obermüller,** Angestellter d. Shell, London E. C. 3, 22. St. Helens Court, Shell Transport u. Trading Co., RSHA IV E 2.
3. **Ochocki, Waclaw Wenzel,** 7.9.93 Dolzig, Bürogehilfe, poln. Agent, RSHA IV E 5, Stapo Liegnitz.
4. **Ochs, Felix, Dr.,** Mitarbeiter d. Merton, London, RSHA III D.
5. **Ocimek, Johann,** 29.5.17 Klein-Lassowitz, Arbeitsdienstmann, RSHA IV E 5, Stapo Oppeln.
6. **O'Donoghue, J. K.,** ehem. Angehöriger der brit. Botschaft in Berlin, RSHA IV E 4.
7. **Oehl,** geb. **Brod, Luise Erna Christl,** 29.10.07 München, Haus-angestellte (Am-Apparat), RSHA IV A 2.
8. **Öhm, Emil,** 29.7.07 St. Joachimsthal, RSHA IV A 1.
9. **von Oertzen, Marie,** geb. **Stewart,** 24.8.78 Rohais/Engl., London, RSHA IV E 4. Stapoleit Hannover.
10. **Öttinghaus, Walter,** 26.2.83 Gevelsberg, Gewerkschaftsbeamter, RSHA IV A 1.
11. **Ogilvie-Forbes, George,** Sir, etwa 45 J. alt, Botschaftsrat, RSHA IV E 4.
12. **Oistros,** Schriftsteller, RSHA IV B 4.
13. **Olden, Rudolf, Dr.,** 14.1.85 Stettin, Rechtsanwalt, Schriftsteller, Cam-bridge oder Oxford, Yatscombe Cottage Boars Hill, RSHA IV A 1, IV A 1 b, IV A 5, II B 5.
14. **Olden, Rudolf,** Sekretär d. „Intern. PEN-Association", Oxford, Yats-combe-Cottage Boars Hill, RSHA IV A 1.
15. **Olden, Rudolf,** Berichterst. d. „Pariser Zeitung", RSHA IV B 4.
16. **Oldenbroek, Jan (Jääpi),** etwa 45 Jahre, Sekretär der ITF., London, RSHA IV A 1.
16a **O'Leary,** brit. ND.-Agent, zuletzt: Kopenhagen, RSHA IV E 4.
17. **Olgin, Konstantin,** 24.6.04 Orel (Rußland), ehem. russ. Emigrant, London, RSHA IV E 4, Stapoleit Berlin.
18. **Oliffers, C. M.,** holl. Hauptmann im ND., zuletzt: Den Haag, RSHA IV E 4, Stapoleit Düsseldorf.
19. **Oliver, E. T.,** 1939, 42—43 J. alt, Leiter der Schiffmaklerfirma Coubro u. Scrutton, zuletzt: Rotterdam, vermutl. England, RSHA IV E 4.
20. **Oliver, Philipps,** zuletzt: Paris, vermutl. England, RSHA IV E 4.
21. **Olivier, Vic,** jüd. Schauspieler, RSHA VI G 1.
21a **Olivier, Christoph Ardon,** Deckname: **Smith,** 10.4.00 Cooktown, brit. N.-Agent, früher Kopenhagen, vermutl. England, RSHA IV E 4.
22. **Ollenhauer, Erich,** 27.3.01 Magdeburg, Parteisekretär (SPD.), vermutl. England, RSHA IV A 1.
23. **Olsen, Hysig,** London, RSHA IV E 4.
24. **Olszar, Karl,** 18.4.14 Neu-Oderberg, Schneider, RSHA IV E 5, Stapo Brünn.
25. **Olszok, Josef,** 12.4.15 Dt.-Leuthen, Schneider, RSHA IV E 0, Stapo Brünn.
26. **Olthof, Jan,** 33 Jahre alt, Sergeant, zuletzt: Holland, vermutl. Eng-land, RSHA IV E 4, Stapo Aachen.
27. **van Oorschot,** niederl. Oberst u. Leiter des niederländischen ND., früher: Den Haag, vermutl. England, RSHA IV E 4, Stapo Aachen.
28. **v. Oosterhout, Geradus,** 27.3.07 Rotterdam, zuletzt: Rotterdam, vermutl. England (Täterkreis: Breijnen), RSHA IV E 4.

29. **Oosterveen, J. W.**, holl. Hauptmann i. holl. Gen. Stab, zuletzt: Den Haag, vermutl. England, RSHA IV E 4, Stapoleit Düsseldorf.
30. **Opl, Adolf,** 12.12.94 Prochomuth, Holowfort bei Sheffield, RSHA IV A 1.
31. **Oppenheim, Arthur,** Mitarbeiter d. Merton, London, RSHA III D.
32. **Oppenheimer, Gertrud, Dr.,** geb. 1893, ledig, Emigrantin, London, RSHA III A 1.
33. **Oppenheimer,** brit. Handelsattaché i. Den Haag, zuletzt: Den Haag, jetzt: vermutl. England, RSHA IV E 4.
34. **Orlowicz, Marian,** 17.9.13 Komarow/Kr. Godecke, Student, RSHA IV E 5.
35. **Ostrer, Isidore,** London W. 1, Upper Brook Feilde, Park Street 47, RSHA II B 2.
36. **Osuski, Pauline,** geb. **Wachova,** 31.3.89, vermutl. England, Ehefrau des Stefan Osuski, RSHA IV E 4, Stapoleit Prag.
37. **Osuski, Stefan,** 31.3.89 Brezova, ehem. tschech. Gesandter in Paris, vermutl. England, RSHA IV E 4, Stapoleit Prag.
38. **Osusky, Stefan, Dr.,** 31.3.98 Brezova, chem. csl. Gesandter in Paris, Staatsminister d. csl. Regierung in London, RSHA IV D 1, II B 5.
39. **Otten, Karl,** 29.7.89 Oberkruechten/Aachen, Schriftsteller, Emigrant, London N. W. 11, 58 Hampstead Way, RSHA II B 5.
40. **Ould, Hermon,** geb. 1886, Schriftsteller, London W. C. 1, 36 Wobern Square, RSHA VI G 1.
41. **Outrata, Eduard, Dr.,** geb. 1898, ehem. Leiter der Brünner Waffen-werke, Finanzmin. d. csl. Regierung in London, RSHA IV D 1.
42. **Outrata, Eduard,** 7.3.98 Caslau, Industrieller, London, RSHA IV E 4, Stapoleit Prag.
43. **Outraty, Eduard, Dr.,** Emigrant, Finanzmin. im tschech. National-ausschuß, London, RSHA II B 5.
44. **Owen, Erna,** geb. **Brückner,** 21.12.04 Oberhausen, England, RSHA IV A 1.

1. **Packe, Edward H.,** Vertr. d. Brit. Regierung, London E. C. 2, Britannic House, Anglo-Iranian-Oil-Co., RSHA IV E 2.
2. **Padding, A. H.,** zuletzt: Eindhoven, jetzt: vermutl. England (Täterkreis: Breijnen), RSHA IV E 4.
3. **Paderewski, Ignacy,** Musiker, Mitgl. d. poln. Nat.-Rates, RSHA IV D 2.
4. **Padt, Ds., N.,** zuletzt: Zutfen/Holl., jetzt: vermutl. England (Täterkreis: Breijnen), RSHA IV E 4.
5. **Paetel, Karl-Otto,** 23.11.06 Berlin, Schriftsteller, vermutl. London, Deckname: **Olaf Harrasin, Alex Afenda** (Boy-Scout International-Büro/Bündische Jugend), RSHA IV B 1.
6. **Pagel, Walter, Dr.,** Privatdozent am Papworth, Settlement, Cambridge, RSHA III A 1.
7. **Pain, Peter,** RSHA VI G 1.
8. **Paish, George,** 1867, Wirtschaftler, RSHA VI G 1.
9. **Palacek, Karl,** 28.1.18 Pilsen, ehem, tschech. Major, London, Kensington W. 8, 53. Lexham Gardens, RSHA IV E 4.
10. **Palecek, Karel,** 28.1.96 Pilsen, ehem. tschech. Major, London (Täterkreis: Moravec, Frantisek), RSHA IV E 6.
11. **Palecek,** 29.1.96 Pilsen, Major OSR., London, Deckname: **Zimmer,** RSHA IV E 3, Stapo Dortmund.
12. **Palmer, R. A.,** Gen.-Sekr. d. Coop. Union Ltd., RSHA VI G 1.
13. **Panefsky, Eugen** (Jude), London (Täterkreis: Ignatz Petschek), RSHA III D 4.
14. **Pankhurst, Sylvia,** Sekret. Int. Frauenliga Matteotti, Woodford Green/Essex, 3 Charteris Road, RSHA VI G 1.
15. **Pannes, Friedrich Gustav,** 23.9.00 Essen, Hausmeister, zuletzt: Amsterdam, jetzt: vermutl. England, RSHA IV E 4.
16. **Panski,** zuletzt: Kowno, jetzt: vermutl. England, RSHA IV E 4, Stapo Tilsit.
17. **van Panthaleon, J. H., Dr.,** Direktor, London E. C. 3, St. Helen's Court, The Asiatic Petroleum Co., RSHA IV E 2.
18. **Pares, Bernhard,** 1867, Prof. für Slawische Kultur an der Universität London, RSHA VI G 1.
19. **Parigger, F. H.,** zuletzt: Holland, jetzt: vermutl. England, RSHA IV E 4.
20. **Parker, John,** geb. 1906, RSHA VI G 1.
21. **Parker, S. J.,** Oberst, RSHA VI G 1.
22. **Parmentier,** ehem. Zivilflieger der KLM., Emigrant, England, RSHA III B.
23. **Pasberg, Maximilian Max,** 26.7.98 Ratibor, Student, Volkswirt, RSHA IV E 5, Stapo Oppeln.
24. **Pascall, Sydney,** RSHA VI G 1.
25. **Passfield, Baron,** RSHA VI G 1.
26. **de Passen,** holländ. Major, zuletzt: Wassonaar, vermutl. England, RSHA IV E 4, Stapoleit Düsseldorf.
27. **Paterson, John,** Leiter des Nachrichteninstitutes I. C. I., London S. W. 1, Buckinghamgate (Täterkreis: s. Informationsheft I. C. I.), RSHA III D 5.
28. **Paty, richtig: Kaspar, Jaroslav,** RSHA IV E 4, Stapoleit Prag.
29. **Paul, Ernst,** 27.4.97 Steinsdorf/Tetschen, Generalsekretär, RSHA IV A 1.

30. **Pawlowitsch, Paul,** richtig: **Paul Dyks,** Oberst, England, RSHA IV E 4.
31. **Paxton,** Geistlicher, RSHA VI G 1.
32. **Pearson, I. W.,** London, Unilever House, Blackfriars, RSHA IV E 2.
33. **Pearson, R. G. (Cecil James?),** brit. Nachr.-Offz., zuletzt: Genf, jetzt: vermutl. England, RSHA IV E 4.
34. **Peartree, Stanley Arthur,** 19.11.02 Leytonstone, Tabaksachverständiger, zuletzt: Griechenland, jetzt: vermutl. England, RSHA IV E 4, Stapoleit Dresden.
35. **Pecher, Anton,** 2.4.90 Neudek, England, RSHA IV A 1.
36. **Pecher, Karl,** 7.4.86 Neudeck, RSHA IV A 1.
37. **Middelton-Peddelton,** richtig: Ustinov, RSHA IV E 4.
38. **Peethick-Lawrence,** Frederic William, geb. 1871, Abgeordneter, RSHA VI G 1.
39. **Peklo, Jaroslav,** 3.8.01 Wilkischen, Manchester, Birsch Polygon Dickenson Road, RSHA IV A 1.
40. **Perabo, Franz, Dr.,** Assistent, geb. 1910, Emigrant, London, RSHA III A 1.
41. **Pernikar, Johann,** 11.1.03 Ober-Cerekwe, ehem. tschech. Stabskapitän (Luftwaffe), vermutl. England, RSHA IV E 4, Stapoleit Prag.
42. **Perry, S. F.,** Sekr. Coop. P., RSHA VI G 1.
43. **Peter, Franz,** 13.2.15 Mährisch-Lodenice, tschech. Leutnant, ND.-Offiz., vermutl. England, RSHA IV E 4, Stapoleit Prag.
44. **Peters, Wilhelm, Dr.,** geb. 1880, o. Prof., Emigrant, Surrey, RSHA III A 1.
45. **Petersen, Jan,** Schriftsteller, RSHA III A 5.
46. **Petigura, Ardeschir,** 21.8.05 Kulangsu, Arzt, England, RSHA IV A 1.
47. **Petschek, Ernst, Dr.** (Jude), London W. 1, Corkstreet (Täterkreis: Ignatz Petschek, RSHA III D 4.
48. **Petschek, Eva Elisabeth,** Ashot-Berks b. London (Täterkreis: Ignatz Petschek), RSHA III D.
49. **Petschek, Fritz,** Sohn Isidor Petscheks, Ashot-Berks b. London (Täterkreis: Julius Petschek), RSHA III D 4.
50. **Petschek, Hans** (Jude), Ashot-Berks b. London (Täterkreis: Julius Petschek), RSHA III D 4.
51. **Petschek, Ina Louise,** Ashot-Berks b. London (Täterkreis: Ignatz Petschek), RSHA III D.
52. **Petschek, Karl** (Jude), London W. 1, Corkstreet, Mayflair-Hotel, St. Regies (Täterkreis: Ignatz Petschek), RSHA III D 4.
53. **Petschek, Paul, Dr.** (Jude), Ashot-Berks b. London (Täterkreis: Julius Petschek), RSHA III D 4.
54. **Petschek, Rita Madelaine,** Ashot-Berks b. London (Täterkreis: Ignatz Petschek), RSHA III D.
55. **Petschek, Victor** (Jude), Ashot-Berks b. London ((Täterkreis: Julius Petschek), RSHA III D 4.
56. **Petschek, Walter** (Jude), Ashot-Berks b. London (Täterkreis: Julius Petschek), RSHA III D 4.
57. **Petschek, Wilhelm** (Jude), London W. 1, Corkstreet, Mayflair Hotel, St. Regies (Täterkreis: Ignatz Petschek), RSHA III D 4.
58. **Pety** richtig **Kaspar, Jaroslav,** RSHA IV E 4, Stapoleit Prag.
59. **Peveling, Hermann,** 7.8.04 Lippstadt, Schriftsteller, Deckname: **Ling** Kossak, London, RSHA IV E 4, Stapoleit Prag.
60. **Pfaffl, Josef,** 15.12.95 Ochsenfurt, RSHA IV A 1.
61. **Pfefferkorn, Olga,** 1.8.16 Frankfurt/M., Liverpool, RSHA IV A 1.

62. **Pfeifer, Heinrich,** 21.3.05 Frankfurt/M., RSHA IV E 5.
63. **Pfeiffer, Heinrich,** 21.3.05 Frankfurt/M., Schriftsteller, Deckname: Hans Jürgen Koehler, RSHA IV B 4.
64. **Pfeiffer, Jan Waclaw,** 31.3.18 Warschau, Student, poln. Offizier, RSHA IV E 5, Stapoleit Stettin.
65. **Pflüger, Kurt,** 12.10.10 Hannover, Student, London (Am-Apparat), RSHA IV A 2.
66. **Philipp, Ursula, Dr.,** geb. 1908, Emigrantin, London (Universität), RSHA III A 1.
67. **Philippovitsch, Jochim,** 9.1.10 Cladle/England, Dipl.-Ingenieur, Manchester, RSHA IV E 4, Stapo Leipzig.
68. **Philips, Christopher John,** 30.6.96 Nottingham, vermutl. England, RSHA IV E 4, Stapoleit München.
69. **Phillips, Ch. J.,** brit. Vizekonsul, vermutl. England, RSHA IV E 4.
70. **Piasetzki, Karl,** 20.1.97 Satorw b. Krakau, Oberstl. Leiter der Offensiv-Abteilung, RSHA IV E 5, Stapo Kattowitz.
71. **Pick, R. H.,** Schriftsteller, Emigrant, London S. W. 5, 62 West Cromwell Road, RSHA II B 5.
72. **Pieniazek, Mieczyslaw,** 27.4.96 Sliwacow, Zollinspektor, Kundschafteroffizier, RSHA IV E 5, Stapo Schneidemühl.
73. **Pieper, Prof.,** Emigrant, vermutl. England, Sozialdemokr. Weltprotestantismus, RSHA VI H 3, II B 3.
74. **Pierson, Allard,** Bankinhaber, zuletzt: Amsterdam, vermutl. England, RSHA IV E 4.
75. **Pietz, Vincenty,** 2.7.97 Czarnikau, Gärtner, RSHA IV E 5, Stapo Oppeln.
76. **Pietzuch, Emil,** 9.3.99 Neurode, Zimmermann, Deckname: Franz Arthur (Am Apparat), RSHA IV A 2.
77. **Pioch Albert,** 8.4.95 Stewnitz, Krs. Flatow, Landwirt, RSHA IV E 5, Stapo Schneidemühl.
78. **Bzdyl-Pioto,** 13.6.98 Polen, protest. Geistlicher, zuletzt: Holland, jetzt vermutl. England, RSHA IV E 4, Stapo Aachen.
79. **Pitcairn, Frank,** Korrespondent, London S. W. 1, Viktoria Street 34, RSHA IV A 1.
80. **Plasczyk, Paul,** 7.10.06 Mikulsschütz, N.-Agent (Polen), RSHA IV E 5, Stapo Oppeln.
81. **van der Plasse, J. M. Z.,** holl. Major, zuletzt: Wassenaar, vermutl. England (Täterkreis: Karel Nihom), RSHA IV E 4, Stapoleit Düsseldorf.
82. **Plaut, Theodor,** geb. 1888, a. o. Prof., Emigrant, Leeds, RSHA III A 1.
83. **Plawski, Eugen Josef Stanislaw,** 26.3.95 Noworosyjsk/Kaukasus, Konteradmiral der poln. Admiralität in England, RSHA III B.
84. **Plesch, Johann, Dr.,** 1878, a. o. Prof., Emigrant, Privatpraxis in London seit 1934, RSHA III A 1.
85. **Plotke, Karl,** Mitarbeiter des Merton, London, RSHA III D.
86. **Podlipnig, Josef,** 21.6.02 Klagenfurt, Redakteur, Deckname: Fritz Valentin, vermutl. England, RSHA IV A 1.
87. **Pöschmann, Karl,** 7.9.03 Eibenberg, RSHA IV A 1.
88. **Pötzsch, Gustav,** 19.8.98 Rixdorf, Metallarbeiter (Am-Apparat), RSHA IV A 2.
89. **Polak, Ernst, Dr.,** Emigrant, London W. 8, Alma Terrace, 7 Allen Street, RSHA II B 5.

90. **Polak, W. C.,** 1.7.97 Zevenberger/Holland, zuletzt: Den Haag, vermutl. England, RSHA IV E 4.
91. **Polanyi, Michael, Dr.,** geb. 1891, a. o. Prof., Manchester (Universität), Emigrant, RSHA III A 1.
92. **Poldermann, Ir. L. J.,** zuletzt: Holland, vermutl. England, RSHA IV E 4.
93. **Poldermans, M.,** zuletzt: Zierikzee/Holl., vermutl. England (Täterkreis: Breijnen), RSHA IV E 4.
94. **Poliakoff, N.,** Journalist, London, RSHA IV E 4.
95. **Poll, W.,** zuletzt: Amsterdam, vermutl. England, RSHA IV E 4, Stapo Aachen.
96. **Pollack, Oskar, Dr.,** 7.10.93 Wien, Journalist, Decknamen: Groß, Smith, Amann, vermutl. England, RSHA IV A 1.
97. **Pollitt, Harry,** geb. 1890, Politiker, RSHA VI G 1, II B 4.
98. **Pomeroy, Henry Ernest,** brit. Vizekonsul, RSHA IV E 4.
99. **Ponsonby, Lord,** geb. 1871, Politiker, RSHA VI G 1.
100. **Poplonek, Wojciech (Albert),** 20.4.96 Trzinice, Maschinenschlosser, Kraftwagenführer, RSHA IV E 5, Stapo Schneidemühl.
101. **Poppinger, Konrad,** 22.2.04 Wien, Schneider, London, RSHA V C 1 e.
102. **Porter, A. E.,** Leiter einer sowjetr. ND.-Zentrale i. Warschau, zuletzt: brit. Vizekonsul in Riga, RSHA IV E 4, Stapo Tilsit.
103. **Pospieszny, Jakob,** 13.7.87 Chajno, Kr. Samter, Tischler, RSHA IV E 5.
104. **Posthuma, A.,** Vertreter, Angest. des Stevens, vermutl. England (Täterkreis: Stevens-Best), RSHA IV E 4.
105. **Potocki, Graf, Josef,** Mitgl. d. poln. Reg., höh. Beamter i. Außenministerium, RSHA IV D 2.
106. **Powell, W. Mansell,** brit. Vizekonsul, vermutl. England, RSHA IV E 4.
107. **Power, Eileen, Prof.,** RSHA VI G 1.
108. **Prager, Emigrant,** London, 513 Endsleighcourt, RSHA II B 5.
109. **Prain, R.,** Gewerkschaftsbeamter, RSHA VI G 1.
110. **Prausnitz, Carl,** 1876, a.-o. Prof., Emigrant, Isle of Wight, RSHA III A 1.
111. **Prausnitz, Otto, Dr.,** geb. 1904, Privatdozent, Emigrant, London, RSHA III A 1.
112. **Prazek, K.,** London, RSHA IV E 4.
113. **Prchala, Leo,** 23.3.92 Mährisch-Ostrau, ehem. tschech. General, England, RSHA IV E 4. Stapoleit Prag.
114. **Preiß, Hans, Dr.,** London W.C.1, Museumstr. 41 a, Emigrantenbuchhandlung, RSHA IV A 1, IV A 5.
115. **Preston, Thomas, Hildebrand,** Diplomat, zuletzt: Kaunas (engl. ND. Litauen), RSHA VI C 2.
116. **Pretorius, Alfred,** 20.10.02 Berlin, Kaufmann, vermutl. England, RSHA IV E 4, Stapoleit Prag.
117. **Le Prevost, H. W.,** Herausgeber der Zeitschrift „Headway", RSHA VI G 1.
118. **Prevsner, Nikolaus, Dr.,** geb. 1902, Priv.-Dozent, Emigrant, London, RSHA III A 1.
119. **Priborsky, Franz,** 27.9.18? Litovel (Hana-Mähren), RSHA IV E 5, Stapo Brünn.
120. **Price-Jones, Alan,** London (Täterkreis: Ignatz Petschek), RSHA III D 4.

121. **Price, George Ward,** 17.2.86 Sonderkorresp. vom „Daily Mail", London, RSHA IV B 4.
122. **Price, Morgan, Philips,** 1885, Politiker, RSHA VI G 1.
123. **Pries, Viktor,** 21.8.08 Hamburg, Schlosser (Am-Apparat), RSHA IV A 2.
124. **Priestley, John Boynton,** geb. 1894, Schriftsteller, RSHA VI G 1.
125. **Prince, Edmund Matthew,** 21.9.96 London, Geschäftsführer, vermutl. England, RSHA IV E 4, Stapo Wesermünde.
126. **Pringsheim, Ludwig,** 4.3.16 Halle/Saale, Wehrpflichtiger, London, RSHA V — D 2 f, Ger. d. Kommand. Berlin.
127. **Prins,** zuletzt: Den Haag, jetzt: vermutl. England, RSHA IV E 4.
128. **Pritt, Denis Nowell,** geb. 1887, London, L. C. 4, 3 Pump Court, RSHA VI G 1.
129. **Prochazka, Karl,** 25.4.05 Brünn, chem. tschech. N.D.-Offiz., vermutl. England, RSHA IV E 4, Stapoleit Prag.
130. **Prochownick, Vilma, Dr.,** 1904, ledig, Ass., Cambridge (Univers.), Emigrant, RSHA III A 1.
131. **Proskauer, Arthur,** 4.8.80 Bauerwitz-Leobschütz, Apotheker, RSHA IV E 5.
132. **Proskauer, Elisabeth,** geb. **Winter,** 23.6.96 Jägerndorf, RSHA IV E 5.
133. **Proskauer, Erich,** 8.9.89 Kreuzburg, Apotheker, RSHA IV E 5.
134. **Przylibski, Jan,** 21.3.93 Jaroslaw, poln. N.-Offiz., Journalist, RSHA IV E 5. Stapo Danzig.
135. **Puciata, Stefan,** Rechtsanwalt, RSHA IV E 5, Stapo Bromberg.
136. **Pugh,** Sir **Arthur,** geb. 1870, Vorsitzender des Generalrates der Gewerkschaften, RSHA VI G 1.
137. **Pulvermann, Heinz** (Jude), Generaldirektor d. Julius Petschek Konzerns, London, Grosvenor House, Park-Lane (Täterkreis: Julius Petschek), RSHA III D 4.
138. **Puppe, Bruno,** 17.1.04 Niederschönbrunn, Ziegeleiarbeiter, Manchester, RSHA IV A 1, Stapoleit Dresden.
* 139. **Gans Edler Herr zu Putlitz, Wolfgang,** 16.7.99 Laaske, chem. Legationsrat b. d. Dtsch. Gesandtschaft, vermutl. England, RSHA IV E 4.

*See notes on pages 266–272

1. **Rabinowitsch, Eugen J., Dr.,** geb. 1898, Ass., Emigrant, London (Univers.), RSHA III A 1.
2. **Raczkiewicz, Mitgl.** d. poln. Reg., Staatspräsident, RSHA IV D 2.
3. **Radatz, Heinrich Hermann Johann,** 2.3.09 Krefeld, Matrose (Heizer), RSHA IV A 1.
4. **Radbruch, Gustav, Dr.,** geb. 1878, o. Prof., Emigrant, Oxford (Universität), RSHA III A 1.
5. **Raddatz, Heinrich,** 2.3.09 Krefeld, in England interniert, Schiffssabotage, RSHA IV A 2.
6. **Rademakers, J. M.,** Schiffskapitän, zuletzt: Holland, vermutl. England, RSHA IV E 4, Stapoleit Düsseldorf.
7. **Rado, Richard, Dr.,** geb. 1906, Sheffield (Universität), Emigrant, RSHA III A 1.
8. **Rahle, Hans,** RSHA VI G 1, II B 5.
9. **Ramsdule,** brit. ND.-Agent, zuletzt: Schiebrock b. Rotte, vermutl. England, RSHA IV E 4, Stapoleit Stuttgart.
10. **Randal, Norman, Sir,** Verbindungsoff. zw. Scotland Yard u. Secret Intell. Service, RSHA IV E 4.
11. **Ratcliffe, Herbert James,** 18.4.88 London, Jeelong., Direktor, Captain, vermutl. England, RSHA IV E 4, Stapo Köln.
12. **Rathbone, Eleonor,** geb. 1872, Abgeordnete, Liverpool, Greenbank, Greenbank Lane, RSHA VI G 1.
13. **Rauch, Harry,** 18.5.13 Berlin, Kürschner, vermutl. England, RSHA IV E 4, Stapo Bremen.
* 14. **Rauschning, Hermann, Dr.,** 7.8.87 Thorn, ehem. Senatspräsident von Danzig, vermutl. England, RSHA IV A 1, IV A 3, II B 5.
15. **Raven, Charles E.,** Geistlicher, RSHA VI G 1.
16. **Rawidowicz, Simon, Dr.,** geb. 1897, London, Emigrant, RSHA III A 1.
17. **Rawita-Gawronski, Sigismund (Zygmunt), Dr.,** 9.12.86 Genf, Handelsrat, Poln. Botsch. Berlin, Deckname: **Gawronski,** RSHA IV E 5.
18. **Rawitzki, Karl, Dr.,** 21.10.79, Emigrant, Jude, vermutl. England, RSHA II B 5.
19. **Masepa-Razumowsky, Jakob, Prinz,** richtig: **Makohin,** vermutl. England, RSHA IV D 3.
20. **Razumowsky, Leon, Prinz,** richtig: **Makohin,** vermutl. England, RSHA IV D 3.
21. **Reader, Ethel,** RSHA VI G 1.
22. **Reading, Marquess of Gerald, Rufus,** 10.1.89 London (Familienname Isaac), Heathfield/Sussex, Great Broadhust Farm, RSHA VI G 1, II B 2.
23. **Reading, Eva Violet,** London S. W. 7, 65. Rutland Gate, RSHA II B 2.
24. **Reed, Douglas,** Schriftsteller, RSHA IV B 4, III A 5.
25. **Reed, Georg,** Generalsekretär d. ITF., England (Schiffssabotage), RSHA IV A 2.
26. **Regnart, Cyril H. (Cyrus),** 65—72 Jahre alt, Kptn., Nachr.-Offz. d. brit. Sp.-Büros in Brüssel, vermutl. England, RSHA IV E 4.
27. **Regulski, Janusz,** 27.12.87 Zawiercie, General, Konsul, Mitglied der poln. Emigrantenregierung i. England, RSHA III B.
28. **Rehbein, Helmut,** 15.2.15 Potsdam, Dienstpflichtiger, zuletzt: Neu-Seeland, RSHA V D 2 f.
29. **Rehwald, Franz,** 16.8.03 Redakteur, RSHA IV A 1.
30. **Reichard, Hans,** 18.12.04 Hamburg, Werftarbeiter (Am-Apparat), RSHA IV A 2.

*See notes on pages 266–272

31. **v. Reichenau-Leuchtmar, Ernst,** 23.5.93 Berlin, Privatlehrer, (Am-Apparat), RSHA IV A 2.
32. **Reichenbach, Bernhard, Dr.,** 12.12.88 Berlin, Schauspieler, Schriftsteller, London, RSHA IV A 1.
33. **Reichenbach, Fritz Ernst,** 11.7.00 Limbach/Sa., vermutl. England, RSHA IV E 4, Stapoleit Chemnitz.
34. **Reichenbach, Hermann,** 6.7.98 Hamburg, Musiker, England, RSHA IV A 1.
35. **Reichenberger, Emanuel,** Pater, RSHA VI G 1, II B 5.
36. **Reichenberger, Erich,** Deckn. des **Alfred Ottomar Baumeister,** RSHA IV A 1.
37. **Reif, Julius,** 5.10.93 Handlawa, London, RSHA IV A 1.
38. **Reilly, Sidney Georg,** 24.3.74 Dublin, brit. Kapitän u. N.-Offizier, vermutl. England, RSHA IV E 4.
39. **Reinhold, Ernst,** 16.11.97 Schönfeld, RSHA IV A 1.
40. **Reinwarth, Adolf,** 26.8.05 Eibenberg, England, RSHA IV A 1.
41. **Reissner, Anton,** 30.12.90 München, Gewerkschaftssekretär, England, RSHA IV A 1.
42. **Reiter, Tiberius, Dr.,** geb. 1903, seit 1936: Privatpraxis in London, Emigrant, RSHA III A 1.
43. **Reitzner, Richard,** 19.8.93 Einsiedel, Parteisekretär, vermutl. England, RSHA IV A 1.
44. **Remitschka, Ella,** 19.12.13 Fischern, RSHA IV A 1.
45. **Reul, Hans,** 13.4.08 Hof/Bayern, vermutl. England, RSHA IV E 4, Stapo Nürnberg.
46. **Reul, Karoline Effi,** 14.4.08 London, London, Ealing 5, RSHA IV E 4.
47. **Reybekiel, von, Helena, Dr.,** 1881, Dozentin, Birmingham (Universität), Emigrantin, RSHA III A 1.
48. **Reynoulds, England,** Antiquitätenhändler (Engl. ND-Lettland), RSHA VI C 2.
49. **Rezler, Franz,** 23.6.15 Pohrelacka, Kapitän, zuletzt: Konstantinopel, vermutl. England, RSHA IV E 4, Stapoleit Wien.
50. **Rhodes, Christopher,** 30.4.14 Gosport/England, brit. Offiz. d. Pass-Controll-Office, zuletzt: Den Haag, vermutl. England (Täterkreis: Stevens/Best), RSHA IV E 4.
51. **Rhondda, Margaret Haig,** Viscountess, geb. 12.6.83, Journalistin, London N. W. 3, 1 B Bay Tree Lodge, RSHA VI G 1.
52. **Richardsohn, John Philipp,** 29.11.90 Preston, Matrose, London, RSHA IV A 1.
53. **Richter, Harry,** 8.5.00 Tischenreuth, Journalist, zuletzt: Den Haag, vermutl. England, RSHA IV E 4.
54. **Richter, Lothar, Dr.,** geb. 1895, Halifax, Emigrant, RSHA III A 1.
55. **Rickards, Esther, Dr.,** RSHA VI G 1.
56. **Rickett, Richard Martin,** 18.3.07, England, RSHA IV A 1.
57. **Riddel (Riddle), James,** Kaufmann, zuletzt: Reval (Engl. ND-Estland), RSHA VI C 2.
58. **Riddle (Riddel), James,** England, Kaufmann, engl. Freimaurer, Wohng.: zuletzt Reval (Engl. ND-Estland), RSHA VI C 2.
59. **Ridley, F. A.,** RSHA VI G 1.
60. **Rieck, Alfred,** 4.7.92 Stettin, Adventist, zuletzt: Maastricht, vermutl. England, RSHA IV E 4, Stapo Aachen.

61. **Rieger, Julius, Dr.,** ev. Geistlicher, London S. E. 3, 1 Ulundi Road Blackheath (Täterkreis: Amsling-Hildebrand-Freudenberg), RSHA II B 3, VI H 3.
62. **Riehl, Jürgen,** 10.10.06 Königsberg, Gerichtsassessor, London (Täterkreis: Boy-Scout Internationales Büro/Bündische Jugend), RSHA IV B 1.
63. **Rieß, Erwin,** 12.10.07 Mannheim, Schlosser (Am-Apparat), RSHA IV A 2.
64. **Rijpma, W. A. F. H.,** zuletzt: Holland, vermutl. England, RSHA IV E 4.
65. **Rinke, Heinz,** 8.6.19 Remscheid, ehem. RAD-Mann, P.SHA IV E 5, Stapoleit Breslau.
66. **Rinner, Erich, Dr.,** 27.7.02 Berlin, vermutl. England, RSHA IV A 1.
67. **Rintelen, Franz,** 19.8.78 Frankfurt/O., dtsch. Korvettenkapitän a. D. u. Schriftsteller, Deckname: **Rintelen v. Kleist,** RSHA IV E 4, IV B 4, III A 5.
68. **Rintelen v. Kleist, Franz,** richtig **Rintelen, Franz,** 19.8.78 Frankfurt/O., dtsch. Korvettenkapitän a. D. u. Schriftsteller, England, RSHA IV E 4.
69. **von Rinteln, Franz,** richtig: **Rinteln, Franz,** 19.8.78 Frankfurt/O., dtsch. Korvettenkapitän, England, RSHA IV E 4.
70. **Ripka, Hubert, Dr.,** 26.7.95 Koderik? Köberwitz? Redakteur, Journalist, Staatssekretär i. Min. f. Ausw. Angel. d. csl. Regierung i. London, RSHA IV D 1, IV E 4.
71. **Ripka, Emigrant,** London, RSHA II B 5.
72. **Robak, Josef,** 5.11.99, Oberleutnant, RSHA IV E 5, Stapoleit Danzig.
73. **Roberts, Frederic Owen,** 1876, Parlamentsmitglied, RSHA VI G 1.
74. **Roberts, Peter,** richtig **Dr. Schiller-Marmorek,** 10.11.78 Wien, Redakteur, Schriftsteller, vermutl. England, RSHA IV A 1.
75. **Roberts, Stephen H.,** Schriftsteller, RSHA IV B 4.
76. **Roberts, Vera,** zuletzt: Prag, vermutl. England, RSHA IV E 4.
77. **Roberts, Wilfried,** 28.8.00 Abgeordneter, London N. W 3, 75 Flask Walk, RSHA VI G 1.
78. **Robertson, H. S.,** Captain, London, Piccadilly 19, RSHA IV E 4.
79. **Robertson, J. M.,** RSHA VI G 1.
80. **Robeson, Paul,** Negersänger, RSHA VI G 1.
81. **Robinson, Helene Elisabeth,** geb. Brunert, 27.2.97 Martenan/Frankr., Ehefrau, vermutl. England, RSHA IV E 4.
82. **Robinson, Jos.,** Rot-Spanienkämpfer, RSHA VI G 1.
83. **Robinson, L. M.,** brit. Gen.-Konsul, vermutl. England, RSHA IV E 4.
84. **Robinson, W. A.,** RSHA VI G 1.
85. **Robinson, William Field,** Vertreter einer brit. Bankengruppe, vermutl. England, RSHA IV E 4.
86. **Robisch, Rudolf,** 14.9.02 Nassengrub, Brauereiarb., RSHA IV A 1.
87. **Rodd, B. H.,** Corford-Chiffs-Bournemouth, Brudderrel-Avenue, RSHA IV E 4, Stapoleit Stuttgart.
88. **Roddy(ie), William,** Stewart, 17.12.82 London, brit. Oberstleutn., vermutl. England (Täterkreis: Gerta Luise v. Einem), RSHA IV E 4.
89. **Rodgers, Frank,** London, Clapham-Road 420, Attentäter, RSHA IV A 2.
90. **Rose, Mandervil,** London, 4 Carmelit Street, RSHA IV E 4, Stapoleit Hannover.
91. **Röhr, Albert,** 5.11.04 Halle, Stukkateur, Birmingham, Deckname: Heinz (Am-Apparat), RSHA IV A 2.
92. **Röhrer, Adolf,** 31.12.98 Georgenthal, RSHA IV A 1.
93. **Roelfsema, P. R.,** zuletzt: Holland, vermutl. England, RSHA IV E 4.

94. **Rösch, Emil,** 15.4.81 Hirschenstand, Kr. Graslitz, London od. Leicester, Wentworth Road 14 b. Mosward, RSHA IV A 1.
95. **Rötz, Franz,** 29.1.87 Altkinsberg, Kr. Eger, RSHA IV A 1.
96. **Rötz, Franz,** 30.9.09 Altkinsberg, Kr. Eger, RSHA IV A 1.
97. **Roghair,** 11.6.86 Linghooten, zuletzt: Den Haag, vermutl. England, RSHA IV E 4, Stapoleit Düsseldorf.
98. **Rohm, Andreas,** 31.7.76 Schönfeld, Krs. Elbogen, RSHA IV A 1.
99. **Rohrschneider, Hildegard,** 17.7.99 Liegnitz, Sekretärin, RSHA IV A 1.
100. **Rommeiss, Ernst,** 2.12.05 Heidelberg, Kaufmann (Am-Apparat), RSHA IV A 2.
101. **Roney-Kougel, Jan,** geb. 1914 Paigton/England, angebl. brit. Offizier, Old Reetory-Codford, Wilts, England, RSHA IV E 4, Stapo Innsbruck.
102. **Roozeboom,** Mitarbeiter d. holl. N.-Dienstes, zuletzt: Den Haag, jetzt: vermutl. England, RSHA IV E 4, Stapoleit Düsseldorf.
103. **Rope, William Sylvester,** 7.12.86 Dresden, brit. N.-Agent, London W. 1, 69 Brookstreet, Savile Club, RSHA IV E 4.
104. **van der Ropp, Freddy,** London W. 1, 69 Brook-Str., RSHA IV E 4.
105. **Rosenau, Helen, Dr.,** geb. 1900, London, Emigrantin, RSHA III A 1.
106. **Rosenau, Wilhelm,** 20.11.15 Graudenz, Arbeiter (ehem. Gefr.), RSHA IV E 5, Stapo Dortmund.
107. **Rosenbaum, Eduard, Dr.,** geb. 1887, London, Emigrant, RSHA III A 1.
108. **Rosenbaum-Docomun, Vladimir,** Rechtsanwalt, vermutl. England, RSHA IV E 4.
109. **Rosenberg, Arthur, Dr. phil.,** 19.12.89 Berlin, Privatdozent, a. o. Prof., Liverpool, Emigrant, RSHA IV A 1, III A 1.
110. **Rosenberg, Hans, Dr.,** 1890 geb., a. o. Prof., Emigrant, London, RSHA III A 1.
111. **Rosenberg, Karl, Dr.,** 1893 geb., Kurator, Cambridge (Harvard Univ.), Emigrant, RSHA III A 1.
112. **Rosenberg, Marie,** 1907 geb., Assistentin, Ambleside, Emigrantin, RSHA III A 1.
113. **Rosenthal, Alfred, Dr.,** 1902 geb., London, Emigrant, RSHA III A 1.
114. **Rosenthal, Erwin, Dr.,** 1904 geb., Prof., Manchester, Emigrant, RSHA III A 1.
115. **Rosin, Paul, Dr.,** 1890 geb., o. Prof., London, Emigrant, RSHA III A 1.
116. **Rosner, Antoni,** 15.1.97 Wien, poln. ehem. Major, RSHA IV E 5, Stapoleit Danzig.
117. **van Rossem, Cornelius,** 5.4.79 Prätoria/Transvaal, angebl. Komponist, Amsterdam, vermutl. England, RSHA IV E 4, Stapoleit Berlin.
118. **Rosser, Enid,** RSHA VI G 1.
119. **Rossmeisl, Rudolf,** 6.6.00 Rothau, RSHA IV A 1.
120. **Rostal, Mac,** Prof., 1905 geb., London, Emigrant, RSHA III A 1.
121. **Roth, Cecil,** Schriftsteller, RSHA IV B 4.
122. **Rotschild, Anthony James D.,** 1887 geb., Bankier, London W 1, 42 Hill-St., Berkeley-Sq., RSHA VI G 1, II B 2.
123. **de Rothschild, Lionel Nathan,** London W. 8, 18 Kensington Palace Gardens, RSHA II B 2.
124. **Rothschild, Paul, Dr.,** 1901 geb., Ass., Emigrant, RSHA III A 1.
125. **Rovers,** zuletzt: Holland, vermutl. England (Täterkreis: Antoine), RSHA IV E 4, Stapoleit Münster.

126. **Roweck, Maria,** geb. **Harnier,** 23.10.90 Maasmünster, zuletzt: Holland, vermutl. England, RSHA IV E 4.
127. **Royden, Agnes Maude, Dr.,** geb. 1876, Publizistin, RSHA VI G 1.
128. **Royden, T.,** Direktor, Liverpool, Cunard Building, RSHA IV E 2.
129. **Rozier,** geb. **de Gay,** London, RSHA IV E 4.
130. **Rubner, Wenzl,** 1.9.86 Oberlohma, Krs. Eger, RSHA IV A 1.
131. **Rudinsky, Josef, Dr.,** 30.7.91 Thurzovska, Journalist, frh. Pfarrer, Deckname: Ing. Thurko, vermutl. England, RSHA IV E 4, Stapoleit Prag.
132. **Runge, Maria,** geb. **Dabrowski,** 18.7.96 Zeznitzere, Sekr. i. ehem. poln. Konsulat, RSHA IV E 5.
133. **Rusche, Georg, Dr.,** 1900 geb., Assistent, London, Emigrant, RSHA III A 1.
* 134. **Russel, Bertrand,** RSHA VI G 1.
135. **Rust, Edmund,** 24.10.00 Litschkau, RSHA IV A 1.
136. **Rychlinski, Stanislaus,** 20.4.06 Stocherowo, Arzt, RSHA IV E 5, Stapoleit Königsberg.
137. **Rys, Franz,** 28.11.05 Schönbrunn, ehem. Hotelier, vermutl. England, RSHA IV E 4, Stapoleit Prag.

*See notes on pages 266–272

1. **Saar, Fritz,** 21.10.87 Minden, vermutl. England, RSHA IV A 1.
2. **Sachs, Rudolf,** Deckname: **Kupfer-Sachs,** 22.5.97 Berlin, Graphiker, vermutl. England, RSHA V C 3 a.
3. **Sachs, Tobias,** brit. Agent, zuletzt: Kowno, vermutl. England, RSHA IV E 4, VI C 2, Stapo Tilsit.
4. **Sack, Julius,** Deckname: **Julijs Zaks,** 26.8.00, brit. Agent, zuletzt: Riga, vermutl. England, RSHA IV E 4, VI C 2.
5. **Safrastian, A.,** brit. N.-Agent, London N. W. 3, 71 Haverstock Hill, RSHA IV E 4.
6. **Sailer, Karl-Hans,** 15.10.00, Redakteur, vermutl. England, RSHA IV A 1.
7. **Sakrewska,** verh. **Baronin Budberg, Maria,** Deckname: „Mura", in Rußland geboren, vermutl. London (brit. ND.-Estland), RSHA VI C 2.
8. **Salinger, Robert,** 9.1.93 Weikersdorf, Kaufmann, vermutl. England, RSHA IV E 4, Stapoleit Berlin.
9. **Salmon, Sir, Isidore,** 1876, London W. 1, 51 Mount Street, RSHA II B 2.
10. **Salmond, John Maitland,** Direktor, London E. C. 3, 22 St. Helens Court, Shell Transport a. Trading Co., RSHA IV E 2.
11. **Salomon, Richard, Dr.,** geb. 1884, o. Prof., London (Universität), Emigrant, RSHA III A 1.
12. **Salomon, Sidney,** Rechtsanwalt, London W. C. 1, Woburn House, Upper Woburn Place, RSHA II B 2.
13. **Salter, Sir, Arthur,** 1881, Prof., Oxford, Parlamentsausschuß für Flüchtlinge, RSHA VI G 1.
14. **Samuel, Herbert Louis,** London W 2, 32 Porchester Terr., RSHA II B 2.
15. **Samuel, P. M.,** Direktor, London E. C. 3, 22 St. Helens Court, Shell Transport a. Trading Co., RSHA IV E 2.
16. **Samuel, Richard, Dr.,** geb. 1900, Assistent, Cambridge (Universität), Emigrant, RSHA III A 1.
17. **Samuel, Viscount,** geb. 1870, Mitglied vom Rat für christliches Judentum, RSHA VI G 1.
18. **Samuels, Harry,** Rechtsanwalt, London N. W. 2, 28 Exeter Road, RSHA II B 2.
19. **Sandbrink,** zuletzt: Winterswijk, vermutl. England, RSHA IV E 4, Stapoleit Münster.
20. **Sander, Wilhelm,** 6.5.95 Dresden, RSHA IV A 1 b.
21. **Sander, William,** 22.2.94 (22.4.84) London, brit. Vizekonsul, vermutl. England, RSHA IV E 4.
22. **Sanders, William Stephan,** 1871, Politiker („Fabian Society"), RSHA VI G 1.
23. **Sankey, Viscount John,** 26.10.66, Jurist, London W. 8, 13 Albert Place („Fabian Society"), RSHA VI G 1.
24. **Sapieha, Fürst,** Mitglied der ehem. poln. Regierung, vermutl. England, RSHA IV D 2.
25. **Sarasin-Fisher,** brit. Major, N.-Agent, vermutl. England, RSHA IV E 4.
26. **Sartori, August,** brit. Vizekonsul, vermutl. England, RSHA IV E 4.
27. **Sassoon, Ellice Victor,** 30.12.81, London EC 3, 86 Grace Church Street, RSHA II B 2.
28. **Sattler, Ernst,** 16.2.1892 Teplitz, vermutl. England, RSHA IV A 1.
29. **Sattler, Josef,** 29.10.05 Graslitz, RSHA IV A 1 b.
30. **Sattler, Josef,** 22.12.12 Eibenberg, vermutl. England, RSHA IV A 1 b.
31. **Savill, Geoffrees,** 23.8.01 Rogston, Ingenieur, East Sheen, Observatory Nr. 50, RSHA IV E 4, Stapolt. Berlin.

32. **Saville, George,** richtig: Grove-Spiro, RSHA IV E 4.
33. **Saxl, Fritz, Dr.,** geb. 1890, a. o. Prof., London (Warburg Institut), (Emigrant), RSHA III A 1.
34. **Scaly,** Pastor, zuletzt Hamburg, vermutl. England, RSHA IV E 4.
35. **Scott, John Russell,** geb. 1879, Vorsitzender d. „Manchester Guardian", „Evening News", RSHA VI G 1.
36. **Scott-Lindsay,** Sekretär, vermutl. England (Nationalrat d. Arbeiterbewegung), RSHA VI G 1.
37. **Sebottendorf,** Baron, Generalvertreter, London (Fa.: Guild Hall Civil Contractes), RSHA IV E 3, Stapoleit Stuttgart.
38. **Sedgwice, E. F. H.,** richtig: Hanfstaengl, Ernst, Dr., 11.2.87 München, London, 28 Gunterstone Road, RSHA IV C 5.
39. **Sedkol, Stan,** brit. Beamter, zuletzt Riga, vermutl. England (brit. ND Lettland), RSHA VI C 2.
* 40. **Sedlarscek, Karl,** 24.9.94 Brüssel, ehem. tschech. Stabskapitän, vermutl. England, RSHA IV E 4, Stapolt. Prag.
41. **Seed, Charl Harry,** 2.8.88 London, London, RSHA IV E 4, Stapo Kiel.
42. **Seeger, Gerhard,** 16.11.96 Leipzig, Schriftsteller (Emigrant), vermutl. England, RSHA II B 5.
43. **Seelig, Louis,** 6.7.02 London, Sekretär, Pilot, früher Westerland, Täterkreis: Grove-Spiro, vermutl. England, RSHA IV E 4.
44. **Seelig, Paul,** 10.6.15 Bandung, zuletzt Holland, vermutl. England, RSHA IV E 4.
45. **Seelig, Siegfried Fritz, Dr.,** 1899 geboren, Privatdozent, Edinburgh, Emigrant, RSHA III A 1.
46. **Segrue, J. C.,** Korrespondent der „News Chronicle", früher Wien, vermutl. England, RSHA IV B 4.
47. **Sekler, Bernhard,** 4.5.95 Kolomea, poln. Offizier, RSHA IV E 5, Stapoleit Breslau.
48. **Seligmann, Leonore (Lore),** 18.5.07 Frankfurt/M., vermutl. London, RSHA IV A 1.
48a **Sell, K. G.,** brit. N.-Agent, zuletzt Kopenhagen, vermutl. England, RSHA IV E 4.
49. **Sellheim, Magda Antonowna,** verh. Webb, gesch. Lauthew, Russin, zuletzt Reval, vermutl. England (brit. ND.-Estland), RSHA VI C 2.
50. **Semoff, Z.,** vermutl. London, 101. Arthur Corat Quinsway Nr. 2, RSHA IV E 4, Stapoleit Wien.
51. **Watson-Seton, R. Williams,** 1879, Prof. (Historiker), vermutl. England (Täterkreis: tschechoslowakisches Komitee „Internationaler Friedensfeldzug"), RSHA VI G 1.
52. **Shacleton,** London, 175 Piccadilly, Tel.: 2448/9, (Täterkreis: Alabert Albseit), RSHA IV E 4, Stapoleit. Wien.
53. **Shadforth, Harald Anthony,** 28.4.92 Piccadilly-Rye, brit. Botschaftsattaché, vermutl. England (Täterkreis: von Einem), RSHA IV E 4.
54. **Shannon, Edmund Cecil,** 11.9.98, brit. Major, London W 1, Piccadilly 96, RSHA IV E 4, Stapo Wesermünde.
55. **Shelley, Richard,** brit. Captain, vermutl. England, RSHA IV E 4.
56. **Shepherd, M.,** brit. Konsul, vermutl. England, RSHA IV E 4.
57. **Sheridan, Klara,** geb. Wreden, geb. 1900 in England, Schriftstellerin, vermutl. London, RSHA IV E 4.
58 **Shinwell, Emanuel,** 1884, Politiker, RSHA VI G 1.
59. **Sieff, Israel Moses,** Präsident der englischen Zionistenorganisation, RSHA VI G 1.
60. **Sieff, Rebecca Doro,** London W 1, Brook House, Parklane, RSHA II B 2.

*See notes on pages 266–272

61. **Sievers, Max,** Deckn.: **Siko,** 11.7.87 Berlin, Verbandssekretär, vermutl. England, RSHA IV A 1.
62. **Sigmund, Rudolf,** 2.5.02 Drahowitz, Albury Chilworth b. Quildforth Surrey, Surrey guest house, RSHA IV A 1 b.
63. **Sik, Alexander, Dr.,** 8.10.00 Sewastopol, Advokatenkonzipient, London, RSHA IV E 4, Stapoleit Prag.
* 64. **Sikorski, Wladislaw Eugenlusz,** 20.5.81 Toszow Nar, ehem. poln. General, vermutl. England, RSHA III B, IV D 2, IV G 1.
65. **Silkin, Lewis,** Jude, Parlamentsmitglied, Londoner Stadtrat, vermutl. London, RSHA VI G 1.
66. **Sillem, James Herbert,** 22.5.98 Sunnighill, Kaufmann, zuletzt: Dorpat, vermutl. England (brit. ND.-Estland), RSHA VI G 2.
67. **Sillem, Walter Oskar,** 16.7.74 Esher, Fabrikant, zuletzt: Dorpat, vermutl. England (brit. ND.-Estland), RSHA VI C 2.
68. **Silley,** ca. 50 Jahre, Hotelinhaberin, Brixham, Nortcliff-Hotel, RSHA IV E 4, Stapo Osnabrück.
69. **Lord Cademan of Silverdale, John,** Präsident, London E. C. 2, Britannic House, Anglo-Iranian-Oil, Co., RSHA IV E 2.
70. **Silvermann,** Abgeordneter, RSHA VI G 1.
71. **Siman, Rudolf,** 10.4.93 Jindr-Hradec, ehem. tschech. Stabskapitän und Journalist, zuletzt Den Haag, vermutl. England, RSHA IV E 4.
72. **Simon, A. P.,** Abgeordneter, vermutl. London, RSHA VI G 1.
73. **Simon, Franz, Dr.,** 1893, o. Prof., Oxford (Universität), Emigrant, RSHA III A 1.
74. **Simon, Sir John Allsebrook,** 1873 geboren, Abgeordneter, RSHA VI G 1.
75. **Simon, Hugo,** 1.9.80 Usch, Bankier, ehem. Finanzminister, vermutl. England, RSHA IV A 1.
76. **Simon, Walter, Dr.,** 1898, a. o. Prof., London, Emigrant, RSHA III A 1.
77. **Simon,** belgischer Artillerist, zuletzt: Lüttich, vermutl. England, RSHA IV E 4, Stapo Trier.
78. **Simon, Dr.,** Direktor, London (Legitimist), RSHA VI G 1.
79. **Simons, Hellmuth, Dr.,** 1893, vermutl. London, Emigrant, RSHA III A 1.
80. **Simpson, F.,** etwa 58 Jahre alt, brit. Agent, zuletzt: Brüssel, vermutl. London, RSHA IV E 4.
81. **Simpson, I. L.,** London, Unilever House, Blackfriars, RSHA IV E 2.
82. **Simpson,** richtig **Black,** ca. 45 Jahre alt, brit. Agent, vermutl. England, RSHA IV E 4.
83. **Simpson, Prof.,** Edinburgh (Universität), (brit. ND-Estland), RSHA VI C 2.
84. **Simpson, Stanley,** Korrespondent der Londoner „Times", RSHA VI G 1.
85. **Sinclair, Sir Archibald,** 1890, Führer der liberalen Partei, RSHA VI G 1.
86. **Sinclair,** Beamter im Ausw. Amt in London, vermutl. London, RSHA IV E 4.
87. **Singer, H. W., Dr.,** 1910 geboren, vermutl. London, Emigrant, RSHA III A 1.
88. **Singer, Karl,** 9.5.90 Wien, vermutl. England, RSHA IV A 1 b.
89. **von Sinowjew,** ca. 50 Jahre, zuletzt: Köln, vermutl. England, RSHA IV E 4, Stapo Köln.
90. **Sinowzik, Franz,** 9.1.00 Orlawen, Hauer u. Dolmetscher, RSHA IV E 5, Stapo Allenstein.

91. **Skapski, Taddäus Marian Viktor,** 7.8.08 Berlin, poln. Agent, vermutl. England, RSHA IV E 5.
92. **Skapski, Viktor,** 29.10.11 Dortmund, Arbeiter, Privatlehrer, RSHA IV E 5, Stapo Schneidemühl.
93. **Skoropadski, Danylo,** 13.2.04 Petersburg, Ingenieur, vermutl. London, RSHA IV D 3 a.
94. **Skoruppa, Wilhelm,** 10.11.94 Paruschowitz, Kaufmann, vermutl. England, RSHA IV E 5, Stapo Oppeln.
95. **Skoszewski, Wladislaus,** 28.4.91 Schliewitz, poln. Polizeibeamter, RSHA IV E 5, Stapo Schneidemühl.
96. **ter Slaa, H.,** zuletzt: Amsterdam, vermutl. England, RSHA IV E 4.
97. **Sladen, Algernon,** brit. Major, Wentworth/Norfolk-Cottage, Surray, (Kraftw.: DYL 417 (GB), Marke Röwer), RSHA IV E 4.
98. **Sladky, Emil,** 11.1.05 Wien, Eisendreher, vermutl. England (RSÖ.-Funktionär), RSHA IV A 1 b.
99. **Slama, Wenzel,** 24.1.93 Ranna, ehem. tschech. Stabskapitän, London, 53 Lexham Gardens, Kensington W 8, Frantisek Moravec, RSHA IV E 4, IV E 6.
100. **Slavik, Juraj, Dr.,** 28.1.90 Dobroniva, ehem. tschech. Gesandter (Täterkreis: Benes), vermutl. England, RSHA IV E 4, IV D 1, Stapoleit Prag.
101. **Slezak,** ehem. tschech. General, (Täterkreis: Benes), vermutl. England, RSHA IV D 1 a.
102. **Smallbones, Robert Tawnsen,** brit. Generalkonsul, vermutl. England, RSHA IV E 4.
103. **Smirnoff, Iwan,** Flieger, zuletzt: Holland, vermutl. England, RSHA III B.
104. **Smith-Atherton, Aline Sybil,** 13.11.75 Ryde, Chantrya, RSHA IV A 1.
105. **Smith, Bertram A.,** Direktor, London S.W.1, Shell Transport & Trading Comp., RSHA IV E 2.
106. **Smith, Cyrus,** brit. Passport-Offizier, vermutl. England, (Täterkreis: Jens Dons), RSHA IV E 4, III D, Stapo Kiel.
107. **Smith, Jackson,** Gehilfe des Handelsattachés, vermutl. England, RSHA IV E 4.
108. **Walker-Smith, Jonah,** London W. C. 1, 21 Russell Square, (Täterkreis: Ignatz Petschek), RSHA III D 4.
109. **Smith, Neville A.,** 1.6.14 Leicester, Börsenmakler, London E. C. 2, 35 Morgate, RSHA IV E 4, Stapo Erfurt.
110. **Smith, Rennie (Renny),** vermutl. London, RSHA VI G 1.
111. **Smith, R. W.,** Sheffield, 10, 214 Cobden Niew R., RSHA IV E 4, Stapo Kiel.
112. **Smith, Wilburn Emmet,** 7.4.82 Port Henry, amerikanischer Major, zuletzt: Brüssel, vermutl. England, RSHA IV E 4, Stapo Aachen.
113. **Smith, W. Gordon,** 16.4.15 England, Geophysiker, Durham, 14 Kitchener Terrace, Garrow Co., RSHA IV E 4.
114. **Smits, Jan,** zuletzt: Holland, vermutl. England, (Täterkreis: Helmers), RSHA IV E 4, Stapo Kiel.
115. **Smitt, Johann,** zuletzt: Rotterdam, vermutl. England, RSHA IV E 4, Stapo Kiel.
116. **Smogarzewski, Kaz.,** vermutl. London, (Täterkreis: „Free Europe"), RSHA VI G 1.
117. **Smolcic, Franz,** 25.5.08 Königsberg, Guildford, Surrey Hills, Guesthouse Chvonthnaz, RSHA IV A 1 b.

118. **Smudek, Johann,** 8.9.15 Weißenschuld, vermutl. England, RSHA IV E 4, Stapoleit Prag.
119. **Smutny, Jaromir,** 23.6.92 Bavorov, ehem. Legationsrat, Gesandter, vermutl. London, (Täterkreis: Benes), RSHA IV E 4, IV D 1, Stapoleit Prag.
120. **Snejdarek, Josef,** 2.4.75 Nepajedla, ehem. tschech. General, vermutl. England, RSHA IV E 4, Stapoleit Prag.
121. **Snejdarek, Mme.,** vermutl. England, RSHA IV E 4, Stapoleit Prag.
122. **Snell, Wilhelm,** 23.7.94 Oranienburg, Gewerkschaftler vermutl. England, RSHA IV A 1.
123. **Snell, Lord,** 1865 geboren, Führer d. Arbeiterpartei im Oberhaus, RSHA VI G 1.
124. **Snow, C. P.,** vermutl. England, Cambridge (Universität), RSHA VI G 1.
125. **Söllner, Karl, Dr.,** 1903, Privatdozent, vermutl. London, Emigrant, RSHA III A 1.
126. **Sokoloff, Celina,** London N. W. 6, 43 Compayne Gardens, RSHA II B 2.
127. **Sokolov, Celina,** geb. Warschau, London N. W. 6, 43 Compayne Garden, RSHA II B 2.
128. **Sokolow, Leonid,** Russe, Handelsvertreter, zuletzt: Reval, vermutl. England (Brit. ND-Estland), RSHA VI C 2.
129. **Soley,** Generalvertreter Vickers-Armstrong, vermutl. London, RSHA IV E 4, Stapoleit Berlin.
130. **Solmsen, Friedrich, Dr.,** 1904, Privatdozent, Cambridge (Universität), Emigrant, RSHA III A 1.
131. **Soltowski, Adam,** Graf, Pole, zuletzt: Kowno, vermutl. England (brit. ND.-Litauen), RSHA VI C 2.
132. **Sommer, Julius,** Mitarbeiter d. Merton, London, RSHA III D.
133. **Sommer,** brit. Agent, vermutl. England, Täterkreis: Gibson, RSHA IV E 4.
134. **Sommerfeld, Martin, Dr.,** 1894 geboren, ao. Prof., Northampton, Smith College, Emigrant, RSHA III A 1.
135. **Sondheimer, Robert, Dr.,** vermutl. London, Emigrant, RSHA III A 1.
136. **Sonikowski,** poln. General, vermutl. England, Angehöriger der ehem. poln. Regierung, RSHA IV D 2.
137. **Sorensen, Reginald William,** vermutl. England (Sozialistische christliche Liga), RSHA VI G 1.
138. **Sosnowski, Georg (Jerzy),** 4.12.96 Lemberg, ehem. poln. Rittmeister, N.-Agent, vermutl. England, RSHA IV E 5.
139. **Southam,** Kaufmann, zuletzt: Reval, vermutl. England, brit. ND.-Estland, RSHA VI C 2.
140. **Southwood, Julius Salter Elias,** Lord, 1873 geboren, Direktor von „Odhams Press Ltd.", vermutl. London, RSHA VI G 1.
141. **Grove-Spiro, Stanley,** Deckname: **Lord Drummond, George Saville,** 18.1.00 Cap Town, Bankier, Makler, brit. Agent, London 5, Suffolk Street Pall-Mall (Büro), London S. W. 1, Kensingtown, London W. 8, Gottesmore Gardens 18 oder de Vere Gardens 46 (privat), RSHA IV E 4.
142. **Spurny, Anezka,** 15.1.95 Doubrawice, ehem. tschech. Abgeordneter, vermutl. London, RSHA IV E 4, Stapoleit Prag.
143. **Squance, W. R. J.,** Gewerkschaftsbeamter, vermutl. England (Internationaler Friedensfeldzug), RSHA VI G 1.

144. **Sramek, Johann, Dr.**, 11.8.70 Grygov, vermutl. England, Täterkreis: Benes, RSHA IV E 4, IV D I a, Stapoleit Prag.
145. **Sudakoff, R. S. Roman**, 9.8.89 Rußland, ehem. russ. Offizier, zuletzt: Riga und Belgrad, vermutl. England, brit. ND.-Lettland, RSHA IV E 4, VI C 2.
146. **Sudakoff, Viktor**, etwa 40 Jahre, Geschäftsführer, zuletzt: Riga, vermutl. England, brit. ND. Lettland, RSHA IV E 4, Stapo Tilsit.
147. **Sulzbach, Herbert**, Schriftsteller, Emigrant, London N. W. 3, 58 b Belsize Park Gardens, RSHA B 5.
148. **Sulzbacher, Max, Dr.**, 1901, Assistent, vermutl. London, Emigrant, RSHA III A 1.
149. **Suszycki, Roman**, 27.5.02, Kamienskoje, Kaufmann, vermutl. England, RSHA IV E 5, Stapo Bromberg.
150. **Susczinski, Roman**, 27.5.02 Kamienskoje, Kaufmann, vermutl. England, RSHA IV E 5, Stapo Bromberg.
151. **Sutton, Chas W.**, Auslandsredakteur b. „Daily Express", London E. C. 4, Fleetstreet, Täterkreis: Panton. RSHA IV E 4.
152. **Swaffer, Hannen**, 1879 geboren, Schriftleiter des „Daily Herald", vermutl. London, RSHA VI G 1.
153. **Swann, F. T. Frederick Thomas**, 22.7.99 St. Petersburg, Kapitän, vermutl. London, RSHA IV E 4, Stapoleit Berlin.
154. **Swaythling, Gladys Helen Rachel**, London W. 8, 28 Kensington Court, RSHA II B 2.
155. **Swaythling, Stuart Albert Samuel Montagu**, Lord, 1898, London S. W. 1, 8 Grosvenor Crescent und Townhill Park, West End bei Southampton, RSHA II B 2.
156. **Swirskik, Jerzy Wlodzimierz**, 5.4.82, Kalisch, poln. Admiral, vermutl. England, RSHA III B.
157. **Syroka, Franz**, 1.1.08 Kurgan, RSHA IV E 5, Stapo Elbing.
158. **Szczerbinski, Josef**, vermutl. England (Polnischer Nationalrat), RSHA IV D 2.
159. **Szeffer, Tadeus**, etwa 36 Jahre, ehemal. poln. Hauptmann, RSHA IV E 5, Stapoleit Danzig.
160. **Szillard, Leo, Dr.**, 1889, Privatdozent, Oxford (Universität), Emigrant, RSHA III A 1.
161. **Szlandak, Hanne Maria**, geb. Paciorkowska, 17.7.89 Pagow, Angestellte, vermutl. England, RSHA IV E 5, Stapo Leipzig.
162. **Szlendak, Henryk**, 17.5.05 Bobrowini, Arzt, vermutl. England, RSHA IV E 5, Stapo Leipzig.
163. **Szliwitzki, Henryk**, 21.2.96 Gnesen, poln. Oberleutnant, N.-Agent, vermutl. England, RSHA IV E 5, Stapoleit Stettin.
164. **Szmidt (Schmidt), Henryk**, 2.1.01 Parlin, poln. Hauptmann, N.-Offizier, vermutl. England, RSHA IV E 5.
165. **Szösz, Roszi**, Tänzerin, zuletzt: Belgrad, vermutl. England, RSHA IV E 4.
166. **Szulz, Gustav**, poln. Offizier, RSHA IV E 5.
167. **Szwaba (Schwabe), Wawrczyn**, 10.9.08 Kopnitz, Tischler, poln. Agent, vermutl. England, RSHA IV E 5.
168. **Szwarcbart, Ignacy, Dr.**, Mitglied des polnischen Nationalrates (Poln. Nationalrat), RSHA IV D 2.
169. **Szymanski, Theofil**, 10.8.06 Königshütte, Destillateur, Kutscher, vermutl. England, RSHA IV E 5, Stapo Oppeln.

1. **Schacleton,** vermutl. London, Tel.: 2448/9 (Täterkreis: Alabert Albscit), RSHA IV E 4, Stapoleit Wien.
2. **Schallamach, Adolf,** geb. 1905, Assistent, vermutl. England, RSHA III A 1.
3. **Scharf, Alfred,** Dr., 1900, Assistent, London, RSHA III A 1.
4. **Scharff, Karl,** Dr., 1911, London, RSHA III A 1.
5. **Schary, August,** 23.11.98 Poremba, Krs. Pleß, Hüttenarbeiter, vermutl. England, RSHA IV E 5, Stapo Oppeln.
6. **Schauroth, von, Robert,** früher Offizier, England, RSHA IV E 4.
7. **Scheiber, Hermann,** 23.2.88 Reutte/Tirol, England, NW 9, Slough Blane, Kings Bury, RSHA IV E 4, Stapoleit Stuttgart.
8. **Scheitler, Josef,** 27.10.99 Chodau, Sheffield, Rustlings Road 149, RSHA IV A 1, Stapoleit Karlsruhe.
9. **Schellenberger, H.,** Vorstandsmitglied der Freien deutschen Kulturliga in England, London, RSHA VI G 1.
10. **Scherbaum, Franz,** 19.1.09 Graslitz, vermutl. England, RSHA IV A 1 b.
11. **Schermuly, Alouis,** 14.7.03 Frankfurt/M., Hilfsarbeiter, vermutl. England (Am-Apparat), RSHA IV A 2.
12. **Scheuer, Ernst,** Dr., Mitarbeiter d. Merton, London, RSHA III D.
13. **Schicht, George,** London, Unilever House, Blackfriars, RSHA IV E 2.
14. **Schiefer, Fritz,** 25.3.89 Ohligs, Schleifer, vermutl. England (Am-Apparat), RSHA IV A 2.
15. **Schiff, Otto,** 1876, London W. 1, 25 Berkeley Square, RSHA II B 2.
16. **Schiff, Viktor,** Mitarbeiter d. „Daily Herald", London, RSHA I B V 4.
17. **Schifrin, Alexander,** Dr., Jude, 11.8.01 Charkow/Rußland, vermutl. England, RSHA IV A 1.
18. **Schijbal, Josef,** 19.6.03 Hrun - Trebinje, ehem. tschech. Stabskpt., vermutl. England, RSHA IV E 4, Stapoleit Prag.
19. **Schild, Gotthard,** 21.1.98 Wohlau, Kaufmann, vermutl. England (Täterkreis: Hans Jäger), RSHA IV E 6.
20. **Schiller-Mamorek,** Dr., 10.11.78 Wien, Deckname: **Peter Roberts,** Redakteur, vermutl. England, RSHA IV A 1.
21. **Schilling, Ernst,** 25.10.01 Berlin, Bäcker, London (Am-Apparat), RSHA IV A 2.
22. **Schlafke, Hermann Erwin Adolf,** 2.11.02 Kattowitz, poln. N.-Agent, RSHA IV E 5, Stapo Oppeln.
23. **Schleicher, Johannes,** 20.2.04 Schwabach, Lehrer, England, RSHA IV A 1.
24. **Schlesinger, Max,** geb. 1905, Ass., London, RSHA III A 1.
25. **Schloßmann, Hans,** Dr., geb. 1894, Cambridge, RSHA III A 1.
26. **Schmettan, Alfons,** 28.4.96 Bukarest, Artist, N.-Agent, Kaufmann, vermutl. England, RSHA IV E 4.
27. **Schmidkunz, Andreas,** 13.12.97 Eger, vermutl. England, RSHA IV A 1 b.
28. **Schmidt, Erich,** 4.8.10 Berlin, vermutl. England, RSHA IV A 1.
29. **Schmidt, Heinz,** 26.11.06 Halle/S., Berichterstatter, RSHA IV A 1, Stapo Halle.
30. **Schmidt, Johanna,** 24.7.89 Frankfurt/M., vermutl. England, RSHA IV A 1.
31. **Schmidt, Ludwig,** 7.4.89 Drahowitz b. Karlsbad, vermutl. England, RSHA IV A 1 b.
32. **Schmidt, Werner,** 18.10.11 Berlin, Photograph, vermutl. England, RSHA IV A 1.

33. **Schmitt, Fritz Eduard, 1**1.8.99 Sobernheim/Rhld., Dipl.-Ing., London S. W. 1, Victoria-Street, RSHA IV E 4, Stapoleit Magdeburg.
34. **Schmitz, Edmund, 1**5.5.18 Hohscheid, Dienstpflichtiger, zuletzt: Palästina, vermutl. England, RSHA V D 2 f.
35. **Schneider, Barbara, geb. Ripper, 18.1.96** Budapest, London N. W. 3, 2 B Winchester Road, RSHA IV A 1.
36. **Schneider, Bruno, 21.1.04** Adorf/Sachsen, Schlosser, London, RSHA IV A 1.
37. **Schneider, Bruno, 6.9.04** Adorf, Bez. Ölsnitz, N.-Agent, London E. G. 4, 35 Bridestreet, RSHA IV E 3, Stapo Halle.
38. **Schneider, Erich, geb. 1903,** Ass., London, RSHA III A 1.
39. **Schneider, Friedrich Wilhelm, 2**0.8.12 Köln-Mülheim, Chauffeur, Diener, zuletzt: Den Haag, vermutl. England (Täterkreis: von Putlitz), RSHA IV E 4, Stapo Köln.
40. **Schneider, Josef, 2**7.6.13 St. Joachimsthal, vermutl. England, RSHA IV A 1 b.
41. **Schnurmann, Robert, 1**904, Ass., Cambridge, RSHA III A 1.
42. **Schönberg, Alexander, 18**92, Prof., Edinburgh, RSHA III A 1.
43. **Schönstein, Karl, 8.3.88** Haslau, Kr. Asch, vermutl. England, RSHA IV A 1 b.
44. **Scholtyssek, Engelbert,** poln. N.-Agent, vermutl. England, RSHA IV E 5, Stapo Oppeln.
45. **Schramek, Jan, Dr.,** Emigrant, Min.-Präs. i. tschechoslow. Nationalausschuß, vermutl. London, RSHA II B 5.
46. **Schreiner, G.,** zuletzt: Amsterdam, vermutl. England, RSHA IV E 4.
47. **Schreiner, Wilhelm Otto, 16.9.92** Laubach, Redakteur, vermutl. England, RSHA IV A 1.
48. **Schröbel (Schröder),** vermutl. England (Täterkreis: Stevens/Best), RSHA IV E 4.
49. **Schröder,** vermutl. England (Täterkreis: Stevens/Best), RSHA IV E 4.
50. **Schubert, Alfred, 1**9.8.00 Schmiedeberg, Hope View/England, Castleton Derbyshire, RSHA IV A 1.
51. **Schürmann, Stanislav, 9.**5.00 poln. Beamter, RSHA IV E 5.
52. **Schürrer, Alfred, 8.5.**11 Kohling, vermutl. England, RSHA IV A 1 b.
53. **Schütz, Arthur,** Schriftsteller, Emigrant, London N. W. 6, 10 Tarranbrae Court, Willesden Lane, RSHA II B 5.
54. **Schütz, Eva,** vermutl. England, RSHA IV E 4.
55. **Schuh, Georg, 3**1.8.17 London, Dienstpflichtiger, London, RSHA V — D 2 f, KP-Stelle Braunschweig.
56. **von der Schulenburg, 13.3.08** Küstrin, zuletzt: s' Gravenhage, vermutl. England, RSHA IV E 4.
57. **Schulz, Gustav, 7.6.15** Freienhuben, Füsilier, vermutl. England, RSHA IV E 5, Stapo Tilsit.
58. **Schulz, Hans Jürgen, 6.11.14** Hersfeld, Schlosser, RSHA IV E 5.
59. **Schuster, George, Sir, 18**81, London S. W. 1, St. James' Pl. und Nether Worton House Middle Barton Oxon, RSHA II B 2.
60. **Schwann, Hans, 5.7.84** München, Kaufmann, vermutl. England, RSHA IV E 5.
61. **Schwarz, Erich, Deckname: Hirsch,** London, RSHA IV A 1.
62. **Schwarz, Ernst, Dr.,** geb. 1889, London, RSHA III A 1.
63. **Schwarz, Georg,** Mitarbeiter d. Merton, London, RSHA III D.
64. **Schwarz, Richard, 8.5.91** Fleißen, Margate-Kent/Engld., RSHA IV A 1.
65. **Schwarzenberger, Georg,** geb. 1908, Ass., London, RSHA III A 1.

66. **Schwarzloh, Georg,** 19.12.11 Lübeck, Deckname: **Steiner,** fr. Pol.-Beamter, vermutl. England (Schwarze Front), RSHA IV A 9.
67. **Schwarzschild, Ernst Lazarus,** 14.12.09 Frankfurt/M., Schriftleiter, London, RSHA IV A 1.
68. **Schweitzer-Detraz, Alfred,** Bankprokurist, zuletzt: Basel, vermutl. England, RSHA IV E 4, III A 1, Stapoleit Karlsruhe.
69. **Schweitzer, Alois,** 1.7.05 Litice, ehem. tschech. Kpt., vermutl. England, RSHA IV E 4, Stapoleit Prag.
70. **Schweitzer,** ehem. evgl. Superintendent, Emigrant, vermutl. England (illegaler Nachrichtendienst der Bekenntnisfront), RSHA VI H 3, II B 3.

1. **Spadrowski, Kasimir Stanislaus,** 1.3.99, poln. Oberstleutn., vermutl. England, RSHA IV E 5, Stapo Oppeln.
2. **Spears, Edward Luis,** 1886, Politiker u. Offizier, vermutl. England, RSHA VI G 1.
3. **Spencer-Davisohn, Ch. Frank,** 10.8.89 Montabu, Rechtsanwalt, RSHA IV E 4, Stapoleit Wien.
4. **Spencer, Maurice,** Oberst, vermutl. England, RSHA VI G 1.
5. **Spender, John Alfred,** 1862, Journalist, vermutl. England, RSHA VI G 1.
6. **Spender, Steffan,** 1909, Schriftsteller, vermutl. England, RSHA VI G 1.
7. **Speth, Helmut,** 29.8.11 Szankow, poln. Agent, vermutl. England, RSHA IV E 4, Stapo Schneidemühl.
8. **Speyer, Alexander Nikolaus,** 6.2.87 Amsterdam, Rechtsanwalt, zuletzt: Holland, vermutl. England, RSHA IV E 4, Stapo Osnabrück.
9. **Spiegel, Annemarie,** geb. **Behrens,** 25.7.01 Altona, vermutl. England, RSHA IV A 1.
10. **von Spiegel-Diesenberg, Felix,** Graf, 19.1.91 Iglau/Mähren, zuletzt: Südmähren, vermutl. England (Täterkreis: von Gerlach), RSHA IV E 4.
11. **Spieker, Karl,** 7.1.88 M.-Gladbach, Min. Direktor a. D., vermutl. London (Deutsche Freiheitspartei, Schwarze Front), RSHA IV A 1, IV A 3.
12. **Spielberg, Isabella,** 13.10.02 England, RSHA IV E 4, Stapoleit Berlin.
13. **Spielbichler, Felix,** 10.1.11 Lendorf, Kr. Spittal, Maurergehilfe, vermutl. England, RSHA IV A 1.
13a **Grove-Spiro, Stanley,** Decknamen: **Lord Drummond, George Saville,** 18.1.00 Cap Town, Bankier, Makler, London 5, Suffolk Street Pall-Mall (Büro), London S. W. 1, Kensington, London W. 8, Gottesmore Gardens 18, oder de Vere Gardens 46 (privat), RSHA IV E 4.
14. **Spithout, C.,** zuletzt: Holland, vermutl. England (Täterkreis: Brijnen), RSHA IV E 4.
15. **Spoor, Mr., J.,** zuletzt: Holland, vermutl. England, RSHA IV E 4.
16. **Sprenger,** zuletzt: Z. O.-Drente/Holland, vermutl. England (Täterkreis: Brijnen), RSHA IV E 4.
17. **Springer, Josef,** 16.8.95 Oporowka, Kr. Lissa, vermutl. England, RSHA IV E 5.
18. **Sprink, Franz,** 20.1.00 Lippstadt, Drahtzieher, vermutl. England (Am-Apparat), RSHA IV A 2.
19. **Spurny, Anezka,** 15.1.95 Doubrawice, ehem. tschech. Abgeordneter, vermutl. London, RSHA IV E 4, Stapoleit Prag.

1. **Stängler, Josef,** 9.8.93 Elbogen, Hilfsarbeiter, Barry Glan, 17 Castel Street, RSHA IV A 1, IV A 1 b.
2. **Stahl, Johannes,** 25.6.00 Heiligenstadt, Deckname: **Franz,** vermutl. England (Am-Apparat), RSHA IV A 2.
3. **Stampfer, Friedrich,** 8.9.74 Brünn, Schriftsteller, Emigrant, vermutl. England, RSHA II B 5.
4. **Stanczyk, Mitgl. d.** poln. Regierung, vermutl. England (poln. Regierung), RSHA IV D 2.
5. **Stanislawski, Jan,** 16.5.98 Woysk, poln. Agent, vermutl. England, RSHA IV E 5, Stapo Köslin.
6. **Stanton, Edmond,** 21.11.81 Cork in Irland, Kaufmann, London W. 1, Cavendish Court, RSHA IV E 4.
7. **von Starhemberg, Rüdiger Ernst,** 10.5.99 Efending, Leiter d. österr. Heimwehr, vermutl. England (österr. Legitimist), RSHA IV A 3.
8. **Starhemberg, Fürst,** brit. Fliegeroffizier, Emigrant, RSHA II B 5.
9. **Starzynski, Adam,** 10.12.93 Jutroschin, chem. poln. Beamter, vermutl. England, RSHA IV E 5, Stapo Dortmund.
10. **Stassen, J. W.,** zuletzt: Holland, vermutl. England (Täterkreis: Brijnen), RSHA IV E 4.
11. **Stedman, P. S.,** Miß, vermutl. England, RSHA VI G 1.
12. **Steed, Wikham,** 10.10.71, Journalist, London, RSHA IV E 4, IV A 5, IV B 4, III B 15, VI G 1.
13. **Steel, C. E.,** I. Botschaftssekretär, England, RSHA IV E 4.
14. **Steen, richtig Campbell, Anjus,** 10.2.61 Sorel/Canada, Rentier, England, RSHA IV E 4, Stapoleit Berlin.
15. **Steenberghe, Maximilian Paul Leon,** 2.5.99 Leiden, chem. holländ. Wirtschaftsminister, zuletzt: Den Haag, vermutl. England, RSHA III B.
16. **Steer, G. L.,** vermutl. England, RSHA VI G 1.
17. **Steers, S. S. J.,** zuletzt: Reval/Estland, vermutl. England (brit. ND. Estland), RSHA VI C 2.
18. **Stegemann, B.,** zuletzt: Winterswyk/Holland, vermutl. England (Täterkreis: Brijnen), RSHA IV E 4.
19. **Stein, Anna, geb. Uhlir,** 31.3.02 Wien, Büroangestellte, vermutl. England, RSHA IV A 1, IV A 1 b.
20. **Stein, H. K.,** Sekretär, London E. C. 8, St. Helen's Court, Shell Mex and B. P. Ltd., RSHA IV E 2.
21. **Stein, Kurt,** 20.2.00 London, England, RSHA IV E 4.
22. **Stein, Moritz,** 4.3.15 Leipzig, poln. N.-Agent, vermutl. England, RSHA IV E 5, Stapo Danzig.
23. **Stein, Oskar,** poln. Agent, RSHA IV E 5.
24. **Steiner, Josef,** 23.12.02 Altenmark, Brotausträger, London, RSHA IV A 1, Stapo Salzburg.
25. **Steinfels, Hilde,** 17.8.03 Birkenfeld, vermutl. England, RSHA IV A 1.
26. **Stempel, Baron,** Nachrichtenagent, vermutl. England, RSHA IV E 4.
27. **Stepanek, Paul,** Filmschauspieler, Emigrant, vermutl. England, RSHA II B 5.
28. **Stephen, Campbell,** 1884, Politiker, vermutl. England, RSHA VI G 1.
29. **Stephens, David,** brit. Beamter, England, RSHA IV E 4, Stapo Innsbruck.
30. **Stephens, Philipp Pembrocke,** 23.9.03 Little, Nissenden/England, Journalist, England, RSHA IV E 4.
31. **Stercks, Pierre,** zuletzt: Brabant, vermutl. England, RSHA IV E 4.
32. **Stern, Karl, Dr.,** 1906, London, RSHA III A 1.

33. **Stern, Kurt,** 1902, Privatdozent, England, Rochester, RSHA III A 1.
34. **Stevens, Moya,** geb. **Godfrey,** 16.2.95 London, Schriftstellerin, London
   · (Täterkreis: Stevens/Best), RSHA IV E 4.
35. **Stewart, Margaret,** Schriftstellerin, vermutl. England, RSHA VI G 1.
36. **Stewart, Marie,** verh. **von Oertzen,** 24.8.78 Rohais/Engl., London
   (Täterkreis: von Oertzen), RSHA IV E 4, Stapoleit Hannover.
37. **Gamma-Stocker, Gustav,** 23.10.04 Zürich, Hotelsekretär, zuletzt:
   Zürich, vermutl. England, RSHA IV E 4, Stapoleit Karlsruhe.
38. **Stockinger, Fritz,** 21.9.94 Wien, früherer Handelsminister, vermutl.
   England (österr. Legitimist), RSHA IV A 3.
39. **Stoddart, H. N.,** zuletzt: Riga, vermutl. England, brit. ND.-Lettland,
   RSHA VI C 2.
40. **Stoeter, Walter Denis,** 5.7.15 London, London, RSHA IV A 1, Stapo
   Lübeck.
41. **Stohwasser, Adolf,** 21.5.07 Altrohlau, vermutl. England, RSHA IV A 1b.
42. **Stockes, R. R.,** Abgeordneter, vermutl. England, RSHA VI G 1.
43. **Stokvis, Zadok,** 19.3.78 Den Haag, zuletzt: Holland, vermutl. England, RSHA IV E 4.
44. **Stoll, Fritz,** 23.7.96 Breslau, Prokurist, zuletzt: Amsterdam, vermutl.
   England (Täterkreis: Kurt Wechselmann), RSHA IV E 4, Stapoleit
   Breslau.
45. **Stolper, Gustav,** Schriftsteller, 25.7.88 Wien, Jude, Emigrant, vermutl. London, RSHA II B 5.
46. **Stolterfoht, Hermann Gustav,** brit. Vizekonsul, England, RSHA IV E 4.
47. **Stopford, Frederic Viktor,** 6.7.00 Wymuth, Commandeur, zuletzt:
   Prag, vermutl. England, RSHA IV E 4.
48. **Stowasser, Otto,** 19.2.98 Altrohlau, vermutl. England, RSHA IV A 1 b.
49. **Stowitz, Heinrich,** 16.10.03 Pechbach, vermutl. England, RSHA
   IV A 1 b.
50. **Strabolgi, Lord,** 1886, vermutl. England, RSHA VI G 1.
51. **Strachey, John,** Schriftsteller, vermutl. England, RSHA IV B 4.
52. **Strachey, Lytton,** 1901, Schriftsteller, vermutl. England, RSHA VI G 1.
53. **Straetman, Gustaf,** 16.6.02 Maastricht, Schiffsfunker, zuletzt: Holland,
   vermutl. England (Täterkreis: Stevens/Best), RSHA IV E 4.
54. **Strankmüller, Emil,** 26.2.02 ehem. tschech. Major, London, 53 Lexham
   Gardens, Kensington W. 8 (Täterkreis: Frantisck Moravec), RSHA
   IV E 4, IV E 6.
 * 55. **Strasser, Otto,** 10.9.97 Windsheim, Schriftsteller, vermutl. England,
   (Schwarze Front), Decknamen: **Baumann, Dr. Berger, Loerbrocks,
   Otto Boostrom,** RSHA IV A 3.
56. **Strasser, Paul,** 21.3.95 Windsheim, Kapuziner-Pater, vermutl. England (Schwarze Front), Deckname: **Pater Bernhard,** RSHA IV A 3.
56a **Strauß, Bert,** jüd. Emigrant, zuletzt: Den Haag, vermutl. England,
   RSHA IV E 4.
57. **Strauß, Bertold,** richtig: **Dr. Halder,** brit. Agent, zuletzt: Den Haag,
   vermutl. England, RSHA IV E 4.
58. **Strauß (Strawson), Frank,** Direktor, vermutl. England, RSHA V G 1.
59. **Strauß, Georg Russell,** Politiker, vermutl. England, RSHA VI G 1.
60. **Strawson-Strauß, Frank,** Direktor, vermutl. England, RSHA V G 1.
61. **Strecker, H. A. Pullar, Dr.,** 1894, Privatdozent, England, RSHA
   III A 1.
62. **Strelka, Karl,** 23.9.96 Prag, ehem. tschech. Major, vermutl. England, RSHA IV E 4, Stapoleit Prag.

63. **Strong, Fray,** brit. Hauptagent, vermutl. England, RSHA IV E 4, Stapoleit München.
* 64. **Strong, K. W. D.,** Korv.-Kpt., England RSHA IV E 4.
65. **Strong, Nic,** zuletzt: Amsterdam, vermutl. England, RSHA IV E 4.
66. **Stronski,** Mitgl. d. poln. Regierung, vermutl. England, RSHA IV D 2.
67. **Stuart, Ruthern,** brit. Oberst, zuletzt: Wien, vermutl. England, RSHA IV E 4.
68. **Stufkens, A. P.,** zuletzt: Holland, vermutl. England (Täterkreis: Brijnen), RSHA IV E 4.
69. **Stutzig, Ernst,** d. 6.98 Pochöfen, vermutl. England, RSHA IV A 1 b.
70. **Styczakowski, Franz,** Kraftfahrer, poln. Feldwebel, vermutl. England, RSHA IV E 5.

1. **Tacke, Richard,** 11.8.77 Berlin, Kunstmaler, zuletzt: Holland, vermutl. England, RSHA IV E 4, Stapo Hamburg.
2. **Tatlow, Charles Edmund,** London, Unilever House, Blackfriars, RSHA IV E 2.
3. **Tauer, Jaroslaw,** 24.2.98 Bela (Weißwasser), ehem. tschechischer Stabskapitän, London, Lexham Gardens, Kensington W. 8 (Täterkreis: Frantisek Moravec), RSHA IV E 4, IV E 6.
4. **Tautz, Max,** 28.6.96 Goldbach, Krs. Glatz, Glasschleifer, RSHA IV E 5, Stapo Kattowitz.
5. **Taylor, Rees Lewell,** RSHA IV E 4.
6. **Taylor, S. W.,** Major im Kriegsamt, London, RSHA IV E 4, Stapoleit Hannover.
7. **Taylor,** ca. 50 Jahre alt, brit. N.-Agent, zuletzt: Rotterdam, vermutl. England (Täterkreis: Hooper), RSHA IV E 4, Stapoleit Hamburg.
8. **Tebarth, Wilhelm,** Deckname: **Schimmel, Schorsch, Michalski, Schneider, Georg Humbold, Hermann, Fritz,** 6.8.02 Düsseldorf, Schriftsetzer, RSHA IV A 2.
9. **Tebbe, Else Johanna,** 7.12.13 Mühlheim, zuletzt: Den Haag, vermutl. England (Täterkreis: Wilhelm Willemse), RSHA IV E 4, Stapoleit Düsseldorf.
10. **Tempel, Hermann,** 29.11.89 Dietzum, Schriftleiter, vermutl. England, RSHA IV A 1.
11. **van den Tempel, Jan, Dr.,** 1.8.77 Willemstad (N. Br.), ehem. holl. Sozialminister, zuletzt: Amsterdam, vermutl. England, RSHA III B.
12. **Temperley, Raleigh,** 50 Jahre alt, brit. Militärattaché in Holland, vermutl. England (Täterkreis: Stevens/Best), RSHA IV E 4.
13. **Tempka-Nowakowski, Siegmund, Dr.,** geb. 1891 Krakau, Journalist, vermutl. England, poln. Emigrantenregierung, RSHA III B.
14. **Tergit-Reifenberg, Gabriele,** Schriftstellerin, Emigrantin, London NW. 3, 23 Belsize Avenue, RSHA II B 5.
15. **Tester, A. A. Artur, Dr.,** London S. W., James Place 14, RSHA IV E 4, Stapoleit Stettin.
16. **Tester, Arthur, Dr.,** Emigrant, 23.8.95 Stuttgart, Schauspieler, Bankdirektor, RSHA II B 5, VI G 1.
17. **Tester, Ingeborg,** 22.12.18 Wiesbaden, zuletzt: Berlin-Halensee, vermutl. England, RSHA IV E 4, Stapoleit Hamburg.
18. **Tewson, H. V.,** geschäftsf. Sekretär des Gewerkschaftsausschusses, RSHA VI G 1.
19. **Thalheimer, August, Dr.,** 18.3.84 Affaltrach/Württ., Schriftsteller, zuletzt: London, RSHA IV A 1.
20. **Thomsen, Mej. Da C. P.,** zuletzt: Gouda/Holl., vermutl. England (Täterkreis: Breijnen), RSHA IV E 4.
21. **Thompson, George Paget,** geb. 1892, Prof. d. Physik i. London, RSHA VI G 1.
22. **Thompson, John,** 2.10.13 Bradford, RSHA IV A 1 b.
23. **Thompson,** Leiter engl. Agenten, zuletzt: Wien, vermutl. England, RSHA IV E 4, Stapoleit Wien.
24. **Thomson, David Yalden,** London N. W. 1, 8 St. George's Terrace, RSHA IV B 1 b.
25. **Thorndike, Sybil,** Nationalrat für zivile Freiheit, RSHA VI G 1.
26. **Thorner, Hans, Dr.,** geb. 1905, Assistent, London, Peckham House (Mental Hospital), RSHA III A 1.
27. **Thorton, James,** Journalist, London, Lexington Road 4, RSHA IV E 4, Stapoleit Karlsruhe.

28. **Thornton,** brit. Kapitän, zuletzt: Brüssel, vermutl. England (Täterkreis: Waldemar Pötsch), RSHA IV E 4.
29. **Thurko,** richtig: **Dr. Josef Rudinsky,** Ing., RSHA IV E 4, Stapoleit Prag.
30. **Thurnwald, Albert,** 27.2.07 Wilkischen, Krs. Mies, RSHA IV A 1.
31. **Thurtle, Ernest,** geb. 1884, Vertreter der Labour Party, RSHA VI G 1.
32. **Tiarks, Frank C.,** Direktor, London E. C. 2, Britannic House, Anglo-Iranian-Oil Co., RSHA IV E 2.
33. **Tichy, Oldrich,** 30.1.98 Nechanicich (Nethanicich), ehem. tschech. Oberstltn., London W. 8, 53 Lexham Gardens, Kensington (Täterkreis: Frantisek Moravec), RSHA IV E 4, IV E 6.
34. **Tille, Gustav,** 7.6.80 Schelkau, Krs. Weißenfels, Schuhmacher, Lagerverwalter, RSHA IV A 1.
35. **Tillett, Ben,** geb. 1859, Gewerkschaftsführer, RSHA VI G 1.
36. **Tiltman-Hessell, Hubert,** 2.2.97 Birmingham, engl. Journalist, London, RSHA IV E 4.
37. **Timperley, Harold J.,** Journalist, RSHA VI G 1.
38. **Tinsley, Bolten Richard,** 14.11.75 Liverpool, zuletzt: Rotterdam, vermutl. England, RSHA IV E 4.
39. **Tischkewicz, Stefan,** Graf (Täterkreis: Camber), RSHA IV E 4, Stapo Tilsit.
40. **Todd, Judith,** RSHA VI G 1.
41. **Tomaszewski, Tadeusz,** Mitgl. d. poln. Nationalrates, RSHA IV D 2.
42. **Tomczak, Ludwig,** 30.7.94 Miemierzyce/Grodzisk, poln. Grenzbeamter, RSHA IV E 5, Stapo Liegnitz.
43. **Tomingas, William,** 6.6.95, brit. Agent, vermutl. England, RSHA IV E 4, Stapo Tilsit.
44. **Tompson, Alfred,** 29.8.01 London, zuletzt: London (Täterkreis: Johan Kreuz), RSHA IV E 4, Stapo Koblenz.
45. **Tompson, Gordon, Dr.,** RSHA VI G 1.
46. **Toot, Joh.,** zuletzt: Holland, vermutl. England, RSHA IV E 4.
47. **Tops,** holl. Eisenbahnbeamter, zuletzt: Blerik/Sportstraat, vermutl. England, RSHA IV E 4.
48. **Torr, Dona,** Schriftsteller, RSHA VI G 1.
49. **Townsend-Warner, Sylvia,** Schriftstellerin, RSHA VI G 1.
50. **Träger, Eva,** 10.11.05 Neukölln, Kinderhortnerin, RSHA IV A 2.
51. **Traube, Isidor, Dr.,** 1860 geb., a. o. Prof., Emigrant, Edinburgh (Universität), RSHA III A 1.
52. **Trautzsch, Walter Ehregott,** Deckname: **Erich Schubert,** 16.3.03 Lengefeld, Metallarbeiter, RSHA IV A 2.
53. **Treffers, J.,** zuletzt: Holland, vermutl. England, RSHA IV E 4.
54. **Treitl, Johann,** 21.6.10 Daßnitz, Krs. Eger (Krs. Falkenau), Fabrikarbeiter, Faversham-Kent, 34 Abbey-Fields, RSHA IV A 1 b, IV A 1, Stapo Karlsbad.
55. **Trenchard, Barnett Herts,** Lord, Marshall der RAF, Dancer's Hill House, Barnett Herts, RSHA III D 2.
56. **Trend, J. B.,** Prof., RSHA VI G 1.
57. **Trenkle, Robert,** 17.11.05, Furtwangen, Polizeibeamter, vermutl. England, RSHA IV A 3.
58. **Trentham, E. N. S.,** Finanzrat der brit. Botschaft in Berlin, RSHA IV E 4.
59. **Trevelyan, Sir, Charles,** 1870 geb., RSHA VI G 1.

* 60. **Treviranus, Gottfried Reinhold,** 20.3.91 Schieder/Lippe, Reichsminister a. D., Sekretär b. Flüchtlingskomitee im Völkerbund, London, RSHA IV E 4, IV 3 a, IV B 1, IV A 1 b, VI G 1, II B 5.
61. **Tribbatts,** geb. **Demmer,** Witwe, Ventnori-of-Wight, Mittchell-Avenue, RSHA IV A 1.
62. **Trünk, Otto,** 18.5.03 Tyczyn, Dipl.-Ing., RSHA IV E 4, Stapoleit Danzig.
63. **Trunkhardt, Arthur,** 10.7.87 Gelsenkirchen, poln. Redakteur, RSHA IV E 5, Stapo Oppeln.
64. **Trupkiewicz, Roman,** 14.6.01 Gradacac, Bosnien, Kaufmann, RSHA IV E 5, Stapo Liegnitz.
64a **Turnball,** ca. 40 Jahre alt, brit. N.-Agent, früh. Kopenhagen, vermutl. England, RSHA IV E 4.
65. **Turner,** dipl. Beamter, zuletzt: Reval/Estland, RSHA IV C 2.
66. **Türkheim, Hans,** geb. 1889, a. o. Prof., Emigrant, London, RSHA III A 1.
67. **Twoja, Alma,** zuletzt: Kutno, vermutl. England (Täterkreis: Norman John Beiles), RSHA IV E 4.
68. **Tynan, Anna H.,** Sekretärin, London, 15 Grosvenor Crescent, RSHA VI G 1.

*See notes on pages 266–272

1. **Ucko, Hans, Dr.,** geb. 1900, Privatdozent, Emigrant, London, Guys Hospital, RSHA III A 1.
2. **v. Uden, W. D.,** zuletzt: Holland, vermutl. England, RSHA IV E 4.
3. **Uhlir, Anna,** verh. Stein, 31.3.02 Wien, vermutl. England, RSHA IV A 1.
4. **Uhlmann, Fred,** Vorstandsmitgl. d. „Freien deutschen Kulturliga" in England, London, RSHA VI G 1, II B 5.
5. **Ulich, Robert, Dr.,** geb. 1890, Emigrant, Cambridge, o. Prof. und Dozent an der Universität, RSHA III A 1.
6. **Ullrich, Erwin,** Deckname: **Rudi Herbert,** 9.8.03 Berlin, RSHA IV A 2.
7. **Unwin, Stanley,** geb. 1884, Verleger, Vorsitzender und Direktor, RSHA CI G 1.
8. **Uppington, A. H.,** Somerset/England, 33 Marlborough, Buildings, RSHA IV E 3, Stapo Trier.
9. **Urch, Thomes,** Journalist, zuletzt: Riga, vermutl. England, RSHA VI C 2.
* 10. **Ustinov,** Journalist, London, Deckname: **Middelton-Peddelton,** brit. N.-Agent, RSHA IV E 4.
11. **Utley, Freda,** Journalistin, RSHA VI G 1.

1. **Vachell, J. L.,** Oberst, Att. für Luftfahrt, England, RSHA IV E 4.
2. **Vahrenhorst, Frieda,** 27.2.15 Hannover, vermutl. England, RSHA IV A 1.
3. **Valentin, Veit, Dr.,** 1885, a. o. Prof., Emigrant, London (Universität), RSHA III A 1.
4. **Vandenheul, Matheus Otto,** 14.10.92 Amsterdam, franz. Agent, zuletzt: Rotterdam, vermutl. England, RSHA IV E 4, Stapo Aachen.
5. **Vanek, verh. Beaumont, Emilie,** 20.3.94 Wien, Agentin, zuletzt: Prag, vermutl. England (Täterkreis: Beaumont), RSHA IV E 4.
* 6. **Vansittart, Robert,** führend im brit. ND., Dipl. Hauptberater des Außenminist., London W. 1, 44 Park Street, RSHA IV E 4.
7. **Varga, Alfred,** 29.9.07 Berlin, Arbeiter, London, Deckname: Karl, RSHA IV A 1, IV A 2.
8. **Vasicek, Josef,** 16.3.96 Tritschein, Handelsreisender, RSHA IV A 1, Stapo Troppau.
9. **Vastelabend, Bram,** etwa 56 Jahre alt, zuletzt: Holland, vermutl. England (Täterkreis: Prins), RSHA IV E 4.
10. **Vaucher, Victor,** richtig: **Jean Lareida,** RSHA IV E 4, Stapo Bremen.
11. **Vaughan, Janet, Dr.,** RSHA VI G 1.
12. **Vedral, Jaroslav,** 17.11.95 Melnik, ehem. tschech. Oberst, vermutl. England, RSHA IV E 4, Stapoleit Prag.
13. **Veit, geb. Kosmack, Imogen,** 12.4.13 Glasgow, Sprachlehrerin, London, RSHA IV E 4.
14. **Velthuis, Jan Gerrit,** zuletzt: Rotterdam, vermutl. England, RSHA IV E 4, Stapoleit Düsseldorf.
15. **Veltmann, Mj. J. A.,** zuletzt: Haarlem, vermutl. England (Täterkreis: Breijnen), RSHA IV E 4.
16. **Venzl, Georg,** 31.7.98 Eger, RSHA IV A 1 b.
17. **Vergoossen,** zuletzt: Holland, vermutl. England, RSHA III A, Stapo Aachen.
18. **Verhoef, J.,** zuletzt: Den Haag, vermutl. England (Täterkreis: Breijnen), RSHA IV E 4.
19. **Vernon, Hilda,** RSHA VI G 1.
20. **Verrat,** Hochschullehrer, England, RSHA III B.
21. **Vevers, G. M., Dr.,** Vize-Vorsitzender der Cult. Rel. USSR., RSHA VI G 1.
22. **Viertel, Berthold,** London, Emigrant, RSHA VI G 1.
23. **Viest, Rudolf (Dr. ?),** 24.9.90 Revuca, ehem. tschech. General, Staatssekretär im Min. für nat. Verteidigung d. csl. Regierung in London, London, RSHA IV E 4, IV D 1, Stapoleit Prag.
24. **Vinke, H. L.,** holl. Hauptmann d. R. im ND., zuletzt: Holland, vermutl. England, RSHA IV E 4.
25. **Vitold,** richtig: **Koc,** Minister (poln. Emigrantenregierung), vermutl. England, RSHA III B.
26. **Vive, Arthur,** Ang. d. belg. Militär-Sureté, zuletzt: Brüssel, vermutl. England (Täterkreis: Bastian), RSHA IV E 4, Stapo Köln.
27. **Vivien,** fr. Offizier d. ind. Polizei, zuletzt: London (Täterkreis: Wolfgang zu Putlitz), RSHA IV E 4.
28. **Vleugels,** vermutl. England, RSHA IV E 4.
29. **Völkl, Anton,** 12.7.02 Neuenbrand, Krs. Asch, RSHA IV A 1 b.
30. **Völkl, Josef,** 20.3.95 Neuenbrand, Krs. Asch, London, 28 Pacre Park, S. E. 13, RSHA IV A 1, Stapo Karlsbad.
31. **Vogel, Johann,** 16.2.81 Oberartelshofen, Vorsitzender der SPD., vermutl. England, RSHA IV A 1.

*See notes on pages 266–272

32. **Vogel, Wilhelm Hans** 11.12.10 Fürth, Parteisekretär (SPD.), vermutl. England, RSHA IV A 1.
33. **Vogelaar,** 15.8.16 Utrecht, Student, zuletzt: s'Gravenhage, vermutl. England, RSHA IV E 4, Stapoleit Düsseldorf.
34. **Vogelenzang, P.,** zuletzt: Gorinchem/Holl., vermutl. England (Täterkreis: Breijnen), RSHA IV E 4.
35. **Voh, Franz,** 6.9.06 Lichtenstadt, Krs. Karlsbad, Porzellandreher, Keswig/England, Haus End Cumberlandstr., RSHA IV A 1 b, Stapo Karlsbad.
36. **Vojtisck,** Ingenieur, London, RSHA VI G 1, II B 5.
37. **Volak, Otokar,** 31.3.02 Zlin, ehem. tschech. Stabskpt., vermutl. England, RSHA IV E 4, Stapoleit Prag.
38. **Vollerth, Max,** 26.8.03 Hamburg, Nieter, RSHA IV A 2.
39. **Vomberg, Josef,** 11.8.16 Brauweiler, RAD-Mann, London, RSHA V D 2 f.
40. **Vonck, Willem Frederik,** 29.8.96 Sido-Hardjo/Nl. Ind., Kapitän, zuletzt: Den Haag, vermutl. England, RSHA IV E 4, Stapo Aachen.
41. **Vondracek, Karl,** 21.1.89 Prag, ehem. tschech. Oberstltn., vermutl. England, RSHA IV E 4, Stapoleit Prag.
42. **Voorbourgh, Albert Peter,** 20.5.17 Rotterdam, Sekretär, zuletzt: Den Haag, vermutl. England (Täterkreis: Best), RSHA IV E 4, Stapoleit Düsseldorf.
43. **Vorstman, Mr. L. D.,** zuletzt: Holland, vermutl. England, RSHA IV E 4.
44. **Vrana, Fritz,** 12.4.15 Türmitz, Krs. Aussig, RSHA IV A 1 b.
45. **de Vries, Adrianus Johannes Josephus,** 13.11.93 Loon op Zand, brit. N.-Agent, richtig: **Vrinten,** zuletzt: Rotterdam, vermutl. England, RSHA IV E 4.
46. **de Vries,** holl. Gastwirt, zuletzt: Nijmegen/Holl., vermutl. England (Täterkreis: Wilhelm Willemse), RSHA IV E 4, Stapoleit Düsseldorf.
47. **de Vries,** zuletzt: Holland, vermutl. England (Täterkreis: Meyendorf), RSHA IV E 4, Stapo Lüneburg.
48. **de Vriessen,** zuletzt: Amsterdam, vermutl. England (Täterkreis: Theodor Franssen), RSHA IV E 4, Stapo Lüneburg.
49. **Vrinten, Adrianus Johannes Josephus,** 13.11.93 Loon op Zand, brit. N.-Agent, Decknamen: **Zwart, A. Emmering, Frinten, de Vries,** Kraftw. „H. 79640" (Täterkreis: Stevens-Best), RSHA IV E 4, Stapoleit Düsseldorf.
50. **Vygen, Ferdinand Hubert Josef,** 29.12.97 Heerlen/Holl., Kaufmann, zuletzt: Heerlen/Holl., vermutl. England, RSHA IV E 4, Stapo Aachen.
51. **Vyth,** zuletzt: Den Haag, vermutl. England, RSHA IV E 4.

1. **Wachova, Pauline,** verehel. **Osuski,** 31.3.89, vermutl. England (Täterkreis: Stefan Osuski), RSHA IV E 4, Stapoleit Prag.
2. **Wachsmann, Klaus, Dr.** geb. 1907, Emigrant, London, RSHA III A 1.
3. **Wagner, Albert Malte, Dr.,** geb. 1886, Privatdozent, Emigrant, London, RSHA III A 1.
4. **Wagner, Fritz,** richtig **Kniefke, Karl,** Agent, zuletzt: Amsterdam, vermutl. England, RSHA IV E 4, Stapo Wilhelmshaven.
5. **Wagner, Linda,** 13.11.13 Asch, vermutl. England, RSHA IV A 1 b.
6. **Wagner, Marie,** geb. **Kohl,** 1.8.08 Haslau, Strickerin, RSHA IV A 1.
7. **Wagner, Rudolf,** richtig **Kleine, Fritz,** 7.3.01 Apolda, RSHA IV E 4, Stapoleit Prag.
8. **Wale,** engl. Oberstltn., RSHA VI C 2.
9. **Walkden, Alexander George,** geb. 1873, Gewerkschaftsbeamter, RSHA VI G 1.
10. **Walker-Smith,** Sir, **Jonah,** London, W.C.1, 21. Russell Square (Täterkreis: Ignatz Petschek), RSHA III D 4.
11. **Walter, Franz,** richtig **Hexmann, Fridrich,** 28.4.00 Brünn, Journalist, vermutl. England, RSHA IV A 2.
12. **Walter, Friedrich,** 8.4.15 London, Wehrpflichtiger, Heath (Kent), 78. Broadway Brexley, RSHA V D 2 f.
13. **Walsh, H.,** zuletzt: Holland, vermutl. England, RSHA IV E 4, Stapo Bremen.
14. **Walzer,** zuletzt: Heerlen, vermutl. England, RSHA IV E 4, Stapo Aachen.
15. **Wanka, Franz,** 14.7.98 Oberleutendorf, RSHA IV A 1 b.
16. **Wanka, Marie,** 20.12.02 Furth i. W., vermutl. England, RSHA IV A 1 b.
17. **Wanner, Johann,** 23.1.19 Seefeld/Tirol, RAD-Mann, vermutl. England, RSHA V D 2 f, KP-Stelle Innsbruck.
18. **Warburg, G.,** Schriftleiter, RSHA IV B 4, IV A 5.
19. **Wardle, W. L.,** Oberhaupt der Methodistenkirche, RSHA VI G 1.
20. **Wardrop, E.,** brit. Konsul, vermutl. England, RSHA IV E 4.
21. **Wark, Nikolaus, Dr.,** 18.1.81 Böwen (Luxemburg), Dozent, zuletzt: Heerlen/Holland, vermutl. England, RSHA IV E 4, Stapo Aachen.
22. **Warminski, Adam,** richtig **Koc,** Minister der poln. Emigrantenregierung, vermutl. England, RSHA III B.
23. **Warner-Townsend, Sylvia,** Schriftstellerin, RSHA VI G 1.
24. **Wassermann, Albert, Dr.,** geb. 1901, Emigrant, London, Privatdozent an der Universität, RSHA III A 1.
25. **Watkins, Olga,** Schriftstellerin, RSHA IV B 4.
26. **Watson, Johnried,** Deckname: **Harald, Eeman,** 25.4.93 Brüssel, geb. 1885 Glasgow, dipl. Beamter, zuletzt: Riga, Stockholm und Kaunas, vermutl. England, RSHA VI C 2.
27. **Watson, Robert I.,** Direktor, London E.C.2, Britannic House, Anglo-Iranian-Oil-Co., RSHA IV E 2.
28. **Watson - Seton, R. Williams,** geb. 1879, Historiker, Prof. f. Zentraleuropäische Geschichte, vermutl. England, RSHA VI G 1.
29. **Webb, Beatrice,** geb. 1859, Ehrenpräsidentin, RSHA VI G 1.
30. **Webb, Magda Antonowna,** geb. **Sellheim,** gesch. **Lauthew,** zuletzt: Reval/Estland (Täterkreis: M. Budberg), RSHA VI C 2.
31. **Weber, Alois,** 27.7.97, Arbeiter, vermutl. England, RSHA IV A 1 b.
32. **Weber, August Karl Wilhelm, Dr.,** 4.2.71 Oldenburg, Bankdirektor a. D., London, RSHA IV A 1 b.

33. **Weber, Editha,** 27.10.05 Düsseldorf, Erzieherin, vermutl. England, RSHA IV E 4.
34. **Weber, Ludwig,** 22.5.02 Pfungsstadt/Darmstadt, RSHA IV A 1, IV A 2.
35. **Wechselmann, Kurt,** 3.2.88 Mleckobitz, Kaufmann, zuletzt: Den Haag, vermutl. England, RSHA IV E 4, Stapoleit Breslau.
36. **Weck, Kurt,** 20.11.92 Werdau/Sa., vermutl. England, RSHA IV A 1 b.
37. **Weckel, Kurt,** 15.3.77 Schedewitz, Volksschullehrer, RSHA IV A 1 b.
38. **Wedgwood, Josiah Clement,** 1872, brit. Oberst, RSHA VI G 1.
39. **van Weegen, Wilhelm,** 1.2.04 Ueden/Holland, zuletzt: Renkum b. Arnheim, vermutl. England, RSHA IV E 4.
40. **Weidmann, Friedrich Wilhelm,** 8.11.02 Erlangen, Arbeiter, London, RSHA III B 3, Stapo Nürnberg.
41. **Weil, Hans, Dr.,** 1905 geb., Assistent, Emigrant, Newcastle-on-Tyne, RSHA III A 1.
42. **Weiler, Gerhard, Dr.,** 1899 geb., Emigrant, Oxford, RSHA III A 1.
43. **Weinberger, Martin, Dr.,** 1893, verh., Emigrant, London, Dozent a. d. Universität, RSHA III A 1.
44. **Weinhart, Josef,** 17.6.97 Gfell, Glan Y Mor, Y. M. G. A., Barry i. Glam, RSHA IV A 1 b.
45. **Weinmann, Fritz,** Emigrant (Jude), London, RSHA III D 4.
46. **Weinmann, Hans,** Hauptaktionär d. Westböhmischen Bergbauaktien-vereins, London, RSHA III D.
47. **Weinstein, Alexander, Dr.,** geb. 1897, London, Privatdozent a. d. Universität, Emigrant, RSHA III A 1.
48. **Weisenfeld, Nathan,** Arzt, London, RSHA IV A 2.
49. **Weiß, Bernhard,** 30.7.80 Berlin, ehem. Pol.-Vize-Präs., RSHA IV A 1, VI G 1.
50. **Weiß, Harry, Dr.,** 1906 geb., Emigrant, London, RSHA III A 1.
51. **Weiß, Joseph, Dr.,** 1905 geb., London, Emigrant, Assistent an der Universität, RSHA III A 1.
52. **Weißenberg, Karl, Dr.,** 1893 geb., Emigrant, a. o. Professor, Southampton, RSHA III A 1.
53. **Weizmann, Chaim,** 1873 oder 1874 in Motyli bei Pinks, Professor der Chemie, Führer der gesamten Judenvereine Englands, London S. W. 1, 104 Pall Mall, Reform-Club, RSHA III B 2, VI G 1.
54. **Welker, Helene,** 13.12.04 Berlin, RSHA IV A 2.
55. **Wells, Herbert George,** 1866 geb., Schriftsteller, London N. W. 1, Regents Park 13, Hanover Terrace, RSHA VI G 1, III A 5, II B 4.
55a **Welsh,** brit. N.-Agent, zuletzt: Kopenhagen, vermutl. England, RSHA IV E 4.
56. **Welter, Charles Joseph Ignace Marie,** 6.4.80 Den Haag, ehem. holl. Kolonialminister, zuletzt: Den Haag, Statenplein 10, RSHA III B.
57. **de Werdestuyn, de Wijkersloot, Robert,** 31.9.12 Utrecht, Student, zuletzt: Nymwegen, vermutl. England, RSHA IV E 4, Stapoleit Düsseldorf.
58. **Wenzel, Johann,** Deckname: Hermann und Bergmann, 9.3.02 Niedau, Schlosser, Schmied, RSHA IV A 2.
59. **Werner, Heinz, Dr.,** 1890 geb., Cambridge, Emigrant, a. o. Prof. an der Universität, RSHA III A 1.
60. **Werner, Hermann,** 27.9.93 Buckwa, vermutl. England, RSHA IV A 1 b.
61. **Werner, Paul Robert,** 16.5.15 Scheidelwitz, Gefreiter, RSHA IV E 5, Stapoleit Breslau.
62. **Wertheimer, Lydia,** Mitarbeiterin d. Merton, London, RSHA III D.
63. **West, Rebeca,** 1892 geb., Journalistin, RSHA VI G 1.

64. **Westhoff, Dr.,** richtig: **Hans Barlson,** 19.12.97 Großbülllesheim, Oberstadtsekretär, vermutl. England, RSHA IV A 2.
65. **Westerlaken, H.,** zuletzt: Holland, vermutl. England, RSHA IV E 4.
66. **Wetzel, Rudolf Paul,** 10.1.09 Rechenberg, Büroangest., Student, London N. 6, 89 Hornsey Lane Highate, RSHA IV A 1, Stapoleit Dresden.
67. **Weyer, D. F.,** zuletzt: Aalsmeer/Holland, vermutl. England (Täterkreis: Breijnen), RSHA IV E 4.
68. **Whately, Monica,** Schriftstellerin, RSHA IV B 4.
69. **White, H. Graham,** 1880 geb., Politiker, RSHA VI G 1.
70. **White-Baker, John,** 12.8.02 W.-Malling-Kent, Captain, N.-Offizier, London, Fracanti Lane, RSHA IV E 4.
71. **Wienzek, Lorenz (Wawrzin),** 15.6.95 Mischinow, Schuhmacher, poln. N.-Agent, RSHA IV E 5, Stapoleit Breslau.
72. **Wiersma, J.,** zuletzt: Heiloo/Holland, vermutl. England (Täterkreis: Breijnen), RSHA IV E 4.
73. **Wigham, Gilbert C.,** Direktor, London E. C. 2, Britannic House, Anglo-Iranian-Oil-Co, RSHA IV E 2.
74. **Wigner, Eugen, Dr.,** Emigrant, Madison, a. o. Prof. an der Universität, RSHA III A 1.
75. **De Wijkersloot, de Werdestuyn, Robert,** 21.9.12 Utrecht, Student, zuletzt: Nymwegen, vermutl. England, RSHA IV E 4, Stapoleit Düsseldorf.
76. **Wildman, B.,** brit. Konsul, vermutl. England, RSHA IV E 4.
77. **Wildman,** Direktor d. brit. Gesellsch. „Becos" in Riga, vermutl. England, RSHA IV E 4.
78. **Wiles, Ph.,** RSHA VI G 1.
79. **Wiliams,** engl. Offizier, London 17, West Bury Avenue, Wordgreen 22 (Täterkreis: Willimse), RSHA IV E 4, Stapoleit Münster.
80. **Wilkinson, Ellen,** Abgeordneter, London W. C. 1, Universität College, Cower Street, RSHA IV A 5, VI G 1.
81. **Willem, II** (Täterkreis: Willms), RSHA IV E 4.
82. **Willems, Gerardus Hubert,** 14.4.03 Kessel, Krs. Limburg, Kraftfahrer, Verkäufer, zuletzt: Venlo/Holland, vermutl. England (Täterkreis: Gerhard Willms), RSHA IV E 4.
83. **Williams, A. M.,** brit. Vizekonsul, RSHA IV E 4.
84. **Williams, Francis,** Herausgeber d. „Daily Herald", RSHA VI G 1.
85. **Williams, James,** Händler, brit. N.-Agent in Litauen, zuletzt: Kaunas, RSHA VI C 2.
* 86. **van der Willik, Piet,** 22.7.90 Den Haag, Direktor, vermutl. England (Täterkreis: Best), RSHA IV E 4.
87. **Willis, Ted,** Vorsitz. d. Jugendliga Arbeiterpartei, RSHA VI G 1.
88. **Willms, Gerhard,** 14.4.03 Kessel, Krs. Limburg, Verkäufer, zuletzt: Venlo/Holland, IV E 4, Stapoleit Düsseldorf.
89. **Wilnarik, Johann,** 5.1.09 Hradzen, Krs. Mies, Tagarbeiter, Watford, 83. the Harebraaks, RSHA IV A 1, Stapo Karlsbad.
90. **Wilnarik, Wilhelm,** 10.11.10 Hradzen, Krs. Mies, Maurer, RSHA IV A 1, Stapo Karlsbad.
90a. **Wilson, Florence,** brit. N.-Agent, zuletzt: Kopenhagen, vermutl. England, RSHA IV E 4.
91. **Wilson, H. J.,** London E. C. 1, 13 Barnstaple, Mansions, Rosebery Avenue, RSHA IV E 4, Stapo Halle.
92. **Wimmer, Paul,** 28.11.05 Gablonz, RSHA IV A 1.
93. **Wind, Edgar, Dr.,** 1900 geb., Emigrant, Privatdozent, London, RSHA III A 1.

*See notes on pages 266–272

94. **Winter, verh. Proskauer, Elisabeth,** 23.6.96 Jägerndorf, RSHA IV E 5.
95. **Winternitz, Arthur, Dr.,** RSHA VI G 1.
96. **Wislicki, Leo, Dr.,** 1901 geb., Emigrant, Ass., Privatpraxis in Manchester, RSHA III A 1.
97. **Wisniewski, Kurt Heinz,** 22.8.19 Schleusenau, Arbeitsdienstmann, RSHA IV E 5, Stapoleit Königsberg.
98. **Wisniewski, Ludwig,** 7.5.79 Szymborze, Krs. Hohensalza, poln. Krim.-Kom., RSHA IV E 5, Stapoleit Berlin.
99. **de Wit, C. W.,** zuletzt: London, RSHA IV E 4, Stapoleit Stuttgart.
100. **De Witte, Euten,** 8.10.82 Karlsbad, Walmer/Kent, Garth Sidney Road, RSHA IV A 1 b.
101. **Wittkower, Erich, Dr.,** 1899 geb., Emigrant, Privatdozent, London, Maudsley Hospital, RSHA III A 1.
102. **Wittkower, Rudolf, Dr.,** 1901 geb., Emigrant, Dozent, zuletzt: Köln, London, Warburg-Institut, RSHA III A 1.
103. **Witzenburg, van, Mej. C. R. C.,** zuletzt: Holland, vermutl. England, RSHA IV E 4.
104. **Wnorowski, Mieczyslaw, Dr.,** 18.10.08 Warschau, Presseattaché b. d. poln. Botschaft Berlin, RSHA IV E 5.
105. **Wohlfahrt, Albert,** 24.2.15 Altersberg b. Geildorf, Dienstpflichtiger, Ashton-Wilts, the Cotswold (Bruderhaus), RSHA V D 2 f.
106. **Wohlwill, Max, Dr.,** Mitarbeiter d. Merton, London, RSHA III D.
107. **Wojars, Leon,** Poln. Grenzbeamter, RSHA IV E 5, Stapo Allenstein.
108. **Wolf, M., Dr.,** Schriftleiter beim Manchester Guardian, London W. C. 1, Nr. 17 St. Joar Street of Theobalds Street, RSHA IV B 1 b.
109. **de Wolff, Pierre,** Direktor der Swiss-Bank-Corp., London E. C. 2, Gresham Street 99 (Täterkreis: Ignatz Petschek), RSHA III D 4.
110. **Wolff, Leon,** 21.4.96 Culmsee, Krs. Thorn, Getreidekaufmann, RSHA IV E 5.
111. **Wolsey, William,** Verleger der Zeitschrift „Kameradschaft", London S. E. 3, 2 Paragon, Blackheath, RSHA IV B 1.
112. **Wondrak, Heinrich,** 16.5.94 Meffersdorf, Manchester, Scholgrove Wittington, RSHA IV A 1 b.
113. **Woodhouse, Josef A.,** 14.1.93 Birmingham, ehem. brit. Polizeibeamter, vermutl. England, RSHA IV E 4, Stapo Köln.
114. **Woodman, Dorothy,** Sekretärin d. Union d. demokratischen Kontrolle, RSHA VI G 1.
115. **Woolf, Leonhard,** 1880 geb., Schriftsteller, RSHA VI G 1.
116. **Woolf, Virginia,** Schriftstellerin, RSHA VI G.
117. **Woudstra, J.,** holländ. Polizeibeamter a. D., zuletzt: Ameland, vermutl. England (Täterkreis: August de Fremery), RSHA IV E 4.
117a **Wright, William Wood,** 17.8.89 Liverpool, zuletzt: Kopenhagen, vermutl. England, RSHA IV E 4.
118. **Wulstrup, Jan,** zuletzt: Rotterdam, vermutl. England (Täterkreis: Waldemar Pötsch), RSHA IV E 4.
119. **Wunderlich, Berta,** 1.6.06 Schönbach, vermutl. England, RSHA IV A 1 b.
120. **Wunderlich, Emil,** 4.12.97 Neuberg, vermutl. England, RSHA IV A 1 b.
121. **Wustra, Jan,** zuletzt: Holland, vermutl. England (Täterkreis: Waldemar Pötzsch), RSHA IV E 4, Stapo Bremen.
122. **Wuttke, Franz,** Deckname: **Georg Paul Rudolf,** 26.11.99 Josefsberg, Krs. Rosenberg, Grubenarbeiter, RSHA IV A 1.

123. **Wreszynsky, Siegfried,** 10.11.93 Gnosen, Kaufmann, London W. 1, 8 Grosvenor Street, Deckadresse: London W. 1, Alfordhouse 10 Parklane, Tel.: Fernsprechamt Primrose, Nr. 8155, RSHA IV E 4, Stapo Kiel.
124. **Wright, John Lifeers,** 12.6.86, Kaufmann, zuletzt: Riga, vermutl England, RSHA IV C 2.
125. **Wright, W. Charles,** Direktor, London E. C. 3, 22. St. Helens Court, Shell Transport u. Trading Co., RSHA IV E 2.
126. **Wynne, T. R.,** Direktor, London E. C. 2, Britannic, House, Anglo-Iranian-Oil-Co., RSHA IV E 2.
127. **Wynyard, J. G. (Ivy),** 4.7.92 Auckland, vermutl. England, RSHA IV E 4.

1. **Yakobsohn, Sergei, Dr.,** 1901, London, Emigrant, Universität, RSHA III A 1.
2. **Yaskiel, David,** Inhaber d. „British International Jewish Agency", London West 1, Southampton Street, Titzroy Square, RSHA IV A 1, IV A 5 a.
3. **Young, E. P.,** Rundfunkautor, Oberstleutnant, RSHA VI G 1.
4. **Young, G. Gordon,** Warschauer Vertreter v. Reuter, RSHA IV B 4.
4a **Younge, Edward Huscarad,** 8.9.92 London, brit. N.-Agent, früh. Kopenhagen, vermutl. England, RSHA IV E 4.
5. **Young,** etwa 45—50 Jahre alt, Techniker, brit. N.-Agent, zuletzt: Holland, vermutl. England (Täterkreis: Wilhelm Willemse), RSHA IV E 4, Stapoleit Düsseldorf.

1. **Zagorski, Woiczech,** 2.9.07 Kozmin, Poln. N.-Agent, RSHA IV E 5.
2. **Zaks, Julijs,** brit. N.-Agent, richtig: **Julius Sack** (Täterkreis: Sudakoff), RSHA IV E 4.
3. **Zaleska, Zofia,** Mitgl. d. poln. Reg., RSHA IV D 2.
4. **Zaleski, August,** Außenmin., Mitgl. d. poln. Reg., RSHA IV D 2.
5. **Zapf, Franz,** 22.2.93 Wintersgrün, London, RSHA IV A 1 b.
6. **Zapf, Robert,** 16.12.90 Doglasgrün, Krs. Elbogen, Sheffield, 147 Rustlings Road, RSHA IV A 1.
7. **Zassenhaus, Herbert Kurt, Dr.,** geb. 1910, Dozent, London, Emigrant, RSHA III A 1.
8. **Zeimer, Arthur,** fr. **Abraham,** 16.10.77 Podwolcziska, Hptm., poln. N.-Agent, RSHA IV E 5, Stapoleit München.
9. **Zeitler, Hans,** 3.9.12 Hamburg, Wehrpflichtiger, zuletzt: Südafrika, vermutl. England, RSHA V D 2.
10. **Zeligowski, Lucjan,** General, Mitgl. d. poln. Nat.-Rat, RSHA IV D 2.
11. **Zernatto, Guido,** 21.7.03 Treffen, Schriftsteller, England, RSHA IV A 3.
12. **Zernick, Rufin Rudolf,** 7.3.01 Nicolai, poln. O. S., Kaufmann, poln. N.-Agent, RSHA IV E 5.
13. **Zernike, J., Dr.,** zuletzt: Holland, vermutl. England, RSHA IV E 4.
14. **Zeuner, Friedrich, Dr.,** 1905, Privatdozent, Emigrant, Universität, London, RSHA III A 1.
15. **Zeylmans, J. W.,** zuletzt: Zaandam/Holl., vermutl. England (Täterkreis: Breijnen), RSHA IV E 4.
16. **Ziaja, Anton,** 7.6.04 Beuthen/O. S., Kellner, poln. N.-Agent, RSHA IV E 5, Stapo Oppeln.
17. **Ziaja, Gerhardt,** 4.9.13 Antonienhütte, Musiker, RSHA IV E 5, Stapo Oppeln.
18. **Zibrid, Anton,** 9.7.96 Graslitz, Margate-Kent, Northdown Road, RSHA IV A 1 b.
19. **Ziehm, Alfred,** 10.2.96 Dresden, Gewerkschafter, RSHA IV A 1 b.
20. **von Zilfhout, J.,** zuletzt: Holland, vermutl. England, RSHA IV E 4, Stapo Bremen.
21. **Zimmern, Alfred,** 1879, Professor, RSHA VI G 1.
22. **Zingler, Alfred,** 6.6.85 Sprottau, Redakteur, vermutl. England, RSHA IV A 1.
23. **Zinner, Josef,** 27.3.94 Janessen, England, RSHA IV A 1 b.
24. **Zowanski,** Generalkonsul, RSHA IV D 2.
25. **Zucker, Arthur,** 21.7.94 Berlin, Redakteur, London, RSHA IV A 1.
26. **Zuckermayer, Karl,** 27.12.96 Nockenheim, London, Schriftsteller, Emigrant, RSHA VI G 1, II B 5.
27. **van Zuiden, Ph.,** zuletzt: Baarn/Holl., vermutl. England (Täterkreis: Breijnen), RSHA IV E 4.
28. **Zuntz, Leonie, Dr.,** geb. 1908, Emigrantin, Oxford (Universität), RSHA III A 1.
29. **Zwart, Adrianus Johannes Josephus,** 13.11.93 Loon op Zand, brit. N.-Agent, richtig: **Vrinten,** zuletzt: Rotterdam, vermutl. England (Täterkreis: Stevens/Best), RSHA IV E 4.
30. **Zweig, Konrad, Dr.,** 1904, Assistent, Emigrant, London, RSHA III A 1.
31. **Zweig, Stefan, Dr.,** 28.11.81 Wien (Jude), Schriftsteller, Emigrant, London W. 1, 49 Hallam Street, RSHA II B 2, II B 5, VI G 1.
32. **Zychon, Jan Henryk,** 1.1.98 Krakau, Kapitän, RSHA IV E 5.

p. 163, 44

Baruch, Berhard should read **Baruch, Bernard**: American business-man, statesman with a London address, chairman of War Industries Board USA 1918, participant in peace negotiations 1919, adviser to President Roosevelt for economic mobilisation. His name possibly included as a former participant in the Peace Conference, also listed **B 27** Barnes, George Nicholl, 80 years old, 'Delegierter bei der Friedenskonferenz'.

p. 164, 65

Beaverbrock, Lord, Zeitungmagnet, Minister should read **Beaverbrook, Lord**: Beaverbrook, (Max Aitkin), first baron, Canadian by birth, advocate of imperial unity, his *Express* group of papers simi-larly campaigned for Empire free trade. Minister of Information in the Lloyd George coalition, Minister of Aircraft Production in the Churchill Government, Minister of State 1941. The press is also rep-resented through a variety of journalists, foreign correspondents and a famous cartoonist, for example **B 43** Vernon Bartlett (*News Chronicle*); **C 70** Claud Cockburn; **D 33** Sefton Delmer (*Daily Express*); **L 137** car-toonist David Low, ('Karikaturist des "Evening Standart"', presumably *Evening Standard*; **P 121** George Ward Price, special correspondent *Daily Mail*; **St 12** Steed, Wikham (should read **Steed, Wickham**).

p. 165, 98

Beneš, Eduard should read **Beneš, Edvard**: Czechoslovak statesman, Prague professor, protégé of Tomas Masaryk, worked in Switzerland with the Czech nationalist movement, delegate at the Versailles Peace Conference, President of Czechoslovakia 1935–8, resigned on German occupation of Sudetenland, exile, president of wartime Czechoslovak government in London. See also under **M 173 Moravec, František**.

p. 169, 192

Boronowski, Georg: A bizarre entry. Boronowski, liable for military service, sought for court-martial. Since his location is given as South Africa, chances of apprehending him seem remote.

p. 172, C 2a

Sir Cadogan: This is presumably Hon Sir Alexander Cadogan, Permanent Under-Secretary of State for Foreign Affairs 1938–46. He is mistakenly described here as 'head of the British Intelligence Service' (Leiter des Brit. ND). The compilers of this list had either not seen, read or understood the text of the *Informationsheft GB*, which gave precise details of the leading personalities of the Intelligence Service.

p. 173, C 37

Chamberlain (Arthur) Neville: The Rt Hon Neville Chamberlain, Prime Minister 1937–40, Lord President of the Council 1940. his speech of 12 October 1939 rejected Hitler's offer of negotiations made on 6 October. Prime minister Chamberlain avoided any phrase or form of language which might encourage the idea of negotiation, while allowing that a Germany able to 'live in amity and confidence' with other nations should not forfeit its rightful place in Europe. Succeeded as Prime Minister in 1940 by **C 49 Churchill, Winston Spencer.**

p. 174, 70

Cockburn, Claude should read Cockburn, Claud: Cockburn, a noted journalist, was a reporter for the London *Daily Worker* during the Spanish Civil War, during which time he became closely acquainted with Mikhail Koltsov, one-time editor of *Krokodil*, confidant and personal agent of Stalin. Koltsov appointed Cockburn the London correspondent of *Pravda,* but with the disappearance of Koltsov during the Stalinist purges Cockburn's tenure with *Pravda* was brief. Cockburn assumed the pen-name **Frank Pitcairn**, which is mentioned in this entry but under **Frank Pitcairn (P 79)**; there is no cross-reference to Cockburn.

p.174, C 87a

Hinchley-Cook, Colonel u. Leiter M.I. 5 (Military-Intelligence) should read **Lieutenant-Colonel W. Edward Hinchley-Cooke**: Described in the German text on the intelligence Service as wearing glasses, 'robust, fresh-faced', speaking fluent German with a mixture of Saxony and Hamburg dialects. The physical description conforms exactly to the photograph in Nigel West, *MI5 British Security Operations 1909–1945* (London 1981). A career counter-intelligence officer, Hinchley-Cooke was a familiar figure at spy trials before the outbreak of WWII, notably in the case of Dr Goertz, who was duly convicted.

p. 175, C 96

Coward, Noel: The famous actor, dramatist, composer, author of *Cavalcade*, *Private Lives*, *Brief Encounter*, needs no introduction, but here he is representative of a category of writers and literary personalities included in the List, for example, **B 227** Vera Brittain (also included under Catlin), **H 209** Aldous Huxley, **P 124** J.B. Priestley, **Sp 6** Steffan Spender (should read Steven Spender), **W 63** Rebecca West and **W 116** Virginia Woolf.

p. 176, D 12a

Dansey, Claude: Claude Edward Marjoribanks Dansey, Lieutenant Colonel, born 1876, a highly controversial figure in intelligence circles, fought in the Matabele wars, seconded to intelligence in France in WWI, ran a country club in the United States, close colleague of Alexander Korda, film producer who was associated with Dansey's intelligence work. Dansey himself became a director of Korda's film company, Korda Films Production Ltd. Dansey was 'exiled' to Switzerland, where he set up a private intelligence organisation, 'Z Organisation', supported financially but not formally acknowledged by SIS, and connecting ultimately with the wartime 'Lucy' spy-ring in Switzerland. The Z Organisation also operated in Holland. See also **W 86** van der Wilklik.

p. 180, D 122

Dunkan-Sendys should read **Sandys, Duncan**: Duncan Edwin, diplomat, politician, soldier, political columnist *Sunday Chronicle* 1937–9, son-in-law of Prime Minister Winston Churchill.

p. 195, H 31a

Hankey, Sir, brit. ND.-Agent: No ordinary 'intelligence agent', rather the Rt Hon Maurice Hankey, 1st Baron Hankey, served in naval intelligence 1906, Secretary of the Cabinet Committee of Imperial Defence 1919–38, member of the Cabinet as Minister without Portfolio 1939–40, Chancellor of the Duchy of Lancaster 1940–1.

p. 210, K 119

Korda, Alexander: film director. See also under **D 12a** Dansey for Korda's presumed intelligence association.

p. 211, K 172
Kukel should read **Kukiel, Marian**: Lieutenant-General, Minister of
National Defence in the London Polish Government in exile.

p 216, L 155
Lockhart, Bruce: Identified here as a journalist, Bruce Lockhart was
a diplomat closely involved with events in Russia in 1917 and the early
days of the Bolshevik regime, author of *Memoirs of a British Agent*
1933.

p. 221, M 83
Masaryk, Jan: full name Masaryk, Jan Garrigue. Czech statesman,
diplomat, son of Tomas Masaryk, Minister to Great Britain 1925–38,
resigned diplomatic service after Munich agreement, Foreign Minister
of the Czechoslovak government in exile, gained US recognition of
Czech government in exile.

p. 223, M 136
Middleton-Peddelton, see under **U 10 Ustinov**.

p.224, M 173
Moravec, František: Head of Czech intelligence, Colonel Moravec
had close relations with the British SIS. Thanks for the local SIS officer Gibson, Moravec was quickly extricated from Prague in March
1939, together with Major Strankmueller and ten Czech staff officers.
The cupboard was bare when the *Abwehr* took over Moravec's headquarters. In London Moravec set up headquarters in West Dulwich,
moving to Bayswater Road after having been bombed out.
It was Moravec's connection with *Abwehr* Major Paul Thummel (Agent
A54) which attracted the special interest of the SIS, a source of invalu-
able intelligence on the *Abwehr* until Major Thummel's arrest in 1942.
After the German invasion of Russia in 1941, Soviet intelligence
approached Moravec for information. Latterly General Sudoplatov disclosed that Moravec was associated with the NKVD and a full-time
KGB agent. See Nigel West, *VENONA: The Greatest Secret of the Cold
War* (London 1999), pp. 66–7. See also under **S 40 Sedlarsček** (should
read **Sedlacek**). The Special Wanted List evidently went to great pains
to trace the 'Moravec network', for example, **C 54 Vladimir Cigna**,
Czech Staff captain, located in London.

p. 234, P 139

Gans Edler Herr zu Putlitz, Wolfgang ehem. Legationsrat b.d. Dtsch. Gesandtschaft: Anti-Nazi diplomat, source of high-grade intelligence on Germany, associated with **U 10** Ustinov.

p. 235, R 14

Rauschning, Hermann: Former President of the Danzig Senate, resigned from the Nazi Party, anti-Nazi publicist, emphasised 'the inability as in 1933–4 to realise the true character of National Socialism' as expounded in *The Revolution of Nihilism: Warning to the West* (1939).

p. 239, R 134

Russel, Bertrand should read **Russell, Bertrand**: Famous philosopher, mathematical logician, who also wrote voluminously on logic, economics and politics.

p. 241, S 40

Sedlarscek, Karl should read **Sedlaček, Karel**: Staff captain, Czech Intelligence Service, specially selected by Moravec, trained as a wireless operator, assigned to Zürich as correspondent for the Czech newspaper *Narodni Listy* under the assumed name of Thomas Selziger. In 1938 in close contact with Swiss intelligence, Bureau Ha, supplying extensive information on German troop movements, details of which were passed on to London. Moravec in turn passed this information to the exiled Czech President Benes in London. One of the sources of this information was Rudolf Rössler, publisher, anti-Nazi, the oft-presumed 'Lucy'. Sedlaček evidently worked for the Swiss, the Russians and the British; he had entered Switzerland on a British passport and had been assigned SIS code number 22505. Rössler, 'Lucy', finally disclosed to his biographer that his prime source was in reality Sedlaček, whose information came largely from London, namely via ULTRA and the Czech radio centre at Woldingham. This through 'Sedlaček-"Lucy"' the Russians obtained crucial intelligence and ULTRA was not compromised. Sedlaček was promoted lieutenant-colonel after 1945, assigned to Berne as Czech Military Attaché and recalled to Prague in 1947.

p. 242, 64

Sikorski, Wladislaw Eugeniusz should read **Sikorski, Wladyslaw**:

Polish general, commander of the Polish legions 1914–18, distinguished in the 1920 Soviet–Polish war, chief of the Polish general staff 1921, Polish Prime Minister 1921–23, Minister of War 1924–5, C-in-C of the Polish Army in France after the defeat of Poland in 1939, Polish C-in-C and Prime Minister of the Polish Government in exile in London.

p. 251, S 55
Strasser, Otto: Politician, writer, editor of the *Berliner Arbeiter Zeitung*, eccentric, doctrinaire, member of the Nazi party 1925, disowned by Hitler, organised Schwarze Front in 1930, left Germany in 1933, lived variously in Vienna, Prague and Zurich. From Prague he operated his 'black radio', directing anti-Hitler speeches into the *Reich*. In 1940 he published *Hitler and I* and moved to Canada. His brother Gregor worked with him and with Goebels to expand the Nazi Party, but like Otto he resigned from the Party and was murdered on Hitler's orders.

p. 252, St 64
Strong, K.W.D.: Incorrectly identified as Naval Captain (Korvetten-Kapitän). Colonel Strong had been Assistant Military Attaché in Germany, in 1940 head of MI 14.

p. 255, T 60
Treviranus, Gottfried Reinhold: Treviranus was a retired Minister of the *Reich*; marked down for death during the 'Röhm putsch', he eluded the gunmen as they rang his doorbell, escaping over his garden wall dressed just as he was, to play tennis, now heading for exile.

p. 256, U 10
Ustinov, Journalist, London, Deckname Middelton-Peddelton, brit. N.-Agent: Presumably this refers to Sir Peter Ustinov's father, described by Peter Wright as 'an old MI5 agent runner'; German by descent with strong connections to the Russian diplomatic community, a committed anti-Nazi, who offered his services to Sir Robert Vansittart, associated with Winston Churchill. His contact was **Baron Wolfgang zu Putlitz** (see under **P 139**), First Secretary at the Germany Embassy, a source of high-grade intelligence. Ustinov and zu Putlitz continued to meet after 1939 when the latter was Air Attaché in Holland. Finally sought by the Gestapo in 1940, zu Putlitz decided on

escape, successfully managed thanks in no small measure to Ustinov senior's personal participation at great risk to himself.

p. 257, V 6

Vansittart, Robert: 'Leading figure in British intelligence', Sir Robert Gilbert Vansittart, Permanent Under-Secretary of State for Foreign Affairs 1930–8, chief diplomatic adviser to the Foreign Secretary 1938, advocate of the total permanent disarmament of Germany. Well known for his anti-German position, he lacked influence with Prime Minister Chamberlain and Lord Halifax; he was opposed by Alexander Cadogan. See also **C 2a** 'Sir Cadogan' 'head of British intelligence'(?), **C 49** Churchill, Winston Spencer, **P 139** zu Putlitz, **U 10** Ustinov.

p. 261, W 86

van der Willik, Piet: Dansey's Z Organisation operated in Holland, employing SIS officer Captain Best (kidnapped by Schellenberg in Venlo in November 1939), who used his firm Menoline Ltd in London as cover for his intelligence work. Best was also director of the Dutch firm N.V. Menoline in The Hague, whose other directors included John Richards and Pieter Nikolaas van deer Willik, the latter one of Best's closest colleagues in the Z Organisation. See also **D 12a Dansey**.